EXEMPLARY WOMEI
OF EARLY CHINA

TRANSLATIONS FROM THE ASIAN CLASSICS

ANNE BEHNKE KINNEY

TRANSLATOR AND EDITOR

EXEMPLARY WOMEN
OF EARLY CHINA

THE *LIENÜ ZHUAN* OF LIU XIANG

COLUMBIA UNIVERSITY PRESS   NEW YORK

Columbia University Press
Publishers Since 1893
New York   Chichester, West Sussex
cup.columbia.edu

Library of Congress Cataloging-in-Publication Data
Liu, Xiang, 77?–6? B.C.
  [Lie nü zhuan]
  Exemplary women of early China : the Lienü zhuan of Liu Xiang / edited and
    translated by Anne Behnke Kinney.
    pages cm. — (Translations from the Asian classics)
  Includes bibliographical references and index.
  ISBN 978-0-231-16308-8 (cloth) — ISBN 978-0-231-16309-5 (pbk.) —
  ISBN 978-0-231-53608-0 (electronic)
  1. Women--China--Biography. 2. Women--China--Conduct of life. I. Kinney, Anne
    Behnke. II. Title.

CT3710.L5813 2014
920.051—dc23

                                                                    2013002987

Cover image: © *The Trustees of the British Museum. 'Nushi zhen', Admonitions of the
  Instructions of the Ladies of the Palace scroll. Zou Yigui & Gu Kaizhi, China. c. 344–405.*
Cover design: Lisa Hamm

FOR MY BROTHERS, BRUCE AND JOHN,
AND MY DAUGHTER, ZOE OLIVIA

CONTENTS

4 THE CHASTE AND COMPLIANT 67

5 THE PRINCIPLED AND RIGHTEOUS 87

8 SUPPLEMENTARY BIOGRAPHIES 157

ACKNOWLEDGMENTS

I gratefully acknowledge the help of many colleagues in the writing of this book. The Columbia University Early China seminars; the meetings of the Warring States Working Group arranged by E. Bruce and Takeo Brooks at the University of Massachusetts; the workshop on the *Huainanzi* organized by Sarah Queen, Michael Puett, and John Major; Clara Wing-chung Ho's conference on the sources for Chinese women's history; and the workshops organized by Moss Roberts at New York University all provided valuable opportunities for enhancing my understanding of numerous issues that bear on the *Lienü zhuan*. Among the scholars who participated in these meetings and others who offered their thoughts on various textual and historical issues connected with this book, I am especially grateful to Barry Blakeley, Yuri Pines, Keith Knapp, Grant Hardy, John Major, Sarah Queen, Michael Puett, Sarah Allan, Constance Cook, Moss Roberts, Andy Meyer, Paul Goldin, Bill Baxter, Margaret Pearson, Li Feng, Wang Hongjie, Melvin Thatcher, Dieter Kuhn, Miranda Brown, Susan Mann, Masatsugu Yamazaki, Michiko Niikuni Wilson, Gustav Heldt, and Wolfgang Behr. My editor at Columbia University Press, Leslie Kriesel, deserves special thanks for her keen eye and careful work. I also thank Anne Holmes, who created the index for this volume.

I am also grateful for the generous support of the American Council of Learned Societies, the National Endowment for the Humanities, the Luce Foundation, the University of Virginia, and the University of Virginia's East Asia Center, which provided the time and the resources essential to the completion of this project. I am thankful for the assistance of the National Library of China, especially Zhang Zhiqing, director of the Rare Books and Special Collections

Department; the Institute for Advanced Technology in the Humanities at the University of Virginia; and the British Museum for their support in the creation of a digital research collection for the study of the *Lienü zhuan*.

My friend and mentor, Eric P. Henry, deserves special thanks. I first met Eric in 1977 in a course on classical Chinese at the Inter-University Center for Chinese Language Studies in Taipei, Taiwan. When I returned to the United States in 1979, I was surprised one day to find that Eric had sent me a copy of Albert O'Hara's translation of the *Lienü zhuan*. I was at turns fascinated, inspired, and appalled by the stories in this collection. It was just my sort of book! And I suspect that is why Eric sent it to me. When I completed my own translation some thirty years later, Eric kindly read through the entire manuscript and offered innumerable insights and suggestions that are reflected on nearly every page. Any errors that remain are my own.

I would also like to thank my daughter, Zoe Olivia, for creating for me a cardboard *Lienü zhuan* "thermometer" with 125 degree-marks for each of the 125 biographies. Each time I completed one biography, I was directed to color a line on the thermometer red until the "mercury" reached the final goal of 125 degrees. I would like to thank my husband, James Daniel Kinney, who provided constant encouragement and thoughtful feedback at each stage of the project and who now knows all 125 women by name. I would finally like to acknowledge three women from the Qing dynasty, Liang Duan (d. 1825), Wang Zhaoyuan (1763–1851), and Xiao Daoguan (1855–1907), who, through their commentaries on the *Lienü zhuan,* have been my constant companions during this project and whose wise counsel has guided my translation at every turn.

INTRODUCTION

Compiled toward the end of the Former Han dynasty (206 BCE to 8 CE), Liu Xiang's (79–8 BCE) *Lienü zhuan*, or *Categorized Biographies of Women*, is the earliest extant book in the Chinese tradition solely devoted to the moral education of women. It consists primarily of biographical accounts of women in early China who were noted for various virtues, though Liu Xiang's final chapter concerns exemplars of feminine wickedness. The *Lienü zhuan* not only inspired generations of Chinese women to cultivate traditional virtues such as filial piety and maternal kindness but also lauded practices such as suicide and self-mutilation as means to preserve chastity. In subsequent periods, collected biographies of women also became a frequent feature of dynastic and local histories.[1] Given the innovative nature of this book in Han times and the continuity of its influence, it deserves our scholarly attention.

HISTORICAL CONTEXT

Liu Xiang

Liu Xiang was a central figure in Former Han thought, politics, and literature. His life spanned the transitional and crisis-ridden reigns of Emperors Zhao (87–74 BCE), Xuan (74–49 BCE), Yuan (48–33 BCE), and Cheng (33–7 BCE). During this period, it is the reign of Xuandi (i.e., Emperor Xuan) in particular that historians often characterize as a major turning point in Han social and political thought. At this time, "reformist" principles began to direct imperial policy and intellectual activity. The reformists favored the mores and institutions of the Zhou dynasty (1056–256 BCE) and emphasized policies of laissez-faire, education, and the moral transformation of the populace. These directives, traditionally associated with Confucianism, contrasted sharply with the "modernist" stance that shaped the policies of the first part of the Former Han, which stressed expansion of the empire's administrative apparatus, maximizing use of state resources, and stressing law as a means of social control.[2] The latter half of the Former Han was also marked by the growing importance of classical texts and Confucian thought in social and political life. As we shall see, this ideological shift intensified the ongoing debate over the role and influence of court women in politics.[3]

Liu Xiang was a scion of the Han imperial family. His great-great-grandfather, Liu Jiao, was King of Chu (r. 201–178 BCE) and the younger half-brother of Liu Bang, the dynasty's founder. Liu Jiao was a man of scholarly interests who, as a youth, had concentrated his studies on the *Book of Odes*.[4] Liu Xiang's father, Liu De (d. 56 BCE), and grandfather, Liu Biqiang (b. ca. 160 BCE), both served terms as Superintendent of the Imperial Clan, a post that Liu Xiang himself filled in 48 BCE.[5] His learned, wealthy, and noble background, however, did not protect him from the usual dangers of public life in Han times. He was imprisoned and faced execution for his role in a costly (and not surprisingly) unsuccessful attempt to produce gold using alchemical techniques.[6] But he was spared when his brother paid fines to redeem him in 56 BCE. In 55 BCE, he was welcomed back to court with a commission to study the Guliang commentary of the *Spring and Autumn Annals*.[7] In the reign of Emperor Yuan (r. 48–33 BCE), as the victim of court rivalries, Liu Xiang once again faced dismissal and imprisonment.[8] But in 33 BCE, when Emperor Cheng came to the throne, he was recalled to office and was soon promoted to the rank of Counselor of the Palace.[9] In 26 BCE, Liu Xiang was ordered to collect ancient texts for collation and incorporation into the imperial library.[10] We can surmise that it was in the course of this work that he began to collect accounts of noteworthy women that would later culminate in the *Lienü zhuan*. He was assisted in the imperial library by a group of scholars that included his son, Liu Xin (46 BCE–23 CE). The end result of their labors was not only the creation of numerous editions of texts, many of which have been transmitted to the present day, but also the compilation of China's first bibliography, called the "Bielu" (Separate Record). The "Bielu" became the basis for Liu Xin's "Qi Lüe" (Seven Summaries), the seven divisions under which Xin classified all the writings in the imperial holdings, and which Ban Gu later incorporated into his bibliography in the *Hanshu*.

In this first comprehensive bibliography, Ban Gu notes some sixty-seven *pian* (sections) of Liu Xiang's own writings, which according to Ban Gu's note, included a lost text entitled *Shishuo* (Tales of the World), as well as Liu Xiang's *Xinxu* (New Collations), *Shuoyuan* (Garden of Eloquence), and *Lienü zhuan song tu* (Categorized Biographies of Women with Verse Summaries and Illustrations).[11] Liu Xiang presented these three texts to the throne sometime around 17 BCE.[12] The *Hanshu* provides the specific impetus for Liu Xiang's compilation of the texts:

> Xiang observed that customs had become extravagant and dissolute and that those who had risen from obscurity, such as Zhao and Wei, had overstepped the rites.[13] Xiang believed that royal teachings proceed from the domestic sphere to the public realm and originate from things close at hand. From the *Odes* and other documents he therefore selected records of worthy consorts and chaste wives who had contributed to the rise of states or made their families illustrious to serve as exemplars. He also included those who were depraved and favored and who caused chaos and destruction. He arranged them according to a specific sequence to create the *Categorized Biographies of Women* in eight *pian* as a warning to the Son of Heaven. He also collected records and accounts of various events and created the *New Collations* and the *Garden of Eloquence* in fifty *pian* and submitted them to the throne.[14]

Thus, according to Ban Gu, the impetus behind Liu Xiang's creation of the *Lienü zhuan* was twofold: to counteract the deleterious influence of women from the lower orders of society on dynastic health and to provide positive exemplars as a standard by which the ruler could judge the moral worth of his consorts and upon which court women could model their own conduct. Ban Gu's statement also makes specific reference to two low-born individuals—Empress Zhao and Favorite Beauty Wei—whose excesses, he claims, contravened the rites.

In Han times, the humble origins of imperial women had already begun to raise eyebrows during the reign of Emperor Wu (141–87 BCE). Sima Qian noted that all of the women Emperor Wu favored had gained the emperor's affection because they were entertainers. Furthermore, because they were not the daughters of nobles or landed gentry, he believed that they were unfit to serve as imperial consorts.[15] Sima Qian did not state specifically why he believed wealthy or noble women were more suited to imperial honors than entertainers from humble families. But we can surmise that in his view, a poor girl was unlikely to have received either the kind of upbringing that would enable her to interact on an equal footing with the elite or the sort of education that would allow her to understand her duties as helpmate to the supreme ruler.

As a scholar, Sima Qian was steeped in classical views that regarded the bond between man and woman as sacred. He noted the priority of this theme in canonical texts: the *Book of Changes*, for example, opens with the male and female trigrams, Qian and Kun; the *Book of Odes* begins with a paean to a virtuous royal consort; the *Book of Documents* praises Yao's bestowal of his two daughters as brides to Shun in its first chapter; and the *Spring and Autumn Annals* in its opening pages warns about neglecting the proper rites of marriage. Moreover, as a historian, Sima Qian was schooled in the belief that the rise and fall of dynasties was at least partly due to the good or destructive influence of the ruler's consorts. He therefore regarded the imperial consort as an essential component in dynastic stability: the right sort of woman would support the imperial house; the wrong sort would topple it. Finally, as an intellectual influenced by the cosmological theories of his own day, Sima Qian subscribed to the notion that the permutations of yin and yang order and produce all things and events. Thus, from his perspective, marriage, particularly imperial marriage, which embodied the union of yin and yang, partook of the cosmic process, and its influence resonated throughout Heaven and earth—it was not a vehicle for self-gratification.[16]

We can attribute the new presence of women, such as the slave-turned-empress Wei Zifu, in the highest echelons of Han society to at least four changes that occurred in elite culture between the Eastern Zhou (771–256 BCE) and the Former Han (206 BCE–8 CE): 1) the transformation of a multistate system into a centralized empire, which resulted in marriages between rulers and consorts who a) were the ruler's social inferiors (because no family possessed status equal to that of the emperor), but b) were from within the realm and thus from families positioned to amass power at court; 2) the discontinuation of the elite practice of sororal polygyny, which provided more opportunities for low-ranking women to assume the position of empress in the event that a ruler's principal wife was barren or died young; 3) the practice of sending the ruler's male relatives away from the capital, which created a power vacuum at court that women and their male kin filled; and finally 4) the expansion of the bureaucracy, which opened the door to more numerous and more lucrative bureaucratic positions for women.[17]

In general, however, the conduct of court women did not become part of a more generalized "women problem" until the time of Chengdi (r. 33–7 BCE). Even Empress Lü's (d. 180 BCE) reign was not curtailed on the basis of gender; she remained in power until her death by natural causes and was given her own imperial annals in Sima Qian's history.[18] Moreover, after she died, there was no initiation of programs for the control of women by moral education. The immediate solution to preventing the emergence of another politically astute empress dowager with a powerful base of male kin was to enthrone a woman with fewer, less aggressive male relatives.[19] This policy worked well until Wudi ascended the throne.

During the reign of Emperor Wu and that of his father, kingdoms originally given to the emperor's paternal kinsmen were eventually stripped away after it became clear that even members of the Liu imperial family could not be trusted with large territories and independent authority. By 154 BCE, kings were no longer permitted to rule over their domains. Wudi dealt the final blow when he decreed that kings could no longer bequeath their kingdoms to a single heir but had to divide up their territories equally among all their sons.[20] Further, by sending all male relatives of the imperial line away from the capital and appointing the male kin of his imperial consorts to key military posts, Wudi unwittingly constructed a firm foundation for the resurgence of consort power at court.

Indeed, once Wei Zifu was appointed empress (128 BCE), Wei Qing and Huo Qubing, her brother and nephew, respectively, became two of the dynasty's most celebrated generals; Huo Guang, her sister's stepson, came to occupy the office of Marshal of State, one of the most powerful positions in the government; her son was named imperial heir apparent; and her great-grandson acceded to the throne as Xuandi.[21]

The machinations of the Huo family, in particular, a plot ascribed to Huo Guang's wife, Huo Xian, would claim the life of Xuandi's Empress Xu, who was poisoned by Xian so that her own daughter could be named empress.[22] In 67 BCE, however, the Huos' influence finally ceased after Xuandi got wind of their plan to seize imperial power.[23] Once the court had been purged of the Huo family, Xuandi filled the vacuum with a number of reformist statesmen whose conservative views on female roles would have far reaching effects on elite women. But these reformers would have to wait until the next reign (Yuandi's) before they could effect any real change.

When Yuandi came to the throne in 49 BCE, he apparently preferred to indulge his interest in music rather than attend to government affairs and left many official matters to his eunuch Shi Xian. Thus, ignoring the lesson of the crisis caused by the Huo family in the previous reign, Yuandi allowed consort power to accrue once again. His maternal relatives—the Xu and Shi clans—conspired with Shi Xian and soon gained control of court politics.[24] It was also thanks to the eunuch Shi Xian that some of the most vocal spokesmen on the dangers of consort clans were ousted. The casualties included Liu Xiang and the unfortunate Xiao Wangzhi, who was forced to commit suicide.[25] But Shi's power ended with Yuandi's death. When Chengdi came to the throne in 33 BCE, Shi Xian resigned, and the reformer Liu Xiang was welcomed back to court.[26] Thus, in contrast to the difficulties posed by the male relatives of imperial consorts, the reign of Yuandi was relatively uneventful in terms of attacks on the morals of court women themselves. This state of affairs may have been due to the fact that Confucian presence at court had averted a potential crisis by convincing Yuandi of the danger of favoring a concubine and her son over the reigning empress and heir apparent.[27]

Yuandi was succeeded by his son, Liu Ao, who ascended the throne as Emperor Cheng (r. 33–7 BCE). In the first ten years of Chengdi's reign, both his empress, née Xu, and his concubine, the Beautiful Companion Ban (Ban Jieyu), bore him sons, but none of these infants survived. Around 20 BCE, Chengdi's mother—the Empress Dowager Wang—and other high officials who were anxious about the line of succession urged Chengdi to distribute his favors more evenly among the palace women so that he might produce an heir. It was at this time that Chengdi became acquainted with a dancer named Zhao Feiyan, who, along with her sister, was brought to court. The Zhao sisters soon dominated the emperor's affections. Around 18 BCE, they engineered the removal of Empress Xu and Ban Jieyu from court by accusing them of practicing sorcery against the emperor and against other palace women who enjoyed the emperor's favors. In 16 BCE, Zhao Feiyan became empress; her sister gained the title Brilliant Companion and soon eclipsed even the empress in Chengdi's affection.

In his description of the motivating forces behind Liu Xiang's composition of the *Lienü zhuan,* Ban Gu makes reference to the excesses of the low-born Zhao Feiyan and the Brilliant Companion Wei. Virtually nothing is known about Wei apart from her humble (and, most likely, slave) background and Ban Jieyu's selfless promotion of her when Ban failed to produce sons for Emperor Cheng.[28] By contrast, records concerning Zhao Feiyan, to which we will return in a moment, provide a great deal of information about this slave-turned-empress. In Chengdi's reign, intellectuals such as Liu Fu, Du Qin, Gu Yong, and Kuang Heng began to address the ruler directly concerning the base origins and untoward behavior of his women.[29] Pointing to the lessons of history, they argued that previous dynasties had been destroyed because of the influence of evil women close to the ruler and that the ethical behavior of court women was essential to a strong empire.

Increased interest in the moral development of women had begun in a symbolic way not long after Chengdi assumed power. In 30 BCE, an eight-year-old girl named Chen Chigong, reacting to reports that a flood was about to engulf the city, fled and eventually wandered into the women's quarters of the Weiyang Palace without being detected by the guards.[30] This event was interpreted as signifying that the power of yin was in the ascendant and that the court was occupied by base individuals whose positions were awarded not on the basis of merit but according to the emperor's partiality toward the relatives of Chengdi's mother, Empress Dowager Wang.[31] From the reign of Xuandi onward, critics began to rely increasingly on the incidence of eclipses, floods, comets, and other natural anomalies to indict powerful court women as well as their male kin. References to portents may have emboldened critics in their accusations, as their claims appeared to be based on the impartial evidence of nature rather than on their own personal judgment alone. Moreover, because the concept of yin and yang had by now become increasingly linked to human gender norms, unnatural phenomena could be used to demonstrate, for example, how yin, associated with feminine powers, might dominate yang, a force identified with the emperor's rightful authority.[32] Nevertheless, because the *Lienü zhuan* is compiled largely of anecdotes from earlier works that do not in their original form draw upon yin-yang thought, this dualistic system plays a very small role in the text.

Thus, in summary, by the late Former Han, reformist officials began to use both omenology and moral instruction to curtail female influence and mold it along more Confucian lines. Chengdi's two empresses, Xu and Zhao, resisted this instruction, arousing the enmity of Chengdi's Confucian counselors, and both eventually died for their defiance. The concubine Ban Jieyu, ironically, embraced such teachings but was never enthroned as empress.

Empress Xu

When Yuandi arranged the marriage of his heir apparent, the future Chengdi, he chose a daughter of the Xu family, in memory of his deceased mother, Xu Pingjun, the empress who had been poisoned at the behest of Huo Xian. The bride's father, Xu Jia, was a first cousin of Yuandi's mother.[33] The bride had been selected in accordance with the recently lauded practice of favoring the maternal relatives of the reigning emperor.[34] When Chengdi finally came to the throne and named Xu as his empress, Xu Jia had already occupied the post of Commander-in-Chief for some time. But now he was made to share the title with Wang Feng, the brother of Chengdi's own mother, Empress Wang. Soon afterward, Xu Jia was asked to retire, and when he died several years later, Xu power began to decline at court and along with it, support for Empress Xu.[35]

In 30 BCE, one year after being installed as empress, Empress Xu still had not produced an heir.[36] Intellectuals concerned about Chengdi's lack of progeny then proceeded to build a case against the empress by pointing to baleful omens as Heaven's negative judgment of her. An earthquake and an eclipse that occurred simultaneously that year were, according to Liu Xiang and Gu Yong, Heaven's warnings about the empress's selfish monopoly of imperial favor.[37] Chengdi was thus urged to spread his affections more widely in the hope of producing an heir. Empress Xu protested, but to no avail. Eventually, in 17 BCE, she was deposed when Chengdi's most recent favorite, the concubine Zhao Feiyan, made accusations against the empress, her sister, and a former favorite, Ban Jieyu. Zhao alleged that they had used magical charms to win back the affections of the emperor and placed curses on palace ladies who were carrying Chengdi's unborn children. Finally, in 8 BCE, the deposed Empress Xu was presented with poison and committed suicide when it was made known that she had attempted to bribe various people to reinstate her as empress.[38] We can attribute her untimely death to shifts in court politics and failure to produce an heir. From another perspective, her failure to choose between two extreme modes of behavior—the Machiavellian cunning of Zhao Feiyan and the Confucian conformism of Ban Jieyu—proved to be her undoing.

Ban Jieyu

After Chengdi was urged to look beyond Empress Xu in his quest for progeny, Ban Jieyu became the emperor's new favorite. Her brother, Ban You (d. 2 BCE), was a learned scholar who worked with Liu Xiang in the imperial library.[39] Although we must remain skeptical of Ban Gu's statements about the virtues of his illustrious great-aunt, the *Hanshu* takes pains to suggest how seriously Ban Jieyu took to heart the teachings represented by female exemplars of ages past. For example, once, when Chengdi suggested that Ban accompany him for a ride in a hand-drawn cart, she refused the offer, explaining, "In the paintings of ancient times one always sees the sage rulers with eminent ministers by their side; it is only the last rulers of the Three Epochs who are shown with their women. Now if you invite me to share your cart, won't that make you look like one of them?"[40] Both the emperor and the empress dowager were deeply impressed by her response. When she failed to produce a child that survived beyond infancy, once again she modeled herself on the virtuous women of antiquity and selflessly recommended to the emperor one of her female attendants, Li Ping, who was soon promoted to the rank of Brilliant Companion. But Chengdi became bored with this woman as well, and his affections were soon focused exclusively on the dancer Zhao Feiyan. In 18 BCE, when Ban was charged along with Empress Xu for cursing the emperor and his women, she was ultimately spared because of her eloquent response to the authorities. She then wisely sought permission to withdraw from the harem in order to serve the empress dowager instead.[41] Ban's attempt to model herself on feminine exemplars from antiquity did not prevent the emperor from favoring the Zhao sisters, but her training in philosophical argumentation and her compliance with Confucian teachings seem to have kept her from harm.

Zhao Feiyan

If we can believe traditional accounts, Zhao Feiyan, a former slave and dancer, lacked scruples to the same degree that Ban possessed Confucian morals. Zhao Feiyan was also barren, but Chengdi felt sufficiently bound to her that he named her empress despite vociferous protests from all quarters. Empress Zhao, moreover, relied on an unofficial form of sororal polygyny to maintain her position once the emperor's affections began to cool. After she became empress, her younger sister became Chengdi's favorite. But because the sister resisted the impulse to pursue the title of empress herself, Zhao Feiyan was able to maintain her position to the end of the reign, even after Chengdi lost all interest in her.

Liu Xiang's concerns about Zhao Feiyan (and her sister) proved well founded. In 12 BCE, sensational events took place that were not made public until the next reign, when officials were asked to investigate the suspicious circumstances surrounding Chengdi's death in 7 BCE.[42] Through a series of interrogations, it came to be known that in 12 BCE, a slave in the empress's palace had given birth to Chengdi's son. Upon being informed of this, the emperor issued orders that the child, its mother, and those who attended at the birth were to be confined to a jail connected to the palace. Three days later, the emperor sent an inquiry to the jail asking if the child was dead yet, signaling his desire to do away with any infant not borne by his empress or her sister. When Chengdi and the Brilliant Companion Zhao learned that the child still lived, they were furious and demanded an explanation. The prison warden replied that whether he disobeyed the emperor's orders or went ahead and killed the child, he would still be guilty of great wrongdoing. He then boldly urged the emperor to reconsider killing the son who constituted his only heir. At this point, Chengdi seems to have changed his mind and assigned a wet nurse to the child. But soon afterward, the mother and the birth attendants were made to commit suicide, and the child disappeared.

Because the Brilliant Companion Zhao had exacted promises of fidelity from Chengdi, when a concubine named Xu gave birth to another son by him in 11 BCE, witnesses reported that the Brilliant Companion was outraged. The child was taken from its mother and delivered in a hamper to Chengdi and the Brilliant Companion. All attendants were asked to leave the room. Some time later, the emperor emerged from the room and ordered the hamper, now containing a dead child, to be buried near the prison wall. The inquisition also revealed that other women who bore the emperor children had been murdered or made to abort.[43] Clearly, Chengdi felt sure he could always produce more sons, and this must have figured in his decision to kill these infants. But his confidence turned out to be misplaced. With no son, he was ultimately forced to choose his successor from the ranks of his male kin. With the support of Zhao Feiyan, Chengdi made Liu Xin, his second cousin, his heir.

Liu Xin was eighteen years old when he assumed the throne.[44] He reigned as Aidi (i.e., Emperor Ai) for the brief span between 7 and 1 BCE. Because Emperor Ai was beholden to Zhao Feiyan for her part in bringing him to the throne, even after an investigation brought to light the Zhao sisters' involvement in the murder of Chengdi's two infant sons, Aidi allowed Zhao Feiyan to serve as empress dowager throughout his reign. After his death, however, in 1 BCE, she was stripped of her rank and committed suicide.[45]

Thus, from the mid–Former Han onward, the resurgence of consort power at court provided Confucian thinkers with a powerful incentive to focus on how to shape women's morals and their impact on dynastic health. It is therefore no coincidence that in the latter half of the Former Han, something entirely new appeared: didactic materials for the moral education of women.

Women's Education

Little is known about female education before the mid–Former Han (ca. 74 BCE). Terse accounts found in bronze inscriptions from the Shang and Zhou dynasties provide hints about women's ritual activities.[46] Among traditionally transmitted texts, one of the earliest sources to mention instruction for women is the *Zhouli* (late fourth century to early third century BCE), a prescriptive text that purports to describe the structure of royal government in the Zhou dynasty. This text lays out the bureaucratic duties of officials assigned to educate court women in "women's rites" (陰禮 *yinli*) as well as in appropriate virtues, speech, bearing, and work. The *Zhouli* simply lists these subject headings without further elaboration, which may suggest that the instruction was nonliterary in nature.[47] Numerous anecdotes from the *Zuo zhuan* also portray women as following well-developed codes of feminine behavior, but no texts (or even titles of texts) setting out these codes have been transmitted from the pre-Qin period.[48]

During the Qin dynasty, the First Emperor seems to have made sporadic efforts to shape women's morals through his public display of inscribed stelae.[49] By the Former Han, particularly during the first half of the period, extant sources generally mention female education only in connection with girls who planned to enter the imperial harem, and their training tended to focus on dance and music; literacy and classical mastery are rarely mentioned.[50] But in the second half of the Former Han, as literacy and classical learning began to assume increasing importance in the culture at large, girls began to receive formal education as preparation for life at court. For example, Ban Jieyu mentions contemplating paintings of famous women as guides to correct deportment, as well as receiving instruction in the lives of female exemplars from a woman versed in the *Odes*:

> I lay out my portraits of women, and make them my mirror,
> I turn to the Women's Counselor and query her on the *Odes*.
> I take to heart warnings about the wife who "announces the dawn,"
> And lament the evil deeds of the voluptuous Bao Si.
> I admire Huang and Ying, the two wives of Shun,
> And glorify Ren and Si, the matriarchs of the Zhou.
> Though I am ignorant and cannot aspire to their examples,
> How could I put them out of mind and forget them?[51]

Her biography adds that in addition to the *Odes*, she could recite (*song* 誦) the texts *The Modest Maiden* (*Yaotiao* 窈窕), *Emblems of Virtue* (*Dexiang* 德象), and *The Instructress* (*Nüshi* 女師), all lost works that appear to have been guides to correct feminine deportment.[52] These texts may well have been precursors to the *Lienü zhuan*. But because they are no longer extant, we can say little about their content apart from noting the Confucian tone of their titles.

Schemes to educate women were one of the few options open to Confucians who sought alternative means to rein in imperial women they could not otherwise control. But the new stress on Confucian learning in female education also reflects a utopian notion that was rapidly gaining currency in the latter half of the Former Han dynasty: that only when the entire population engages in self-cultivation will the empire achieve an era of great peace (太平 *taiping*).[53] The *Lienü zhuan*, with lessons that guide women from all levels of society, is the earliest extant text that sought to shape the entire female population in the Confucian mold. Furthermore, in the reign of Xuandi we begin to see Han imperial interest in rewarding the exemplary behavior of female subjects as another means of promoting a specific moral code.

Two imperial commands specifically targeted the female population. In 63 BCE, Xuandi rewarded with salaries, houses, and precious objects the women who had saved his life by suckling him in the aftermath of the black magic affair of 91 BCE.[54] This edict represents the first recognition of service to the emperor that extended down to the very lowest ranks of the female population. In 58 BCE, in conjunction with special honors Xuandi conferred on Huang Ba, the grand administrator of Yingchuan commandery, chaste widows and obedient daughters in Huang Ba's district were awarded gifts of silk.[55] This is the first mention in the dynastic histories of female subjects being officially recognized for their high morals. The next mention, however, did not come until a half-century later, when in 1 CE, during the regency of Wang Mang, one chaste wife was chosen from each village to receive tax-exempt status.[56]

Early evidence that girls who married high-ranking officials were, like their husbands, beginning to feel pressured to cultivate Confucian virtues also appears in the mid to late Former Han. For example, Wang Ji (d. ca. 48 BCE), grandee remonstrant under Emperor Xuan, divorced his wife for what was in his view a form of stealing, specifically, picking jujubes from the branch of a neighbor's tree that overhung the Wangs' yard. The story suggests that the behavior of women married to Confucian bureaucrats needed to correspond to the high ideals professed by their husbands.[57] As extreme as this case was, such incidents must have made an impression on young girls who hoped to marry ambitious officials.[58] At this early period, there are few recorded incidents illustrating such radical concern on the part of Confucian officials for the morals of their womenfolk; what attracted far more attention was the behavior of women at court.

Dynastics

With very few exceptions, the *Lienü zhuan* seeks to demonstrate how the actions of women either support or weaken the health and reputation of a family or dynasty. The unifying theme of the collection as a whole can thus be best understood with reference to "dynastics," by which I mean an ideology for reinforcing habits of deference to a family-based hierarchy for the sake of its ongoing continuity and prestige. In many respects, dynastics resembles the ideology of filial piety in the broadest sense of that term, specifically, in its directive to maintain the health and luster of one's ancestral legacy by producing and educating a continuous line of heirs who sustain and enhance social standing. Dynastics incorporates those individuals included in the most capacious definition of filial piety, promoting not only the flourishing of the enduring family or dynastic unit but also a concern for family or dynasty on the part of nonfamily members, such as servants or slaves who are bound to a family, as well as others concerned with the family writ large—subjects of a political unit, such as a state or a dynasty in which the ruler is envisioned as the "father and mother of the people."[59] The broad scope of individuals included in this self-perpetuating agenda thus renders the word "filial" inappropriate. And while the notion of dynastics incorporates filial piety (*xiao*), it also encompasses other virtues, such as loyalty (*zhong*), righteousness (*yi*), compliance (*shun*), and faithfulness (*xin*). At times, however, the dynastic agenda is divorced from ethical considerations and involves amoral or even immoral directives, such as the vaunting of self-serving and ruthless ambition to further family power, position, or wealth. This aspect of dynastics is exemplified, for example, in the *Lienü zhuan* biography of Jiang of Qi, wife of Duke Wen of Jin, who without apology or regret put to death an innocent servant who overheard politically sensitive information and thus represented a threat to state security.[60] The term "piety" in the standard translation of *xiao* thus also seems ill-suited to the moral exigencies frequently broached in fulfilling the dynastic imperative.

Dynastics is also distinct from patriarchy, which can be defined as a system of authority that is gendered male. In contrast to the gender-based notion of patriarchy, dynastics focuses on the *transmission* and *perpetuation* of a specific power structure. Dynastics is thus more concerned with maintaining continuity than with shoring up masculine power. Because patriarchy often monopolizes power, the two converge on a regular basis. Dynastics, however, is concerned with perpetuating and rationalizing hegemony that is already entrenched. It is a verbal and behavioral mechanism for perpetuating power, whether it is masculine or not. We therefore see in the narratives of the *Lienü zhuan* and elsewhere in early Chinese literature not just women subordinating themselves to men but also husbands, sons, and brothers who are directed to defer to women as a means to sustain dynastic power or family prestige.[61]

In the *Lienü zhuan*, there is little in the way of morality that does not support a dynastic status quo. One of a small handful of exceptions is the biography of Xu Wu, a poor woman who could not afford to supply her own candles and asked to work in the candlelight provided by others.[62] With its emphasis on an act of charity by one ordinary woman to another, it is one of the few stories that ignores the dynastic imperative and is thus anomalous in the collection. In many cases, however, overlooking a dynastic agenda will render the actions of the protagonist as bizarre or foolish. For example, in the story of Fan Ji of Chu, Fan might be mistaken as a woman so witless as to undermine her own relationship with her husband by introducing scores of women into his bed. But if we read the story through the perspective of dynastics, we come to understand her as never having conceived of her marriage in personal terms from the onset. Her relationship to the ruler is depersonalized to allow the dynastic mentality to predominate. Thus, just as a minister should promote worthies, even when he might be supplanted by those whom he introduces into the ruler's service, so too a woman is enjoined to refrain from jealousy and promote other women who might excel her in their ability to please, advise, or produce progeny for the ruler.

In the biography of Fan Ji, the relationship between husband and wife is presented as professional and impersonal, with the interests of all individuals placed beneath those of the enduring family or dynastic unit. Thus, a woman must perform her occupational duties for the greater glory of her husband's line in the same way as a minister performs his. Fan Ji explains her desire to supply her husband with worthy women as follows: "I have heard that there should be many women filling one's hall so that you can have a chance to observe their abilities. I cannot use my personal desires to conceal the public good but prefer your majesty to observe many women and understand their abilities."[63] The implication is presumably that there may be other women who can excel Fan in producing progeny or who are able through their moral influence to enhance the health of the dynasty. Furthermore, the didactic nature of the *Lienü zhuan* forces us to read her incentive for introducing more women to the king as driven by morality or the desire to promote dynastic continuity; otherwise she is simply encouraging her husband to indulge in excess and lust, acts associated with the female exemplars of evil found in the final chapter of the *Lienü zhuan*. Liu Xiang presents her motivation as arising in connection with enhancing the public good [公 *gong*]. This reference again underscores the professional nature of her marital relationship and the way it overlaps with the duties of the minister.

It is also due to the dynastic imperative that many of the lessons of the *Lienü zhuan* veer away from a direct concern for women and concentrate on how women can support those in power. For example, in the "Outcast Orphan Maid of Qi," what begins as a story about a woman who overcomes her great ugliness by developing her inner beauty ultimately becomes a lesson on how to encourage worthy men to serve the state.[64] Stories involving acts of personal kindness or charity between women that do not directly bolster state or family concerns are therefore an infrequent feature of this text.

Women in the Breach

A large number of narratives in the *Lienü zhuan* also portray women as mediators who must step in to assist menfolk who, for a variety of reasons, fail to fulfill their duties to either family or ruler. Thus, when the affairs of the "outer realm," that is, the male-dominated public sphere, go awry, the *Lienü zhuan* deems it appropriate and commendable for women to step into the breach and set things right. For example, a daughter might stand in for a filial son in a family with no male offspring, or a wife might set her husband straight on affairs of state when he either neglects or fails to understand his duty.[65] We might term the dynamic of this mediation as "inner versus outer," "male versus female," or "provisional versus institutional," as the moral solution to the problem involves dissolving or negotiating the boundaries that usually separate these pairs. The moral territory negotiated in this sort of dynamic reveals the cultural contradictions, fault lines, or gaps in societal, religious, or political norms that clearly weakened or threatened the stability of both family and state.

A frequent concern of the *Lienü zhuan* is how inferiors can effectively criticize their superiors, particularly in cases where the gap between them is especially great (e.g., commoner vs. aristocrat), but also when there is a gender divide that forces a woman to move outside her normal sphere of activity. In such cases, women are doubly challenged in terms of their positions in both the hierarchy of social rank and the hierarchy of gender. All of these dynamics point to the ways the established system breaks down. The *Lienü zhuan* is thus concerned with how best to overcome these systemic weaknesses and ideological inconsistencies while leaving the status quo intact. The text thus frequently sanctions crossing gender boundaries, moving from the domestic sphere into the world of politics and statecraft in order to right a wrong that no one else is willing to address. But while the *Lienü zhuan* prompts women to step outside traditional roles, it also suggests that after the task is completed, women must then resume their roles as daughters or wives. Often, women in this text who successfully address problems receive no material reward or elevation in social status. The result is the return of equilibrium to the existing social structure. Nevertheless, the female protagonist is elevated in the eyes of the reader as a worthy, and one who is more extraordinary than her male counterparts by virtue of her operating in an unfamiliar sphere.

In the majority of narratives found in the *Lienü zhuan*, women are generally portrayed as acting in response to some form of conflict, crisis, or dangerous trend that threatens family or dynasty. Thus, the primary dynamic or set of opposing principles is often that of a provisional solution offered by women, who are normally not supposed to meddle in public affairs, and a critical situation that men have failed to address. At the same time, the women act with the knowledge that they must return to the status quo; that is, resume their normal gender roles. In the context of criticizing superiors, this dynamic differs from that in which men operate in that the filial son is permitted to admonish his father, but eventually he will grow into the role of the father and assume that authority. A filial wife, however, may criticize her husband's political acts, but she will never completely assume his authority. The filial wife thus does not offer political advice to replace her husband any more than the filial son attempts to replace his father. Both must step back to their original roles after offering their critique, though the son steps aside only until his father dies. There is however no official place in the outer realm for a woman as a decision maker or governor. But she is valued as an outside observer who is encouraged to intervene when those in charge fail in their duties.

Thus, the *Lienü zhuan* is not arguing for an inflexible separation of the sexes or for rigid adherence to various oppositions between men and women, such as inner versus outer, superior versus inferior, but suggests the ways women can mediate or temporarily transcend those distinctions. It acknowledges that power predicated on a strict system of division can easily break down and that women's contributions are key to dynastic health and survival. But women are nevertheless welcome to participate in a provisional and temporary way. A large number of biographies in the *Lienü zhuan* thus focus on the ways a woman can uphold the legacy of her husband's family, and many of these tales depict the delicate dance between a woman's participation in the management of his family, dynasty, or kingdom in times of danger or crisis and the cultural imperatives that bar her from that participation.

Like his grandfather and father before him, Liu Xiang served as the Superintendent of the Imperial Clan. It is therefore no surprise that dynastic health should figure as a central concern of the text. The examination of how women can contribute to the health and continuity of family and dynasty is furthermore linked to what Liu Xiang perceived as the primary threat to Han power: court women who selfishly furthered their own interests and the interests of their natal families over those of the dynasty. Nevertheless, although the dynastic crisis that threatened the reign of Emperor Cheng was the result of specific historical conditions and particular individuals who occupied the court, because Liu Xiang drew upon narratives that predated his own age to compile the *Lienü zhuan*, it is clear that the problem, in its broader outlines, was not entirely new. What is new is the compilation of a text designed to address it.

"Speaking truth to power" is always a delicate business, and even more difficult for those crossing gender boundaries. The *Lienü zhuan* was thus almost certainly meant to provide more than an array of lessons for quiet contemplation; it was, in some important respects, also a textbook of rhetoric that accommodated women and prepared them to voice their concerns in both the private and public sphere. When we take into account the stress the *Lienü zhuan* places on words, reason, and skill in argumentation, this text may also be viewed as a companion piece to Liu Xiang's *Shuo yuan* or *Garden of Eloquence*. As Eric Henry has noted in the introduction to his translation of the *Shuoyuan*, "Among the tools of statesmanship, Liu Xiang placed paramount importance on skill in speech, hence the title of the collection: *The Garden of Eloquence*. Upon this skill, he felt, the survival or destruction of states, dynasties, and individuals depended."[66] In many cases, the biographies of the *Lienü zhuan* serve primarily as vehicles for formal speeches that exemplify successful rhetorical strategies and are less intent on providing details about the subjects' lives. Still, whether highlighting the life or the rhetoric of its biographical subjects, the *Lienü zhuan* was unique in its focus on women's crucial role in dynastic health.

THE TEXT

Sources

The *Zuo zhuan*, *Shijing*, *Shiji*, *Guoyu*, and *Hanshi waizhuan* comprise the primary texts from which much of the narrative material of *Lienü zhuan* is derived, but textual parallels can be found in a large body of other works.[67] In his magisterial work, *Ryū kō Retsujoden no kenkyū*, Shimomi Takao distinguishes how stories found in the *Lienü zhuan* relate to previous sources, noting: 1) biographies for which the apparent source text is known and that use the source as a basis for the story; 2) biographies for which it is possible to surmise the source text but that contain different elements or a different sequence of events; 3) biographies for which it is difficult to identify a specific source but that may be linked to earlier material and may have been significantly modified by Liu Xiang; 4) biographies whose sources cannot be ascertained but that concern known historical events or personages; and 5) biographies with no known precursors.[68] He categorizes roughly half of the stories as the first type and less than one-fifth of the biographies as having no known precursors. For each biography, Shimomi explores the relationship between *Lienü zhuan* narratives and their sources in extensive annotations and philological notes. The precise relationship between an individual biography and earlier texts is complex and varies from biography to biography.[69] But in general, when the *Lienü zhuan* departs from early sources, it is most often when female characters are given speaking parts that occupy less space or are entirely absent in earlier texts, or when narratives include female characters that do not appear in precursors. Much ink has been spilt arguing whether these variations were created by Liu Xiang or not. The sheer variety of lessons for women found in the *Lienü zhuan*, especially the contradictory messages they convey, suggest that Liu Xiang often let earlier sources speak for themselves rather than rigorously editing them to conform to one coherent vision. The most glaring example is the pronouncement that a woman must obey her son after her husband dies and the many stories that portray women who dominate their sons with unshakeable resolve. At the same time, it was a general practice of writers from mid–Warring States times through the Han to alter earlier sources to conform to their individual styles and ideological concerns. In keeping with this practice, it is more than likely that Liu Xiang also changed and embellished earlier accounts to accord with the specific tone, style, and agenda of the *Lienü zhuan*.[70] Ultimately, however, in the case of textual variants, it is impossible to know if Liu was working from some earlier source that is no longer extant or simply inventing plots, characters, or dialogues to suit his didactic needs.

Structure and Content

Most modern editions of the *Lienü zhuan* include Liu Xiang's original seven chapters plus one chapter of biographies that were added in the Later Han (25–220 CE). But the process by which it achieved this final form was long and complicated. The *Lienü zhuan* is mentioned twice in the *Hanshu*. It is listed in the catalog of the imperial collection, the "Yiwen zhi" (Treatise on Arts and Letters), as one work entitled *Lienü zhuan song tu* (Categorized Biographies of Women with Verse Summaries and Illustrations), along with several other works included in the sixty-seven *pian* of Liu Xiang's opus.[71] In Liu Xiang's biography, however, the *Hanshu* records the title as simply *Lienü zhuan* (*Categorized Biographies of Women*) in eight *pian* with no reference to illustrations or verse summaries.[72] The text is also mentioned in a fragment of Liu Xiang's "Bielu" (Separate Record) that has been preserved in the Tang dynasty compendium *Chuxue ji,* where it is described as consisting of seven sections.[73]

Various scholars, such as Zeng Gong 曾鞏 (1019–1083) and Wang Yuansun 汪遠孫 (1764–1836), have understood the eight sections of the *Lienü zhuan* to refer to the first seven chapters of biographies of the modern edition and one section of *song* (頌) "verse summaries."[74] Citing the bibliographical chapter of the *Suishu,* Zeng Gong tells us that the *Lienü zhuan* had been edited and annotated by Cao Dagu (i.e., Ban Zhao, b. ca. 48 CE) in an edition of fifteen sections.[75] Zeng then argues that Ban Zhao divided each of Liu Xiang's original seven chapters into two sections, which, along with the one section of verse summaries, totaled fifteen sections.[76] To these, Zeng claims that Ban Zhao inserted into the seven original chapters of biographies additional accounts of women from the Later Han that were not in Liu Xiang's original text. Zeng further states that in the middle of the Jiayou period of the Song dynasty (1056–1063), Su Song 蘇頌 (1020–1101) reorganized the text to follow Liu Xiang's original eight sections.

Another Song scholar, Wang Hui 王回 (1048–1101), also created an edition of the *Lienü zhuan.* In his preface, which is the only remaining portion of his effort, he also mentions a fifteen-section edition, adding that it was annotated by Ban Zhao (Cao Dagu). Wang also states that Ban's was the most popular edition of his day.[77] Unfortunately, only a few fragments of Ban Zhao's commentary remain.[78] Wang Hui, however, considered that this edition was marred by interpolations. He therefore edited the book himself and restored it to the eight chapters of Liu Xiang's original text (i.e., seven chapters of biographies plus one chapter of verse summaries), then titled it *Gu Lienü zhuan* (Ancient Categorized Biographies of Women). To these eight chapters he appended the 續列女傳 "Xu Lienü zhuan" (Supplementary Categorized Biographies of Women), which consisted of twenty biographies that began with "The Woman of the Suburbs of Zhou" and ended with "Lady Liang Yi," a sequence that reflects the position of those two biographies in the text that has been transmitted to this day.[79] These twenty biographies may be the same as the material Ban Zhao inserted into Liu Xiang's original seven chapters.

In the "Ba" 跋 "Postscript" of yet another edition, that of Cai Ji 蔡驥 (fl. 1214 CE), Cai states that "At present the eight sections of the book are counted as including the seven sections of Liu Xiang's *Lienü zhuan* and the twenty biographies of the "Supplementary Biographies."[80] Cai Ji also tells us that he placed Liu Xiang's "Major Preface in Verse Summary" (頌義大序 Songyi Daxu), which is no longer extant, at the beginning of the table of contents, the "Minor Prefaces" (小序 Xiaoxu), which summarize each chapter, within the table of contents, and the individual verse summaries after each biography. This ordering of the various sections of the text reflects the current state of the transmitted text as found in sources such as the *Sibu beiyao*.

Wang Yuansun noted that among the editions that were circulating in his day, the oldest was the Southern Song dynasty edition of a Mr. Yu of Jian'an. This was based on the edition of Cai Ji.[81] Wang notes that Yu's edition was not ideal.[82] It was missing one biography in the first chapter ("Maternal Models") as well as the "Major Preface." Thus, all but the first of the seven sections of the *Lienü zhuan* contain fifteen biographies, while the eighth section, the "Supplementary Biographies," includes twenty. The original book is no longer extant, but copies exist, and all modern editions are based on this text.

The text of the *Lienü zhuan* as it has been transmitted to the present day has thus passed through many hands over the course of nearly two millennia.[83] It has been taken apart and put back together several times. We can only speculate on the degree to which the received text differs from Liu Xiang's original. The earliest archaeological evidence of the *Lienü zhuan* dates to the late Former Han period. In 1993, a tomb in Jiangsu was found to include the *Lienü zhuan* in an inventory of objects interred with a deceased couple.[84] Unfortunately, the text itself was not in the tomb. In 1907, Sir Aurel Stein uncovered a bamboo slip bearing the title *Lienü zhuan* from a Han settlement in Dunhuang, which is dated to 75 CE based on evidence from other documents recovered in the area.[85] A handful of fragments of the text found in encyclopedias and commentaries, such as Li Shan's (fl. 689) notes to the *Wenxuan*, occasionally provide variant readings of the received text.[86] Nevertheless, while we must rely for the most part on the Southern Song edition, the text as a whole seems consonant with the language and conventions of Warring States and Han literature.

In his Song dynasty preface to the *Lienü zhuan*, Zeng Gong comes close to admitting that he excised part of the text's opening biography, "The Two Consorts of Youyu." He says, "The passage concerning Xiang's plan to kill Shun and the means by which Shun escaped are in accord with the *Mencius*. But what was not relayed in the *Mencius* is not worth recounting."[87] As Yuan Ke points out in his study of Chinese myth, pre-Song and Song dynasty texts preserve versions of Shun's legend in which his consorts advise Shun to cloak himself in protective clothing for "bird work" and "dragon work" to escape being burned and drowned by his evil brother Xiang.[88] Shun thus dons these magical garments and is able to fly away from a burning granary and to tunnel his way to safety from a blocked well. A fifth-century painting on a lacquered coffin also portrays Shun standing atop a blazing granary with arms outstretched, poised for flight.[89] Not surprisingly, these fanciful elements played no role in Mencius' account of this myth.[90] But because the received version of the *Lienü zhuan* describes Shun as "flying forth" and "tunneling out" of his difficulties, without detailing how he might have achieved these feats, it is more than likely that references to the magical garb were deleted by Zeng Gong. Nevertheless, this case may be exceptional, as Zeng Gong seems to have taken some pains to alert the reader to his editorial decision.[91]

Finally, we need to take into account that the *Hanshu* "Yiwen zhi" records the title of Liu Xiang's work as the *Lienü zhuan song tu* (Categorized Biographies of Women with Verse Summaries and Illustrations), which suggests that illustrations were part of Liu Xiang's original text. Further evidence is supplied by a fragment of Liu Xiang's "Bielu," which says that the work was "illustrated on four panels of a screen."[92] Significantly, the *Hanshu* mentions that Emperor Cheng (r. 32–7 BCE) owned a screen that depicted the story of Da Ji, the favorite concubine of King Zhow of the Shang dynasty.[93] Wu Hung speculates that it is at least possible that this screen might have been the one designed by Liu Xiang.[94]

There are numerous references to and preserved examples of art that depict stories found in the *Lienü zhuan*.[95] In the Former Han, texts mention portraits of contemporary exemplary women that decorated the walls of palaces.[96] For example, Emperor Wu of the Han commissioned a portrait of the mother of his advisor, Jin Midi (d. 86 BCE), whom the emperor praised for her ability to raise sons of high moral reputation.[97] Wang Yanshou's (fl. 118–138) "Rhapsody on the Hall of Numinous Brilliance" describes murals in the palace of King Gong of Lu (r. 154–128 BCE) that depicted both exemplary women and debauched consorts who contributed to dynastic decline.[98]

The increased popularity of artwork depicting female exemplars in the Eastern Han may be linked to the dissemination of Liu Xiang's *Lienü zhuan*. Earlier, we mentioned exemplar paintings that Ban Jieyu consulted. In addition, at least two accounts from the *Hou Hanshu* describe both an emperor and an imperial consort who possessed pictures of virtuous women.[99] The great scholar Cai Yong (132–192) is also said to have executed paintings of exemplary women.[100] In addition to textual references to illustrations of exemplars, there is also extant art from the Later Han that represents virtuous women, such as the inscribed stones of the Wu Liang Shrines in Shandong, the inscribed stone murals from the temple of Li Gang (d. 172 CE) of Jingzhou, an inscribed stone coffin from Xinjing in Sichuan, and the Helinger murals of Inner Mongolia, which depict more than twenty women, many of whom can be identified by name and correspond to biographies in the *Lienü zhuan*.[101] Whether or not the growing numbers of exemplary women illustrated in Later Han art are linked to Liu Xiang's work, it is clear that interest in female exemplars, both in image and in text, was gaining ground across a broad geographical area at this time.

In the following sections, I shall consider the title of the text, the "Minor Prefaces," the components of each chapter, and the formal features of the biographies.

The Title

The word *zhuan* (傳) in the title *Lienü zhuan*, which I have translated as "biography," is associated with the term *liezhuan* (列傳), as first used in Sima Qian's *Shiji* to designate accounts "concerning the lives of individuals and peoples."[102] Sima Qian was the first to use the term *liezhuan* but never defined it. Its precise meaning therefore remains controversial. The term *zhuan* is often understood as meaning "traditions" or "transmissions." Some translators have argued that in the *Shiji, zhuan* carries the meaning of "commentary" with the sense that the *liezhuan* "supplement or complement the narrative line presented in the *benji* (basic annals)."[103] Liu Xiang had access to the *Shiji* through his work in the imperial library and is noted in the *Hanshu* for his admiration of this text.[104] But he was the first to bring together a collection of biographies that were not complements to separate historical apparatus such as the "Basic Annals" (本紀 *benji*) and the "Accounts of the Hereditary Houses" (世家 *shijia*) as found in the *Shiji*. In the case of the *Lienü zhuan*, the biographies form the entire basis of the work and therefore cannot be construed as supplementary in nature. I therefore translate the term as "biography," though "account" would also be a suitable rendering for those less comfortable with the strict identification of the term with biographical writing.

The word *lie* in the title *Lienü zhuan* poses a more complex problem. The *Shuowen jiezi* defines *lie* as "to divide" (分解 *fenjie*).[105] From this sense are derived other meanings such as "to rank in order" (次 *ci*), "to distinguish" (別 *bie*), and "to set forth" (陳 *chen*).[106] The Tang dynasty commentators of the *Shiji*, Sima Zhen (early eighth century) and Zhang Shoujie (fl. ca. 737), both understood the term *lie* to mean "to rank," or "to place in order" (i.e., 敘 *xu*, also written as

序).[107] *Lie,* as used in the term "various states" (列國 *lieguo*), also functions as a plural marker and has thus led some translators to render the term *liezhuan* as "biographies" or "memoirs."[108] Finally, *lie* is also used in early Chinese texts to mean "illustrious" (烈 *lie*) and "exemplary" (例 *li*).[109] But among the seventeen instances in which the term is used in the *Lienü zhuan* itself, in ten cases it is used as the verb "to rank" or the adverb "according to rank" and is generally applied to people; in the other seven cases it means "to set forth" and is generally used in reference to ideas or examples in the context of a discussion or argument. In Ban Gu's discussion of the *Lienü zhuan* in Liu Xiang's *Hanshu* biography, Ban Gu also describes Liu Xiang as gathering accounts of women, which he "arranged in order" or "arranged according to a specific sequence" (序次 *xuci*).[110] The fragment of Liu Xiang's "Bielu" that has been preserved in the *Chuxue ji* also states that he "arranged [the accounts] according to category (種類相從 *zhonglei xiangcong*)."[111] Thus, given the organizational structure of the *Lienü zhuan,* which places each biography into one of seven categories, the title can be best translated as the *Categorized Biographies of Women.*[112]

The Prefaces

As mentioned earlier, Cai Ji placed Liu Xiang's "Major Preface in Verse Summary," which is no longer extant, at the beginning of the table of contents and the "Minor Prefaces" within the table of contents, following their respective chapter titles. In my translation, I have placed the "Minor Prefaces" at the beginning of each chapter. Each preface rhymes and is written in ten four-character lines, except the one preceding the "Depraved and Favored," which is incomplete. This format resembles the table of contents of the *Shiji*, which provides rhymed abstracts in four-character lines for some but not all of the chapters.[113] Six of the prefaces make reference to a female readership, clearly indicating that while the text was presented to the emperor, its message was also to be shared with his women. The prefaces may also represent the first time a text directly addressed female readers.

Components of Each Chapter

The seven categories of female exemplars that Liu Xiang devised are 1) the Maternal Models (母儀 *muyi*); 2) the Worthy and Enlightened (賢明 *xianming*); 3) the Sympathetic and Wise (仁智 *renzhi*); 4) the Chaste and Compliant

(貞順 *zhenshun*); 5) the Principled and Righteous (節義 *jieyi*); 6) the Accomplished Rhetoricians (辯通 *biantong*); and 7) the Depraved and Favored (孽嬖 *niebi*). The categories are arranged so that the *Lienü zhuan* opens with a topic appropriate to beginnings: the impact of women on the beginnings of life, namely, the "Maternal Models." Similarly, the exemplars of wickedness, the "Depraved and Favored," are relegated to the least prominent position, at the end of the book. Each chapter follows a roughly chronological order, beginning with exemplars from the earliest phases of Chinese history and ending with those closest to Liu Xiang's own age.

THE MATERNAL MODELS

The *Lienü zhuan* appropriately begins with the starting point of life itself: the mother–child relationship. As the opening chapter, the "Maternal Models" structurally prioritizes the role of motherhood as critical to the foundation of dynastic success. Five of the biographies describe how mothers contributed to the founding of the great dynasties of antiquity, the Xia, Shang, and Zhou.

The "Maternal Models" is furthermore the earliest extant work to focus on fostering the moral development of children, and thus represents a radical departure from all previous expositions on Confucian education by setting forth in more than a few scattered comments methods for moral training in early childhood.[114] In the educational theory of the Warring States philosopher Xunzi (fl. 298–238 BCE), who exerted significant influence on Han Confucianism, nothing is said about the moral instruction of young children. For Xunzi, moral education began with the memorization of the Five Classics (the *Odes*, *Annals*, *Music*, *Documents*, and *Rites*), an enterprise that normally began no earlier than age ten *sui* (age nine by modern reckoning) and as late as age fifteen *sui*. Liu Xiang's program of education as found in the *Lienü zhuan* therefore advances beyond Xunzi's theories in two crucial respects: it makes early childhood (including the prenatal stage) the starting point in a person's education, and it grants women an important role in the moral development of their children and charges.

For Han thinkers, the dynastic implications of early childhood education were paramount. Moral and well-educated princes, the early Han emperors were told, would allow the house of Liu to preserve its control of imperial power. To drive the point home, thinkers such as Jia Yi (200–168 BCE) argued that the Qin's downfall (207 BCE) was due in good part to the First Emperor's failure to educate his son properly and surround him with wise teachers, for it was when this ignorant and easily swayed youth ascended the throne that the dynasty plunged into a precipitous collapse. The increasing interest in mothers as educators among Han intellectuals thus owes much to their preoccupation with discovering the underlying reasons for the rise and fall of dynasties as a means to control such events. Reflecting this interest, more than a third of the biographies describe the efforts of women who raised the progenitors and founders of the great dynasties of Chinese antiquity.

The "Maternal Models" chapter is, however, not exclusively concerned with the upbringing of children and youths. In fact, only five of the fourteen biographies concern minors. The bulk of the chapter focuses on a mother's influence on adult sons as well as nephews, daughters-in-law, and adult stepchildren, and, in one case, on the influence of a governess upon her charge. The greater focus on a mother's relationship with adult offspring reflects the perceived need for a mother's counsel on adult concerns, including those specific to the outer realm, such as statecraft.

Several features distinguish this chapter from all others in the *Lienü zhuan*. In his 1403 preface to the *Lienü zhuan*, Ming Emperor Chengzu (r. 1403–1424) expressed his perplexity as to why Liu Xiang opened his chapter on "Maternal Models" with an account of the two wives of Shun but included no discussion of their role as mothers.[115] Materials concerning their father Yao's own mother were almost certainly available.[116] Ultimately, Emperor Chengzu speculates that if Liu Xiang had not opened with an account concerning Yao, "the book could not be considered a book." This rather cryptic remark may mean that any proper survey of Chinese history needs to begin with the sage ruler Yao. According to one early Chinese account, dynastic history was preceded by the reigns of two illustrious rulers, Yao and Shun, whose civilizing influence and great virtue provided a model for all subsequent sovereigns. The *Book of Documents* thus begins with the reign of Yao. Confucian scholars in Han times who venerated the Five Classics also recognized this period as the earliest reliable starting point of history.[117] This categorical aberration (i.e., substituting wives for mothers) may thus represent the impulse toward chronological comprehensiveness colliding with and trumping that of topical classification. A further possibility is that because the Liu imperial family traced its descent from Yao, Liu Xiang might have thought it would be appropriate to begin his book with the story of Yao's daughters, who were most well known for their roles as Shun's wives rather than for their roles as mothers.[118]

The "Maternal Models" is anomalous for two additional reasons. As mentioned earlier, since Song times it has included fourteen rather than the standard fifteen biographies found in the other six biographical chapters of the original *Lienü zhuan*. As a possible clue concerning the lost biography, Liang Duan (d. 1825) in her *Lienü zhuan jiaozhu* notes that the *Yiwen leiju* and *Taiping yulan* cite a *Lienü zhuan* biography of Mo Mu, the consort of Huangdi.[119] Another candidate for the lost biography is "The Mother of the Shi Family of Lu" (魯師 氏母), a story attached to the ode "Ji Ming" of the *Qi Feng* section of the *Book of Odes,* which Kong Yingda cites in his commentary on the *Odes* as deriving from the *Lienü zhuan*.[120] Finally, the "Maternal Models" chapter is also the only section of the *Lienü zhuan* that categorizes its subjects according to biological or social roles, in contrast to the other chapters, which focus on the moral qualities or skills of the biographical subjects.

THE WORTHY AND ENLIGHTENED

In the section entitled the "Worthy and Enlightened," Liu Xiang sets forth fifteen narratives that cover a range of exemplary behavior as broad and all-encompassing as the title itself. It is the most thematically heterogeneous chapter of the *Lienü zhuan.* Thirteen of its narratives focus on women who admonish husbands who have strayed from the path of virtue or common sense, while the remaining two biographies describe women whose handling of their husbands' funerals was exemplary. The majority of narratives in this chapter converge in their focus on the ways a wife can uphold the prominence and continuity of her husband's lineage or state. Two biographies, however, show how a woman may protect her natal lineage when it comes into conflict with that of her husband.[121] The lessons of these two accounts can, perhaps, be reconciled with the prevailing theme of the chapter by demonstrating that the husband's mercy redounds to his favor by demonstrating his ability to moderate his own anger and promote peace among the states. For example, in the account of "Ji of Wey, Wife of Duke Huan of Qi," Ji is able to becalm her husband's rage at her natal state of Wey by pointing out the recklessness of his behavior.[122] The incident ends with Duke Huan of Qi stating, "If I rely upon Guan Zhong to manage the outer realm and my wife to manage the inner quarters, even though I am dim-witted, it will be sufficient to establish me in the world!" The "Wife of Jieyu of Chu," along with the two biographies that follow it in the "Worthy and Enlightened," are also somewhat anomalous in the *Lienü zhuan* for their promotion of the ideal of reclusion rather than political engagement.[123] But even these narratives fall into line with the dynastic imperative of the text by portraying reclusion as a means to preserve the purity of the family reputation.

The diversity of lessons conveyed in this chapter occasionally gives rise to contradictory directives. For example, according to "The Woman of Distinction, the Wife of Bao of Song," a husband may divorce a wife, but it is not permissible for a woman to leave her husband.[124] In contrast, three biographies in this chapter portray wives who are able to prompt their husbands to mend their ways by threatening to leave them.[125] Here, as in other sections of the text, some of the more extreme messages of the *Lienü zhuan* are often tempered by accounts that express opposing points of view.

THE SYMPATHETIC AND WISE

In the category "Sympathetic and Wise" (仁智 *ren zhi*), the term *ren,* which is normally understood as "benevolence" or "humanity," refers not so much to feelings of kindness but to the ability to understand others intuitively and empathetically through close observation of the minute details of their behavior, and from these inferences to predict correctly a person's future. Thus, *ren* connotes a form of sympathetic resonance, and *zhi* (智), which is usually translated as "wisdom" or "knowledge," refers to a form of prescience. The meaning of this title can also be understood with reference to a passage in *Huainanzi:* "From knowing the near, he knows the distant; from knowing himself, he knows others. This is the operative similarity between Humaneness and Wisdom."[126] For example, in the *Lienü zhuan* account of "Shu Ji of Yang of Jin," when Shu Ji's grandson Boshi was born, Shu Ji went to look at him. But when she heard his cry, she said, "It is the voice of a wolf. A wolflike child will have a wild heart. The one who destroys the Yangshe lineage will surely be this child." After this she refused to see him. As predicted, when he grew up, he eventually brought about the destruction of the lineage.[127] Other accounts are less fatalistic and involve predictions based on the observation of ritual violations and moral missteps. For example, in "The Wife of Bo Zong of Jin," we learn that

> Bo Zong was virtuous but fond of using direct language to insult others. Whenever he went to court his wife would always warn him, saying, "Thieves despise lords and the people hate their superiors. If there are those who are fond of a man, then there are bound to be those who hate and envy him as well. You, sir, are fond of straight talk, but wrongdoers despise it. So you are sure to meet with misfortune."[128]

Many of the biographies in this chapter are dark and portentous. In two-thirds of the accounts, the exemplar's advice is ignored with disastrous results.

Unlike the first two chapters of the *Lienü zhuan,* which focus on mothers and wives, respectively, the biographical subjects of the "Sympathetic and Wise" represent a greater variety of female social roles: mothers, wives, daughters, sisters, and ordinary citizens. A few narratives, for example, portray ordinary women who express concern not for their own families, but for the stability of the state. The "Woman of Qishi of Lu," for example, is an eloquent document in which the exemplar argues for the necessity of women's political involvement.[129] It thus represents the utopian vision of Liu Xiang and other like-minded individuals of the Former Han, which enjoined all subjects of the imperial house of Han, noble and common, male and female, to work toward the goal of "Great Peace" as the crowning achievement of dynastic success.[130]

THE CHASTE AND COMPLIANT

The "Chaste and Compliant" takes as its central theme the ritual responsibilities of married women. Two-thirds of the narratives praise women who exemplify purity and devotion in their refusal to remarry or in their compliance with rules concerning sexual segregation and movements outside of the domestic sphere. The remaining biographies portray women who express their deep convictions about the sanctity of marriage through their insistence on upholding all of the rites prescribed for betrothal and marriage. Given the centrality of ritual in early Chinese texts, these ideals come as no surprise. But modern readers generally find the extreme means by which these exemplars pursue the goals of chastity, devotion, purity, and ritual correctness profoundly disturbing. When commanded to remarry or prompted to act in violation of the rites, a third of the exemplars in this chapter either commit or attempt suicide, and one cuts off her nose to discourage unwanted suitors.

Historical accounts of women in Han times supply few examples of those who martyred themselves for the sake of ritual correctness. Thus, when we read early Chinese accounts of ethically motivated suicide, it is important to keep in mind that most people in early China probably viewed the extreme behavior lauded in some of these stories as acts that were to be admired but not followed to the letter. For example, the *Lienü zhuan* biography "Bo Ji, Consort of Duke Gong of Song," which portrays a woman who chooses to burn to death rather than venture out alone at night, was almost certainly meant not to promote self-destructive compliance with ritual but to demonstrate that a woman should avoid as much as possible appearing in public alone at night.[131] Even the *Zuo Commentary to the Spring and Autumn Annals* argued that Bo Ji's behavior was unnecessarily extreme.[132] However, we cannot neglect the simultaneous presence of those who admired the extreme observance of ritual laws and who believed that a woman's decision to burn to death rather than violate the rites was a beautiful thing.[133] The story of Bo Ji of Song in particular reveals Liu Xiang's affiliation to the Guliang interpretation of the *Spring and Autumn Annals,* which states that "Women make chastity their practice, and Bo Ji fulfilled to the utmost the Way of Womanhood."[134] Although the Han histories suggest that few women tried to emulate the ideals of the female martyrs of earlier texts, Empress Wang, the consort of the last emperor of the Former Han dynasty, Emperor Ping (r. 1 BCE to 6 CE), is said to have burned to death to absolve herself from the crimes of her father, Wang Mang.[135]

Thus, while early Chinese texts express a broad spectrum of views on ethically motivated suicide, ranging from enthusiastic endorsement to staunch disapproval, martyrdom features prominently as a praiseworthy practice in the *Lienü zhuan,* especially as an act of resistance against remarriage.[136] Furthermore, while these issues pose complex questions concerning the interplay of gender, sexuality, and religious views of purity, the dynastic implications are clear. A woman's remarriage represented a threat to her husband's line, specifically to the well-being of both his offspring and his parents. Caring for children and elderly parents-in-law was the responsibility of the wife, who, once remarried, was no longer in a position to fulfill these obligations. At the same time, the chapter's extreme concern for purity has little to do with virginity, paternity, or marital fidelity to a living spouse. These issues are treated elsewhere, cast in negative terms in the adulterous and promiscuous women described in the "Depraved and Favored" chapter of the *Lienü zhuan.* Instead, the accounts found in the "Chaste and Compliant" tend to focus on the iron resolve of women who successfully resist betraying an obligation of fidelity to a first husband or who refuse to disobey a ritual rule concerning marriage.

In contrast to the issue of remarriage, the concern with precisely observed marriage rites stems from a sense that the manner in which an endeavor begins will affect all of its subsequent development. Thus, a man who neglects the rites leading up to marriage not only fails to treat his bride with all due courtesy but also reveals a more general tendency to disregard the rules and sacred rites crucial to the ancestral legacy and the orderly governance of the family.[137] That women are portrayed as willing to die rather than wed such a spouse suggests a conviction that, by ignoring even one rite, one creates an "anything goes" atmosphere, which in turn emboldens others to flout any number of rules. To violate rules without fear of reprisal, however, actors must rely on the complicity of others who will turn a blind eye to their misconduct. The reciprocal willingness to countenance wrongdoing is thus conceived as generating an endless chain of disorder, a series of actions and reactions that swing between the domestic sphere and the political. The unyielding view of ritual espoused by exemplars in this chapter is thus part of a more generalized ethic that calls for the sacrifice of individuals to uphold the enduring family or dynastic unit.[138]

THE PRINCIPLED AND RIGHTEOUS

The lives of women designated "Principled and Righteous," like the "Chaste and Compliant," often end in suicide. But in contrast to the chaste and compliant, the principled and righteous do not kill themselves as a sign of their affectionate devotion to husbands but often as a powerful rebuke for a husband's unforgiveable offense. The biographies in this chapter portray women facing ethical dilemmas that are often resolved by the heroine's suicide. The dilemma is generally one of conflicting loyalties, for example, when a heroine must choose between her own death and that of her father. In other cases, the choice is between preserving the life of her own child or of the child of her sibling, sovereign, or husband's first wife. Usually the heroine chooses to sacrifice either herself or her own child for the sake of preserving the reputation or dynastic continuity of a hierarchical superior, usually a husband or a ruler. These highly fictionalized accounts make gripping if somewhat melodramatic reading. But it is worth noting the connection between some of the narratives and historical events. For example, two of the biographies extol wet nurses who make great sacrifices to protect their royal charges. These accounts must have possessed special significance for Liu Xiang. The life of Emperor Xuan depended in part on the women who saved his life by suckling him after a political purge annihilated three generations of his family, leaving him as the sole survivor.[139] The prevailing ethic of this chapter is embodied in Confucius' statement, "The determined officer and the person of virtue will not seek to live at the expense of injuring their virtue. They will even sacrifice their lives to preserve their virtue complete."[140]

THE ACCOMPLISHED RHETORICIANS

In the biographies of the "Accomplished Rhetoricians," women use their rhetorical skills either to advise incompetent rulers on state policy or to extricate themselves or, more typically, a male family member from difficulties. Liu Xiang portrays the accomplished rhetoricians as conversant with the lessons of history and thus supplies tacit approval for educating women on matters that go well beyond the ritual and practical concerns of the domestic realm. Here, perhaps more than in any other chapter of the *Lienü zhuan*, we see the importance attached to the idea of "women in the breach"; that is, women who must step in to address a situation in place of men who are either absent or incompetent.

For example, the female protagonist in "The Woman of the Injured Locust Tree of Qi" pleads her case with an official when her father has been unjustly sentenced to death for injuring a tree treasured by Duke Jing of Qi. In this narrative, she must assume the role of the worthy and bring the injustice to the attention of the duke, taking great care not to undermine her efforts by angering her superiors. Her immediate goal is the release of her father, but the means by which she can achieve this is through her attention to how her father's plight figures in the larger political landscape. By defending her father in the public realm, she is treading the path normally reserved for the filial son. But as is the case in other accounts in the "Accomplished Rhetoricians," the achievement of the Woman of the Injured Locust Tree covers far more than the filial duty of a woman to stand in for absent males to promote the dynastic health of her father's or husband's lineage. It also illustrates that when filial piety is perceived as a larger political duty—in this case, protesting an unjust law that affects the state as a whole—rather than a merely personal concern, for example, saving one's father from execution, the act has far-reaching implications; it transforms and enhances the entire sphere for all. In this way, the Woman of the Injured Locust Tree is performing the work of a worthy. Filial piety is thus imbued with the power to radiate from the inner quarters and affect the outer realm.[141]

While many of the stories in this chapter fall within the category of legend, there is some factual basis for the account found in "The Daughter of the Chief of the Treasury of Qi," in which a filial daughter's argument results in the abrogation of mutilating punishments under Han Emperor Wen.[142] In these narratives, the highly delicate and potentially dangerous task of begging to differ with one's superiors makes rhetorical skill crucial. Three narratives, all of which focus on women who are ill-favored, deformed, and rejected by society, but who nevertheless gain honor through their ability to admonish erring rulers, convey well the difficulties of such honest counsel. The stories thus represent the idea that although the truth is often ugly, it shines more beautifully than pleasing but ultimately bad counsel. If the ill-favored women of this chapter represent the unvarnished and unpleasant truth, the alluring qualities of many of the women in the next chapter, "Depraved and Favored," signifies beauty's power to deceive.

THE DEPRAVED AND FAVORED

The first and last chapters of the *Lienü zhuan,* the "Maternal Models" and the "Depraved and Favored," respectively, provide a frame for the entire work, the first chapter focusing on how felicitous maternal influences give rise to great dynasties, and the final chapter demonstrating how the wrong sort of women destroy them. The first four biographies of the "Depraved and Favored" thus trace how various women instigated the decline of the Xia, Shang, and Western Zhou dynasties. This theme is an old one, with early examples appearing, for example, in the *Book of Odes*, the *Guoyu*, and the *Zuo zhuan*.[143] In most of the *Lienü zhuan* accounts, the most serious crime with which these women are charged is tampering with succession. Records from the Spring and Autumn, Warring States, Qin, and Han periods record with disturbing regularity the bloody disputes over the succession of emperors, kings, dukes, and clan heads. We can attribute much of the conflict to the practice of polygyny and, later, concubinage. While these practices provided a man with an heir in the event that his wife did not produce sons, they also frequently generated conflict and bloodshed. The title "Depraved and Favored" itself points to the danger of unscrupulous women who gain the affection of a ruler or family head. In these accounts, murder, slander, and adultery feature prominently as favored methods for acquiring access to power and position. In some cases, such as in the biography of Xia Ji, it is no single action that is reviled as much as the power of her beauty and sexuality to precipitate strife among all the men who contend for her.[144] Positioned as the final chapter of the *Lienü zhuan*, the "Depraved and Favored" and those it describes are thus ranked, both structurally and morally, in the lowest position.

SUPPLEMENTARY BIOGRAPHIES

Zeng Gong's preface tells us that Ban Zhao supplemented Liu Xiang's text with additional biographies. Wang Hui's preface is less clear about their origin, but he tells us that he created a separate chapter for the twenty "Supplementary Biographies" that lacked corresponding verse summaries and arranged them chronologically. In modern editions, the supplementary biographies include four pre-Han exemplars, twelve from the Former Han, and four from the Later Han. Because Wang Hui's edition is not extant, it is impossible to say whether or not the biographies found in the "Supplementary Biographies" as transmitted to this day are consistent with those Wang Hui originally placed in his edition.

According to a third account, found in Cai Ji's "Postface" of 1214, the supplementary biographies were originally distributed among the seven chapters of Liu Xiang's original work.[145] His table of contents indicates the chapter in which each supplementary biography was placed as well as its order within that chapter. For example, the first biography, "The Woman of the Suburbs of Zhou," was categorized as one of the "Sympathetic and Wise." While the themes of these biographies are consistent with those used in Liu Xiang's text, the stories concerning women from Liu Xiang's own age and those from the Later Han differ from earlier accounts in their greater length, attention to detail, and at times, in their easily demonstrable connection to actual historical events.

Components of Each Biography

In keeping with Sima Qian's model, the aim of Liu Xiang's biographies was not to provide a detailed account tracing a woman's life from birth to death but to preserve for memory or emulation the signal acts that made her life worthy of consideration and exemplified the crucial moral messages of her age. The biographies generally begin by stating the exemplar's name and those of her father, husband, and offspring, as well as her geographical affiliation. In a large number of cases, the exemplar's name is not stated and she is simply identified by reference to her husband or son, as, for example, in the case of "The Wife of Duke Ling of Wey." While most narratives focus on one main event, some biographies, such as that of "Jing Jiang of the Ji Lineage of Lu," contain several separate narratives.[146] Exemplars often deliver their moral message through dialogues, poems, and set speeches, though occasionally the entire account is narrated in the third person. In the original seven chapters, each biography generally concludes with four components: a comment attributed to a "man of discernment" (君子 *junzi*) on the main lessons to be derived from the story, a quotation from the *Book of Odes*, a brief statement on the purport of the cited ode, and a verse summary.[147]

The man of discernment's comments followed by the citation of a passage from the *Odes* replicates a convention used in the *Zuo zhuan*.[148] Recent scholarship suggests that the comments found there were written by the author, namely, Mr. Zuo.[149] In the case of the *Lienü zhuan,* we can likewise assume that Liu Xiang is the author of the "man of discernment's comments," unless otherwise specified.[150] Some, for example, are attributed to Confucius.

Like the comments appended to the narratives of the *Zuo zhuan*, those found in the *Lienü zhuan* briefly summarize for the reader the moral of the story. From one perspective we can understand this formula as a modest ploy; instead of simply stating his view, Liu Xiang was able to attribute his opinions to an imaginary man of quality or discernment. Yet there is a sense in which the comments also represent how Liu Xiang imagined *the* man of discernment, that is, Confucius, might have judged the individuals under examination, as a number of the comments are direct quotations from the *Analects*. The comment is then morally guaranteed, as it were, by an appropriate quotation from the *Odes*, demonstrating that the exemplar's actions are consistent with classical models. In most cases, the cited ode is followed with a further comment, usually the phrase "these [words] apply well to her" (此之謂也 *ci zhi wei ye*), but occasionally several lines of more specific commentary are included.[151] The comments of the "man of discernment" in the *Lienü zhuan* thus serve to affirm and clarify the moral message of the narrative.[152]

"Verse summaries" (頌 *song*) conclude each biography of the original seven chapters of Liu Xiang's text. The term *song* is variously defined. In early sources it refers to the "hymns" section of the *Book of Odes*, but also to one of six expository principles whereby the odes convey meaning.[153] Zheng Xuan defines the technique of *song* as "to relate; to recite" (誦 *song*) and "to encompass" or "embody" (容 *rong*). He states that "By relating the virtues of the present, one expands upon it and extols it."[154] In Lu Ji's (261–301 CE) "Rhapsody on Literature," which categorizes ten genres of writing, the term *song* is commonly translated as "eulogy" and is described as follows: "The Eulogy is relaxed and leisurely, lush and luxuriant."[155] His contemporary, Zhi Yu (d. 312 CE), described the *song* as a form that "praises the concrete appearance of consummate virtue" and represents "the finest form of poetry."[156] All these definitions of the term assume that the *song* is a vehicle of praise. Yet in the *Lienü zhuan,* the *song* that follow accounts of negative exemplars criticize rather than laud, rendering the translation "eulogy" inappropriate. Liu Xie (465–522) addresses this issue in his *Wenxin diaolong* (Literary Mind and the Carving of Dragons). He states that the function of *song* "is to praise great virtue and describe the rites honoring it."[157] Liu Xie then goes on to criticize *song* that mix praise and blame as examples of "the corrupt style of an age of decline."[158] From the perspective of Liu Xie's divisions of literary genres, the *song* of the *Lienü zhuan* are more in keeping with the "pronouncement" (讚 *zan*), which, according to Liu Xie, "expresses both praise and censure" (託讚襃貶 *tuo zan bao fan*) in the critical remarks at the end of biographies in the historical works of Sima Qian and Ban Gu.[159] Liu Xie also states that *zan* provide "summaries," (總錄 *zonglu*), "pronounce judgment" (論辭 *lunci*), and are couched in tetrasyllabic verse. Still, he acknowledges the connection between the two forms in his classification of *zan* as a subdivision of *song*.[160] In keeping with its use for both praise and blame in the *Lienü zhuan*, its verse format, and the space it devotes to summarizing the biography in contrast to merely pronouncing judgment, I translate the term "verse summary."

The authorship of the verse summaries is controversial; some claim they were written by Liu Xiang himself, others argue that they were written by his son, Liu Xin. In my view, by specifically including the verse summaries in the name of the text, i.e., *Lienü zhuan song tu*, the *Hanshu* "Yiwen zhi" implicitly attributes the verse summaries to Liu Xiang. Later editors of the text, such as Zeng Gong, agree with this attribution.[161] However, other scholars have argued that the verse summaries were composed by Liu Xin, citing the *Suishu*, which lists in its bibliography a text in one section called *Lienü zhuan song* by Liu Xin.[162]

Recently, Chen Liping has made a case for Liu Xin's authorship of the verse summaries. She bases her argument on the following: 1) an attribution found in a fragment of the "Bielu" in the Tang-dynasty compendium, the *Chuxue ji*; 2) the fact that Yan Zhitui (ca. 531–590) and virtually all other pre-Song sources apart from the "Yiwen zhi" cite Liu Xin as the author of the verse summaries; and 3) the view that we should not expect Liu Xin to be mentioned in the *Hanshu* "Yiwen zhi" as author of the verse summaries, just as the illustrator of the text is not mentioned.[163] I am personally inclined to accept the attributions of the *Hanshu* "Yiwen zhi" over those derived from a Tang-dynasty fragment. The multiple pre-Song texts that attribute the verse summaries to Liu Xin may simply be a case of multiple texts repeating misinformation from one early source.

Editions

The most important Ming and Qing dynasty editions of the *Lienü zhuan* that are extant, including collections of annotations, have been conveniently assembled in the *Lienü zhuan huibian*, a massive ten-volume set that also includes illustrated editions.[164] The digital research collection, *Traditions of Exemplary Women*, also provides both clear page images of additional significant early editions of the *Lienü zhuan* and searchable transcriptions of text.[165] I have consulted all of these for my translation but have found the editions of the three women scholars Wang Zhaoyuan (1736–1851), Liang Duan (d. 1825), and Xiao Daoguan (1855–1907) the most useful in terms of annotations. Of these three, I have found Liang's to be the most judicious in her editorial decisions and follow her text unless otherwise noted.[166]

The field of early China studies is an intellectual world largely composed of texts written and explicated by men. It has been an extraordinary experience to have been guided in my study by three women from the premodern period. But the *Lienü zhuan* has long been the domain of women's scholarly efforts. Ban Zhao (ca. 48–120 CE), also known as Cao Dagu (曹大家), wrote the earliest known commentary to the *Lienü zhuan*, which now exists only in fragments.[167] Another early commentary was written by a woman known as Mother Zhao (趙母), who is also referred to by the names Zhao Yi, "Imperial Concubine Zhao" (趙姬), and Yu Zhenjie (虞貞節). She was a member of the Zhao family of Yingchuan and the wife of Yu Wei, and her reputation for scholarship earned her an appointment at the court of the Wu ruler Sun Quan (r. 239–252 CE). She is said to have died in 243 CE. Her commentary has been lost and now exists in fragments only.[168] One additional early commentary, now lost except for a few fragments, was written by the Jin dynasty scholar Qiwu Sui (綦毋邃) (fl. ca. 345–365 CE).[169]

For modern annotated editions, I have relied upon Shimomi's *Ryū kō Retsujoden no kenkyū*, the *Xinyi Lienü zhuan* of Huang Qingquan and Chen Manming, and Zhang Tao's *Lienü zhuan yizhu*.[170] D. C. Lau's *Gu Lienü zhuan zhuzi suoyin* also serves as an essential tool in the study of the *Lienü zhuan*.[171]

I have tried to maintain as much fidelity to the original text as possible and some consistency in translating frequently used terms. I have also cast some of the verse summaries in rhyme, but for the most part utilized free verse to preserve the meaning of the text. Notes direct readers to both primary and English-language sources to facilitate the use of this translation by both specialists and general readers alike. When only an English-language source is cited for a Chinese text, it is because the Chinese text is included in that work along with the English translation. Digital editions of the *Lienü zhuan* and of many other early Chinese texts in both Chinese and English translation can be found at my website, *Traditions of Exemplary Women*.[172]

Transliteration of names follows standard *pinyin* conventions, apart from the use of Hann (韓), Wey (衛), Shaanxi (陝西), and Zhow (紂) to distinguish these names from Han (漢), Wei (魏), Shanxi (山西), and Zhou (周). Because naming conventions vary greatly across the centuries spanned in this book, I have provided explanatory notes for individual names in the text of the translation.

For names from the Spring and Autumn period, I gratefully acknowledge and have followed the models provided by David Schaberg, Li Wai-yee, and Steven Durrant in their forthcoming translation of the *Zuo zhuan*. In general, however, a person's family name comes first, followed by a given name or, in some cases, a "style" name (*zi* 字). The style name (sometimes translated as "courtesy name") was conferred on an individual at adulthood. I have tried to explain the conventions of women's names in the notes to individual biographies, as these follow many different rules and often incorporate various kinship terms, such as "wife" or "concubine," which themselves are expressed in a great variety of ways.

In all cases, I translate the title *gong* (公) as "duke" but here remind the reader that this title was given as a posthumous honorific to all territorial rulers and in some cases to high court officers, most of whom, in life, did not bear this title or the prestige that it conferred.[173] The title *dafu* (大夫), which I translate as "grandee," designated powerful court officers who were also often heads of large aristocratic lineages. I generally translate the term *shi* (士) as "officer," to account for both the military and civil nature of this rank, but with the understanding that frequently these men merely aspired to rather than actually held official positions. In its oldest sense, it referred to a low-ranking member of the aristocracy who served in a military capacity, but later it came to refer to scholar-officials. Finally, I translate the term *junzi* (君子) as "man of discernment," when it appears at the end of each biography as a descriptive title of the commentator who summarizes the moral of the biography. The term, in this context, designates one who demonstrates the powers of sound moral judgment and occasionally refers to Confucius. Elsewhere, it is generally used to designate a person of superior moral and intellectual ability. In some cases, I have translated it as "gentleman," "man of quality," or simply "the discerning" to best accord with the specific meaning and stylistic demands of a particular passage.

CHRONOLOGY

Shang/Yin ca. 1554–1045 BCE
Zhou
      Western Zhou ca. 1045–771 BCE
      Eastern Zhou 770–256 BCE
         Spring and Autumn Period 770–476 BCE
         Warring States Period 475–222 BCE
Qin 221–207 BCE
Han
      Former/Western Han 206 BCE to 8 CE
      Xin 9–25 CE
      Later/Eastern Han 25–220 CE

EXEMPLARY WOMEN
OF EARLY CHINA

1

THE MATERNAL MODELS

PREFACE

It is only through those such as the Maternal Models
That worthies and sages possess wisdom.
Their actions are emblems of correct behavior,
And their words are aligned with righteousness.
From the time of conception, they nurture sons and grandsons,
Gradually instructing and transforming them.
Having established them with virtue,
They bring about their achievements and accomplishments.
Female kin and mothers who examine these exemplars
Should make them their models.

1.1 THE TWO CONSORTS OF YOUYU

The two consorts of Youyu were the two daughters of Emperor Yao.[1] The elder
was Ehuang, the younger was Nüying. Shun's father was perverse and his mother
was duplicitous. His father was called Gusou.[2] His younger brother was called
Xiang and was given to idle roaming. Shun was able to harmonize and placate
them. He served Gusou with filial reverence. Shun's mother hated Shun and
loved Xiang. But Shun still maintained his composure and harbored no ill will.

The chiefs of the Four Mountains recommended Shun to Yao.[3] Yao thereupon gave Shun his two daughters in marriage so that he could observe Shun's

conduct within [the family]. The two women served Shun in the fields and did not presume upon their status as daughters of the Son of Heaven to behave in an arrogant, overbearing, or disrespectful manner. They proceeded with humility, reverence, and frugality, being ever mindful of the Way of Wives.[4]

Gusou and Xiang plotted to kill Shun and ordered him to plaster the granary. Shun thus returned home and told the two women, "Father and Mother have ordered me to plaster the granary. Shall I go?" The two women said, "By all means, go!" When Shun went to repair the granary, the ladder was removed, and Gusou set the granary on fire. But Shun flew forth and escaped.

Xiang once again plotted with his father and mother, and Shun was ordered to dig a well. Shun then reported this to the two women, and the two women said, "Yes, by all means go!" Shun went forth and dug the well. [Gusou] blocked the exits and entrances and then sealed it shut. But Shun tunneled his way out.

Up to this point they had been unable to kill Shun. So Gusou tried once again and invited Shun to drink wine, hoping to make him drunk and then kill him. Shun reported this to the two women. The two women thereupon made Shun bathe in a pool with a potion they had given him. He then went forth. Shun drank wine all day long but never became drunk.

Shun's younger sister, Xi, pitied him and was in accord with her two sisters-in-law. Although Shun's parents wanted to kill him, Shun never harbored resentment toward them. They raged against him incessantly, so that Shun would go forth into the fields, wailing and weeping. Daily he cried out to merciful Heaven; he cried out to his father and mother. Though they tried to harm him, his feelings of affection for them endured.[5] He bore no resentment against his younger brother but treated him with sincere and unfailing generosity.

When he was appointed as the General Regulator, he received guests from the four quarters. He went into the forests and entered the foothills. Yao tested Shun in a hundred ways, and in each matter Shun consulted with the two women. When he succeeded [Yao], he was raised to the rank of Son of Heaven. Ehuang became queen and Nüying his consort.[6] He granted Xiang a fief in Youbei and in serving Gusou continued to be in accord with him.[7] All under Heaven praised the two women as intelligent, perceptive, chaste, and benevolent.

While making a tour of inspection, Shun died at Cangwu.[8] His honorary title was Chonghua.[9] His consorts both died in the region between the Jiang and the Xiang rivers and were commonly referred to as the "Ladies of the Xiang."[10]

A man of discernment would say, "The virtue of the two consorts was pristine and their conduct was magnanimous." A passage from the *Odes* says, "What is most distinguished is being virtuous;—/It will secure the imitation of all the princes."[11] These words apply well to them.

The Verse Summary says,

In the beginning there were the two consorts,
The daughters of Emperor Yao.
Both, in proper order, wed Youyu,
Sustaining and following him as his subordinates.
Though nobly born, they willingly served the humble,
And to the end they were able to labor and bear hardships.
They placated Gusou,
And finally enjoyed happiness and blessings.

1.2 JIANG YUAN, MOTHER OF QI

Jiang Yuan, the mother of Qi, was the daughter of the Marquis of Tai.[12] In the time of Yao, while she was out walking, she saw the footprint of a giant.[13] She was delighted and trod upon it. But after she returned home, she found that she had conceived a child.

Gradually she became bigger. She regarded her condition as unnatural and loathsome, and thus divined with the turtle shell and milfoil and made *yin* and *si* sacrifices so that she might be childless.[14] When the child finally came, she regarded him as inauspicious and abandoned him in a narrow lane. But the cattle and sheep stepped around him and did not trample him. Then she left him on a wooded plain, but later, the woodsmen of the plain covered him with a mat of grass. She then placed him on cold ice, but the birds protected him with their wings. Jiang Yuan regarded these events as extraordinary, so she retrieved him and took him home. It is for this reason that he was called Qi, "The Abandoned."

By nature, Jiang Yuan was pure, serene, and unwavering in purpose. She was fond of sowing and harvesting grain. When Qi was older, she taught him to plant mulberries and hemp. Qi, by nature, was perspicacious and benevolent. He was able to cultivate her teachings and thereby achieved renown.

Yao commanded Qi to occupy the post of Minister of Agriculture. Moreover, he established the territory of Tai as a kingdom, enfeoffed Qi with Tai, and gave him the name Hou Ji.[15] When Yao died, Shun ascended the throne and commanded him, saying, "Qi, the black-haired people are plagued by starvation. Take charge of agriculture and sow the hundred grains."[16] Generation after generation of his progeny oversaw agriculture, until the time of Kings Wen and Wu, when they rose up as Sons of Heaven.

A man of discernment would say, "Jiang Yuan was serene and could educate and transform others." The *Odes* says, "Highly distinguished was Jiang Yuan,/ Of virtue undeflected./God regarded her with favor"[17]; and, "Oh, accomplished Hou Ji,/Thou didst prove thyself the correlate of Heaven;/Thou didst give grain-food to our multitudes."[18] These words refer to Jiang Yuan and her son.

The Verse Summary says,

Qi's mother, Jiang Yuan,
Was pure, serene, and resolute.
She trod upon a footprint and conceived a child;
In fear, she abandoned him in the wilds.
When birds and beasts sheltered and protected him,
She took him up again and cared for him.
When finally he served as the Emperor's aide,
The Way of Mothers was made complete.[19]

1.3 JIANDI, MOTHER OF XIE

Jiandi, mother of Xie, was the eldest daughter of the Yousong lineage.[20] In the time of Yao, she went bathing with her sister in the waters at Xuanqiu.[21] A dark-colored bird carrying an egg in its mouth passed by and dropped the egg, which was multicolored and very fine. When Jiandi and her sister raced to get the egg, Jiandi got it first and put it in her mouth. She mistakenly swallowed it, and as a result, gave birth to Xie.[22]

By nature Jiandi was skilled at managing human relationships. She also understood the patterns of the stars on high and delighted in extending kindness to others. When Xie grew up, she taught him about moral principles and the various degrees of precedence in human relationships. Xie, by nature, was intelligent and benevolent. He was able to cultivate her teachings and thus finally established his reputation. Yao appointed him as Director of the Multitudes and enfeoffed him with the territory at Bo.[23]

When Yao died, Shun ascended the throne and commanded him, saying, "Xie, the hundred surnames are not on good terms with one another, and they do not observe the five orders of human relationships.[24] Assume the post of Minister of Education and honor and promote the five teachings. Be lenient."[25]

Generation after generation of his descendants resided at Bo, down to Tang of the Yin, who rose up as Son of Heaven.[26]

A man of discernment would say, "Jiandi was benevolent and mindful of ritual." The *Odes* says, "When the Yousong began to be great,/[God] appointed their child to bear the Shang."[27] It also says, "Heaven commanded the Dark Bird to descend and engender the Shang."[28] These words refer to her.

The Verse Summary says,

Xie's mother, Jiandi,
Esteemed benevolence and exerted herself reverently.
Swallowing an egg, she gave birth to a son,
And proceeded to cultivate her capacity to instruct.[29]
She taught according to the correct principle of things,
Extended mercy, and possessed virtue.
That Xie served as aide to the ruler
Was no doubt due to his mother's efforts.

1.4 TUSHAN, MOTHER OF QI

The mother of Qi was the eldest daughter of the Tushan lineage.[30] Yu of Xia took her as his consort. When she gave birth to Qi, for the four days of *xin*, *ren*, *gui*, and *jia*, Qi wept and wailed. Yu then left to regulate the waters, planning with all his might his labors on the land.[31] Three times he passed by his dwelling but did not enter its doors. Alone, Tushan taught with great insight and thereby brought about Qi's education. When Qi grew up, transformed by her virtue and following her teachings, he established his renown. Yu became the Son of Heaven, and Qi, as his successor, upheld unabated his achievements.

A man of discernment would say, "Tushan conveyed her teachings with great power." The *Odes* says, "You are given a heroic wife/And from her shall come [a line of] descendants."[32] This saying applies well to her.

The Verse Summary says,

Qi's mother, Tushan,
Was mate to Emperor Yu.
After the days *xin*, *ren*, *gui*, and *jia*,
Yu went forth to divide the land.[33]
While Qi wept and wailed,

Alone, his mother ordered their affairs,[34]
She taught him about goodness
Until finally he succeeded his father.

1.5 YOUSHEN, CONSORT OF TANG

Tang's consort, Youshen, was a maiden of the Youshen lineage.[35] Tang of Yin married her and made her his consort. She gave birth to Zhongren and Wai-bing.[36] She understood well how to teach them and thus brought about their achievements. As consort to Tang, Youshen led the nine concubines and created order in the rear palace so that there were no women who were jealous or refractory.[37] In this way she helped bring about the king's achievements.

A man of discernment would say, "The consort was enlightened and brought about order." The *Odes* says, "The modest, retiring, virtuous young lady;/A fine match for our lord."[38] This ode expresses the idea that a worthy woman is able to harmonize the ruler's many concubines, and indeed describes Youshen.

The Verse Summary says,

Tang's consort Youshen—
In character and in deed, enlightened.
Following her bridal party was Yi Yin,[39]
Who traveled with her from Xia to Yin.
She applied herself to governing the inner chambers with diligent care,
And brought the nine concubines into line.
Teaching and transforming within and without,
She committed not the slightest fault.

1.6 THE THREE MATRIARCHS OF THE HOUSE OF ZHOU

The Three Matriarchs were Tai Jiang, Tai Ren, and Tai Si.[40] Tai Jiang was the mother of Wang Ji and a daughter of the Youtai lineage.[41] Tai Wang married her and made her his consort.[42] She gave birth to Tai Bo, Zhong Yong, and Wang Ji.[43] She was pure, accommodating, and able to lead and guide others so that they were without fault.[44] During the time when Tai Wang was laying plans to move, he always consulted Tai Jiang.[45]

A man of discernment would say that Tai Jiang's greatness lay in her moral teachings.[46]

Tai Ren was the mother of King Wen and the second daughter of the Ren lineage of Zhi.[47] Wang Ji took her as his consort. By nature Tai Ren was devoted, reverent, and unfailingly virtuous in her conduct. When she was with child, her eyes beheld no evil sights, her ears heard no perverse sounds, and her mouth uttered no careless words. She was able to teach her child in the womb. When she went to relieve herself in [the privy over] the pigpen, she gave birth to King Wen.[48] At birth King Wen was brilliant and sagacious. When Tai Ren instructed him, from one [of her precepts] he was able to understand one hundred [principles]. In the end he founded the Zhou dynastic lineage.

A man of discernment would say that Tai Ren was adept at fetal instruction. In ancient times, a woman with child did not lie on her side as she slept; neither would she sit sideways or stand on one foot. She would not eat food with odd flavors; if the food was cut awry, she would not eat it; if the mat was not placed straight, she would not sit on it. She did not let her eyes gaze on lewd sights or let her ears listen to depraved sounds.[49] At night she ordered blind musicians to chant the *Odes*.[50] She spoke only of proper things. In this way she gave birth to children of correct physical form who excelled others in talent and virtue. Thus, during pregnancy, one must always be cautious about [external] stimuli. If one is stimulated by something good, then [the child] will be good. If one is stimulated by something evil, then [the child] will be evil. People's resemblance to various things at birth is in every case due to the mother's being stimulated by external things, so that in form and voice they come to resemble these things.[51] The mother of King Wen can indeed be said to have understood simulative transformation.

Tai Si was King Wu's mother.[52] She was a daughter of Yu's descendants, the Youshen lineage of the Si clan. She was benevolent and understood the Way. King Wen treasured her, and personally went to the River Wei to welcome her, making a bridge of boats.[53] Upon her arrival, Tai Si was thoughtful and solicitous in her treatment of Tai Jiang and Tai Ren. Morning and night she strove to perfect the Way of Wives. Tai Si was called "Cultured Mother." King Wen ruled the outer realm and Tai Si ruled the inner quarters.

Tai Si gave birth to ten sons. The eldest was Boyi Kao, the next was Fa, King Wu; the next was Dan, Duke of Zhou; the next was Guan Shu Xian; the next was Cai Shu Du; the next was Cao Shu Zhenduo; the next was Huo Shu Wu; the next was Cheng Shu Chu; the next was Kang Shu Feng; and finally there was Dan Ji Zai.[54] Tai Si taught her ten sons so that from the time they were small until they were grown, they never laid eyes upon evil or perversion.[55] After they were grown, King Wen continued to instruct them, finally completing the virtue of King Wu and the Duke of Zhou.[56]

A man of discernment would say, "Tai Si was benevolent, enlightened, and virtuous." The *Odes* says,

> In a great state there was a lady,
> Like a fair denizen of Heaven.
> The ceremonies determined the auspiciousness [of the union],
> And in person he met her on the Wei.
> Over it he made a bridge of boats;
> The glory [of the occasion] was illustrious.[57]

It also says, "Tai Si inherited her excellent fame,/And from her came a hundred sons."[58] This ode describes her.

The Verse Summary says,

> The Three Matriarchs of the house of Zhou,
> Were Tai Jiang, Tai Ren, and Tai Si.
> The rise of Kings Wen and Wu
> Began with them.
> The most worthy was Tai Si,
> Who is called "Cultured Mother."
> Yet the virtue of all three women
> Was very great indeed.

1.7 DING JIANG, A LADY OF WEY

Ding Jiang, a lady of Wey, was the wife of Duke Ding of Wey and the mother of the duke's son.[59] The duke's son had already married when he died, but his wife had no sons. So after completing three years of mourning, Ding Jiang sent his wife back home, personally accompanying her beyond the outskirts of the city. Filled with loving kindness and thoughts of sorrow, her grieving heart was stirred. She stood gazing after her and shed many tears. She then composed an ode that said:

> The swallows go flying about
> With their wings unevenly displayed.

This lady is going home,
And I escort her far into the country.
I looked till I could no longer see her,
And my tears fell down like rain.[60]

After seeing her off, Ding Jiang returned home weeping and gazing back at her in the distance. She also composed an ode that said, "I think of our deceased lord,/ To rouse myself."[61]

A man of discernment would say, "Ding Jiang was a loving mother-in-law; she exceeded the call of duty but arrived at great kindness."[62]

Duke Ding hated Sun Linfu.[63] After Sun Linfu fled to Jin, the Marquis of Jin sent Xi Chou to request permission for Sun to return.[64] Duke Ding wanted to refuse the request. Ding Jiang said, "That won't do! Sun Linfu is the heir of our former ruler's minister. Moreover, a large state is making this request on his behalf, so to refuse is to court disaster. Even though you despise him, isn't acceding to this request better than perishing? You, my lord, should be more tolerant. Is it not indeed appropriate to maintain peace on the behalf of the people and treat leniently a minister of your own clan?" Duke Ding thereupon granted him permission to return.

A man of discernment would say, "Ding Jiang was capable of keeping disaster at bay." The *Odes* says, "His conduct is irreproachable;/He thereby rectifies the four quarters of the State."[65] These words can be used to describe her.

After Duke Ding died, Kan, the son of Jing Si, came to the throne.[66] This was Duke Xian. Duke Xian was negligent in the mourning [of his father]. Ding Jiang, having wept and lamented, and seeing Duke Xian's lack of sorrow, refused to eat or drink. She sighed, saying, "This [man] will destroy the state of Wey. He will first harm good people, and then it will be Heaven that brings ruin on Wey.[67] Alas, that I could not bring it about that Zhuan should preside over the altars of soil and grain."[68] When the grandees heard this, they were all afraid. From this time onward, Sun Wenzi did not dare to store his valuables in Wey.[69]

Zhuan was Duke Xian's younger brother and was called Xian. Because he was virtuous, Ding Jiang wanted him to succeed his father, but it didn't come about. Later, Duke Xian proved tyrannical and cruel. He was contemptuous and rude to Ding Jiang and was finally expelled. In the course of his flight he reached the border of the state. He charged the chief invocator to report his departure in the ancestral temple and at the same time to report that he was without fault. Ding Jiang said, "This is unacceptable! If he reports that he is without [fault], the spirits cannot be so deceived. Since he is at fault, how can he report that he is faultless?[70] Moreover, in all his dealings, he ignored his great ministers and made plans with the lesser ones. This was his first offense. Our former ruler selected his prime minister as his tutor, yet he treated him contemptuously. This is his second offense. I served our former lord with towel and comb, yet he oppressed me as if I were a concubine. This is his third offense. Report his departure and be done with it; do not report that he is without fault!" Later, with Zhuan's support, Duke Xian was allowed to return to the state.[71]

A man of discernment would say, "Ding Jiang was able to use her words to instruct others." The *Odes* says, "My words address [present urgent] affairs."[72] This phrase applies well to her.

Huang Er of Zheng led troops to attack Wey.[73] Sun Wenzi divined about pursuing them and presented the omen to Ding Jiang, saying, "The omen resembles a hill. There are men who go to battle, but they will lose a hero."[74] Ding Jiang said, "That there are men going into battle who will lose a hero is to the advantage of those who resist the attack. Let the grandees devise a plan!" The people of Wey then pursued and captured Huang Er at Quanqiu.

A man of discernment would say, "Ding Jiang understood the nature of events." The *Odes* says, "To the left, to the left,/The nobles are possessed of the ability."[75] These words apply well to this case.

The Verse Summary says,

The lady of Wey, Ding Jiang,
Bade farewell to the wife and composed an ode.
Merciful, loving, and kind,
She wept and gazed at her in the distance.
Often she admonished Duke Xian,
But only reaped his recriminations and contempt.
Her intelligence and far-seeing wisdom
Are displayed in her cultivated speech.[76]

1.8 THE TUTOR MATRON OF THE WOMAN OF QI

The Tutor Matron was the tutor matron of the woman of Qi. The woman was the wife of Duke Zhuang of Wey.[77] She was called Zhuang Jiang.[78] Jiang was ravishingly lovely. When she first arrived, her manner was careless and indolent. She was flirtatious in her behavior and promiscuous at heart. The tutor matron, seeing that she did not behave in accordance with correct womanly principles, told her, "Your family for generations has been honored and illustrious, so it is appropriate that it should serve as a model for the people. By nature you have been endowed with an understanding of affairs, so it is appropriate that you should serve as an example for others. You are beautiful in face and form; it is therefore essential for you to cultivate yourself properly. [When you came to our court, you] wore over your brocade robe a plain coat, attired to ride in a horse-drawn carriage. Was this not a matter of esteeming virtue?"[79] She then composed a poem that said,

> Buxom was she and tall,
> In her embroidered robe, with a [plain] single garment over it:—
> The daughter of the Marquis of Qi.
> The wife of the Marquis of Wey,
> The sister of the Heir-son of Qi,
> The sister-in-law of the Marquis of Xing,
> The Viscount of Tan also her brother-in-law.[80]

The tutor matron used lofty principles to cut and polish the girl's heart, considering that as the offspring of a ruler of men and the wife of a ruler of a state, she must never engage in depraved or vulgar behavior. The lady was then moved and practiced self-cultivation. A man of discernment would praise the tutor matron for her ability to prevent that which had not yet come about.

Zhuang Jiang was the younger sister of Dechen, Qi's heir apparent.[81] She was childless but served as mother to the son of Dai Gui, who became Duke Huan [of Wey].[82] Duke Zhuang's son, Zhouxu, was the son of one of the duke's favored ladies. He was much loved by the duke, arrogant, and fond of weapons. Duke Zhuang did nothing to restrain him. Later Zhouxu in fact killed Duke Huan.[83] The *Odes* says, "Don't teach monkeys to climb trees."[84] These words describe this situation well.

The Verse Summary says,

> The tutor matron of the woman of Qi
> Prevented the lady from doing what had not yet come to pass.
> She set forth the lady's ancestors,
> None of whom was without glory.
> She composed a poem to make her point clear,
> Enjoining the lady to bring no shame to her forebears.
> Zhuang Jiang as mother and sister,[85]
> At last proved able to cultivate herself.

1.9 JING JIANG OF THE JI LINEAGE OF LU[86]

Jing Jiang, of the Ji lineage of Lu, was a woman of Ju; she was also called Dai Si.[87] She was the wife of the Lu grandee Gongfu Mubo, the mother of Wenbo, and the paternal great-aunt by marriage of Ji Kangzi.[88] She was far-ranging in her wisdom and understood the rites. Mubo predeceased Jing Jiang, and she maintained her chastity.[89]

Wenbo left home to study and when he returned, Jing Jiang observed him discreetly. She saw that when his friends entered the hall, they came down the back steps and humbly skulked about, handing him his sword and straightening his shoes as if they were serving a father or elder brother. Wenbo now thought of himself as a grown man.

Jing Jiang called him over and upbraided him, saying, "Once, in antiquity, when King Wu dismissed his court, he noticed that his stocking garter had snapped.[90] All of his attendants saw what had happened, but among them there was no one he could order to fasten it, so he bent over and tied it himself.[91] He was therefore able to perfect the way of true kings. Duke Huan of Qi had three friends who were not afraid to confront him about his faults, five ministers whose duty it was to admonish him, and thirty people who would daily point out his errors.[92] Therefore he was able to achieve the position of hegemon. The Duke of Zhou in the course of one meal would be interrupted three times; and in the course of one bath, he would emerge three times grasping his unbound hair.[93] Bearing ceremonial gifts, he would give audience to more than seventy people in poor villages and narrow alleys. Thus he was able to preserve the house of Zhou. These two sages and one worthy were all rulers capable of leading their peers, yet they placed themselves under the scrutiny of others in this way. The people they consorted with all surpassed them. This is how they were able to improve daily without ever being aware of it. At present, you are young and your status is low, but the people you consort with all render service to you. Your lack of progress is abundantly clear." Wenbo thereupon admitted that he was at fault.

After this he chose strict teachers and worthy friends to serve him. Those with whom he lived and socialized were all very elderly, toothless gentlemen with yellowed hair. Wenbo would adjust the lapels of their robes, roll up their sleeves for them, and personally serve them food. Jing Jiang said, "Now you are a grown man."

A man of discernment would say, "Jing Jiang perfected transformative teaching." The *Odes* says, "Numerous is the array of officers, / And by them King Wen enjoys his repose."[94] These words describe this case well.

When Wenbo served as minister in Lu, Jing Jiang told him, "I will tell you how the essentials of ruling a country can be found in [the art of weaving]: everything depends upon the warp![95] The 'temple' is the means by which the crooked is made straight.[96] It must be strong. The temple can therefore be thought of as the general. The reed is the means by which one makes uniform what is irregular and brings into line the unruly. Therefore the reed can be thought of as the director. The 'hairpin' is the means by which one organizes the coarse and dense fibers [that have become entangled]. The hairpin can therefore be thought of as the capital grandee. That which can maintain connection without losing control of [the threads] moving inward and those moving outward is the batten.[97] The batten can be thought of as the great envoy. That which pushes and goes out and which pulls and comes back is the heddles.[98] The heddles can be thought of as the commander of the populace within the passes. That which manages [the threads] in numbers great and small is the warp-spacing reed.[99] The warp-spacing reed can be thought of as the clerk of the capital. That which fulfills a key role, travels a long way, is exact, upright, and firm is the cloth-beam.[100] The cloth-beam can be thought of as the prime minister. That which unrolls without limit is the warp-beam.[101] The warp-beam can be thought of as the Three Excellencies."[102] Wenbo bowed twice and received her teaching.

Once, when Wenbo was returning from court, he paid a visit to Jing Jiang.[103] At the time, Jing Jiang was spinning. Wenbo said, "In a family such as mine, though you are the matriarch, you continue to spin. I'm afraid this will provoke Jisun's anger.[104] Won't he think that I'm incapable of providing for you?" Jing Jiang sighed, saying, "Lu must be going to perish. They order youths who know nothing about such things to fill office. Sit. Let me explain this to you.

"In antiquity, when the sage kings settled the people, they chose poor land and settled them there. They utilized the populace by putting them to work, so their rule of all under Heaven endured. Now, when the people labor they become thoughtful, and if they are thoughtful they develop hearts that are good. If they are idle they become dissolute, if they become dissolute they forget goodness, and if they forget goodness they develop hearts that are bad. The people of fertile land are not of much use; they are dissolute. People of infertile lands tend toward righteousness; they are hard-working.

"For this reason, when the Son of Heaven, decked in the greater-colored robes, saluted the appearance of the sun, he consulted with the Three Excellencies and the Nine Ministers to enhance his understanding of the virtues of the earth.[105] At midday he examined the state of the government, concerning himself with the administrative affairs of the hundred officials. He then ordered the grandees to present to the officers and governors a full and prioritized account of their duties to the people. At the sacrifice to the moon, wearing the lesser-colored robes, he consulted with the Grand Astrologer and the Grand Recorder on their reverent observations of celestial laws.[106] At sundown, he inspected the nine ranks of his concubines, ordering them to prepare pure and abundant grain offerings for the ancestral and suburban altars, and only then would he rest.

"As for the feudal lords, in the morning they received orders from the Son of Heaven. During the day they inspected the affairs of their kingdoms, at dusk they examined laws and ordinances, and at night they cautioned the hundred officials against indolence and dissolution, and only then did they rest.[107] As for the ministers and grandees, in the morning they attended to their official duties, during the day they discussed the governance of the commoners, at dusk they arranged their duties in due sequence, at night they put in order the affairs of their families, and only then did they rest. As for the officers, in the morning they received their instructions, during the day they lectured and studied, in the evening they reviewed, at night they contemplated their errors, and if they had no regrets, only then did they retire. As for the common people and all those ranked beneath them, at daybreak they all sprang into action.[108] When night fell, they rested, spending no day in idleness.

"The queen personally wove the black fringe that hung down the sides of the ruler's cap. To this, the wives of the marquises added the chin straps and the flat top of the hat.[109] The wives of the ministers made the great sash. The wives of the grandees made sacrificial robes, and the wives of the high-ranking officers contributed court robes. From the lower-ranking officers and common people on down, all of the women clothed their husbands. In the sacrifices to the soil they contributed their labor; in the winter sacrifices they offered the fruits of their labor. Men and women put forth effort, and those who did not were punished. This was the rule of ancient times.

"The man of discernment labors with his mind, the humble man labors with his strength. This is the teaching of the kings of former times. From the highest to the lowest, who would dare to indulge themselves or shirk responsibility? As for me, I am now widowed and you occupy a lowly position. From morning to night we attend to affairs and are still fearful of forgetting the tasks set for us by our ancestors. And how much more the case if we were truly indolent, how then could we escape punishment? I had hoped that morning and evening you would help me by saying, 'Do not cast off our ancestors!' Now, however, you say, 'Why don't you relax your efforts?' If this is how you carry out official duties, then I fear that Mubo's line will soon end!"

Zhongni heard this and said, "Disciples, take note of this. The wife of the Ji lineage was not self-indulgent!"[110] The *Odes* says, "The women have no public duties,/They abide by their silkworm work and weaving."[111] This means that women make weaving and spinning their official occupation, and to refrain from it contravenes ritual.

Wenbo once invited Nangong Jingshu to a drinking party and made Lu Dufu the guest of honor.[112] He was served a turtle, but it was very small. Dufu was angry, and as the other guests were receiving and eating their turtles, Dufu announced his departure, saying, "Let the turtle grow up, then I'll eat it." Then he left.

When Jing Jiang heard about this incident she became angry, saying, "I have heard that our former lord used to say, 'Sacrifices provide for the deceased; banquets provide for honored guests.' Exactly which [ritual] were you following when you offered this person a turtle and angered him so?"[113] She then expelled Wenbo from the house. After five days, the grandees of Lu made supplications and secured his return.

The man of discernment would say, "Jing Jiang was practiced in exercising care over minutiae."[114] The *Odes* says, "I have good wine,/To feast and make glad the hearts of my admirable guests."[115] Its message is to honor guests.

When Wenbo died, Jing Jiang admonished his concubines, saying, "I have heard that when a man favors the inner quarters his women will die for him; when he favors public life his officers will die for him. Now my son has died prematurely, and I hate to think that he might be known for favoring the inner quarters. I therefore entreat the concubines who bear the burden of offering sacrifices to the ancestors to not become emaciated, to not [make a show of] wiping away your tears, to not beat your breast, and to not wear a sorrowful countenance. Reduce the degree of your mourning clothes, do not increase it. Follow the rites and remain tranquil. This will make my son illustrious."[116]

Zhongni heard this and said, "A girl's wisdom is not as great as a woman's; a boy's wisdom is not as great as a man's. The wife of the Gongfu lineage was indeed wise. She wished to add further luster to her son's good reputation." The *Odes* says, "May our prince maintain his goodness,/And transmit it to his descendants!"[117] These words apply well to her.

When Jing Jiang was in mourning, in the morning she wept for Mubo and in the evening she wept for Wenbo. Zhongni heard about it and said, "The wife of the Ji lineage can indeed be called one who understands ritual. In her expression of love she was impartial and maintained proper distinction between superiors and inferiors."[118]

Jing Jiang once went to the Ji residence. Kangzi was holding court and spoke to her, but she did not respond.[119] He followed her, and when she reached the door to the inner apartments, she did not respond and went in. Kangzi then took leave of the court and went in to speak to her, saying, "I did not manage to hear your command. It is not because I have offended you, is it?"

Jing Jiang said, "Have you not heard that the Son of Heaven and the feudal lords settle the affairs of the common people in the outer court [and settle the affairs of the spirits] in the inner court?[120] For the ministers and grandees on down, they settle official duties in the outer court and settle family affairs in the inner court. Inside the inner apartments, women attend to their affairs. Superiors and inferiors are all alike in this respect. Now, the outer court is where you attend to the affairs of our ruler, and the inner court is where you manage the affairs of the Ji lineage. I would not dare to speak about either of them."

Once, when Kangzi arrived, Jing Jiang opened the door and spoke to him but would not allow him to cross the threshold.[121] When she sacrificed to Daozi, Kangzi took part.[122] When Kangzi pledged an offering of wine, she would not accept it, nor did she share in the banquet in which sacrificial offerings of food were consumed.[123] If the lineage official in charge of ritual was not present, she would not sacrifice. When partaking in the sacrifice, she would leave before draining the cup of wine.[124] Zhongni said, "Jing Jiang made the distinction between men's and women's rites." The *Odes* says, "The woman did not err."[125] These words describe her well.

The Verse Summary says,

Wenbo's mother
Was called Jing Jiang.
She was perceptive and conversant with ritual;
Her virtuous actions provide a shining example.
She corrected her son when he erred,
Teaching him with reasoned principles.
Zhongni saw a worthy in her,
And classified her as a caring mother.

1.10 THE MOTHER OF ZIFA OF CHU

The Mother of Zifa of Chu was the mother of the Chu general Zifa.[126] When Zifa attacked Qin, his supply of grain was cut off. He sent a messenger to request assistance from the king and took advantage of the opportunity to inquire about his mother as well. His mother asked the messenger, "Have the officers and men managed to avoid falling ill?" The messenger responded, saying, "The officers and men have all been apportioned beans and grain to eat."[127] She also asked, "Has the general managed to avoid ill health?" The messenger said, "Mornings and evenings the general has grain-fed pig and millet."

After Zifa defeated Qin and returned home, his mother closed the door and refused him entry. She sent someone to reprimand him, saying, "Have you never heard of King Goujian of Yue's attack on Wu?[128] When a guest once offered the king a flagon of fine wine, the king requested that he pour it into the river upstream so that the officers and men downstream could partake of it. Although the taste of the water was not really any more savory, the officers and men each went on to fight with the strength of five men. On another day someone presented the king with a sack of dried rice cakes. Again, the king divided them up for his army to eat, and though their sweetness never reached their throats, each went on to fight with the strength of ten men.

"Now, however, you serve as general and the officers and men are apportioned beans and grain to eat, while day and night you alone enjoy grain-fed pig and millet. Why? Have you not heard what the *Odes* says: 'Let us not be wild in our love of enjoyment./The good man is ever diligent'?[129] It means that one should not lose goodwill. Now you send men to the place of death, while you yourself preside over them in good health and comfort. Although you managed to win a victory, it was not due to your skill. You are not my son and you will not enter my door!"

Zifa then apologized to his mother, and only then did she allow him to come in.

A man of discernment would say, "Zifa's mother was skilled in teaching and training. The *Odes* says, "Teach and train your sons,/And they will become as good as you are."[130] These lines describe her well.

The Verse Summary says,

The mother of Zifa
Attacked her son's arrogance and extravagance.
The general enjoyed rice and millet,
While the soldiers ate beans and grain.
She admonished him, saying that without propriety,
He would never win the help of others.
A man of discernment would find her praiseworthy,
And thus include her as an example of maternal virtue.

1.11 THE MOTHER OF MENG KE OF ZOU

The mother of Meng Ke of Zou was called Mother Meng.[131] She lived near a graveyard. During Mencius' youth, he enjoyed playing among the tombs, romping about pretending to prepare the ground for burials. Mother Meng said, "This is not the place to raise my son." She therefore moved away and settled beside the marketplace. But there he liked to play at displaying and selling wares like a merchant. Again Mother Meng said, "This is not the place to raise my son," and once more left and settled beside a school. There, however, he played at setting out sacrificial vessels, bowing, yielding, entering, and withdrawing. His mother said, "This, indeed, is where I can raise my son!" and settled there. When Mencius grew up, he studied the Six Arts, and finally became known as a great classicist.[132]

A man of discernment would say, "Mother Meng was good at gradual transformation."[133] The *Odes* says, "That admirable person,/What shall I give him?"[134] These words apply well to her case.

Once, when Mencius was young, he returned home after finishing his lessons and found his mother spinning. She asked him, "How far did you get in your studies today?" Mencius replied, "I'm in about the same place as I was before." Mother Meng thereupon took up a knife and cut her weaving. Mencius was alarmed and asked her to explain. Mother Meng said, "Your abandoning your study is like my cutting this weaving. A man of discernment studies in order to establish a name and inquires to become broadly knowledgeable. By this means, when he is at rest, he can maintain tranquility and when he is active, he can keep trouble at a distance. If now you abandon your studies, you will not escape a life of menial servitude and will lack the means to keep yourself from misfortune. How is this different from weaving and spinning to eat? If one abandons these tasks midway, how can one clothe one's husband and child and avoid being perpetually short of food? If a woman abandons that with which she nourishes others and a man is careless about cultivating his virtue, if they don't become brigands or thieves, then they will end up as slaves or servants."

Mencius was afraid. Morning and evening he studied hard without ceasing. He served Zisi as his teacher and then became one of the most renowned classicists in the world.[135]

A man of discernment would say, "Mother Meng understood the Way of the Mother." The *Odes* says, "This admirable person,/What shall I tell him?"[136] This phrase applies well to this case.

Once, after Mencius had married, as he was about to enter his private apartments, he encountered his wife, who was inside the room in a state of undress. Mencius was displeased, so he left without going in. His wife then went to bid farewell to Mother Meng and requested permission to leave, saying, "I have heard that in the husband–wife relationship, the private rooms are not subject to the same rules that govern our behavior elsewhere. Just now when the master saw me, I was in a state of disarray in my room. He was abrupt and displeased, which is tantamount to treating me as one of his retainers. Don't the rules of conduct for wives dictate that they are not to be treated as retainers lodging for the night? I beg to return to my father and mother."

Mother Meng then summoned Mencius and told him, "According to ritual, when you are about to enter a room, you ask if anyone is there, and that is how to convey respect. When you go into the hall, you must raise your voice to alert others to your presence. When you are about to go through a door, you must avert your gaze lest you see another's misdeed.[137] If you fail to investigate ritual yet fault the ritual behavior of others, then you are far from being correct yourself!" Mencius then apologized and kept his wife.

A man of discernment would say, "Mother Meng understood ritual and was perceptive in the Way of the Mother-in-Law."

Once, when Mencius was living in Qi, he began to look worried. Mother Meng noticed and asked him, "You look worried—why is that?" Mencius said, "I'm not."[138] On another day, when he was at leisure, he leaned against a pillar and sighed. Mother Meng saw him and said, "Earlier you look worried but said it was nothing. Now you are leaning against a pillar and sighing. Why?" Mencius said, "I have heard that the gentleman weighs his talents and then seeks an appropriate position. He does not receive rewards gained through illicit means. He does not covet glory or emolument. If his lord does not listen to him, then he does not persist in communicating with him. If his lord listens but does not put his ideas into practice, then he does not frequent his lord's court. At present the Way is not carried out in Qi. I would like to leave, but you, Mother, are old. That is why I am worried."

Mother Meng said, "The rites for a wife require that she purify the five grains, strain the wine, care for her father-in-law and mother-in-law, and sew clothing, and that is all. Thus, she takes care of the inner quarters but has no ambitions beyond that sphere. The *Book of Changes* says, 'She prepares the food within but pursues nothing beyond that.'[139] The *Odes* says, 'She has no transgressions and no authority to decide,/Wine and food are her only concerns,' to explain how a woman does not usurp authority but practices the Way of the Three Obediences.[140]

Therefore, according to the rites, when she is young she obeys her parents, when she marries she obeys her husband, and when her husband dies she obeys her son.[141] Now you are a grown man and I have become old. You should act in accordance with duty, and I will act according to ritual."

A man of discernment would say, "Mother Meng understood the Way of Women." The *Odes* says, "With meaningful looks and smiles,/Teaching without anger."[142] These words describe her well.

The Verse Summary says,

> The mother of Mencius
> Was able to teach, transform, judge, and discriminate.
> With skill she selected a place to raise her son,
> Prompting him to accord with the great principles.
> When her son's studies did not advance,
> She cut her weaving to illustrate her point.
> Her son then perfected his virtue;
> His achievements rank as the crowning glory of his generation.

1.12 THE MOTHER TEACHER OF LU

The Mother Teacher of Lu was a widowed mother of nine sons from the state of Lu. During the La festival, when people rested from their labors and the new year sacrifices had been completed, she summoned all of her sons and told them, "The moral conduct for a woman requires that unless there is a compelling reason, she does not leave her husband's home. Yet there are many children in my parents' home who can't manage the annual rituals. I request your permission to go there to oversee their preparations."[143] All of her sons bowed, touching their heads to the ground, and gave their assent.

She also summoned all of the wives and told them, "A woman has the duty of the Three Obediences, and there are no actions over which she wields complete authority.[144] When she is young she is bound to her father and mother, when she is grown up she is bound to her husband, and when she is old she is bound to her son. Just now my sons all agreed to let me go visit my own family. Although this goes against the proper etiquette, I would like my youngest son to accompany me in order to accord with the rules that govern a woman's movements outside of the home. Ladies, be sure to take care of securing the doors and windows. I'll be back in the evening."

Ordering her youngest son to drive the carriage, she then returned to her home to help take care of matters there. When it began to get dark she returned, but having miscalculated, she arrived at the outskirts of the village early. So she stayed there until night fell and then went home.

A grandee of Lu had been watching her from his tower. Thinking it strange, he sent someone to spy on her at her residence. Ritual observances were tended to with great care and the household was run in a very orderly fashion. When the messenger returned, he reported the situation. The grandee then summoned the mother, asking her, "The day that you came back from the north, you got to the village gate and then just stopped there for a good while, waiting until evening to enter. I couldn't understand why you had done this and thought it strange, so that is why I'm asking you about it now."

The mother replied, "Unfortunately, I lost my husband early on and now live with my nine sons. During the La festival, after finishing the ritual preparations, I asked my sons if I could return to the home of my own family. I settled with their wives and children that I would not return until evening. I was afraid that they would be celebrating together, drinking and eating their fill. After all, it's only human nature! But I returned too early and didn't dare go back at that time. So I waited outside the village gate until the appointed time and then went in."

The grandee praised her and related the story to Duke Mu.[145] He awarded the mother with the honorary title "Mother Teacher," and ordered her to call on his wife the next day. His wife and all of his concubines honored her as their teacher.

A man of discernment would say, "The Mother Teacher was able to teach by her own example. According to the rites, before a woman is married, she regards her father and mother as Heaven. After she is married, she regards her husband as Heaven. When she mourns her parents, she reduces the period in which she wears mourning garments for them by one degree, which signifies that there are not two Heavens."[146] The *Odes* says, "When I came forth, I lodged in Ji,/And we drank the cup of parting at Ni./When a young lady goes to be married,/She leaves her parents and brothers."[147]

The Verse Summary says,

The mother of nine sons
Knew well the ritual rules.
She asked to return home, and when she came back,
There was no need to hide what was only human nature.
Her virtuous conduct having been perfected,
She received honors in the end.

The ruler of Lu regarded her as worthy,
And gave her an honorary title.

1.13 THE KIND MOTHER, MANG OF WEI

The Kind Mother, Mang of Wei, was a daughter of the Mengyang lineage of Wei and the successor wife of Mang Mao of Wei.[148] She had three sons. The former wife had five sons, none of whom felt any love for the Kind Mother. She treated them exceptionally well, but they still felt no love for her. So the Kind Mother told her own three sons that they could no longer be considered the equals of the sons of the first wife, and that their clothing, food, and drink, their rising and retiring, their advancing and withdrawing would all differ greatly. But the sons of the first wife still felt no love for her.

Then it happened that the middle son of the former wife violated a law of the King of Wei and was condemned to death. The Kind Mother was so grief-stricken that her sash had to be made smaller by one *chi*.[149] Day and night she labored to save him from his punishment. Someone said to her, "People who do not love their mothers are the most [despicable], so why do you labor and worry like this?" The Kind Mother said, "He is like one of my own sons. If one of them did not love me, I would still try to save him from disaster and remove him from harm's way. If I refused to do this only in the case of my stepson, how would that be different from treating him as if he were just an ordinary person?[150] Because he is an orphan, his father asked me to be his stepmother. A stepmother is like a mother. If one serves as a mother but is incapable of loving one's child, how can she be considered kind? If one cares only for one's kin and is biased against those who are not, how can she be considered righteous? Being without kindness and righteousness, how could I take my place in the world? Although he doesn't love me, how can I disregard what is right?" She then proceeded to appeal his case.

When King Anxi of Wei heard about her plight, he was awed by her righteousness, and said, "With a kind mother like this, how can I refuse to redeem her son?"[151] He then pardoned her son and released the family [from tax and labor obligations]. From this time forward the five sons became attached to the Kind Mother, and they all lived harmoniously like one family. The Kind Mother, through the influence of propriety and right conduct, guided her eight sons so that all of them became grandees or chief counselors in the state of Wei, and each of them became renowned for propriety and right conduct.

A man of discernment would say, "The Kind Mother with one heart [regarded all with equal concern]." The *Odes* says,

> The turtledove is in the mulberry tree,
> And her young ones are seven.
> The virtuous man, the princely one,
> In his conduct, treats all with equal concern.
> In his conduct, treats all with equal concern;
> His heart is as if it were tied to what is correct."[152]

This ode describes a heart that is extended to all equally. The turtledove with one heart nourished seven chicks. The man of quality with one standard of conduct nourishes the ten thousand things. A heart with one intention can serve one hundred masters, but a heart with one hundred intentions cannot serve even one master. This lesson applies here.

The Verse Summary says,

> The wife of Mang Mao
> Was stepmother to five sons.
> With loving kindness, benevolence, and righteousness,
> She raised her stepsons.
> Although they felt no love for her,
> She embraced them as her own.
> A stepmother such as this
> Should indeed be honored.

1.14 THE MOTHER OF TIAN JI OF QI

The mother of Tian Ji of Qi was the mother of Tian Jizi of Qi.[153] Tian Jizi was the prime minister of the state of Qi. He once collected bribes from his subordinate officials in the amount of one hundred *yi* of cash, which he presented to his mother.[154] His mother said, "You have served as prime minister for three years now, yet your salary has never amounted to this much. Surely you are not presenting me with money at the expense of your officials! Where did this come from?"

He replied, "In fact, I received it from my subordinates."

His mother said, "I have heard that an official cultivates himself, is pure in his conduct, and does not involve himself in ill-gotten gain. He exhausts all efforts to be truthful and does not carry out deceptions. If something is not right, he does not scheme about it in his heart. If a profit comes through unprincipled means, it does not enter his house. His words and actions are one, and his thoughts and outward appearance are in accord. At present, the ruler has established this position to accommodate you and offers a generous sum as your salary. Your words and actions should therefore be used to repay him.

"Now a subject serves his ruler in the same way as a son serves his father. He exerts all of his efforts and exhausts all of his abilities; he is loyal, trustworthy, and does not deceive. He is devoted to demonstrating his loyalty and if he must die, he still obeys the ruler's command. When he is incorruptible, pure, just, and upright, then he can proceed without misfortune. Now your behavior is quite the contrary and far removed from loyalty. Indeed, one who acts as a disloyal subject will be an unfilial son. Wealth that is tainted is not among my possessions, and a son who is unfilial is not my son. You should leave now."

Tian Jizi was ashamed and left. He returned the cash, confessed his crime to King Xuan, and requested immediate punishment.[155] After King Xuan had heard all the details of the case, he greatly rewarded Tian's mother for her correct conduct. He then pardoned Jizi's crime, restored his position as prime minister, and presented his mother with a gift of cash.

A man of discernment would say, "Jizi's mother was incorrupt and possessed transformative powers." The *Odes* says, "Oh that superior one,/Who would not eat the food of idleness!"[156] To be without merit but to receive a salary is something that should not be done, how much more so in the case of receiving cash!

The Verse Summary says,

The mother of Tian Ji
Was incorrupt, pure, honest, and upright.
She reprimanded her son for accepting cash,
Considering it to be immoral.
To fulfill the duties of loyalty and filial piety,
One should exhaust one's wealth and expend all effort:
The superior man who receives a salary
To the end will not eat the food of idleness.

2

THE WORTHY AND ENLIGHTENED

PREFACE

Only those such as the Worthy and Enlightened[1]
Can be perfectly pure and correct.
Their actions were measured
And their words, most felicitous.
With complete knowledge of the principle of things,
They grasped the precepts and rules of the world.
By observing the law at work and in rest,
Not one, to the end, did misfortune distress.
Consorts and empresses who attend to these phrases
Will bring to their names lauds and praises.[2]

2.1 QUEEN JIANG, CONSORT OF KING XUAN OF ZHOU

Queen Jiang, consort of King Xuan of the Zhou dynasty, was the daughter of the Marquis of Qi.[3] She was wise and virtuous, so that in all matters she did not mention what was not in accord with propriety, and in all actions she did not initiate what was not in accord with propriety.

King Xuan habitually went to bed early and rose late, and the royal consorts tended to remain in his chamber. Once, after Queen Jiang [had left his chamber], she took off her hairpins and earrings and went to await punishment in the Lanes of Perpetuity.[4] She sent her tutor matron to convey a message to the king, which said, "I am incompetent and my dissolute heart has now manifested itself, to the extent that I have caused my ruler to engage in improprieties and to arrive late to court, showing that he loves women but has forgotten virtue. Now if a man delights in women, he will also be fond of extravagance and give free rein to his desires, and that is how disorder begins. The beginning of this disorder finds its origin in me. I, your servant, therefore request to accept blame for this turn of events."

The king said, "I am not virtuous, and in fact, I am myself responsible for this offense. It is not your fault!" He then restored Queen Jiang and applied himself diligently to governmental affairs, rising early and retiring late, so that he finally achieved renown for the restoration of the house of Zhou.

A man of discernment would say, "Queen Jiang was virtuous and skilled at maintaining a dignified and majestic bearing. Indeed, according to ritual, when a queen or consort waited upon the ruler, she approached with a candle, and when she arrived at his quarters, she put out the candle. When she arrived inside his chambers, she removed her court robes and put on her sleeping attire. She then approached and served the ruler. When the cock crowed and the music master struck a drum to announce the dawn, the consort would sound the pendants on her sash and leave."[5] The *Odes* says, "May they manifest all self-restraint in deportment,/And their virtuous fame be without fail!"[6] It also says, "In the low wet grounds, the mulberry trees are beautiful,/And their leaves are dark./When I see my lord,/His virtuous fame binds us closely."[7] Thus, a woman uses beauty to gain affection but uses virtue to make that affection secure. The virtuous actions of Lady Jiang can indeed be regarded as a powerful bond.[8]

The Verse Summary says,

How admirable this Queen Jiang,
Her virtue so revered.
Her actions all derived from propriety,
Thus, she aided King Xuan.
She brought up his transgression with all humility,
So that King Xuan soon understood.
Till day and night revering the Way,
He ruled a dynasty restored.

2.2 JI OF WEY, WIFE OF DUKE HUAN OF QI

Ji of Wey was the daughter of the Marquis of Wey and the wife of Duke Huan of Qi.[9] Duke Huan was fond of dissolute music, and because of this, Ji of Wey would not listen to the tunes of Zheng and Wey.[10]

Duke Huan employed Guan Zhong and Ning Qi and practiced the Way of the Hegemon.[11] And though all of the feudal lords attended his court, Wey alone did not come. Duke Huan and Guang Zhong therefore planned to attack Wey.

After holding court, Duke Huan entered the women's quarters, whereupon Ji of Wey observed him from afar. She then removed her hairpin and earrings, untied her jeweled sash, and went to the lower part of the hall, where she bowed twice and said, "I wish to accept the blame for Wey's offense." The duke said, "I have no quarrel with Wey. Why do you make such a request?"

Ji of Wey replied, saying, "I have heard that a ruler has three demeanors. Bright and joyful, with a countenance of extreme pleasure—this look accompanies bells and drums, feasting and drinking. Silent, pure, and still, with mind and mood subdued—this look bespeaks mourning and misfortune. Full of anger, with reckless movement of arms and legs—this look signals attack and invasion. Just now I saw you raising your legs in a powerful stride; your expression was severe and your voice was raised, all while your mind was fixed on Wey. That is why I made this request."[12] The duke then acceded to her wishes.[13]

The next day at court, Guan Zhong hastened forward, saying, "While Your Majesty held court, you were respectful, your temper was calm, your speech was composed, and you were disinclined to attack other states—this means Wey will be spared." Duke Huan said, "Indeed."

The duke then established Ji of Wey as his wife and began to address Guan Zhong as "Uncle," saying, "If I rely upon my wife to manage the inner quarters and Guan Zhong to manage public affairs, even though I am dim-witted, it will be sufficient to establish me in the world!"

A man of discernment would say, "Ji of Wey was trustworthy and took action." The *Odes* says, "Ah! Such a woman as this!/The beauty of the country!"[14]

The Verse Summary says,

Ji of Wey, wife of Duke Huan of Qi,
  Was loyal, true, sincere, and trustworthy.

The duke was fond of dissolute music,
But Ji continued to cultivate herself.
Gazing at his demeanor from afar, she asked to bear the blame,
And the duke was well pleased with her.
He then ordered her to take charge of the inner quarters
And made her his wife.

2.3 JIANG OF QI, WIFE OF DUKE WEN OF JIN

Jiang of Qi belonged to the lineage of Duke Huan of Qi and was the wife of Duke Wen of Jin.[15] Earlier, Duke Wen's father, Duke Xian, had taken Li Ji as his concubine. She slandered and brought about the death of the Crown Prince Shensheng.[16] Duke Wen was then known as Prince Chonger.[17] He fled with his uncle Fan to the Di people and then went to Qi, where Duke Huan of Qi gave him one of his own kin as a wife.[18]

The duke treated Chonger very well, so that Chonger now possessed twenty teams of four horses and planned to die in Qi, saying, "Life has no aim but peace and enjoyment! Who cares about anything else?" Zifan, who was aware of Duke Wen's contentment with Qi, wanted to leave and was troubled by this state of affairs. He therefore devised a plan with the duke's followers beneath a mulberry tree.

A serving girl who tended silkworms and who happened to be present told Jiang about the plan. Jiang then killed the servant and said to the prince, "Your followers are planning to take you away. Moreover, I have already done away with a servant who happened to overhear their conversation. You must go along with them and not be of two minds. If you are of two minds, you will not realize your destiny. Since you left Jin, it has not enjoyed one year of peace. But Heaven has not yet destroyed it. If anyone is to possess Jin, who should it be, if not you? You must rouse yourself into action! 'The Lord on High draws near to you,/To be of two minds is inauspicious.'"[19]

The prince said, "I refuse to go. I'll end my days here!" Jiang said, "That won't do. The *Zhou Odes* says, 'Well prepared and alert was the messenger with his suite,/Ever anxious lest he should not succeed.'[20] Morning and night they moved forward, as if afraid of not reaching their destination. How much more should this be so for one who thinks only of his own comfort? How will you ever succeed? If a person doesn't seek success, how can he obtain it? The disorder in Jin will not last forever. Jin must be yours!" But the prince would not listen.

Jiang and the prince's uncle Fan then plotted to get the prince drunk and carry him off. When he awoke from his drunkenness, he grabbed a spear and chased Uncle Fan, saying, "If we succeed, then fine! But if we don't, then I will eat your flesh as if I can never get my fill!"

Thus, they made their way, passing through Cao, Song, Zheng, and Chu until they entered Qin. Duke Mu of Qin provided them with troops and took them into Jin.[21] The people of Jin then killed Duke Huai and set up Prince Chonger as Duke Wen.[22] He brought Jiang of Qi [to Jin] and made her his wife, and then proceeded to rule as hegemon over all, serving as the master of covenants.[23]

A man of discernment would say, "Jiang of Qi was uncompromising but not abrasive. She was able to nurture her ruler's goodness." The *Odes* says, "That beautiful, eldest Jiang,/Can respond to you in conversation."[24] These lines describe her well.

The Verse Summary says,

Jiang of Qi was public-spirited and upright,
In words and actions, never careless.
She urged Duke Wen of Jin
To put aside all hesitations and return home.
Though the duke at first refused to listen,
Jiang and Uncle Fan devised a scheme:
They made him drunk and carried him away,
So that in the end, he became hegemon.

2.4 JI, WIFE OF DUKE MU OF QIN

Mu Ji, the wife of Duke Mu of Qin, was the daughter of Duke Xian of Jin, elder sister to Crown Prince Shensheng by the same mother, and sister of Duke Hui of Jin by a different mother.[25] She was worthy and righteous.

Duke Xian killed the Crown Prince Shensheng and expelled the other princes.[26] Duke Hui, who was then known as Prince Yiwu, fled to Liang.[27] When Duke Xian of Jin died, Yiwu relied upon the aid of Duke Mu of Qin to ascend the throne of Jin.[28]

At the beginning of Duke Hui's reign, Mu Ji arranged for all of the sons of Duke Xian to be conveyed [back to Jin], saying, "The ducal clan is the ruler's foundation." Yet Duke Hui did not employ any of them.[29] He also went back on his promise of a gift to Qin.[30] Also, when Jin suffered from famine, Jin asked

Qin for grain, and Qin gave it to them. When Qin suffered famine, Qin asked Jin for grain, but Jin refused to oblige. Qin then raised troops to attack Jin and captured the Duke of Jin in order to bring him back to Qin.[31] Duke Mu of Qin said, "Sweep and purify our ancestral temple. I am going to send the Duke of Jin to visit [the ancestors]!"[32]

When Mu Ji heard this, she took the Crown Prince Ying, Prince Hong, and her daughter, Jianbi, all dressed in coarse hempen mourning robes and bands, and awaited him, standing on firewood [which they had spread on the ground].[33] She told Duke Mu, "Heaven on high is sending down misfortune, causing you two rulers to meet each other not with gifts of jade and silk but with brandished weapons. I, your servant, as an elder sister, have been unable to instruct my younger brother and have thus shamefully neglected your commands. If the Duke of Jin is brought in this morning, then I, your servant, as well as your children will die tonight. You, my lord, should consider this!"

The duke was alarmed and therefore put Duke Hui in the Ling Tower.[34] When the grandees asked that the duke be brought into [the city], Duke Mu said, "When I captured the ruler of Jin, I thought that I was returning with a great achievement, but now it is only destruction that I bring back with me. How can that be of any use?" He therefore housed the ruler of Jin and presented him with food for seven *lao* sacrifices.[35]

After Mu Ji died, her younger brother Chonger came to Qin. Qin escorted him to Jin, and it was he who became Duke Wen of Jin. Crown Prince Ying, thinking of his mother's mercy, accompanied his uncle and composed an ode, which said, "I escorted my uncle/To the north of the Wei./What did I present to him?/Four bay horses for his carriage of state."[36]

A man of discernment would say, "A kind mother produces a filial son." The *Odes* says, "With reverent care of the outward demeanor,/One will become a pattern for the people."[37] These words apply well to Mu Ji.

The Verse Summary says,

> The wife of Duke Mu of Qin
> Was the elder sister of Duke Hui of Jin.
> When Qin took Jin's ruler prisoner,
> This wife's tears flowed.
> Pained that she could not save him,
> She prepared to meet her death.
> Duke Mu regarded her as righteous,
> And therefore released her brother.

2.5 FAN JI OF KING ZHUANG OF CHU

Fan Ji was a consort of King Zhuang of Chu.[38] When King Zhuang came to the throne, he was very fond of hunting.[39] Fan Ji admonished him, but he would not desist. She therefore refused to eat the flesh of wild game. The king then corrected this fault and assiduously applied himself to governmental affairs.[40]

Once the king was presiding over court and did not finish until very late.[41] Fan Ji came down to the hall to meet him, asking, "How can you work so late without feeling hungry or tired?" The king said, "When I speak to worthy men I never feel hungry or tired." Ji said, "When you say 'worthy,' to whom are you referring?" The king said, "Yu Qiuzi." Ji covered her mouth and laughed. The king said, "What are you laughing at?" She replied, "If it is a question of being worthy, then Yu Qiuzi is certainly worthy. But he cannot yet be considered loyal." The king said, "Why do you say that?"

She replied, "In the eleven years I have served you with towel and comb, I have [constantly] sent people to Zheng and Wey to look for beauties to present to Your Majesty. Thus, at present, there are two who are worthier than me and seven who can be ranked as my equals. Naturally I would like to monopolize your love and favor. But I have heard that there should be many women filling your halls so that you have a chance to observe their abilities. I cannot let my personal concerns obstruct the public good because I hope that Your Majesty will observe many and learn about their capabilities. Now Yu Qiuzi has been a minister of Chu for more than ten years, yet the people he has recommended are either his sons or younger brothers or men from his clan. I have not heard of him promoting worthy men or demoting those who are incompetent. This is a case of deceiving one's ruler and obstructing the path of the worthy. To know of worthies and not promote them is disloyal. To be unaware of their worthiness is ignorance. So isn't it in fact appropriate that I should laugh?" The king was pleased.

The next day the king reported Ji's words to Yu Qiuzi. Qiuzi moved backward on his mat and did not know how to reply.[42] He then vacated his residence and asked someone to bring in Sunshu Ao and present him to the king.[43] The king made Sunshu Ao chief counselor.[44] He governed in Chu for three years, and with his help King Zhuang became hegemon.

The Historian of Chu wrote, "The hegemony of King Zhuang was due to the efforts of Fan Ji." The *Odes* says, "Early retire, ye great officers,/And do not make the ruler fatigued!"[45] The "ruler" here refers to a "female ruler." The *Odes* also says, "Be mild from morning to night,/And reverent in discharging service."[46] These words apply to her.

The Verse Summary says,

Fan Ji was humble, yielding,
And without jealousy.
She recommended and advanced beauties
Who were ranked as her peers.
She criticized Yu Qiuzi
For blocking the path of the worthy.
King Zhuang of Chu applied these lessons,
And his efforts soon made him hegemon.

2.6 THE WIFE OF ZHOUNAN

The wife of Zhounan was the wife of a grandee of Zhounan.[47] The grandee received orders to level the floodplain. When the appointed time passed but he still did not return, his wife feared that he had been negligent in his service to the king.[48] So, recounting to her neighbors some of the things she had often discussed with her husband, she said, "When one's kingdom or family faces many difficulties, one must try one's best to address them without blame or resentment in order to ease the anxieties of one's father and mother. Formerly, Shun plowed on Mount Li, fished at Lei Marsh, and made his own crockery on the banks of the Yellow River.[49] These tasks were not appropriate for Shun, but his willingness to do them was for the sake of taking care of his father and mother.

"With a poor family and elderly parents, he was willing to serve as an official regardless of the position.[50] He himself carried out the tasks of drawing water from the well and grinding grain in the mortar, and he was willing to marry without being selective about a wife. Thus, as long as his parents were alive, he thought it appropriate to live more or less in harmony with the times, to avoid violating any important moral principles, and to escape harm—that and nothing more.[51]

"Thus, the phoenix does not fall into the fine-meshed net, the qilin does not venture into the pitfall, and the scaly dragon does not approach the dried marsh.[52] If birds and beasts know how to avoid harm, then how much more the case for human beings? If one is born in an age of disorder and cannot obtain principled treatment, but is oppressed by cruel tyranny and cannot act in accord with what is right yet still holds office, one does so because one's parents are still alive."

She then composed an ode, which said, "The bream is showing its tail all red;/The royal house is like a blazing fire./Though it be like a blazing fire,/Your parents are very near."[53] Under such circumstances, there was nothing more that could be done. For the discerning, this incident demonstrates that the wife of Zhounan was able to aid her husband.

The Verse Summary says,

The wife of the Zhou official
Saw her husband go out to manage the floodplain.
She cautioned him not to be idle,
To exert himself for his parents' sake,
And in all he did to keep harm at a distance,[54]
Because his parents were still alive.
She wrote the ode about the bream,
In order to warn her husband.

2.7 THE WOMAN OF DISTINCTION, THE WIFE OF BAO OF SONG

The Woman of Distinction was the wife of Bao Su of Song.[55] She was most diligent in the care of her mother-in-law. Bao Su held an official position in Wey for three years and had a mistress there. But the Woman of Distinction continued to care for her mother-in-law with even greater solicitude.

Whenever travelers passed through, she asked them for news about her husband and learned that her husband had given his mistress many valuable gifts. The Woman of Distinction's sister-in-law told her, "You are entitled to leave him now." When the Woman of Distinction asked why, her sister-in-law replied, "He has found what he wants, so why should you stay here?"

The Women of Distinction said, "Once a woman drinks from the marriage cup, she does not waver. When her husband dies, she does not remarry.[56] She manages hempen fibers, processes the silk cocoons, weaves silk fabric, and fashions cords to supply clothing and provide for her husband. She purifies the wine and prepares food in order to serve her father- and mother-in-law.[57] She understands devotion to one [man] as purity and the capacity to follow his lead as obedience. Purity and obedience are the highest achievements of women.[58] How then can I consider it right to monopolize my husband's love? If I allow myself to be motivated by my own passions and try to control my husband's affections, I don't know how that would improve my lot!

"According to the rites, the Son of Heaven has twelve consorts; the feudal lords have nine; the ministers and grandees, three, and the officers, two. Now as my husband is indeed an officer, isn't it appropriate that he should have two women? Furthermore, there are seven reasons wives may be divorced, while there is not one principle upon which a husband can be divorced. According to the Seven Reasons for Divorce, jealousy is most properly the chief reason, while lasciviousness, stealing, loquaciousness, arrogance, childlessness, and suffering from a repulsive disease are all secondary. Because, my sister, you do not instruct me in the proprieties of domestic life but instead urge me to do something that will result in my being sent away, how can I make use of this advice?" She therefore disregarded her sister-in-law and served her mother-in-law with even greater diligence.

When the Duke of Song heard about her, he honored her village and gave her the title, "Woman of Distinction."

A man of discernment would say, "The Woman of Distinction was humble and understood propriety." The *Odes* says, "Good is his deportment;/Good his looks;/The lessons of antiquity are his law;/He is strenuously attentive to his deportment."[59] These words describe her well.

The Verse Summary says,

The Woman of Distinction, the wife of Bao of Song,
Loved the rites and understood moral principles.
When her husband took a mistress,
She did not waver in the least.
She exemplified the Way of Wives
And disregarded her sister-in-law.
The Duke of Song considered her a worthy
And honored her village.

2.8 THE WIFE OF ZHAO CUI OF JIN

The wife of Zhao Cui of Jin was the daughter of Duke Wen of Jin.[60] She was called Zhao Ji.[61] In the beginning, when Duke Wen was still a prince, he fled to Di territory with Zhao Cui.[62] The Di people presented him with two women,

Shu Wei and Ji Wei.[63] The duke gave Shu Wei to Zhao Cui as a wife. She gave birth to Dun. When Duke Wen and Zhao Cui returned to their state, the duke gave his daughter, Zhao Ji, to Zhao Cui as a bride. She gave birth to Yuan Tong, Ping Kuo, and Lou Ying.[64]

Zhao Ji asked to bring into their home Dun and his mother. Zhao Cui, not daring to do so, refused. Ji said, "That is not acceptable! To find favor and then forget one's old acquaintances is to abandon righteousness. To be fond of the new and mistreat the old is to be lacking in kindness. To tax others in times of difficulty and neglect them in times of wealth is to lack propriety. If you abandon these three principles, then how will you be able to lead others? And though I am only your wife, I too would be unable to go on serving you with towel and comb.[65] Does not a passage in the *Odes* say, 'When we gather the mustard plant and earth melons,/We do not reject them because of their roots./While I do nothing contrary to my good name,/I should live with you till our death'?[66] If one person shares with another cold and suffering, even though that person may have some small fault, the two should remain together till death and not part. How much more should this be kept in mind when one is pleased with someone new but forgets old acquaintances? The *Odes* also says, 'You feast with your new wife,/And think me not worth being with.'[67] How can this not hurt them? My lord, you should welcome them and not abandon the old for the new!" Zhao Cui agreed and then welcomed Shu Wei and Dun.[68]

When they arrived, Ji considered Dun to be worthy and asked that he be established as his father's heir and made her three sons be placed on a level below him. She had Shu Wei made primary wife, while Ji herself assumed a lower status. When Dun achieved the rank of high minister, thinking of Zhao Ji's yielding and kindness, he requested that Ji's middle son, Ping Kuo, serve as a grandee of the ducal clan, saying, "He is the much-loved son of the ruler's wife, Ji. If not for her, I would still be considered a person of the Di. How else would I have obtained my present status?"[69] Duke Cheng agreed.[70] Ping Kuo, as leader of his lineage, thereupon served as a grandee of the ducal clan.[71]

A man of discernment would say, "Zhao Ji was reverent and yielding." The *Odes* says, "The mild and respectful man/Possesses the foundation of virtue."[72] These words describe Zhao Ji well.

The Verse Summary says,

Zhao Cui's consort Ji
Clearly understood the distinctions of rules and ranking.
Although she herself was noble,

She harbored no jealousy toward the other wife.
She personally served Shu Wei
And had her son made heir.
Gentlemen praised her
Because of the perfection of her conduct.

2.9 THE WIFE OF DAZI OF TAO

The wife of Dazi of Tao was the wife of the grandee Dazi of Tao.[73] Dazi governed
Tao for three years, and though he was not known for any particular achievement, his personal wealth increased threefold. His wife repeatedly admonished
him, but it was of no use. After five years, he took leave and returned home with
one hundred teams of horse-drawn carriages following him. His clan members
slaughtered an ox to congratulate him. But his wife stood alone, holding their
child and weeping.

Her mother-in-law became angry, saying, "Why are you behaving in such an
inauspicious manner?" The wife said, "My husband's talents are meager, yet the
official position he holds is very important. This is known as 'dashing into harm's
way.' To be without merit while one's family becomes prosperous is known as
'accumulating misfortune.' Formerly, when the Chief Counselor of Chu, Ziwen,
governed the state, his family was poor while the state prospered.[74] The ruler was
respected and the people were sustained.[75] Therefore his good fortune extended
to his sons and grandsons, and his name was handed down to later generations.
At present, my husband is not like this but instead lusts after wealth and strives
for power without regard to future harm.

"I have heard that on South Mountain there was once a black leopard. For
seven days he exposed himself to mist and rain and did not come down to feed.
Why was this? He hoped thereby to moisten his fur so that it would become
spotted. He was therefore able to conceal himself to keep harm at a distance.[76]
Dogs and pigs, on the other hand, will eat anything to fatten themselves, preferring to stay in one place until they die. Now, while my husband governs Tao, our
family prospers but the city is poor. The ruler is not respected and the people are
not sustained—all clear omens of destruction. I wish to take leave with my child."
The mother-in-law was furious and expelled them.

After a period of a few years, Dazi's family was indeed put to death for graft
and only his elderly mother was spared.[77] Dazi's wife and young child thus
returned home to care for her, so that she lived out her Heaven-appointed days.

A man of discernment would say, "The wife of Dazi was able to use her sense of what was right to scorn profit. Although she violated the rites by asking to leave her husband, ultimately she embraced them wholeheartedly. This can indeed be called far-reaching wisdom." The *Odes* says, "The hundred plans you think of/ Are not equal to the course I was going to take."[78] These words describe her well.

The Verse Summary says,

Dazi governed Tao,
And his family's wealth increased threefold.
His wife admonished him, but he refused to listen.
Knowing that he would not change,
Alone, she cried, angering her mother-in-law,
And was sent back to her mother's home.
When Dazi met with disaster,
She returned to care for her mother-in-law.

2.10 THE WIFE OF LIUXIA HUI

The wife of Liuxia Hui was the wife of the Lu grandee Liuxia Hui.[79] During Liuxia's stay in Lu, he was dismissed three times but did not leave because he was distressed about the people and wished to avert disorder. His wife said, "Won't this, in fact, stain your reputation? For the gentleman there are two forms of disgrace. To be honored by an immoral state or disregarded in a moral one is to be disgraced in either case. At present, we live in a chaotic world. To be dismissed three times but not to leave is indeed approaching disgrace."[80]

Liuxia Hui said, "The people in great throngs are about to fall into harm's way; how can I stop now? Moreover, other people are what they are, and I am what I am. Though another person should stand next to me stark naked, how can he defile me?"[81] He therefore was content to stay with [the people of Lu], filling an office of inferior rank.

After Liuxia Hui died, his disciples were about to write a dirge for him. But his wife said, "If you are going to eulogize my husband's virtues, then none of you knows him as well as I do." She therefore composed the following dirge:

Alas, my husband was not boastful,
Tireless was he.
He was trustworthy and never visited harm upon others.

He was yielding and gentle, respectful of custom and never severe.

Alas, he suffered disgrace to aid the people; how abundant was his virtue!

Though he thrice met with dismissal, he did not end his days in obscurity.

This kindly gentleman was ever determined;

What a pity that he should now leave this world!

Though he had only begun to approach old age, he has now passed away.

How lamentable that his spirit and soul have departed.

Alas, how fitting that he now be known by the name "Kind."

His disciples used her composition for the dirge, and none of them found it necessary to correct a single word.

A man of discernment would say, "The wife of Liuxia Hui was indeed able to glorify her husband." The *Odes* says, "They know one thing,/But they only know that one."[82] These words apply well to this case.

The Verse Summary says,

The wife of Liuxia Hui

Was worthy, enlightened, and cultured.

After Liuxia died,

His disciples were intent on preserving [his memory].[83]

They were about to write Xiahui's eulogy,

But his wife had already composed one.

She set forth his deeds so well,

No one could improve it.

2.11 THE WIFE OF QIAN LOU OF LU

[This lady was] the wife of Master Qian Lou of Lu.[84] At the time of the master's death, Zengzi and his disciples came to offer condolences.[85] When the master's wife came out of the door, Zengzi condoled with her.[86] They went into the hall, where they saw the master's body beneath the window, resting on a pillow of earthen bricks and a mat of straw. He was dressed in a padded robe with no upper garment over it. He was also covered with a cloth quilt that did not completely cover his head and feet. When it was moved to cover his head, his feet were exposed, and when it was moved to cover his feet, his head was exposed.[87] Zengzi said, "Place the quilt on the bias and then it will cover him completely."

[Qian Lou's] wife said, "If it is on the bias then it will be too long [on either side]. It is better to place it squarely even though it is not quite big enough. Because the master was himself never biased, he was able to achieve what he did. Placing the shroud on the bias in death, when he was never biased in life, would not be in accord with the master's disposition."

Zengzi was not able to respond, so he wept for him, saying, "Alas, the master has met his end. What shall we use for his posthumous name?" His wife said, "I would like to use 'Kang' (Contentment) as his posthumous name." Zengzi said, "When the master was still alive, he did not have enough food to satisfy his hunger or enough clothing to cover his frame. When he died, his hands and feet were not covered and there were no offerings of wine or meat by his side. When he was alive, he did not obtain the finer things of life, and in death he obtained no glory. What contentment did he enjoy that he should be given the posthumous name Kang?"

His wife said, "In the past, the ruler once wished to confer office on him and make him the chief minister of state, but he declined and would not do it because it was an excessive honor. The ruler once tried to give him thirty measures of fine grain, but the master declined and would not accept it because it was excessive wealth.[88] The master savored the world's blandest tastes and was content with the world's most humble rank. He was not distressed by poverty or low position, and he was not pleased by wealth and honor. He sought benevolence and obtained benevolence. He sought righteousness and obtained righteousness. Is it not appropriate indeed that his posthumous name should be Kang?" Zengzi said, "No one but this man would have such a wife."

A man of discernment would say, "Qian Lou's wife was happy in poverty and practiced the Way." The *Odes* says, "That beautiful, virtuous lady/Can respond to you in conversation."[89] This saying describes her well.

The Verse Summary says,

When Qian Lou died,
His wife presided over the funeral alone.
And Zengzi came to condole with her.
The shroud was plain cloth and the coverlet was coarse,
But Qian Lou had been content with the humble and savored the bland,
And never sought abundance or luxury.
His corpse was barely covered,
Yet his posthumous name was Contentment.

2.12 THE WIFE OF THE CHARIOTEER OF QI'S PRIME MINISTER

[This lady] was the wife of the charioteer of Prime Minister Yanzi of Qi.[90] She came to be referred to as the "Commissioned Wife."[91]

Once, when Yanzi was about to go out, the Commissioned Wife secretly observed how her husband discharged his duty as the prime minister's driver. Sheltered under a large umbrella, he whipped his team of four horses and struck an attitude of overbearing arrogance and self-regard. When he returned home, his wife said, "Your humble and lowly position is most appropriate for you!" Her husband said, "Why is that?"

The wife said, "Yanzi is not fully six *chi* tall, yet he serves as Qi's prime minister and his name is illustrious among all the feudal lords.[92] Just now, through this crack in the door, I observed that his bearing was reverent and humble, and he seemed deep in thought. Now, while you are eight *chi* in height and serve only as his driver, your manner is that of an overbearingly arrogant man who is very pleased with himself. For this reason I want to leave."

Her husband apologized, saying, "Let me try to change. How should I go about it?" The wife said, "Embrace the wisdom of Yanzi and add to that your eight *chi* in height. If you are benevolent and serve an enlightened ruler, your reputation will certainly flourish! Moreover, I have heard that it is better to be humble and glorious in your righteousness rather than honored and full of empty pride." Thereafter, her husband became unrelenting in the demands he placed on himself. He studied the Way and cultivated humility as if no amount of effort would ever suffice.

Yanzi was intrigued, and when he asked about it, the driver told him the whole story. Afterward, Yanzi thought highly of his ability to submit to good counsel and correct himself. So he promoted him to the service of Duke Jing, who made him a grandee and honored his wife with the title "Commissioned Wife."[93]

A man of discernment would say, "The Commissioned Wife understood goodness. For a worthy to reach perfection, the Way must be broadly conceived. It is not just a matter of being cut and polished by teachers and friends. One's spouse also contributes much to the enterprise." The *Odes* says, "The high mountains, I look up at them;/The great road, I travel it."[94] These lines say that one should always aspire to goodness.

The Verse Summary says,

The wife of the Minister of Qi's charioteer
Corrected her husband according to the Way.
She spoke clearly of arrogance and respect,
And with great care he labored to put her words into practice.
Her husband changed his behavior
And studied without ceasing.
Yanzi promoted him,
And he was ranked as a man of discernment.

2.13 THE WIFE OF JIEYU OF CHU

[This lady] was the wife of the madman Jieyu of Chu.[95] Jieyu personally tilled the land to feed himself. The King of Chu thus ordered a messenger to approach him with a gift of cash in the amount of one hundred *yi* and two chariots, each fitted with two teams of four horses, saying, "The king would like to invite you, sir, to rule Huainan."[96] Jieyu laughed and did not respond. The messenger was not able to elicit a word from him and finally left.

When his wife returned from the market, she said, "When you were young, you acted according to your principles. Now that you are approaching old age, have you decided to abandon them? Why are the carriage tracks outside our door so deep?" Jieyu replied, "The king doesn't realize that I am unworthy and wants me to govern Huainan. He sent a messenger who came to invite me with a gift of money and a team of four horses."

His wife said, "You didn't consent, did you?" Jieyu said, "Wealth and honor are what all people desire. Why should you dislike these things? I consented!"[97] The wife said, "For a man of principle, if something is not in accord with the rites, he does not do it. He does not alter his moral principles because of poverty, and he does not deviate from his course because he occupies a humble position. Since I have come to serve you, we have plowed to feed ourselves and spun to clothe ourselves. We are able to eat our fill and dress in clothing that keeps us warm. We act in accord with what is right, and the joy that this provides is in itself sufficient. If you accept high salaries from others, ride in their sturdy carriages with fine horses, and eat the delicacies they offer, then how will we deal with them in the future?"

Jieyu said, "I will decline." The wife said, "To disobey a ruler's command is disloyal. But to obey yet go against one's own principles is immoral. We'd better flee!" Thereupon, the husband shouldered their cooking vessels and the wife carried away her loom, balancing it on top of her head. They changed their names and fled far away so that no one knew where they were.

A man of discernment would say, "Jieyu's wife was able to rejoice in the Way and keep harm at a distance. Being content with poverty and a humble position yet not negligent of the Way—only one of the highest virtue can accomplish this." The *Odes* says, "Carefully adjusted are the rabbit nets;/Clang, clang go the blows on the pegs."[98] These lines indicate that one should not be negligent of the Way.

The Verse Summary says,

> The wife of Jieyu
> Was indeed content with poverty and a humble status.
> Though Jieyu at first wanted to serve in office,
> He saw that the times were violent and chaotic.
> The King of Chu invited Jieyu with gifts,
> But his wife begged to flee their home.
> She carried off her loom and they changed their names,
> So that in the end they did not meet with disaster.

2.14 THE WIFE OF LAO LAI OF CHU

[This lady] was the wife of Lao Laizi of Chu.[99] Laizi had fled the world and farmed at the south side of Meng Mountain.[100] His fence was made of rushes and his house was fashioned of sticks. He had a bed of wood, and his mat was made of milfoil. He wore clothing padded with hemp, and his food consisted of beans. He had opened the barren lands of the hills and sowed seed there.

Someone told the King of Chu about him, saying, "Lao Lai is a worthy man." The king wanted to send him gifts of jade and silk but was afraid that he would still not come.[101] So the King of Chu rode in his carriage to Lao Lai's door. At the time, Lao Lai was weaving a basket. The king said, "I am quite incompetent and must guard our ancestral altars all on my own, so I am requesting that you, sir, do me the favor of coming to court." Lao Laizi said, "I am just a man from the back hills and not competent to oversee the government." The king replied, "I, the orphaned one and protector of the state, request that you alter your ambitions."[102] Lao Laizi said, "I will." The king then left.

His wife, who had just arrived carrying a winnowing basket on her head and clasping kindling under her arm, said, "Why are there so many carriage tracks?"

Lao Laizi said, "The King of Chu wants to employ me in overseeing the government." The wife said, "Did you consent?" He said, "Yes."

The wife said, "I have heard: 'One who can be fed with wine and meat can be made to fall into line with the whip. One who can be given office and salary can be made to fall into line with the axe.' If you now eat the wine and meat of others and accept from them office and salary, you will also be controlled by them. Will it then be possible to escape disaster? I cannot be controlled by others!" She then threw aside her basket and left. Lao Laizi said, "Come back! For your sake I will reconsider!" So they left and never looked back.

When they arrived south of the Yangzi River, they halted, saying, "Loose feathers and the fur of beasts can be woven to clothe us. We can glean grain and it will be sufficient to feed ourselves." Lao Laizi was then in accord with his wife and settled there. After a year, the people who followed them and made their homes there were numerous enough to form a hamlet, and after three years, they formed a whole village.

A man of discernment would say, "The wife of Lao Laizi was determined in her pursuit of goodness." The *Odes* says, "Under a cross-beam door,/One can be at rest./Where the spring flows by,/One can cure hunger."[103] These lines apply well to this case.

The Verse Summary says,

> Lao Lai and his wife
> Fled the world and went to the south of the mountain.
> They built a house of sticks
> With a roof made of rushes.
> When the King of Chu invited him with gifts,
> Lao Laizi was about to go to court.
> But his wife said, "The world is in disorder."
> So they fled instead.

2.15 THE WIFE OF WULING OF CHU

[This lady] was the wife of Wuling Zizhong of Chu.[104] The King of Chu heard that Wuling Zizhong was worthy and wanted to make him his minister. So he sent a messenger to summon him, bearing a gift of one hundred *yi* of cash. Wuling Zizhong said, "I, your servant, have a wife who serves me with basket and broom.[105] I ask that I may go inside and consult with her."

When he went inside, he told his wife, saying, "The King of Chu wants me to serve as his minister and has sent a messenger here bearing a gift of cash. Today I could be made a minister, and tomorrow I could be riding in a carriage tethered with four horses accompanied by an outrider and eating at a table ten square *chi* in size! What do you think?"

His wife said, "Husband, though you only weave straw sandals to provide our food, you have managed our material needs well.[106] To your left is your lute and to your right, your books. In these things we can also find happiness. Now the comfort provided by [a carriage with] a team of four horses and mounted escort is still nothing more than a place to rest your legs. And what you can actually enjoy at a ten-foot table spread with food is still just one dish of meat. Now, for the sake of comfort for your legs and the savory taste of meat, is it reasonable to take on the troubles of the state of Chu? In this disordered generation there is much danger. I fear that you will not be able to preserve your life." Thereupon, Zizhong went out and thanked the messenger but did not accept his offer. Then both of them fled and took up work caring for someone's garden.

A man of discernment would say, "Wuling's wife can be considered a woman of virtuous action." The *Odes* says, "Tranquil and serene is the good man,/With his virtuous fame spread far and near."[107] These words apply well to her.

The Verse Summary says,

> Wuling was dwelling in Chu
> When the king's messenger approached him with gifts.
> He went in and discussed it with his wife,
> But she feared the troubles of a disordered age.
> To enter officialdom would be to meet with harm;
> How much better to be safe,
> With one's lute to the left and one's books to the right,
> Tending someone else's garden!

3

THE SYMPATHETIC AND WISE

PREFACE

Only those such as the Sympathetic and Wise
Know beforehand what is difficult and what is easy.
By fathoming the Way of Heaven,
They understand changes in bad and good fortune.
By returning to righteousness and seeking accord,
They are able to avoid danger.
They are single-minded and cautious,
Ever fearful and never indolent.
Wives who cultivate these qualities
Will gain glory and renown.

3.1 THE MOTHER OF DUKE KANG OF MI

The mother of Duke Kang of Mi held the clan name Wei.[1] Once, King Gong of Zhou traveled to the Upper Jing River with Duke Kang in his entourage. [In the course of this excursion] three women eloped with Kang.[2]

His mother said, "You must present the women to the king. One may observe that three wild animals make a herd, three people make a group, and three women make a "splendid array." When the king goes out hunting, he does not take the entire herd, and when a feudal lord goes out, he descends [from his carriages upon encountering] a group.[3] When the king marries, he never takes three women from one family.[4] Now this "splendid array" is a thing of beauty. [But even though these women have] attached themselves to you, what virtue makes you worthy of such a possession? If even the king is not worthy of it, how could a petty wretch like you be considered worthy?" But Duke Kang did not offer the women to the king, and the king went on to destroy Mi.[5]

A man of discernment would say, "The Mother of Mi may be regarded as one who knew how to discern subtle signs." The *Odes* says, "But let us not go to great excess./Let us first think of the duties of our position."[6] These lines apply well to this case.

The Verse Summary says,

The mother of Kang of Mi
Had foreknowledge of the cycle of flourishing and decline.
She faulted Duke Kang
For receiving but not returning the array.
When the feudal lords go out, they dismount for a group,
For abundant possessions soon turn to loss.
When urged he refused to make a gift of the women,
And in the end Mi was destroyed.

3.2 DENG MAN, CONSORT OF KING WU OF CHU

Deng Man was the wife of King Wu of Chu.[7] It came to pass that the king ordered Qu Xia to serve as general and attack Luo.[8] Qu Xia bore the title "Moao."[9] When he set out with a group of officers and all of Chu's troops, Dou Bobi, commenting to his charioteer, said, "The Moao, with his swaggering strut and volatile temper, is sure to be defeated!"[10] He therefore advised the king, saying, "You must aid the troops."

When the king relayed this conversation to his wife, Deng Man said, "The grandee was not suggesting that you should augment the troops but that you, my lord, should assist the common people with your faithfulness, instruct your officials by means of your virtue, and awe the Moao with the fear of punishment.[11] The Moao, accustomed to success after the battle at Pusao, will make too much of his own ability and too little of Luo's might.[12] If you do not keep watch and offer assistance, won't his preparations be inadequate?"

After this the king sent a man from Lai to pursue the Moao, but he did not catch up with him.[13] The Moao issued a command to his troops, saying, "Anyone who criticizes me will be punished!" When they reached the river Yan, the line of troops became disorganized in crossing.[14] When they arrived at Luo, Luo along with Lurong attacked and greatly defeated them.[15] The Moao hanged himself at Huanggu, while the officers were imprisoned and awaited punishment at Yefu.[16] But the king said, "It is my fault," and released all of them.

A man of discernment would say, "Deng Man can be regarded as one who understands people." The *Odes* says, "You will not listen to them,/And so your great appointment is being overthrown."[17] These words apply well to this case.

Later, the king planned to attack Sui.[18] As he was about to leave, he said to Deng Man, "My heart is agitated, why is this?" Man said, "Your majesty's virtue is scant, but your wealth is great; what you give is small, but what you receive is abundant. Once things flourish they will surely decline; at noon the sun begins to sink. Replete and then agitated—this is the Way of Heaven. The kings of former times knew this. Therefore before the battle, when you were about to issue a great command, they agitated your majesty's heart.[19] If your troops sustain no losses, even if your majesty dies along the way, it will prove to be good fortune for the kingdom." The king therefore set out, but died beneath a *man* tree.[20]

A man of discernment would say, "Deng Man may be considered one who understood the Way of Heaven." The *Yijing* says, "When the sun reaches the meridian, it begins to decline. When the moon becomes full, it begins to wane. The interaction of Heaven and earth is now abundant, now insubstantial, diminishing or growing according to the seasons."[21] These words apply well to this case.

The Verse Summary says,

> Deng Man, the consort of King Wu of Chu,
> Perceived the source from which events arise.
> She said Qu Xia's troops would be defeated
> And knew the king would die.
> She acknowledged that in Heaven's Way,
> What flourishes must soon decline.
> In the end it was as she said,
> Earning gentlemen's laud and praise.

3.3 THE WIFE OF DUKE MU OF XU

The wife of Mu of Xu was the daughter of Duke Yi of Wey and the wife of Duke Mu of Xu.[22] In the beginning, [the state of] Xu sought her in marriage; Qi sought her as well. Duke Yi was about to give her to Xu, but speaking through her tutor matron, she told him, "In antiquity, the feudal lords utilized their daughters as precious gifts for binding themselves to large states. At present, Xu is small and distant, while Qi is large and nearby, and in our current generation, the strong are considered the victors. If our borders are threatened with military incursions, and if for the sake of holding together the four quarters of our state, we appeal to a large state, wouldn't it be better if I were there? If you put aside those who are nearby and approach the distant, forsake the great and cleave to the small, and one morning face chariots and swift horses in a military crisis, then who will be there to assist you in your concern for our ancestral altars?"[23] But the duke would not listen and married her to the Duke of Xu.[24]

Later the Di attacked Wey, causing massive destruction, but Xu could not rescue them.[25] The Duke of Wey therefore fled, crossing the river, and made his way south to Chuqiu.[26]

Duke Huan of Qi went there to assist him and built a walled city in Chuqiu for him to live in. After this the Duke of Wey regretted not heeding his daughter's advice. At the time of the defeat, the wife of Duke Mu of Xu set out with great haste to condole with him. But because she was frustrated in her efforts, she wrote the following ode:

> I galloped my horses and whipped them,
> Returning to condole with the Marquis of Wey.
> I would have urged them all the long way,
> Till I arrived at Cao.[27]
> But a great officer has gone, over the hills and through the rivers,[28]
> And my heart is full of sorrow.
> You disapproved of my [proposal],
> And I cannot return to [Wey];
> But I regard you as in the wrong
> And cannot forget my purpose.[29]

A man of discernment would praise her compassion and her farsighted wisdom.
The Verse Summary says,

> Before the woman of Wey was married,
> She considered both Xu and Qi.
> She responded by way of her tutor,
> Saying that Qi was large and could be relied upon.

But the ruler of Wey would not listen,
So that later, he was indeed forced to flee.
When Xu was unable to rescue him,
His daughter composed the ode "Zai Chi."

3.4 THE WIFE OF XI OF CAO

The wife of Xi of Cao was the wife of Xi Fuji, a grandee of Cao.[30] When Prince Chonger of Jin fled his state, he passed through Cao,[31] where Duke Gong treated him discourteously.[32] Duke Gong had heard about Chonger's fused ribs.[33] He therefore approached his quarters to spy on him as he was about to bathe, arranging a screen from which he could observe him.

Fuji's wife told her husband, "I have been observing the Prince of Jin. His three followers are all competent to serve as ministers of state. With these three men, all of whom excel at working together to assist others, the prince will certainly go on to rule Jin. If he is able to return to his state, he is also certain to preside over all the feudal lords as hegemon. And when he punishes those who have been discourteous to him, Cao will certainly be first! Thus, if Cao comes under attack, you will not be spared. Wouldn't it be better if you distinguished yourself from the Duke of Cao as soon as possible?

"Furthermore, I have heard that if one does not know the child, then look at the father, and if one does not know the ruler, then look at those whom he commands. If his followers are all servitors capable of acting as chief ministers of state, then their ruler is sure to become hegemon over all the feudal lords. If you treat him with courtesy, he will surely be able to repay you in kind. But if you offend him, he will clearly be able to punish any affront. If you don't make plans soon, it won't be long before disaster appears." Fuji thereupon sent Chonger a warm meal in a tureen with a jade disk placed on top. The prince accepted the meal but returned the jade.

After the prince returned to his state, he attacked Cao but placed a marker in Fuji's village prohibiting the troops from entering. In response, gentry and commoners alike, supporting their elders and leading their children by the hand, came to the village gate in numbers so great they covered an area the size of a market.

A man of discernment would say, "The wife of Xi was farsighted indeed." The *Odes* says, "Intelligent and wise is he;/Protecting his own person."[34] These words apply well to her.

The Verse Summary says,

The wife of Xi
Possessed wisdom of great brilliance.
She observed the Prince of Jin
And knew that he would rise to greatness.
She prompted her husband to offer him a meal,
And to entrust himself to the prince.
When Duke Wen attacked Cao,
Only Fuji's village was spared.

3.5 THE MOTHER OF SUNSHU AO

The mother of Sunshu Ao was the mother of the Chu Chief Counselor, Sunshu Ao.[35] When Shu Ao was a young child, he once went out to play and saw a two-headed snake, which he killed and buried. When he returned home and saw his mother, he began weeping.

When his mother asked why he was crying, he said, "I have heard that whoever sees a two-headed snake will die. I saw one today when I went out to play." His mother said, "Where is the snake now?" He said, "I was afraid that other people would also see the snake, so I killed it, then buried it."

His mother said, "You are not going to die! Whoever performs acts of virtue in secret will be rewarded in the clear light of day. Virtue overcomes the inauspicious, and benevolence dispels the hundred misfortunes. Heaven resides on high but hears even the most humble [below]. Doesn't the *Book of Documents* say, 'Great Heaven has no affections; it helps only the virtuous?'[36] Say no more. You will rise to greatness in Chu!" When Shu Ao grew up, he became chief counselor.

A man of discernment would say, "Sunshu Ao's mother understood the workings of virtue." The *Odes* says, "Our Mother is wise and good."[37] These words apply well to her.

The Verse Summary says,

Shu Ao's mother
Possessed great insight into Heaven's Way.
When Shu Ao saw a snake
With its two heads each separately formed,
He killed and buried it,

Then wept, fearing his demise.
But his mother said, "For your secret act of virtue,
You will live long and not die."

3.6 THE WIFE OF BO ZONG OF JIN

The Wife of Bo Zong of Jin was the wife of the Jin grandee Bo Zong.[38] Bo Zong was a worthy man but fond of using direct language to insult others. Whenever he went to court his wife would invariably warn him, saying, "'Brigands despise lords and the people hate their superiors.'[39] If there are those who are fond of a man, then there are bound to be those who hate and envy him as well. You, sir, are fond of straight talk, but wrongdoers despise it. You are therefore sure to meet with misfortune."

But Bo Zong disregarded her advice. After attending court, he returned with a pleased expression on his face. His wife said, "Why do you look so pleased?" Bo Zong said, "When I spoke at court, the grandees all compared my wisdom to that of Yangzi."[40] His wife said, "Ripe grain does not flower, and direct speech is not ornamented. Now, Yangzi's [speech] was florid but bore no fruit, and when he spoke, he lacked solid plans. This is how one brings disaster upon oneself. Why should you be happy about this?" Bo Zong said, "I will invite the grandees to drink with me, and when I talk to them you could listen in." His wife said, "Agreed."

Thereafter he held a great meeting where he drank with all the grandees. Afterward he asked his wife, "How do you interpret the situation?" She said, "Not one of the grandees is your equal, and because this is the case, the people have been unable to support their superiors for a long time now. This will cause difficulties for you. Your character is firmly established and cannot be changed. Moreover, many of the families of the state are of divided loyalties, so that you can expect the danger that this poses to present itself immediately. Why don't you make plans to bind yourself to some worthy grandee and entrust [our son] Zhouli to him?" Bo Zong said, "I will." He then found Bi Yang and befriended him.[41]

At the time of Luan Buji's difficulties, the Three Xi attacked Bo Zong, first slandering and then killing him.[42] Bi Yang then took Zhouli to Jing, where [the latter] was able to escape with his life.[43]

A man of discernment would say, "Bo Zong's wife understood the Way of Heaven." The *Odes* says, "The troubles will multiply like flames,/Till they are beyond help or remedy."[44] This sums up the case of Bo Zong.

The Verse Summary says,

Bo Zong disparaged others,
And his wife foretold his end.
Repeatedly she admonished Bo Zong
To secure an agreement with Bi Yang.
Entrusting Bi with Zhouli
He delivered his son from misfortune.
When Bo Zong met with disaster,
Zhouli fled to Jing.

3.7 THE WIFE OF DUKE LING OF WEY

[This lady] was the wife of Duke Ling of Wey.[45] One evening as Duke Ling of Wey and his wife were sitting together, they heard the rumbling sound of a carriage. When it reached the tower, it stopped. The carriage then passed the tower, and the noise resumed.[46]

The duke asked his wife, "Do you know who this could be?" His wife said, "It is sure to be Qu Boyu."[47] The duke said, "How do you know?" His wife said, "I have heard that according to ritual, one should dismount one's carriage at the gate of a ruler and bow before his horses.[48] This is how one promotes respect. Now the loyal minister and the filial son do not engage in ostentatious display of virtue, nor become derelict in their duties when they cannot be observed. Qu Boyu is a worthy officer of Wey. He is benevolent, wise, and respectful in serving his superiors. This sort of person would surely not use the cover of darkness to abandon ritual. This is how I know."[49] The duke sent someone to go look and discovered that it was, in fact, Boyu.

But in order to play a joke on his wife, the duke suggested the contrary, telling her, "You are wrong." His wife then poured a goblet of wine, bowed twice, and congratulated the duke. The duke said, "Why are you congratulating me?" His wife said, "At first, I thought Wey had only one Qu Boyu. But now I see that we have yet another who is his equal, so that you have two worthy ministers. A state with many worthy officers is a fortunate state! That is why I congratulated you." Astonished, the duke said, "Well said!" Then he told his wife the truth of the matter.

A man of discernment would say, "The wife of Wey was well versed in the art of knowing people. So great was her wisdom that she could be tricked but not deceived." The *Odes* says, "I heard him,/ But did not see his person."[50] These words apply well to her.

The Verse Summary says,

Ling of Wey one night sat,
Together with his wife.
A carriage came rumbling by
And stopped when it reached the gate.
Well his wife knew
That this must be Boyu.
Knowing how to discern the worthy,
When she inquired, it was indeed true.

3.8 ZHONG ZI, WIFE OF DUKE LING OF QI

Zhong Zi of Ling of Qi was the daughter of the Marquis of Song and the wife of Duke Ling of Qi.[51] Earlier, Duke Ling had married Sheng Ji of Lu, who gave birth to a son named Guang. He was made heir apparent.[52] The duke's consorts Zhong Zi and her younger sister, Rong Zi, were both his favorites.[53] Zhong Zi gave birth to a son named Ya.[54] When Rong Zi requested that Ya be made heir apparent and replace Guang, the duke granted her request.

Zhong Zi said, "This is unacceptable. To discard the regular [rules of succession] is inauspicious, and the resistance you will encounter from the feudal lords makes this a plan that will fail.[55] Since Guang has been established as your successor, he has already taken his place among the feudal lords. Now, to depose him for no reason is to take it upon yourself to degrade a feudal lord. And because of the ensuing difficulties, it will be condemned as inauspicious. My lord, you are sure to regret it."

[The duke replied,] "It's my decision and that's that."

Zhong Zi said, "I cannot go along with your plan—it will only sow the seeds of disaster, and I will fight it until I die." But in the end the duke would not listen. He therefore expelled the heir apparent Guang and established Ya as his heir, making Gao Hou his tutor.[56]

When Duke Ling was ill, Cui Zhu secretly welcomed Guang to return to the state.[57] When the duke died, Cui Zhu established Guang as duke and killed Gao Hou.[58] Because the duke did not make use of Zhong Zi's advice, the disaster reached these proportions.[59]

A man of discernment would say, "Zhong Zi was a perceptive judge of the logic of events." The *Odes* says, "Hear and follow my counsels;/Then shall you have no cause for great regret."[60] These words apply well to Zhong Zi.

The Verse Summary says,

Zhong Zi of Ling of Qi
Was benevolent, wise, and enlightened.
The duke wanted to make Ya his heir
And depose Ji's son Guang.
Zhong Zi admonished him forcefully,
Explaining that deposing the eldest son would be inauspicious.
Because the duke disregarded her advice,
Disaster was the result.

3.9 THE MOTHER OF ZANGSUN OF LU

The mother of Zangsun was the mother of the Lu grandee Zang Wenzhong.[61] Once, when Wenzhong was about to set out on a diplomatic mission as Lu's envoy to the state of Qi, his mother, while seeing him off, said, "You are harsh and without mercy. You are fond of exhausting the strength of others and weaken them with fear. The state of Lu cannot tolerate you any longer, so you have been sent to Qi. When treachery is about to take place, it is always in the midst of change and upheaval. Won't those who wish to harm you use this opportunity to take action? You should beware. Lu and Qi share a border; they are neighboring states. In Lu there are many favored ministers who resent you and who also have connections to Gaozi and Guozi of Qi.[62] They will almost certainly cause Qi to scheme against Lu and then seize and detain you. It will be difficult to escape. You must extend many favors to people so that later, after you have left, you can seek help from them." Thereafter Wenzhong entrusted himself to the Three Families, showed generosity to the officers and grandees, and then went to Qi.[63] Qi did in fact seize him and raised troops to attack Lu.

Wenzhong secretly instructed someone to send a letter to the duke. Fearing that his letter would be intercepted, he veiled the meaning of his words and wrote: "Gather the small vessels and put them in the vat. Feed the hunting dogs, and fashion a sheepskin coat. The harmony of the *qin*, how I long for it![64] Take care of the sheep—the sheep have a mother. Feed me with jagged-scaled fish.[65] The chin strap of my cap is inadequate, but my belt is slack." The duke and all of the grandees discussed the message, but not one of them understood it.

Someone said, "Zangsun's mother comes from one of the great hereditary houses. Why don't you try summoning her and ask her about it?" So the duke summoned her and explained the situation to her, saying, "I sent Zangzi to Qi, and now we have received a letter from him. What does it mean?"

Zangsun's mother wept, bedewing the collar of her robe, and said, "My son has been seized and fettered with wooden manacles." The duke said, "How do you know this?"

She said, "As for 'Gather the small vessels and put them in the vat,' it means to take all of the people who are outside the city walls and lodge them inside the city. 'Feed the hunting dogs, and fashion a sheepskin coat' means to quickly feast the warrior knights and make ready their armor and weapons. 'The harmony of the *qin*, how I long for it' means that he misses his wife. 'Take care of the sheep—the sheep have a mother' means to tell his wife to take good care of his mother. As for the meaning of 'feed me with jagged-scaled fish'—something that is jagged has a serrated pattern. To make something serrated is how one makes a saw. A saw is used to work with wood. The meaning is that he has been fettered with wooden manacles and placed in prison. As for 'the chin strap of my cap is inadequate, but my belt is slack,' it means that his hair is matted and cannot be combed and that he is starving and cannot obtain food. This is how I know that my son was seized and manacled."

Afterward, in response to the conversation with Zangsun's mother, Lu sent troops to the border. When Qi was about to call out troops to attack Lu, it heard that [Lu's] troops now occupied the border. So [Qi] returned Wenzhong and did not attack Lu.

A man of discernment would say, "Zangsun's mother understood the meaning of subtle signs and saw what the distant future held." The *Odes* says, "I ascend that bare hill,/And look toward the residence of my mother."[66] These words apply well to this case.

The Verse Summary says,

Zangsun's mother
Criticized her son's harshness.
Knowing it would surely lead to harm,
She made him bestow favor on those he would later need.
He treated the Three Families generously,
And when he was, in fact, seized by Qi,
Zang's mother explained his letter,
And he was able to return.

3.10 SHU JI OF YANG OF JIN

Shu Ji was the wife of Yangshezi and the mother of Shuxiang and Shuyu, who were also known by the lineage name Yang.[67] Shuxiang's given name was Xi and Shuyu's given name was Fu. Yangshezi was fond of upright behavior and not tolerated in Jin, so he left and went to the city of Sanshi.

Some people from Sanshi stole a sheep and presented it to Yangshezi, but he would not accept it. Shu Ji said, "When you lived in Jin, you were not tolerated and left for Sanshi city. If once again you are not accepted in Sanshi city, it will be due to your own lack of tolerance. You had better accept [the sheep]."

So Yangzi took it and said, "Prepare it for Xi and Fu." But Shu Ji said, "That won't do! In the south there is a bird called the *qianji*. It is not particular about the meat it chooses to feed its young, so its offspring often do not reach maturity. Now Xi and Fu are still children. Since they learn from your example, you cannot feed them with meat obtained through illicit means. You'd better bury it to make clear that you did not partake of it." He then put it in a pot and buried it on the north side of a shed.

Two years later, the affair of the stolen sheep came to light. When an official from the capital arrived, Yangshezi told him, "I received it but did not dare to eat it." When they found the [sheep carcass] and examined it, its bones were all still intact. The capital official said, "He is indeed a man of quality! Yangshezi had no part in the affair of the stolen sheep."

A man of discernment would say, "Shu Ji was able to prevent harm and keep suspicion at bay." The *Odes* says, "Do not say, 'This place is not public;/No one can see me here.'"[68] These words apply well to this case.

Shuxiang wanted to marry the daughter of Wuchen, the Duke of Shen, and Xia Ji.[69] She was beautiful and beguiling, but Shu Ji did not want him to marry into this family.[70] Shuxiang said, "Your family, mother, is noble but small in number, and I am apprehensive about my maternal uncles." Shu Ji said, "Ziling's wife caused the death of three husbands, a ruler, and a son, and destroyed one state and two ministers.[71] How can you *not* be forewarned by these events but instead be apprehensive about *my* family? Moreover, I have heard that those who have extraordinary good fortune are also certain to have extraordinary misfortune, and those who have extraordinary beauty are certain to be possessed of extraordinary evil. Now, [Xia Ji] was the daughter of Duke Mu of Zheng's lesser concubine, Yao Zi, and the younger sister of Zihe.[72] Zihe died young without offspring.

Because Heaven concentrated so much beauty in her, it will also use her to effect great destruction.

"Formerly, the Youreng family gave birth to a daughter. Her hair was black and very beautiful, and shone so brilliantly that one could see one's reflection in it. She was called 'The Dark Consort.' Kui, the Regulator of Music, made her his wife.[73] She gave birth to Bofeng, who was dissipated and possessed the heart of a pig. He was filled with insatiable greed and implacable rage. People called him the 'Great Swine.' Yi, the Prince of Youqiong, destroyed him.[74] Because of this, Kui had no one to continue his sacrifices. Moreover, the ruin of the three dynasties down to the deposal of Crown Prince Gong was due to creatures of this sort.[75] Why are you so intent on doing this? It is a generally applicable principle that things endowed with great beauty have the power to move others [from their principles].[76] If one is not virtuous and principled, then disaster will ensue."

Shuxiang was frightened and did not dare proceed with his marriage plans. But Duke Ping forced him to marry the girl.[77] She gave birth to Yang Shiwo. Shiwo was also called Boshi. When Boshi was born, a serving woman reported it to Shu Ji, saying, "Eldest sister-in-law has given birth to a boy." Shu Ji went to look at him, but when she reached the hall she heard his cry and returned, saying, "It is the voice of a wolf. A wolflike child will have a wild heart. The one who destroys the Yangshe lineage will surely be this child."

After this she refused to see him. When he grew up, he and members of the Qi lineage brought about great disorder.[78] The people of Jin killed Shiwo, and it was because of him that the Yangshe lineage was destroyed.

A man of discernment would say, "Shu Ji was able to reason by analogy." The *Odes* says, "We are like the stream flowing from a spring,/And will sink together in a common ruin."[79] These lines apply well to this case.

When Shu Ji first gave birth to Shuyu, she looked at him and said, "He has the eyes of a tiger and the snout of a pig, the shoulders of a kite, and the chest of an ox. What could fill a mountain gorge would still not be enough to satisfy him. He is sure to die because of corruption."[80] After this she would not look at him.

When Shuyu grew up, he served as his state's Assistant Supervisor of Men-at-Arms. [At the time], Xing Hou and Yongzi were involved in a dispute over land.[81] Seeking a verdict of innocence, Yongzi offered his daughter to Shuyu. But Xing Hou slew both Shuyu and Yongzi at court. Han Xuanzi was troubled by this turn of events.[82] Shuxiang said, "The three culprits are guilty of the same crime. I request that you kill the one who is still alive and [further] punish the ones who are dead." Thus, he annihilated Xing Hou and his lineage and exposed the corpses of Shuyu and Yongzi in the marketplace.

In the end, Shuyu died because of his covetousness. Shu Ji can be called wise indeed. The *Odes* says, "The covetous men try to subvert their peers."[83] These words apply here.

The Verse Summary says,

Shuxiang's mother
Examined disposition and character.
She extrapolated from the manner of a person's birth,
And was able to know a person's fate.
Shuyu and Shiwo
Were both covetous and immoral.
They were bound to die because of corrupt dealings.
Indeed, divisive and contentious, they met their end.

3.11 THE MOTHER OF THE FAN LINEAGE OF JIN

The mother of the Fan Lineage of Jin was the wife of Fan Xianzi.[84] Once, her three sons went to spend some leisure time at the Zhao lineage [estate]. At the time, Zhao Jianzi was riding his horse in the orchard.[85] In the orchard there were many stumps, so he asked the three sons, saying, "What can be done about it?"

The eldest said, "The enlightened ruler does not act without first making inquiries. The muddled ruler acts without inquiring first." The middle son said, "If a man is concerned about his horse's hoofs, then he will not be concerned about belaboring his people. If he is concerned about belaboring his people, then he will not be concerned about his horse's hoofs." The youngest said, "You can mobilize the people with three acts of virtue. [First] issue an order to clear the stumps on the mountain, and you will then be able to accomplish all that needs to be done.[86] When this [first step] has been completed, then open up your park lands and show the people the stumps there.[87] The mountain is distant but the park is nearby. This will be the first reason for the people to rejoice. That they have left behind the difficult terrain of the mountains to clear stumps on level land will be the second reason for the people to rejoice.[88] Once they are finished, sell them the wood cheaply, and that will be the third reason for the people to rejoice." Jianzi followed his plan, and the people did in fact rejoice three times.

The youngest son prided himself on his plan and returned home to tell his mother. His mother heaved a sigh and said, "The one who will finally destroy the Fan lineage will be this child. One who brags about his ability to assign work is seldom able to extend benevolence; and no one who deceives others to perpetrate acts of dishonesty will live long." Later, Zhi Bo annihilated the Fan lineage.[89]

A man of discernment would say, "The mother of the Fan lineage can be regarded as one who knew where the sources of trouble lay." The *Odes* says, "Do not disgrace your ancestors,/And it will save posterity."[90] These words apply well to her.

The Verse Summary says,

The mother of the Fan lineage
Honored virtue and esteemed honesty.
When the "Three Virtuous Acts" of the youngest son
Were used as a means to deceive the people,
She knew he would surely be destroyed
And fall short of benevolence.[91]
Later he did in fact meet with misfortune:
He lost his life and his state was partitioned.

3.12 THE ELDER SISTER OF GONGCHENG OF LU

The elder sister of Gongcheng of Lu was the elder sister of Gongcheng Zipi of Lu.[92] After the death of a family member, she cried very bitterly. Zipi tried to restrain her, saying, "Please calm yourself. I will arrange a marriage for you now." But even after [the mourning] period had passed, he did not speak of it again.[93]

The ruler of Lu wanted to make Zipi a minister. Zipi asked his sister about it, saying, "The ruler of Lu wishes to appoint me as minister. Shall I agree to it?" His sister said, "You should not agree." Zipi said, "Why?" His sister said, "While in mourning, you spoke of arranging a marriage for me. How could you be so completely ignorant of propriety? After that time had passed, you did not bring it up again. How could you be so utterly unfamiliar with human affairs?[94] Because you are ignorant of the rules that should be observed within the family and unfamiliar with human affairs outside of it, it is impossible for you to serve as minister."

Zipi said, "Sister, if you wanted to marry, why didn't you say so earlier?" His sister said, "In matters concerning women, they wait for others to 'sing the first note' and then join in harmoniously.[95] But do you think I am criticizing you because I want to be married? If you are indeed ignorant of propriety and unfamiliar with [basic] human affairs but go on to serve our state as minister and take charge of large numbers of people, how will you manage? It would be like covering your eyes and trying to distinguish black from white. Still, if you covered your eyes and tried to distinguish black from white, there would be no disaster. But to be unfamiliar with basic human affairs and yet serve as our state's minister, if no Heaven-sent disaster ensues, then a man-made calamity will surely strike. You should definitely not serve."

Zipi did not listen and in the end accepted the post of minister. Before he had served a full year, as anticipated, he was found guilty [of an offense] and died.

A man of discernment would say, "Gongcheng's elder sister understood how affairs are connected and thus knew her younger brother would meet with disaster. She can indeed be called wise. She took action only after attending to the rites and did not allow herself to be swayed by emotion; she can indeed be called pure." The *Odes* says, "Ye withered leaves! Ye withered leaves!/How the wind is blowing you away!/Oh ye uncles,/Give us the first note and we will complete the song."[96] It also says, "The hundred plans you think of/Are not equal to the course I was going to take."[97] These words apply well to her.

The Verse Summary says,

Zipi's elder sister
Could predict events and analyze principles.
If Zipi served as minister in Lu,
She knew disaster would arise.
She advised Zipi
That it would be better to abandon his plan.
Zipi did not listen,
And in the end brought shame to the lineage.

3.13 THE WOMAN OF QISHI OF LU

The woman of Qishi was a woman of the city of Qishi in Lu.[98] She was an unmarried woman who had now passed [marriageable] age.[99]

During the time of Duke Mu of Lu, the ruler was old and the crown prince was very young.[100] The woman leaned against a pillar and moaned. Of all the passersby who heard her, not one was not grieved on her behalf.

A neighbor woman who had gone out with her said, "Why are you moaning so pitifully? Is it because you want to marry? I will find a husband for you." The woman of Qishi said, "Alas! At first I thought you were possessed of some understanding, but now I see that you have none! I would not grieve merely because I am unhappy about not being married! I worry that the ruler is old and the crown prince is so young." The neighbor woman laughed, saying, "This is the concern of the grandees of Lu. What does a woman have to do with it?"

The woman of Qishi said, "This is not the case. You simply don't understand. Formerly a guest from Jin stayed at our house. He tied up his horse in our garden. But the horse got loose and went on a rampage, trampling all of our mallows and causing us to go for a whole year with no mallows to eat. Then the daughter of a neighbor eloped, running away with a man. Her family asked my elder brother to go after her. But he encountered a heavy rain and died, drowning in floodwaters. Now, for the rest of my life I will have no elder brother.[101]

"I have heard that when the river floods [the land] for nine *li*, it dampens the area for another three hundred paces. Now the ruler is old and unreasonable and the crown prince is young and ignorant, so that acts of ignorance and guile arise on a daily basis. When misfortune strikes the state of Lu, ruler and subject, father and son will all suffer humiliation, and the disaster will spread to affect ordinary people as well. How is it that women alone should escape? I am deeply concerned. How then can you say that women have nothing to do with this?"

The neighbor woman conceded the point, saying, "I'm afraid I cannot match your powers of thought!" Three years later Lu was in fact thrown into upheaval. Qi and Chu attacked, and thereafter Lu was continuously plagued by marauders. The men fought in battles, while the women transported supplies without respite.

A man of discernment would say, "Far-reaching indeed were the thoughts of the woman of Qishi!" The *Odes* says, "Those who knew me/Said I was sad at heart./Those who did not know me/Said I was seeking something."[102] These words apply well to her.

The Verse Summary says,

> The woman of Qishi—
> How subtle were her powers of foresight.
> Seeing that disorder would plague Lu,
> She leaned against a pillar and moaned,
> For the ruler was old and his heir was young,
> And ignorance and perversity grew.
> Lu indeed suffered upheaval
> When Qi invaded her walls.

3.14 THE OLD WOMAN OF QUWO OF WEI

The Old Woman of Quwo was the mother of the Wei grandee Ru Er.[103] When Qin established Prince Zheng as Wei's heir apparent, King Ai of Wei ordered an emissary to find a bride for the prince.[104] [The woman who was selected] was a great beauty, so the king was about to take her for himself.

The Old Woman of Quwo told her son Ru Er, "The king is debauched and indiscriminate. Why don't you correct him? At present, the powerful among the warring states become leaders, while those among them who are righteous are regarded as illustrious. If Wei cannot muster [the requisite] power and the king is moreover without righteousness, then by what means can the state be sustained? The king is a middling sort of person who is not aware that he is creating a disaster. If you don't speak to him, Wei will not escape disaster. And if there is a disaster, it will extend to our family. If you admonish him with the utmost loyalty, and your loyalty is sufficient to prevent calamity, then this is an opportunity you cannot afford to lose!"

But Ru Er never found the right moment and was then sent to Qi on a diplomatic mission. The old woman therefore knocked on the king's door herself and submitted a written statement saying, "I am an old woman from Quwo. My heart is filled with concerns that I would like the king to hear." The king summoned her to enter.

The old woman said, "I have heard that the separation of the sexes is an important regulation of the state.[105] A woman's resolve is fragile and her mind is weak, so one cannot expose her to evil. For this reason, by age fifteen she must 'receive the hairpin,' marry at age twenty, and early on have her [adult] name determined so that she can complete [her life in accordance with its import].[106] When a formal betrothal petition is made, then a woman becomes a wife.[107] When a woman marries without preliminary formalities, then she becomes a concubine. In this way one can encourage goodness and restrain lust. When a woman is fully grown, she is promised in marriage. Only after she is fetched in person does she follow [her mate].[108] These are the principles that guide a pure woman. At present, you went to find a wife for the crown prince. But if you keep her in the women's quarters of your own palace for yourself, you will destroy the moral standing of a pure woman and throw into disarray the proper separation of men and women.

"From antiquity the sage kings have always maintained proper order among their consorts. When proper order was maintained among their consorts [states] flourished, and when it was not maintained they were thrown into chaos. Thus, when the Xia flourished, it was because of Tushan. When it was destroyed, it was because of Mo Xi.[109] When the Yin flourished, it was because of Youshen; and when it was destroyed, it was because of Da Ji.[110] When the Zhou flourished, it was because of Tai Si; and when it was destroyed, it was because of Bao Si.[111] The wife of King Kang of the Zhou was late in leaving [the king's chamber].[112] But the ode, 'Guan, Guan Cry the Ospreys,' prompted thoughts of obtaining a pure maiden as a good match for a ruler.[113] As for the osprey, even these birds have never been known to pair off and couple indiscriminately.[114]

"When a man and woman are in their prime, if you unite them by way of ritual, then the father and child relationship arises from this union and the ruler and subject relationship is perfected through it. It is therefore the origin of the ten thousand things. The three relationships of ruler and subject, father and child, and husband and wife are the world's great bonds.[115] When these three are in order, then order prevails. When these three are in disarray, then disorder reigns. At present, you have brought disorder to the most essential of human relationships and cast aside the principles associated with the great human bonds. Wei has five or six enemies: in the south is the Vertical Alliance of Chu and in the west the Horizontal Alliance of Qin.[116] Wei is situated between them and is just barely able to survive. If Your Majesty is not concerned about this and continues to behave without restraint and discrimination, taking a woman promised to your son, then I fear your state is headed for ruin."

The king said, "What you say is true. I was unaware of these matters." He then gave the bride to the crown prince and rewarded the old woman with thirty *zhong* of grain.[117] When Ru Er returned, the king conferred a title on him. The king then assiduously engaged in self-cultivation and labored for his state so that Qi, Chu, and the mighty Qin did not dare to raise troops against them.[118]

A man of discernment would say, "The Old Woman of Wei understood the rites." The *Odes* says, "Let me be reverent, let me be reverent,/[The Way of] Heaven is clear."[119] These lines apply well to this case.

The Verse Summary says,

The Old Woman of Wei was intelligent and perceptive.
She criticized King Ai.
When the king took his son's bride,
He proved blind to ritual distinctions.[120]
The Old Woman knocked on the king's door

And set forth the principles of the Three Bonds.
The king reformed and cultivated himself,
And was no longer troubled by enemy troops.

3.15 THE MOTHER OF GENERAL KUO OF ZHAO

[This lady] was the wife of the Zhao General Zhao She, [known as] the lord of Mafu, and the mother of Zhao Kuo.[121]

When Qin attacked Zhao, King Xiaocheng of Zhao ordered Zhao Kuo to replace Lian Po as general.[122] When he was about to leave, Kuo's mother sent a letter to the king saying, "Kuo cannot be made general."

When the king asked why, she replied, "In the beginning, when I first married, Kuo's father served as general. The men to whom he personally served meals numbered in the dozens, and those whom he befriended numbered in the hundreds.[123] All of the gifts bestowed upon him by the king and the royal clan he gave to his military subordinates, officers, and grandees. From the day he first received the king's charge, he did not inquire about our family's affairs. Yet on the first day that Kuo served as general, he assembled his military officers and held court, taking the position of honor, facing east. Not one of the military officers dared to look him in the face. He took home and hoarded all of the cash and silks presented to him by the king, and then spent each day looking for conveniently located fields and houses that he could purchase. Do you think he is like his father? Father and son are not alike; temperamentally they are quite distinct. I hope that you will not send him [on this mission]."

The king said, "Leave it be. I have already made my decision." Kuo's mother then said, "If in the end you do send him and he does not fulfill his responsibility, will I be exempt from punishment?"[124] The king said, "You will be exempt."

Kuo then set out for his mission, replacing Lian Po. After some thirty days, Zhao's forces were indeed defeated. Kuo was killed and his army was vanquished. Because she had spoken up earlier, the king did not subject Kuo's mother to punishment.

A man of discernment would say, "Kuo's mother can be regarded as empathetic and wise."[125] The *Odes* says, "An old man, [I speak] with entire sincerity;/ But you, my juniors, are full of pride./It is not that my words are those of age,/ But you make a joke of what is sad."[126] These words apply well to her.

The Verse Summary says,

King Xiaocheng employed Kuo
To replace Po and oppose Qin.
Kuo's mother submitted a letter,
Knowing that the army would be vanquished.
Hoping but failing to stop the king,
She asked to be spared punishment.
Kuo died at Changping,
And his wife and child were spared.

4

THE CHASTE AND COMPLIANT

PREFACE

Only those such as the Chaste and Compliant
Cultivate the way with unerring progress.
They avoid suspicion and keep deeply sequestered
To ensure their fidelity.
To the end they forsake all others,
Even the most eminent in the land.
Diligent in pursuing what is proper and in practice chaste,
They are devoted and ever cautious,
All women, observe these lessons well,
And consider them your teaching.

4.1 THE WOMAN OF SHEN, SHAONAN

The woman of Shen of Shaonan was the daughter of a man of Shen.[1] She had been promised in marriage to a man from Feng.[2] Though the ritual preparations of the husband's family were incomplete, they still planned to bring her to their home.[3] The woman spoke with her go-between, saying, "The relationship of husband and wife is the beginning of all human relationships, and so it must be correct.[4] A commentary says, 'If you make the fundamentals correct, then all things will be well ordered. But mismanaging them by even a small margin will result in an error of a thousand *li*.'[5] Thus, when the fundamentals are established, the Way arises.

When the wellspring is [carefully] tended, the water is pure. Marriage is therefore the means whereby one transmits a family's most important legacies, provides continuity for one's ancestors and [descendants] to preside over the ancestral temple.[6] My husband's family makes light of ritual and disregards the rules, so I cannot proceed." She was therefore unwilling to go to him.

The husband's family went to the authorities to file a case against her and had her brought to trial.[7] To the very end, if even one item was missing or if one ritual was not complete, she was determined to guard her purity and uphold her righteousness, preferring to die rather than to go to his home. Accordingly she wrote a poem that said, "But though you have forced me to trial,/Your ceremonies for betrothal were not sufficient," to describe how the ritual preparations of her husband's family were incomplete and inadequate.[8]

The man of discernment considered that her conduct was in accord with the Way of Wives and therefore upheld her as an example worthy of praise. He transmitted her story and set her up as a model to put an end to demands that transgress the rites and to prevent debased practices in such situations.[9] She also wrote: "But though you forced me to trial,/I will still not follow you."[10] These words describe the situation well.

The Verse Summary says,

> For the woman of Shen in Shaonan,
> Purity was the unifying principle of her aspirations and bearing.
> As long as her husband left the ceremonies incomplete,
> She refused to follow him,
> Even to the point of death.
> When he brought her to trial,
> She composed an ode to make her intentions clear
> That was praised and recited by later generations.

4.2 BO JI, CONSORT OF DUKE GONG OF SONG

Bo Ji was the daughter of Duke Xuan of Lu and the younger sister of Duke Cheng.[11] Her mother, who was called Mu Jiang, married Bo Ji to Duke Gong of Song.[12] The duke did not personally go to fetch her, but Bo Ji, being forced to do so by the command of her father and mother, proceeded [to her husband's home].[13] She entered Song, and after three months, she was to appear in the ancestral temple where the couple would assume their roles as husband and wife.[14] But because Duke Gong had failed to come personally to fetch Bo Ji [from her parent's home], she refused to obey the command. When the people of Song reported this to Lu, Lu sent the grandee Ji Wenzi to Song to convey orders to Bo Ji.[15]

When he returned and reported on his mission, the duke entertained him with a feast.[16] Mu Jiang emerged from the side chamber and bowed to him twice, saying, "You, sir, have labored hard over distant roads, suffering the indignity of accompanying our child, not forgetting our former ruler and his posterity. If the departed were aware of this, it would certainly be all that he hoped for.[17] I therefore make bold to salute you again for this indignity."

After Bo Ji had been married to Duke Gong of Song for ten years, the duke died and Bo Ji became a widow. One night during the reign of Duke Jing, Bo Ji's [dwelling] caught fire.[18] People called to her, saying, "Fire! Madam! Flee!" Bo Ji said, "The rules of correct deportment for a married woman require that unless her governess and tutor are both present, she does not leave the house at night. I will wait until the governess and tutor come."[19] The governess finally arrived, but the tutor matron had still not come. People called out to her once again, saying, "Fire! Madam, flee!" Bo Ji said, "According to the rules of correct conduct for a married woman, if the tutor matron is not in attendance, she must not leave the house at night. To die preserving one's principles is better than transgressing the rules to stay alive." She was then encompassed by the fire and died.

The *Chunqiu* made a detailed record of these events in order to honor Bo Ji, considering that among women who made purity a practice, Bo Ji had indeed perfected the Way of Womanhood. At the time, when all of the feudal lords heard about her [death], they were deeply saddened, thinking that while the dead could not be made to live again, [the losses] in property could be restored. Therefore they assembled at Chanyuan and indemnified Song for its losses, for which the *Chunqiu* praised them.[20]

A man of discernment would say, "According to the rites, a woman should not go out at night if she is not accompanied by her tutor matron, and if she does go out, she must carry a candle.[21] Bo Ji exemplifies this rule." The *Odes* says, "Watch well over your behavior,/And allow nothing wrong in your demeanor."[22] Bo Ji can indeed be called one who did not err in her conduct.

The Verse Summary says,

Bo Ji was devoted at heart,
And single-mindedly adhered to the rites.
One night the palace caught fire,

But neither her governess nor her tutor was present.
The fire encompassed her and she died,
Without the least regret in her heart.
The *Chunqiu* considered her a worthy,
And recounted this event in detail.

4.3 THE WIDOWED WIFE OF WEY[23]

The [widowed] wife was the daughter of the Marquis of Qi. She was to be married to [the ruler of] Wey. But when she arrived at the city gates, the ruler of Wey died.[24] So her governess said, "We can return now!" But the woman would not hear of it and went to [his home] and observed three years of mourning.

When she had completed [the mourning observances], her husband's younger brother, who had now ascended the throne, extended an invitation to her, saying, "Wey is a small country and cannot accommodate two separate kitchens. I would like to ask you to share a kitchen with me."[25] The woman said, "Only husband and wife may share a kitchen," and ultimately rejected the plan. So the ruler of Wey sent a messenger to make a plea to her brothers in Qi. Her brothers all wanted her to accept the newly established ruler's proposal and sent a messenger to inform her of their view. But to the very end the woman refused to agree.

She then composed an ode that said, "My mind is not a stone;/It cannot be rolled about./My mind is not a mat;/It cannot be rolled up."[26] For it is only by suffering hardship without complaint and enduring indignities without resorting to what is improper that one can finally achieve one's goal. This means that it is only by not erring that one can be saved from difficulty.[27] The *Odes* says, "My deportment has been dignified and good;/You cannot measure it."[28] These lines express [her view that] there were no worthy men among the officers at court; they all simply followed their lord's wishes. The man of discernment found the woman's purity and devotion praiseworthy and therefore set her up as an example and included her in the *Odes*.[29]

The Verse Summary says,

The woman of Qi was to wed in Wey.
But when she reached the city gates,
Though the duke had died, she did not return.
She entered and stayed for three years.
When the next duke proposed a union,

To the very end she refused to sully herself.
She composed an ode in protest,
And remained true to her deceased lord.

4.4 THE WIFE OF THE MAN OF CAI

The wife of the Man of Cai was the daughter of a man from Song.[30] After she had already been married in Cai, her husband contracted a loathsome disease. Her mother then began making plans to find a new husband for her. The woman said, "A husband's misfortune is in fact his wife's misfortune. How can I leave him? In marriage, once [a woman] partakes of the libation rites with her husband, she must remain devoted to him to the end.[31] If he has the misfortune of contracting a noxious disease, she must not waver in her resolve. Now, when picking the plantain, though its smell is foul when first plucked, one will finally tuck it into one's bosom. After being steeped in [its scent], one becomes increasingly fond of it. How much more is this the case with husband and wife? He has done no great wrong, nor has he sent me away. So how can I leave?" In the end she did not listen to her mother but went on to write the ode "The Plantains."[32]

A man of discernment would say, "The intentions of the daughter of Song were profoundly pure and devoted."

The Verse Summary says,

The woman of Song was devoted and loyal;
She was steadfast and unrelenting in her affection.[33]
Her husband contracted a noxious disease,
But she was strong in her resolve.
When her mother tried to persuade her to leave and remarry,
She composed an ode and refused to listen.
Later ages praise her,
Regarding her as mindful of purity.

4.5 THE WIFE OF ZHUANG OF LI

The wife of Zhuang of Li was a daughter of the Marquis of Wey and the wife of Duke Zhuang of Li.[34] After she had already gone [to live with the duke], she discovered that they shared nothing in common and that there were great differences in what each one regarded as essential. Furthermore, never having been summoned into his presence, she was profoundly disappointed.

Her tutor matron, lamenting the fact that the lady was worthy but had nevertheless been rejected by the duke, sympathized with her disappointment. But she also feared that once the lady had been sent away, she would fail to leave at an opportune time.[35] So she told her, "The Way of Husband and Wife is such that when there is devotion, then [the couple] forms a bond; when there is no devotion, they part. Since you are dissatisfied, why don't you leave?" She then composed an ode that said, "It is no use! It is no use! Why not return?"[36]

The lady said, "The Way of Wives rests in single-minded devotion; that and nothing more. Although he rejects me, how can I not cleave to the Wifely Way?" She then composed an ode that said, "If it were not for you O prince,/How should I be here on the road?"[37] To the very end she maintained her purity and devotion, never once deviating from the Wifely Way while awaiting her lord's summons. The man of discernment therefore included her in his edition of the *Odes*.[38]

The Verse Summary says,

> The wife of Zhuang of Li
> Remained firm in her conduct and did not waver.
> Duke Zhuang would not see her;
> His conduct was unreasonable and perverse.
> The tutor matron urged her to leave,
> And wrote the ode "It Is No Use."
> But the lady maintained her devotion,
> And to the end was unwilling to return.

4.6 MENG JI OF DUKE XIAO OF QI

Meng Ji was the eldest daughter of the Hua lineage and the wife of Duke Xiao of Qi.[39] She was fond of the rites, pure, and devoted, but had passed the usual time for marriage without having made a match.[40] Suitors from Qi had pursued her, but because their observance of the rites had been lacking, in the end she did not go forth [to marry] any of them. She would not share a mat with a man, and her conversation never touched upon the affairs of the outside world.[41] She remained deeply sequestered to avoid suspicion. In Qi no one was able to complete the rites in pursuit of her. All of Qi praised her for her purity.

When Duke Xiao heard about her, he applied himself to mastering the ceremonies and personally went to fetch her at the home of the Hua lineage. Her father and mother accompanied Meng Ji but did not leave the hall.[42] Her mother offered her the libation cup in the side chamber, then fastened her lapel and sash and exhorted her, saying, "Be reverent! Be cautious! Do not neglect your duties in the palace!"[43] Her father from the top of the eastern stairway exhorted her, saying, "Rise early and retire late! Do not disobey commands! And if there are any who oppose the king's commands, do not follow them!" All of [her father's] concubines, standing on both sides of the steps, exhorted her, saying, "Be reverent! Be reverent! Fulfill the commands of your father and mother! Day and night, be not indolent! When you look upon your lapel and sash, remember what your father and mother have told you!"[44] Inside the gate her aunts exhorted her, saying, "Day and night, be without fault. When you look upon your lapel and sash, do not forget the words of your father and mother!"

The duke then personally came to fetch Meng Ji from her mother and father.[45] Upon leaving, he handed her the mounting cord.[46] [The duke] then drove the [bride's] carriage for three revolutions of the wheels, averting his gaze and looking only at the baseboard of Meng Ji's [carriage].[47] She was then received in the palace. After three months, she made her appearance in the ancestral temple and only then entered into the Way of Husband and Wife.

After they had lived together a long while, the duke made a trip to Langye, and Hua Meng Ji accompanied him.[48] It so happened that on the way, the carriage ran off the road, whereupon Meng Ji fell out, and the carriage was damaged. Duke Xiao then [returned and] sent a chariot drawn by four horses in which there was only room to stand, to take Meng Ji back home.[49]

Ji ordered the carriage driver to unroll the curtain so that she would be concealed, and then asked her tutor matron to respond to the messenger, saying, "I have heard that when a royal consort ventures beyond her threshold, she must ride in a covered carriage with seats.[50] When she leaves the hall, she must follow her tutor matron and governess.[51] When entering or withdrawing, she sounds her jade sash pendants.[52] At home, her attire is well fastened and bound. When she goes beyond the city, she is concealed by curtains in her carriage. This is how she maintains an upright mind, concentrates her thoughts, and exercises self-restraint.[53] Because the vehicle you sent requires that I stand in it and lacks screens, I dare not accept your command. And because I am outside of the city without protection, I dare not dwell here for long. These three conditions represent grave violations of ritual. Indeed, it is better to die an early death than to live without the rites."

The messenger then sped back and reported her words to the duke, who then sent a carriage with seats. By the time he returned to her, she was already in the process of hanging herself, but the tutor matron was able to rescue her and she did not die. The tutor matron said to her, "The messenger has arrived with a carriage complete with screens." Meng Ji then revived and returned home in the carriage.

A man of discernment would say, "Meng Ji was fond of the rites. According to the rites, when a woman goes out, she uses a carriage with screens, and her clothing is properly wrapped and bound. When she is married and returns home, she inquires after her sisters, but not her brothers, in order to maintain maximum segregation [of the sexes]."[54] The *Odes* says, "Those ladies of the noble houses,/ With their hair so thick and straight!"[55] These words apply well to her.

The Verse Summary says,

Meng Ji was fond of the rites;
She maintained her chastity with great reverence.
To avoid suspicion, she remained deeply sequestered;
To the very end, she avoided an alluring appearance.[56]
She refused to ride in a carriage with no seats,
Practicing only what ritual preached.
The discerning praise her for this,
And from ancient times, few have matched her.

4.7 THE WIFE OF THE LORD OF XI

[This lady] was the wife of the Lord of Xi.[57] [The King of] Chu attacked Xi and conquered it. He took the [Lord of Xi] captive and ordered him to guard the gate.[58] [The king also] took the Lord of Xi's consort. He made her his wife and installed her in his palace.

Once, when the King of Chu went out traveling, [the Lord of Xi's] wife went out to see her husband and told him, "In life, one must die once and then it is over. Why should we allow ourselves to suffer? I will never forget you, my lord, for even a moment, and I will never allow myself to partake of a second wedding libation.[59] We live apart in this world. How could that compare to dying and returning [to dwell together] in the underworld?" She then composed an ode that said, "While living, we occupy different rooms;/But in death, we share the same grave./If you say that I am not sincere,/By the bright sun, I swear that I am."[60]

Though the Lord of Xi tried to stop her, she wouldn't listen and proceeded to kill herself. The Lord of Xi then also killed himself, so that they both died on the same day. The King of Chu admired the worthiness the wife had shown in guarding her chastity and maintaining her integrity. He therefore had them buried together with the ceremonies appropriate to a feudal lord.

A man of discernment would say, "The wife delighted in putting virtue into practice, and for this reason was included in the *Odes*." Indeed, righteousness moves a person of quality, while profit moves a petty person. The wife of the Lord of Xi could not be moved for the sake of profit. The *Odes* says, "While I do nothing contrary to my good name,/I should live with you till our death."[61] These words apply well to her.

The Verse Summary says,

[The King of] Chu captured the Lord of Xi,
And took his chief consort.
She remained resolute
To the end of time, never relenting.
She composed an ode about a shared tomb,
Thinking only of her former lord and paying no heed to the new.
Without a second thought, she chose to die,
And has thus been ranked among the chaste and worthy.

4.8 THE WIFE OF QI LIANG OF QI

The wife of Qi Liang of Qi was the wife of Qi Liang Zhi of Qi.[62] Duke Zhuang once made a surprise attack on Ju. Zhi fought in the battle and died.[63] When Duke Zhuang returned home, he encountered Zhi's wife and sent a messenger to convey his condolences to her on the road. Qi Liang's wife said, "If Zhi has committed an offense, then why, my lord, do you demean yourself by issuing a decree [of condolence] for him?[64] If you have found Zhi guilty of no crime, then there is the humble abode of our ancestors [for this purpose]. But it will not do for me, your lowly servant, to accept your condolences here in the wilds."[65] After this, Duke Zhuang returned to his carriage and went to [Qi Liang's] home, where he completed the [condolence] ritual and then left.

Qi Liang's wife had no children, and in both her husband's and her natal family there were no relatives of the five categories.[66] Because she had nowhere to go, she went to her husband's corpse beneath the city wall and wept for him. Her sincerity so greatly moved all passersby that not one of them failed to shed tears for her. After ten days [her weeping] had caused the wall to collapse.

After she buried her husband, she said, "Where shall I go? A woman must have someone she can rely on. When her father is alive, she depends on her father; when her husband is alive, she depends on her husband; when her son is alive, she depends on her son. Now, in the generation that came before me I have no father, in my own generation I have no husband, and in the generation after me I have no son. At home I have no one to rely on and for whom I can express my sincerity. Beyond, I have no one to rely upon and for whom I can establish my integrity.[67] I cannot bring myself to remarry. My only alternative is to die." She then threw herself into the River Zi and died.[68]

A man of discernment would say, "Qi Liang's wife was pure and understood ritual." The *Odes* says, "My heart is wounded with sadness!/Oh, that I could return with you!"[69] These words apply well to her.

The Verse Summary says,

When Qi Liang died in battle,
His wife arranged for his burial.
Duke Zhuang of Qi went to condole with her on the road,
But she avoided him, not daring to receive him.
When she wept for her husband at the city wall,
The wall collapsed in response.
Because she had no family left,
She threw herself in the River Zi and died.

4.9 BO YING OF KING PING OF CHU

Bo Ying was the daughter of King Mu of Qin, the wife of King Ping of Chu, and the mother of King Zhao.[70] During the reign of King Zhao, Chu and Wu fought a battle at Boju.[71] Wu defeated Chu and then entered Ying.[72] King Zhao fled, and He Lü, the King of Wu, took as wives all the women of the rear palace.[73]

When he came to Bo Ying, she grasped a sword and said, "I have heard that the Son of Heaven is a model for all under Heaven, and the dukes and marquises serve as exemplars for each state. If the Son of Heaven disregards the rules, then all under Heaven will become disordered. If the feudal lords disregard regulations, then their states will be endangered.

"The Way of Husband and Wife is clearly the beginning of all human relationships and thus the starting point for all royal teachings. For this reason the regulations of enlightened kings demand that men and women do not touch each other when giving and receiving objects; when sitting, they do not share the same mat; when dining, they do not share the same dish; and they maintain separate clothing racks and use different towels and combs. [74] This is how [the king] instructs them. [75]

"If a feudal lord behaves in a licentious manner outside of his own home, he will be exterminated; if a minister or grandee behaves in a licentious manner outside of his home, he will be banished; if an officer or commoner behaves in a licentious manner outside of his home, he will be castrated. [76] Nevertheless, if benevolence is neglected, then it can be restored by means of righteousness. If righteousness is neglected, then it can be restored by means of ritual.

"When [proper relations between] men and women are lost, chaos and destruction ensue. [77] Now, initiating chaos and destruction is what dukes and marquises punish with extermination and what the Son of Heaven settles with execution. But in the present case, if your majesty abandons exemplary behavior and gives free rein to destructive desires, or commits crimes punishable by extermination and execution, how can he issue commands and instruct the people?

"Moreover, I have heard that to live in disgrace is not as good as to die in glory. If Your Majesty abandons exemplary behavior, then you will lack the means to govern your state. If I engage in depravities, then I will not be able to go on living. This one act will disgrace us both. I will therefore embrace death to guard [my virtue] and dare not obey your order. Furthermore, you desire me for your pleasure, but if you approach me and I die, what pleasure is there in that? If you first kill me, then of what benefit is that to Your Majesty?"

The King of Wu was ashamed and withdrew. He then released Bo Ying and her governess and shut the gates to the Lanes of Perpetuity, placing it under the watch of armed guards. [78] After thirty days, Qin came to their aid, and King Zhao was then restored. [79]

A man of discernment would say, "Bo Ying was courageous and profoundly devoted." The *Odes* says, "Luxuriant are the dolichos and other creepers,/Clinging to the branches and stems;/Easy and self-possessed was our prince,/Seeking for happiness by no crooked ways." [80] These words describe her situation well.

The Verse Summary says,

He Lü conquered Chu
And entered the palace chambers.

He made wives of the women of the rear palace,
And not one did not quake in fear.
But Bo Ying protected herself,
Firmly maintaining her devotion.
The discerning praise her
As one who was chaste.

4.10 CHASTE JIANG OF KING ZHAO OF CHU

Chaste Jiang was the daughter of the Marquis of Qi and the wife of King Zhao of Chu.[81] Once, when the king went out on an excursion, he settled his wife at a pavilion on the water, then left.[82] When the king heard that the river was about to flood, he ordered a messenger to fetch his wife, but the messenger forgot to take along the tally.[83]

When the messenger arrived, he asked the lady to come out. She replied: "The king has made an agreement with those who live in the palace, stating that when he issues an order to summon someone from the palace, it must be accompanied with a tally. Now, because you did not bring a tally, I do not dare to follow you."

The messenger replied, saying, "The waters have begun to rise. If I return to get the tally, I'm afraid it will be too late!" The lady said, "I have heard that it is the duty of a chaste woman to abide by an agreement, and that the brave are not afraid to die. They maintain their principles under all circumstances. I know that if I follow you I will live, and that if I remain I will die. But to abandon the agreement and trespass against righteousness while seeking life is not as good as remaining here and dying."

The messenger then went back to get the tally, but when he returned the water had risen, the pavilion had collapsed, and the lady had been swept away to her death.

The king said, "Alas, you held fast to righteousness and died for your principles, refusing to live dishonorably. You held to the agreement and maintained your fidelity, thereby making your chastity complete." He therefore gave her the name "Chaste Jiang."

A man of discernment would say, "Chaste Jiang possessed wifely integrity." The *Odes* says, "The virtuous man, the princely one,/Has nothing wrong in his deportment."[84] These words apply well to her.

The Verse Summary says,

King Zhao of Chu went for an outing,
Leaving Jiang at a pavilion on the water.
The river began to rise,
But without a tally, she refused to leave.
She held fast to her principles,
Was washed away, and died without hesitation.
For the discerning who appraise her,
She ranks on high with Bo Ji.[85]

4.11 CHASTE JI OF DUKE BAI OF CHU

Chaste Ji was the wife of Sheng, Duke Bai of Chu.[86] When Duke Bai died, his wife took up spinning and did not remarry. The King of Wu, hearing of her beauty and accomplishments, sent a messenger carrying one hundred *yi* of cash and a pair of white jade disks, as a formal petition of betrothal to her.[87] He sent thirty curtained carriages to fetch her, hoping that she might become his wife.

When a grandee presented the wife of Duke Bai with the gifts, she refused them, saying, "When Duke Bai was alive, I was fortunate to serve in the rear palace. There I wielded dust basket and broom, took care of clothing and shoes, brushed pillows and mats, and was entrusted with the duties of a consort.[88] Duke Bai unfortunately has died, and your handmaiden wishes to tend his grave until the end of her Heaven-appointed days. But now, Your Majesty wants to give me betrothal gifts of money and jade and the position of wife. Your foolish handmaiden has never heard of such a thing!

"Moreover, to abandon righteousness and follow after one's desires is to be defiled; to see profit and then forget the dead is covetousness. What use does Your Majesty have for a person who is defiled and covetous? I have heard that the loyal subject does not loan his strength to others, and the pure woman does not loan her beauty to others. How could that be the case only for one's service to the living? It should be the same for the dead. And because I am uncaring, I was unable to follow [my husband] in death. Now, if in addition, I leave and remarry, wouldn't that be utterly egregious?" She therefore declined and did not follow him. The King of Wu greatly esteemed her integrity and righteousness and gave her the name Chaste Ji of Chu.

A man of discernment would say, "Chaste Ji was scrupulous, pure, sincere, and faithful. Indeed, 'the burden is heavy and the road is long.'[89] When one makes benevolence one's burden, is that not indeed a heavy burden? And to do so unto death, is that not indeed a long road?" The *Odes* says, "That beautiful eldest Jiang,/Her virtuous fame is not to be forgotten."[90] This applies well to Chaste Ji.

The Verse Summary says,

> The wife of Duke Bai
> Kept to her widowhood, spinning and reeling silk.
> The King of Wu admired her,
> And proposed to her with gifts of cash and jade.
> The wife firmly maintained her principles,
> And though her husband was dead, would not change him for another.
> The discerning regard her as great
> And laud her accomplishments.

4.12 THE TWO COMPLIANT WOMEN OF THE HOUSE OF WEY

The two compliant women of the house of Wey were the wife and the attendant concubine of Lord Ling of the hereditary house of Wey.[91] When Qin destroyed Lord Jiao of Wey, [the emperor] enfeoffed the hereditary line of Lord Ling and allowed him to maintain their sacrifices.[92]

When Lord Ling died, his wife was childless and maintained her widowhood, while the attendant concubine had a child. But the concubine served the wife for eight years without slackening, reverently caring for her needs with increasingly greater dedication.[93]

The wife told the concubine: "You have cared for me with great diligence.[94] Your son now maintains the sacrifices, and yet you serve me in the manner of a concubine.[95] This is not a happy state of affairs. Moreover, I have heard that a lord's mother does not serve others in the capacity of concubine. Because I am childless, according to the rites I am someone who should be expelled.[96] Yet that I have been allowed to stay and fulfill my commitment [to my deceased husband] is my great good fortune. Furthermore, I feel great shame that I inconvenience you by maintaining this commitment. I would like to leave and live elsewhere, and if we can see each other from time to time I would be most pleased."

Beginning to cry, the concubine replied, "Madam, is it your intention to make Lord Ling suffer misfortune on three counts? That our lord died young was his first misfortune; that his wife bore him no son, while his humble concubine produced a son was his second misfortune. Now, that his wife wishes to leave and dwell outside of his home while his maidservant dwells inside his home is his third misfortune. I have heard that when a loyal minister serves his ruler, he has no time for idleness, and when a filial child cares for parents, he only regrets that the days may be too few. How would I dare to alter my duties as concubine for a small measure of honor? Reverent care is in fact the duty of a concubine, so how is it that the wife should be troubled by such a thing?"

The wife said, "For a childless woman to abuse the mother of our [young] lord, even though it accords with your wishes, will be interpreted by others as my ignorance of ritual. I will move out, and that's that." The concubine withdrew and told her son, saying, "I have heard that a person of quality dwells in a state of compliance, attending to the ceremonies between superiors and inferiors and cultivating the rituals of antiquity. This is the Way of Compliance. If the wife finds me troublesome and plans to move out, forcing me to stay here, then [my actions can only be seen as a form of] rebellion. How could living in a state of rebelliousness ever compare with remaining compliant and dying?" She then tried to kill herself.

Her son wept and tried to stop her, but she would not listen. The wife heard them and became afraid. She then promised the concubine that she would stay. To the end of her days the concubine reverently served the wife with unremitting dedication.

A man of discernment would say, "These two women who yielded to each other are truly persons of distinction.[97] It can indeed be said that what they accomplished within the family established a reputation for all later generations." The *Odes* says, "My mind is not a stone;/It cannot be rolled about."[98] These words apply well to this case.

The Verse Summary says,

> The two compliant women of the house of Wey,
> Were both resolved in their actions.
> Though the succession went to the concubine's son,
> She provided reverential care as of old.
> The wife was ashamed to concede,
> Seeking instead to dwell elsewhere.[99]
> To the end the concubine would not agree,
> But observed the rites undaunted.[100]

4.13 THE WIDOW TAO YING OF LU

Tao Ying was a daughter of the Tao family of Lu. She was widowed early and had to raise her young orphaned children without the help of older brothers. So she took up spinning as her livelihood. A man of Lu heard of her virtue and sought to marry her. When Ying heard about this turn of events, she feared that she would not be able to evade him. She therefore composed a song that explained her decision to refrain from remarriage. The song went,

> How sad, the yellow swan, bereft so young.
> For seven years it sought no other,[101]
> But bowed its head and retired alone,
> Dwelling apart from all the rest.
> Deep in the night it mournfully called,
> Thinking of its former mate.
> Since Heaven decreed an early widowhood,
> What harm to retire alone?
> When the widowed wife thinks of this,
> She weeps many tears.
> Alas, how sad indeed;
> Yet the dead cannot be forgotten!
> What is true of winged creatures
> Must be doubly so for the good and pure.
> Though there might be a worthy mate,
> I will not wed again.

When the man from Lu heard it, he said, "This woman is unobtainable." Thereafter he did not dare approach her again. Widow Ying, to the end of her days, did not remarry.

A man of discernment would say, "Tao Ying was pure, devoted, and thoughtful." The *Odes* says, "My heart is grieved,/I chant and sing."[102] These words describe her well.

The Verse Summary says,

> Tao Ying, widowed early,
> Spun silk to raise her brood.
> When someone sought her in marriage,

She stood firm in her principles.
She composed a song to make her intentions clear,
And her suitor soon desisted.
The man of discernment praises her,
So that women may take note.

4.14 THE "EXALTED-CONDUCT" WIDOW OF LIANG

[The Widow of] Exalted Conduct was a widow from Liang.[103] She was beautiful in appearance and refined in conduct. Her husband died, and though she was widowed early, she did not remarry. Many nobles of Liang competed to marry her, but no one could obtain her. When the King of Liang heard about her, he sent his prime minister to make a formal proposal to her.

The Widow of Exalted Conduct said, "My husband suffered the misfortune of dying early. I buried him even before his dogs and horses were laid to rest.[104] Though it would have been fitting for me to follow him to the grave, I must care for his young orphans and therefore cannot fulfill this wish to express my total devotion to him.[105] Though many nobles have sought me, I have fortunately managed to evade them.

"Now Your Majesty is also [entreating] me. I have heard that a wife's duty is to never change once she has gone out to marry, so that she can maintain intact the principles of purity and fidelity. If I were now to forget the dead and rush toward the living, this would be infidelity, and if I were to see only honor and forget the humble, this would be impurity. If I were to discard righteousness and follow profit, I would have nothing left with which to maintain my humanity." She thereupon took up a mirror and a knife and cut off her nose, saying, "Consider my punishment now complete![106] The reason I do not choose death is that I cannot bear to make my children orphaned a second time. The king has pursued me because of my beauty. Now, with what is left of me after my punishment, I can be free."

When the messenger reported this incident to the king, he considered her righteousness to be very great indeed and her conduct to be exalted. He then freed her from obligations to the state for the rest of her life and honored her with the title Exalted Conduct.[107]

A man of discernment would say, "She was exalted in conduct, firm in ritual principles, and single-minded in her devotion." The *Odes* says, "If you say I am not sincere,/By the bright sun I swear that I am."[108] These phrases describe her well.

The Verse Summary says,

The Widow of Exalted Conduct dwelt in Liang;
She was single-minded in her purity.
Never coveting a life of privilege,
She labored to maintain her devotion.
Rejecting all proposals in Liang,
She cut off her nose in self-inflicted punishment.
The man of discernment exalts her
And distinguishes her for future generations.

4.15 THE FILIAL WIDOWED WIFE OF CHEN

The Filial Wife was a young widow of Chen.[109] When she was sixteen she married, and before she had any children, her husband was conscripted to serve on the frontier. When he was about to leave, he enjoined the Filial Wife, saying, "Whether I will live or die is impossible to tell. I am fortunate that my elderly mother is still alive. Since I have no brothers, in the event that I do not return, will you be willing to care for my mother?" The Filial Wife promised him, saying, "I will."

When her husband, in fact, died and did not return, the Filial Wife cared for her mother-in-law unstintingly, becoming increasingly devoted in her loving kindness. She spun at home as a means of livelihood and to the end never wished to remarry.

After she had observed mourning for three years, her parents lamented the fact that she was so young, yet widowed and childless. So they went to fetch her with the intention of arranging a marriage for her. The Filial Wife said, "I have heard that fidelity is the foundation of one's humanity, and righteousness is the standard for all conduct. I have been fortunate to have left my swaddling clothes, received the command of my parents, and finally, to have served a husband. Moreover, when my husband left, he charged me to care for his elderly mother, and I gave him my promise. When one commits oneself to an obligation to another person, can one simply cast it aside? Casting aside an obligation is faithlessness, and turning one's back on the dead is immoral. These are things that must not be done."

Her mother said, "That you have been widowed so long fills me with pity!" The Filial Wife said, "I have heard that it is better to die encumbered by righteousness than to live unencumbered by the world.[110] Moreover, if I take on the responsibility of caring for a person's elderly mother without completing the task and make a promise to someone without keeping my word, then how could I ever hope to establish myself in this world? To act as a man's wife includes caring for his mother. Unfortunately, my husband died before me, so he was unable to fulfill the ritual duties of a son. Now, if you make me leave, with no one to care for his aged mother, it will make my husband look cruel and reveal me as unfilial. If I am unfilial, faithless, and without righteousness, how can I go on living?"

Because of this, she wanted to kill herself. In a state of alarm, her parents did not dare to arrange a marriage for her but allowed her to care for her mother-in-law for the next twenty-eight years. Her mother-in-law died at age eighty-four, after which the Filial Wife sold all of her land and fields to provide for her burial, and to the end of her days carried out sacrifices for her.[111]

When the governor of Huaiyang brought this story to the attention of the throne, Filial Emperor Wen extolled her righteousness, honored her fidelity, and praised her achievements.[112] He ordered a messenger to present her with forty catties of gold. He also released her from obligations to the state for the rest of her life and honored her with the title "Filial Wife."[113]

A man of discernment would say, "The Filial Wife fulfilled to the utmost her duties as wife." The *Odes* says, "No ordinary person was he,/In his steadfast heart he was sincere and profound."[114] These words describe her well.

The Verse Summary says,

The Filial Wife dwelt in Chen;
Her husband died and she was childless.
Her mother was about to marry her off,
But to the end she would not obey.
With complete devotion she cared for her mother-in-law,
Having married once with no wish to change.
The sage ruler praised her,
And gave her the title Filial Wife.

5

THE PRINCIPLED AND RIGHTEOUS

PREFACE

Only those such as the Principled and Righteous
Will not flee the prospect of death.
Fond of goodness, admiring principle,
To the end they will not turn their backs on righteousness.
Sincere, trustworthy, brave, and bold,
How can there be any thought of danger?
Where righteousness dwells,
There they hasten without hesitation.
Women: model yourselves accordingly,
Considering these principles the foundation of the world.

5.1 THE RIGHTEOUS NURSE OF DUKE XIAO OF LU

The righteous nurse of Xiao was the nurse of Cheng, Duke Xiao of Lu.[1] She was
a widow of the Zang family. Earlier, Duke Xiao's father, Duke Wu, with two of
his sons, Kuo, the eldest, and Xi, the middle son, went to the court of King Xuan
of Zhou for an audience with the king.[2] King Xuan established Xi as Lu's heir
apparent.[3] When Duke Wu died, Xi came to the throne as Duke Yi.[4] At the time,
[the future] Duke Xiao was called Prince Cheng.[5] He was the youngest [son].
The righteous nurse had entered the palace along with her own son to care for
Prince Cheng.

Kuo's son, Boyu, along with the people of Lu, revolted.[6] He attacked and murdered Duke Yi, set himself up as ruler, then sought Prince Cheng in the palace with the intention of killing him. When the righteous nurse heard that Boyu was planning to kill Cheng, she dressed her own son in Cheng's clothing and laid him down in Cheng's place. Boyu then murdered him. Meanwhile, the righteous nurse had gathered up Cheng and fled.

Outside [of the palace] she encountered Cheng's maternal uncle, who was a grandee of Lu. The uncle asked, "Is Cheng dead?" The nurse said, "He is not dead; he is here!" The uncle said, "How did you manage to escape?" The nurse said, "I substituted my own son for Cheng." The righteous nurse then fled with him.

In the eleventh year of [Boyu's reign] the grandees of Lu all knew that Cheng was with his nurse, so they asked the Zhou Son of Heaven to kill Boyu and put Cheng on the throne.[7] He was called Duke Xiao. The people of Lu all held him in great esteem.

The *Analects* says, "This person can be entrusted with a young orphan [prince]."[8] This saying applies well to the righteous nurse.

The Verse Summary says,

> Boyu raised a rebellion,
> Which started in the palace of Lu.
> The wet nurse of Duke Xiao
> Was a matron of the Zang family.
> She fled and hid Duke Xiao,
> Exchanging him for her own son.
> A nurse like this
> Can indeed be relied upon!

5.2 ZHENG MAO, CONSORT OF KING CHENG OF CHU

Zheng Mao was a woman of Zheng sent as a secondary bride to accompany the [principal bride from the clan of] Ying.[9] She was the wife of King Cheng of Chu.[10]

Once, soon after [Zheng Mao had arrived in Chu], King Cheng ascended a tower that overlooked the rear palace. All of the palace women looked up at him. But Zimao [i.e., Zheng Mao] walked straight ahead and did not look, maintaining her dignified stride.[11]

The king said, "You, the one walking there, look at me!" But Zimao did not look. Then the king said, "Look at me and I will make you my wife!" But once again Zimao did not look. The king then said, "Look at me and I will also give you one thousand cash and enfeoff your father and elder brother." But Zimao continued to walk and did not look at him.

So the king came down from the tower and asked her, "The status of wife is very highly regarded and the income of a noble is very generous. With one glance, these things could have been yours, but you refused to look at me. Why?"

Zimao said, "I have heard that a woman comports herself with propriety and dignity.[12] If I had looked at your majesty when you were on the tower, I would have failed to observe the rules of correct deportment. If at first I wouldn't look at you, but then looked only after being offered the great honor of being your wife and the generous grant of a noble rank, I would be guilty of coveting honors and relishing profit at the expense of moral principles. If I overlook moral principles, how can I serve Your Majesty?"

The king said, "Well put!" and then established her as his wife.[13]

After several years, the king was about to establish Prince Shangchen as heir apparent.[14] The king consulted his prime minister, Zishang, about it.[15] Zishang said, "You are not yet old, and you favor many of your sons. If you establish one and later demote him, he will create an upheaval. Furthermore, he has the eyes of a wasp and the voice of a wolf. He is a cruel man and should not be made heir apparent."[16] The king withdrew and asked his wife about it. Zimao said, "The prime minister has spoken the truth. You can follow his advice." But the king didn't listen and established Shangchen as heir apparent. Later, Shangchen employed Zishang in the rescue of Cai, but then slandered Zishang and had him killed.[17]

Zimao told her nurse, saying, "I have heard that the concerns of women lie exclusively in the realm of providing food. Nevertheless, I cannot conceal what my heart has observed. Formerly, Zishang said that the heir apparent could not be established as his father's successor. The heir resented it and then slandered him and had him killed. The king did not make a thorough investigation and therefore had an innocent man punished. This is to turn white into black and to mistake high for low. The king is fond of many of his sons, and all of them want possession of the kingdom. The heir apparent, being greedy and cruel, is afraid that he will lose his position. The king, moreover, does not understand the situation, and with no way to bring him to his senses, his sons will contend with each other and disaster is sure to arise because of this."

Later the king wanted to establish Prince Zhi as his heir. Zhi was Shangchen's younger brother by a concubine. Zimao withdrew and told her nurse, "I have heard that the trustworthy are not regarded with suspicion. At present, the king is going to replace the heir apparent with Zhi. I am afraid that this will bring about chaos and disaster. But when I said as much to the king, he did not respond. Does he suspect that I am working against Zhi because he is not my son?[18] Indeed, if one goes on living while being regarded with suspicion, who will ever know that the suspicion is without basis? To be regarded as unrighteous and live is not as good as dying in order to make the truth known. Moreover, when the king hears that I am dead, he will awaken to the fact that the heir apparent cannot be deposed."

She then killed herself, and her nurse conveyed her words to the king. At this time, the heir apparent was aware of the fact that the king wanted to depose him. So he raised troops and rebelled, surrounding the king's palace. The king asked to eat bear's paws before he died, but his request was denied and he hanged himself.[19]

A man of discernment would say, "Only the truly benevolent would offer their own lives as a reproach." The *Odes* says, "He is steadfast unto death."[20] These words apply well to her.

The Verse Summary says,

Zimao was prescient;
How constant was her integrity.
What began as her refusal to turn around and look
Concluded in her marriage to King Cheng.
She understood Shangchen's rebelliousness
And spoke of it forcefully.
But, charged with resenting that Zhi was not her son,
She killed herself to make the truth known.

5.3 HUAI YING, CONSORT OF YU OF JIN

Huai Ying was the daughter of Duke Mu of Qin and the wife of Duke Hui of Jin's heir apparent.[21] When [the heir apparent] Yu was residing in Qin as a hostage, Duke Mu gave him Ying as a wife.[22] After six years, when Yu was about to escape to his home, he told Ying, "It has been a number of years since I left my own state.[23] Your father has been remiss in his treatment of me, and the friendly relations between Qin and Jin have not improved. 'Alas, the bird takes flight, returning to its home,/And the fox near death heads toward his den.'[24] Shouldn't I, then, head back to Jin to die, and won't you go with me?"

Ying responded, saying, "You are the heir apparent of Jin. You have been poorly treated in Qin, and so your desire to leave is indeed appropriate. My father ordered your handmaiden to wait on you with towel and comb so that you might stay.[25] But now, my inability to bind you is due to my own worthlessness. If I follow you to your home, I will be abandoning my ruler. If I report your plan, I will be failing in my duties as wife. Of these three situations, not one is acceptable. So although I will not accompany you, you must go. I would not dare to divulge your plans, just as I would not dare to follow you." Ziyu then left and returned home.

A man of discernment would say, "Huai Ying was skilled at managing relations between husband and wife."[26]

The Verse Summary says,

When Yu of Jin became hostage in Qin,
He was wed to Huai Ying.
When Yu was about to flee,
Ying would not accede to his wishes,
Nor would she divulge his plan.
She took great pains to be even-handed
And did not report his plan for her to follow.
She was without partiality or bias.

5.4 KING ZHAO OF CHU'S LADY OF YUE

King Zhao of Chu's Lady of Yue was the daughter of Goujian, King of Yue, and the consort of King Zhao of Chu.[27]

Once King Zhao went on a leisure outing. The Lady of Cai sat to his left in the carriage and the Lady of Yue sat on his right. The king himself took the reins of his team of four horses, galloping ahead at great speed. Then they ascended the Fushe Tower to gaze at Yunmeng Park.[28]

Watching the officers and grandees passing by below, he felt very happy. He then turned to the two consorts and said, "Are you pleased?" The Lady of Cai said, "I'm pleased." The king said, "I wish to live with you like this and also to die with you like this." The Lady of Cai said, "Formerly, when the ruler of my state offered the labor of his people to serve in Your Majesty's stables, he also presented me as a gift for your amusement. And now, having entered the ranks of your wives and concubines, naturally I wish to live with you and I am also pleased to die with you." The king turned to his historian and told him, "Write that down! The Lady of Cai promises to follow me in death!"

He then repeated the question to the Lady of Yue, who said, "All this is pleasurable, to be sure, but it cannot last long." The king said, "I wish to live with you like this and to die with you like this. Will it not be granted me?"

The Lady of Yue said, "In the past, our former lord, King Zhuang, indulged in pleasure for three years and did not attend to the affairs of state. In the end, he was able to change and finally ruled all under Heaven as hegemon.[29] Your handmaiden believes that if your majesty can model yourself on our former lord, you will be able to transform your interest in pleasure and apply yourself to governing. But at present, since this is not the case, how can you obtain your wish that I should die with you?

"Furthermore, the king came with bolts of silk and a team of four horses to fetch me from my humble state. When my own ruler accepted these things in his ancestral temple, he did not agree that I should die with you. I have heard from my aunts that a woman dies in order to honor the benevolence of her lord and to increase devotion toward him.[30] I have never heard that recklessly following an unenlightened lord in death will redound to his glory. I dare not obey your order."

King Zhao was startled, but he respected what the Lady of Yue had to say. Nevertheless, he still favored the Lady of Cai.

Twenty-five years later, the king went to the aid of Chen, and the two ladies accompanied him.[31] Stationed with his soldiers, the king fell ill. There was a red cloud around the sun that looked like birds in flight. The king asked the scribe of Zhou about it.[32] The scribe said, "It portends harm to the king's body, but [the harm] can be transferred to your generals or ministers."

When the generals and ministers heard this, they requested to be used as sacrifices to the spirit. The king said, "My generals and ministers are like my own arms and legs! If I transfer my misfortune to them, how could that possibly remove me from harm?" He therefore ignored the directive.

The Lady of Yue said, "How great is the king's virtue! I am now willing to follow Your Majesty [in death]. On our earlier outing, [your greatest devotion] was to the pursuit of pleasure, so I dared not agree. Now that Your Majesty has returned to ritual propriety, all of the capital populace will be willing to die for you. So how much more must someone like me be willing to do the same? Please allow me to go before you and drive away the fox of the underworld!"

The king said, "What I said during that leisure outing was only in jest. If you really intend to die, it will only magnify my lack of virtue." The Lady of Yue said, "At that time, though I did not say so, I had already promised in my heart. I have heard that the faithful do not deny what is in their hearts, and the righteous do not make empty promises. I will die for the king's righteousness; I will not die for his pleasure." She then killed herself.

When the king's illness was at its most serious, he ceded his throne to his three younger brothers, but all three of them declined.[33] The king died with his army, but in the end the Lady of Cai was unable to die with him. The king's younger brothers, Zilü, Zixi, and Ziqi, devised a plan, saying, "If the mother is faithful, then the child will certainly be benevolent." They therefore concealed [the king's death] from the army, sealed off the roads, and fetched the Lady of Yue's son, Xiongzhang. He was established as King Hui.[34] The troops were then dispersed, and they returned to bury King Zhao.

A man of discernment would say, "The Lady of Yue was truly able to die for righteousness." The *Odes* says, "Not betraying the fair name that is mine,/I shall join you in death."[35] This passage describes the Lady of Yue well.

The Verse Summary says,

> King Zhao of Chu, while on a leisure outing,
> Asked his consorts to follow him in death.
> The Lady of Cai promised the king,
> But only the Lady of Yue held fast to propriety.
> Ultimately, only she died for her principles,
> So that all of the ministers praised her.
> Of these two ladies,
> Her virtue was beyond compare.

5.5 THE WIFE OF THE GENERAL OF GE

The wife of the General of Ge was the wife of the Assistant General Qiuzi.[36] When the Rong attacked Ge, they killed its lord and issued an order to all the ministers of Ge, saying, "We will execute the wives and children of anyone who commits suicide."[37] Qiuzi attempted suicide, but someone rescued him and he did not die.

When he returned, his wife said to him, "I have heard that bravery is the moral principle of a general and that he refuses to be taken alive. In this way officers and commoners will exert themselves to the utmost without fear of death, battles will lead to victory, attacks will end in occupation, and one can therefore preserve the nation and secure the ruler. But to wage war and forget valor is unfilial; to see one's ruler perish and not to die oneself is disloyalty. At present, the army has been defeated and the ruler has died, so how is it that you alone are still alive? Having lost your sense of loyalty and filial duty, how can you bear to return?"

Qiuzi said, "Ge is small and the Rong are great. I exerted my strength and abilities to the utmost, but our ruler unfortunately perished. Naturally I tried to kill myself, but because someone rescued me, I did not die." His wife said, "Your rescue is a thing of the past; what prevents you from acting now?" Qiuzi said, "It is not that I begrudge giving my life. The Rong issued a decree, saying, 'We will execute the wives and children of those who kill themselves.' That is why I did not die. Furthermore, of what use am I to my ruler if I am dead?"

His wife said, "I have heard that if a ruler is distressed, his ministers should suffer disgrace, and when a ruler suffers disgrace, his ministers should die. Our ruler is now dead, but you have not died. Can this be called righteousness? Many officers and commoners were killed. You could not protect your country, and yet you yourself are still alive. Can this be called benevolence? You worry about your wife and children, but you have forgotten about benevolence and righteousness. You turned your back on your former ruler, but deferred to the powerful and violent. Can this be called loyal? Can a man who is deficient in the Way of the Loyal Minister and in acts of benevolence and righteousness be called worthy?

"The *Book of Zhou* says, 'The ruler is given priority over the minister, parents are given priority over brothers, brothers are given priority over friends, and friends are given priority over wife and children.'[38] Taking into consideration one's wife and children is a matter of personal affection; serving one's ruler is a public duty. Now, for the sake of your wife and children, you have neglected the moral principles of the minister and failed in the ritual duty to serve your ruler. You have abandoned the public Way of the Loyal Minister to indulge a personal affection for wife and children. You have stolen life to live dishonorably. We women would be ashamed by this, so how much greater must your shame be? I cannot go on living with you while enduring this shame." She then killed herself.

The ruler of the Rong regarded her as a worthy, performed a *tailao* sacrifice for her, and had her buried with the rites of a general.[39] He presented her younger brother with a gift of one hundred *yi* of cash and gave him the rank of high minister, and ordered that another person should rule over Ge.[40]

A man of discernment would say, "The wife of the general of Ge was pure and loved righteousness." The *Odes* says, "A pure, noble person,/Whose virtue does not swerve."[41] These words describe her well.

The Verse Summary says,

The wife of the General of Ge
Maintained her principles with fierce determination.
After the Rong destroyed Ge,
Only Qiuzi was left alive.
His wife was ashamed that he did not die,
And set forth the Five Glories.[42]
She preceded her husband in death
And left behind an illustrious name.

5.6 THE RIGHTEOUS AUNT OF LU

The Righteous Aunt of Lu was a woman of Lu's countryside. Once, when Qi attacked Lu, upon arriving at the border the [troops] surveyed the scene and saw a woman carrying one child and holding the hand of another as she fled. When the army drew near, she cast aside the child she was holding, picked up the one whose hand she was holding, and headed for the hills. The child [she left behind] followed after her, crying, but the woman kept going and didn't look back. The Qi general questioned the child, saying, "Is the person running away your mother?"

The child said, "Yes, she is." The general asked, "Who is the one your mother is carrying?" The child said, "I don't know." The Qi general then pursued the woman and, as the soldiers drew their bows to shoot her, said, "Stop! If you don't stop, I will shoot you!"

When the woman returned, the Qi general asked, "Who is the child you are carrying, and who is the one you abandoned?" She replied, "The one I am carrying is my elder brother's child. The one I abandoned is my own child. When I saw the army approaching, I knew I was not strong enough to take both of them, so I abandoned my child."

The Qi general said, "A child's relation to its mother is one of great love and represents the heart's deepest affection. Why then did you abandon him and take the son of your elder brother?"

The woman said, "With my own son, it is a matter of personal affection. But in the case of my elder brother's son, it is a matter of public duty. Thus, if I turn my back on my public duty and follow after personal affection, denying my brother's son and preserving my own child, though I might be fortunate enough to escape, the ruler of Lu would not harbor me, the grandees would not see to my welfare, and the commoners and the capital populace would have nothing to do with me.[43] In such a case, no matter how small I might make myself, there would be no place that would harbor me, and no matter how I might place my feet, there would be no place to tread. Although I love my child, when it comes to my duty, what choice do I have? I can bear to abandon my child to practice righteousness, but without righteousness I can't live in the state of Lu."

The general of Qi then ordered his soldiers to halt and desist. He commissioned someone to tell the ruler of Qi, "Lu cannot be attacked. When we arrived at the border, even an old woman from the hills and marshes knew enough to maintain her integrity, practice righteousness, and refrain from pursuing personal matters at the expense of the public good. So how much more would this be the case for the ministers and grandees of the court? We request to return." The ruler of Qi granted them permission. When the ruler of Lu heard it, he presented the woman with one hundred bolts of cloth and gave her the title "Righteous Aunt."

[A man of discernment would say, "The aunt of Lu] was public-minded, correct, sincere, and trustworthy, and resolute in her righteous act.[44] How great was her righteousness! Though she was a common woman, the state still depended upon her. How much more imperative it is then to employ ritual and righteousness to rule the state!" The *Odes* says, "To an upright virtuous conduct,/All in the four quarters of the State render obedient homage."[45] These words apply well to this case.

The Verse Summary says,

When the ruler of Qi attacked Lu,
The Righteous Aunt maintained her principles.
She saw the army and fled to the hills,
Abandoning her son and taking her nephew.
When the Qi general questioned her,
He admired her moral reasoning.
One woman practiced righteousness,
And the army of Qi was halted.

5.7 CONSORT ZHAO OF DAI

Consort Zhao of Dai was the daughter of Zhao Jianzi, the elder sister of [Zhao] Xiangzi, and the consort of the King of Dai.[46]

After Jianzi's burial, and before Xiangzi had stopped wearing mourning garments, he traveled north and ascended Xiawu mountain.[47]

Then, in a ruse designed to dupe the King of Dai, [Xiangzi] ordered his cook to bring a long-handled ladle for serving the King of Dai and his followers. When they were about to serve the wine, he secretly directed Steward Ge, armed with the ladle, to strike and kill the King of Dai and his followers. He then raised troops to gain control of Dai and went to fetch his elder sister, Lady Zhao.[48]

The lady said, "Since I received the order from our former lord to serve the King of Dai, it has now been more than ten years. Though Dai committed no great offense, you, my lord, have destroyed it. And now that Dai has been devastated, where can I go? Moreover, I have heard that it is the principle of women to not serve two husbands, so how can I take a second husband? And just where do you intend to take me? To treat one's husband with contempt for the sake of one's brother is not right. To resent one's brother for the sake of one's husband is unkind. While I would not presume to feel resentment, I will also not return." She wept and cried out to Heaven, then killed herself in the "Place of the Sharpened Hairpin."[49] The people of Dai all cherished her.

A man of discernment would say, "Consort Zhao was adept at managing the husband and wife relationship." The *Odes* says, "Be not untruthful, do no harm;/ And few will not make you their pattern."[50] This phrase describes her well.

The Verse Summary says,

Zhao Xiangzi,
Was the brother of the Lady of Dai.
He attacked and destroyed the King of Dai,
Then went to fetch his sister.
But she adduced moral principles,
And spoke of chastity and the rites.
Without returning, without resentment,
She remained in the wilds and died.

5.8 THE RIGHTEOUS STEPMOTHER OF QI

The Righteous Stepmother of Qi was a mother from Qi who had two sons. During the time of King Xuan, a man was killed in a fight on the road.[51] When an official investigated, he learned that one man had been injured by another. Two men, an older and younger brother, were standing next to the victim. When the official questioned the men, the elder brother said, "I killed the man." But the younger brother said, "It was not my elder brother. It was actually I who killed him."

After a year elapsed, the official was still unable to make a determination. He explained the situation to the prime minister, but the prime minister was unable to decide, so he spoke of the matter to the king. The king said, "If I pardon both of them, I will be releasing a criminal. If I execute both of them, I will be punishing an innocent man. I think the mother will be able to tell us which son is innocent and which is guilty. Let's ask the mother and see who she thinks should live and who should die."

The prime minister then summoned the mother and questioned her, saying, "One of your sons killed a man. Since each son wishes to die for the other, the officials were unable to come to a decision, so they referred the case to the king. Because of the king's great kindness and benevolence, he is asking you which one you think should live and which should die."

The mother wept and answered, saying, "Kill the youngest." The minister accepted her answer, but then questioned her further, saying, "Since the youngest child is usually the one people cherish most, why do you think that it is he who should die?"

The mother replied, "The youngest is my son. The eldest is the son of my husband's first wife. When their father was ill and about to die, he entrusted the boy to me, saying, 'Take good care of him,' and I said, 'I will.' Now, having agreed to a person's request and having given one's word to that person, how can one simply forget about the request and not honor the agreement? Moreover, to have the elder brother killed and allow the younger to live is to abandon my public duty for a personal affection. To turn one's back on one's word and forget one's pledge is to defraud the dead. Indeed, if one does not keep one's word or carry out what one has already promised to do, how can one live in this world? Although I love my son, if I consider what my duty is, what choice do I have?"[52] She then wept, soaking the lapels of her robe with her tears.

The minister sent word to the king, whereupon the king praised her righteousness and extolled her conduct. Both sons were pardoned and spared execution, while the mother was honored with the title "Righteous Stepmother."

A man of discernment would say, "The Righteous Stepmother was trustworthy and loved righteousness. She was perceptive and willing to yield." The *Odes* says, "O happy and courteous sovereign,/You are a pattern to the four quarters."[53] These words apply to her.

The Verse Summary says,

The Righteous Stepmother was truly faithful;
She was unbiased, upright, and understood propriety.
When her son and stepson were accused of a crime,
They persisted in yielding to each other.
The officials could not come to a decision,
So the king questioned the mother.
Because she maintained good faith and followed righteousness,
Both her sons were finally spared.

5.9 THE CHASTE WIFE OF QIU OF LU

The chaste wife was the wife of Qiu Huzi of Lu. Five days after their marriage, Qiu left to assume an official position in Chen. He did not return until five years later. Before arriving at his home, he saw a woman picking mulberry leaves by the side of the road. Qiu Huzi took a fancy to her, alighted from his carriage, and addressed her, saying, "Since you are here in the open air picking mulberry leaves, and I have a long way to travel, may I avail myself of the shade of the mulberry to eat, put down my bags, and rest a while?"

But the woman continued picking mulberries without stopping. Qiu Huzi then said to her, "Laboring in the fields cannot compare with coming across an abundant harvest, and laboring with mulberries is no match for gaining an audience with a minister of state! I have money that I would like to give you."

The wife said, "I beg your pardon? I labor at picking mulberry leaves and spin and weave to provide clothing and food to offer my parents-in-law and to take care of my husband and children. I don't want your money! But I do want you to put an end to these inappropriate proposals! I have absolutely no intention of engaging in debauchery, so you can pack up your bags and the money from your carrying case now!" Qiu Huzi thereupon left.

When Qiu arrived home, he politely offered the money to his mother as a gift. When he ordered someone to call his wife and she arrived, he found himself facing the woman who had been picking mulberries. Qiu Huzi was mortified.

His wife said, "You bound up your hair, subjected yourself to training, and left your family to become an official. After five years you have returned. You should have been happily racing home in a cloud of dust, eager to arrive. But instead you took a fancy to a woman on the road, set down your bags, and offered her money.

This was to forget your mother. To forget your mother is unfilial. To be obsessed with women and sensuality is impure conduct, and impure conduct is immoral. Now, one who is unfilial in serving one's parents will be disloyal in serving one's ruler. One who is immoral in managing one's family will be unfit to administer official duties. When filial piety and morality have both perished, there is no way to succeed. I cannot bear to look at a man who is unfilial and immoral.[54] You should remarry, but I do not wish to marry again." She therefore left, traveling east, where she cast herself into a river and died.

A man of discernment would say, "The chaste wife was intent upon goodness. As for unfilial conduct, there is nothing worse than not loving parents and loving other people instead.[55] Such was the conduct of Qiu Huzi." The man of discernment would [also] say, "'Contemplate goodness and pursue it as if it could not be reached; and contemplate evil and shrink from it as one would from thrusting one's hand into boiling water.' These words apply well to the wife of Qiu Huzi."[56] The *Odes* says, "It is his shallow disposition/That makes him a subject for criticism."[57] This phrase also applies well to this case.

The Verse Summary says,

Qiu Hu went west to take up an official post;
Five years later he returned.
When he met a married woman he did not know,
His heart was filled with lustful thoughts.
The wife upheld her belief that she should cleave to no other,
But upon returning, she recognized him.
Ashamed that her husband was so lacking in morals,
She fled east and cast herself into a river.

5.10 THE LOYAL CONCUBINE OF THE MASTER OF ZHOU

The loyal concubine of the master of Zhou was a concubine who accompanied the bride of a grandee of Zhou upon her marriage.[58] The grandee, who was referred to as "the master," had come from Wey to serve in Zhou. After two years he returned home. Meanwhile, his wife had an affair with a neighbor. The neighbor became worried, fearing that the master would find out about the affair. So the wife said, "Don't worry! I have prepared some poisoned wine. I've already set it aside for him!"

Three days later, when the master arrived home, his wife said, "Allow me to see to your comfort! I've set aside some wine for you." She ordered the concubine to bring out the wine and serve it.

The concubine knew that the wine was poisoned, so she thought, "If I serve the wine, then I will kill the master, which is not right. But if I say something about it, my mistress will be killed, and that would be disloyal." She hesitated, and then, pretending to trip, spilled the wine.

The master became angry and caned her. When he was finished, the wife was afraid that the concubine would talk, so on the pretext of some other offense, the wife also caned the concubine with the intention of killing her. The concubine knew she was about to die but said nothing. It so happened that the master's younger brother had heard about the affair and proceeded to tell the master everything. The master was shocked. He then released the concubine and beat his wife to death.

He then had someone discreetly question the concubine, saying, "You knew about the affair; why didn't you say anything even when you were on the verge of dying?"

The concubine said, "How could I see my mistress die to preserve my own life, and how could I besmirch her reputation? If I had to die, then I would just die. How could I possibly say anything?"

The master, deeply impressed with her principles and full of admiration for her presence of mind, wanted to take her as his wife. But the concubine declined, saying, "Because my mistress has been disgraced and died while I still live, it would not be proper. To take the place of my mistress would go against ritual. As far as ritual improprieties go, what has already happened is bad enough. If I were to add to it now, I would find it difficult to go on living."

She planned to kill herself, but when the master learned of her intentions, he presented her with generous gifts and arranged a marriage for her. The neighbors all vied to wed her.

A man of discernment would say, "The loyal concubine was benevolent and unselfish. There is no name so obscure that it cannot become known. There is no conduct so hidden that it cannot become manifest." The *Odes* says, "Every word finds its answer,/Every good deed has its recompense."[59] These words apply well to this case.

The Verse Summary says,

The loyal concubine of the master of Zhou
Was kind and good, and understood her place.
The mistress was lustful and evil,

Poisoning the wine to kill her husband.
When the concubine was ordered to serve it,
She tripped to avoid doing harm.
Her loyalty saved her master,
And in the end she received good fortune.

5.11 THE PRINCIPLED WET NURSE OF WEI

The principled wet nurse of Wei was the wet nurse of the Prince of Wei.[60] Qin launched an attack on Wei and destroyed it, killing King Xia of Wei and executing the all of the king's sons apart from one who was not captured.[61] Orders went out to the state of Wei, saying, "Whoever apprehends the prince will be rewarded with one thousand *yi* in cash. Anyone found harboring him will be exterminated along with his entire clan."

The principled wet nurse fled with the prince. A former minister of Wei happened upon the nurse and, recognizing her, said, "Nurse, is all well?" The wet nurse said, "Oh dear, oh dear! What can be done about the prince?" The minister said, "Where is the prince now? I have heard that Qin issued an order stating that whoever captures the prince will be given one thousand *yi* in cash, and whoever hides him will be exterminated along with his entire clan.[62] If you, Nurse, provide information, then you stand to gain one thousand in cash. But if you know and don't tell them, then your brothers will all be [executed] without exception."

The wet nurse said, "I don't know where the prince is!" The minister said, "But I heard that you and the prince escaped together." The nurse said, "Although I know where he is, I cannot tell you under any circumstances." The minister said, "The kingdom of Wei has already been destroyed and the royal family has been exterminated. You continue to hide him, but for whom?"

The nurse sighed and said, "Seeing an opportunity to profit by turning on one's superiors is betrayal. Abandoning righteousness because one fears death is lawlessness. Now to resort to betrayal and lawlessness in order to chase after profit is something I cannot do. Furthermore, those who take care of other people's children are devoted to keeping them alive, not to seeing them killed. How could I be motivated by reward or intimidated by execution to abandon what is right and sacrifice my principles? I could not allow the prince to be captured and then go on living myself."

She then gathered up the prince and fled deep into the marshes. The minister proceeded to report them to the Qin army. When the army managed to track them down, the soldiers contended with one another to shoot them. But the nurse used her body to shield the prince. Dozens of arrows pierced her so that both she and the prince died.

When the King of Qin heard about this incident, he was deeply impressed with her loyalty and willingness to die for righteousness. He therefore arranged a burial for her using the ceremony reserved for high ministers of state and set forth a *tailao* sacrifice for her.[63] He honored her elder brother with the title of grandee of the fifth rank and bestowed upon him one hundred *yi* in cash.

A man of discernment would say, "The righteous wet nurse was kind and generous. She valued righteousness and disdained wealth. According to the *Rites*, 'For a [newborn] child, an apartment was prepared in the palace. From all the concubines and other attendants, there was chosen one known for her generosity, benevolence, kindness, gentle nature, virtue, respectful bearing, caution, and reticence, who was appointed as the child's teacher. Another was chosen to be its "kind matron" and another to be its "guardian matron." They all lived in the child's apartment, where they nourished and sustained the child. Others were not allowed to enter unless they had some special business there.'[64] Indeed, it is kindness that enables love. A suckling dog will attack a tiger; a brooding hen will strike a fox. This is because mercy comes from the heart."[65] The *Odes* says, "On the road there is a dead man;/Someone will bury him."[66] These words apply well to this case.

The Verse Summary says,

After Qin destroyed Wei,
It offered a reward for its royal scion.
So the prince and the wet nurse fled together.
She held fast to her principles and took charge,
Not swayed by profit.
She faced death without concern.
And her illustrious name will be transmitted forever.

5.12 THE PRINCIPLED AUNT OF LIANG

The principled aunt was a woman of Liang.[67] A fire broke out in her home while her elder brother's son and her own son were inside. When she tried to retrieve her brother's son. she managed to get her own son out but failed to reach the son of her brother. Because the fire was at its height, she could not go back in.

Nevertheless, she was about to dash into the flames when a friend stopped her, saying, "Your original intention was to rescue your brother's child, but in such a state of alarm you mistakenly took your own son. You did all you could do in good conscience.[68] Why go to the extreme of going back into the fire?"

The wife said, "Will I be able to go from house to house in the state of Liang to make people understand my intentions? With a reputation for this ignoble act, how can I face my brothers or my countrymen? I would like to cast my own child into the fire, but that would be a breach of maternal love. I cannot go on living in this way." So she cast herself into the fire and died.

A man of discernment would say, "The righteous aunt was pure and not defiled." The *Odes* says, "That great-hearted man/Will give his life rather than transgress."[69] These words apply well to her.

The Verse Summary says,

> The principled aunt of Liang
> Upheld righteousness and cherished moral principles.
> Her son and nephew were both inside
> When a great fire burst forth.
> She went to save her nephew,
> But could only find her son.
> At its height, she threw herself into the fire,
> Wishing to make clear her unselfish intentions.

5.13 THE TWO RIGHTEOUS WOMEN FROM ZHUYAI

The two righteous women of Zhuyai were the second wife of the mayor of Zhuyai and the daughter of his first wife.[70] The daughter's name was Chu, and she was thirteen years old.[71]

Zhuyai was rich in pearls, and the stepmother had strung together a number of large pearls to make a bracelet. When the mayor died, she made preparations to accompany the funeral cortege.[72] According to the law, anyone caught concealing pearls when crossing the border would be sentenced to death. The stepmother had cast aside her pearl bracelet, but her nine-year-old son was fond of it and had retrieved it, placing it in his mother's toiletry case. No one was aware of what he had done.

After attending the funeral, they returned home. When they reached the customs office, the head of customs and other officials searched their luggage and found ten large pearls in the stepmother's toiletry case. The official said, "This [offense] is [punishable] by law.[73] Since no exceptions can be made, who should be tried for this crime?"

Chu stood there as onlookers stared. She feared that her mother might confess that she had placed the pearls in the toiletry case, so she said, "I should be tried for this crime." The official said, "How did all of this come about?" She replied, "When my poor father passed away, my mother took off her bracelet and cast it aside. I pitied her and retrieved it, placing it in her toiletry case. She knew nothing about it." When the stepmother heard this she hurried to Chu's side and questioned her. Chu said, "I picked up the pearls you cast aside and put them in your case. So I should stand trial."

The stepmother thought that Chu was telling the truth and felt compassion for her, so she said to the official, "Please wait! I hope you will not charge this child. She actually knows nothing about it. The pearls came from my bracelet. When my husband died, I took it off and put the pearls in my case. Because I was burdened with arranging the funeral and traveling far away with two children, I simply forgot all about them. So I should stand trial."

But Chu stubbornly insisted, "It was actually I who took them." The stepmother then said, "The child is merely taking the blame for me. It was actually I who put them there." She then began to cry uncontrollably.

The girl then said, "My mother pities me because I am an orphan, so she is trying to persuade you to let me live. She actually knows nothing about this." She then began to cry as well until the tears streamed down her neck. Then everyone in the funeral cortege began to cry, and their sorrow moved bystanders until there was no one who was not sniffling and sobbing.

The customs inspector picked up his brush and was about to write out an accusation, but could not complete even one word, and for the entire day the head of customs shed tears and could not bear to pass judgment. He finally said, "This mother and child are so full of righteousness, I would rather stand trial for the crime myself than apply the law. Furthermore, because each one wants to take the blame for the other, how do I know which person actually did it?" He thereupon tossed away the pearls and sent them away. After they had left, they finally learned that it was the boy who had retrieved the pearls.

A man of discernment would say, "The two righteous women were kind and filial." The *Analects* says, "The father conceals the misconduct of the son, and the son conceals the misconduct of the father. Uprightness is to be found in this."[74] A stepmother and stepdaughter who were willing to yield and competed to die for each other, and who so moved onlookers, can indeed be called upright.

The Verse Summary says,

The woman of Zhuyai
Was full of maternal love.
The stepdaughter who was willing to take the blame
Was a virtuous daughter indeed.
When a pearl was brought through customs,
Each one accepted the guilt.
Two righteous women like these
Should have their names transmitted for all generations.

5.14 THE LOVING YOUNGER SISTER OF HEYANG

The loving younger sister was the wife of Ren Yanshou of the town of Heyang.[75] Her polite name was Jier, and she had three children.

Jier's elder brother, Jizong, once had a dispute with Yanshou over the burial of his father. So Yanshou and his friend, Tian Jian, secretly had Jizong killed. Tian Jian alone suffered the death penalty, while Yanshou, because of a general amnesty, went free.[76] When he told Jier what had happened, she said, "Why are you only telling me this now?" She then straightened her clothes, preparing to leave, and asked, "Who was the person who helped you kill my brother?"

Yanshou said, "Tian Jian. Tian Jian is already dead, so I alone must accept the guilt. Kill me and be done with it." Jier said, "To kill one's husband is wrong, but to serve the enemy of one's elder brother is also wrong."

Yanshou said, "I would not dare to make you stay, so I will give you the carriage, the horse, and all of the valuables in our home. I'll agree to your going wherever you want to go."

Jier said, "Where can I go? My elder brother is dead, and his enemy has not been avenged. I share pillow and mat with you, yet you had my brother killed. I am unable to live in peace with your family. Furthermore, if I let my elder brother's enemy go free, how can I live with Heaven above or tread the earth below?"

Yanshou was ashamed and left, not daring to look at Jier. Jier then told her eldest daughter, "Your father killed my elder brother. It would not be right to stay here, but I also cannot marry again. I am leaving you so that I may die. Please take good care of your two younger brothers."

She then hanged herself with swaddling bands and died. When the Metropolitan Superintendent Wang Rang heard about this incident, he admired her righteousness.[77] He ordered her district to exempt her three sons from compulsory labor service and display on her tomb an acknowledgment [of her virtue].[78]

A man of discernment would say, "The loving younger sister understood well how to requite her elder brother's enemy." The *Odes* says, "Committing no excess, doing nothing injurious,/There are few who will not take you for their pattern."[79] Jier could indeed serve as such a pattern.

The Verse Summary says,

Jier upheld righteousness
When her husband killed her elder brother.
She longed to punish her brother's enemy,
Yet her sense of righteousness would not allow it.
She could neither stay nor go,
So she visited misfortune upon herself.
The Metropolitan Superintendent displayed on her tomb
His admiration for her righteousness.

5.15 THE PRINCIPLED WOMAN OF THE CAPITAL

The principled woman of the capital was the wife of a man from the Dachang district of Chang'an. Her husband had enemies who wanted to take vengeance on him but could not find a way. They heard that his wife was benevolent, filial, and righteous, so they seized her father and then made him demand that she become their accomplice.

When her father summoned her and explained the situation, she tried to devise a plan, thinking, "If I disobey, they will kill my father, which would be unfilial. If I obey, they will kill my husband, which would be unrighteous. If I am unfilial and unrighteous, then although I might remain alive, I cannot go on in this world. So I will forfeit my life for theirs." She therefore went to them and agreed to their demands, saying, "Tomorrow, my husband will bathe and then lie down in the eastern part of the upper story [of our house]. I will open the window and await you there."[80]

When she returned home, she told her husband that she wanted to sleep where he usually slept. She herself then bathed in the upper story, opened the window on the eastern side, and lay down. At midnight, her husband's adversaries came to her house, cut off her head, and took it with them. The next day when they looked at it, they discovered that it was the head of their [intended victim's] wife. They were greatly saddened by this discovery, and in consideration of her righteousness, they relented and did not kill her husband.

A man of discernment would say, "The principled woman was benevolent and filial. Her compassion and righteousness were profound. Indeed, to value benevolence and righteousness, while thinking nothing of death, is the highest form of conduct." The *Analects* says, "People of quality will sacrifice their lives to preserve their virtue complete. They will not seek to live at the expense of injuring their virtue."[81] This saying applies well to her.

The Verse Summary says,

The principled woman of the capital
Saw her father seized by her husband's enemies.
They forced her to cooperate,
And she did not dare to refuse.
After settling on a time and place,
She changed places with her husband.
She sacrificed her life in an act of benevolence,
And her righteousness reigned supreme under Heaven.

6

THE ACCOMPLISHED RHETORICIANS

PREFACE

Only those such as the Accomplished Rhetoricians
Convey words worth heeding.
They use analogies and cite examples
To ward off trouble and disaster.
They promote and prohibit all manner of things,
Without ever repeating themselves.
To the very end, with unfailing devotion,
They elaborate their thoughts for the sake of the public good.
Wives and concubines who make them their models
Will be praised by the whole world.

6.1 JING, CONCUBINE OF GUAN ZHONG

The concubine Jing was the concubine of Guan Zhong, prime minister of Qi.[1]

[A man named] Ning Qi once wanted to see Duke Huan but had no way to bring this about.[2] So he took a job as another man's driver and drove a cart to the east gate of Qi, where he stopped for the night. When Duke Huan came out, Ning Qi tapped the horn of his ox and sang a song in the tone of *shang*.[3] It was full of sorrow. Duke Huan was intrigued by this, so he ordered Guan Zhong to receive him. Ning Qi then declared, "How vast, the white water." But Guan

Zhong did not understand what he meant. So for five days he did not attend court and looked worried.

His concubine came to him and said, "You, my lord, look worried and have not attended court for five days now. If I may ask, is it because of state business? Or perhaps because of one of your own affairs?" Guan Zhong said, "It's nothing you would understand."

Jing replied, "I have heard, 'Do not treat the old as old, the humble as humble, the young as young, or the weak as weak.'" Guan Zhong said, "What do you mean?"

"Formerly, Taigong Wang at age seventy butchered oxen in the marketplace of Zhaoge.[4] At eighty he was tutor to the Son of Heaven, and by ninety he was enfeoffed with the state of Qi.[5] Taking this into account, should one treat the old as old? As for Yi Yin, he served as part of Youshen's bridal entourage.[6] When Tang established him as one of the Three Ducal Ministers, all under Heaven was well governed and peaceful.[7] From this perspective, should one treat the humble as humble? Gaozi was only five years old when he assisted Yu.[8] Should the young then be treated as young? A *jueti* mule is able to outrun its mother seven days after it is born.[9] Taking this into consideration, should the weak be treated as weak?"

Guan Zhong moved back on his mat and apologized to her, saying, "Please allow me to explain to you.[10] The other day when the duke ordered me to receive Ning Qi, Ning Qi said, 'How vast, the white water.' I have no idea what he meant. That is why I have been worried." His concubine smiled, saying, "He has already as much as told you. Don't you recognize those lines? Aren't they from the old poem 'White Water' that goes,

> Vast, vast, the white water,
> Small, small, the fish.
> My lord is coming to summon me,
> So I will settle there.
> The country is in turmoil,
> So why not follow me there?[11]

This poem expresses Ning Qi's wish to assume office in our state.'"

Guan Zhong was delighted and reported the news to Duke Huan. Duke Huan then prepared an official residence, and fasted for five days before holding an audience with Ningzi. He gave him the post of minister, and the state of Qi was well governed thereafter.

A man of discernment would say, "The concubine Jing can be regarded as one who was worth consulting." The *Odes* says, "The ancients had a saying:/'Consult the grass and firewood gatherers.'"[12] These words apply well to this case.

The Verse Summary says,

When Duke Huan encountered Ning Qi,
He ordered Guan Zhong to receive him.
But when Ning Qi recited "White Water,"
Guan Zhong became anxious.
After the concubine went in and inquired about it,
She was able to explain the ode for him.
Guan Zhong commended Ning to the duke,
And Qi thereby secured the means to good government.

6.2 THE MOTHER OF JIANG YI OF CHU

The mother of Jiang Yi of Chu was the mother of the Chu grandee Jiang Yi.[13] Once, in the time of King Gong, when Yi served as a grandee in Ying, a burglar entered the royal palace.[14] The prime minister held Yi responsible for the crime and asked the king that he be dismissed.

Not long after Yi had returned home, his mother lost eight yards of cloth. She went to speak to the king, saying, "Last night eight yards of cloth went missing. The prime minister has stolen them."

At the time, the king was in the Xiaoqu Terrace, where the prime minister was in attendance. The king told the mother, "If the prime minister has in fact stolen from you, I will apply the law without consideration of his wealth or position. But if he did not steal and you are slandering him, the state of Chu has a standard law for that as well."[15] The mother said, "The prime minister did not steal it himself but rather caused someone else to steal it." The king said, "How is it that he caused someone to steal it?"

She replied, "Formerly, when Sunshu Ao served as prime minister, no one picked up things left on the road, doors were never bolted shut, and theft and burglary stopped of their own accord.[16] But now, under the rule of the present prime minister, no one seems to be watching or listening, so burglars and thieves act openly. Because of this, he has caused a burglar to steal my cloth. How is this any different from inciting people to steal?"

The king said, "The prime minister moves in the highest circles, whereas a bandit occupies the lowest. What crime is there in his not knowing what they are up to?" The mother said, "Alas, Your Majesty could not be more mistaken! Formerly, when my son served as grandee in Ying, someone burgled the palace. My son was charged with the crime and dismissed. He too knew nothing about it, yet in the end he was charged with the crime. What makes the prime minister an exception and thus not held accountable for this crime?

"Formerly, King Wu of Zhou stated, 'If any of the common people commits a fault, the responsibility rests in me.'[17] If superiors are unenlightened, then their inferiors will not be well ruled. If ministers are not worthy, the state will not be at peace. The phrase 'The state lacks people' doesn't mean that there are no people, but that it lacks people who are capable of ruling others. Your Majesty should look into this."

The king said, "Well said! You have not only admonished the prime minister, you have admonished me as well!" The king then ordered an official to repay her for the cloth and present her with ten *yi* of cash. But she refused the cloth and cash, saying, "I would never have challenged Your Majesty because I thought I might stand to gain from it. It was simply a case of my dissatisfaction with the rule of the prime minister!" She then left, refusing to accept anything. The king said, "The son of a mother who is this wise is clearly no fool." He then summoned Jiang Yi and reinstated him.

A man of discernment would say, "Yi's mother was skilled at subtle instruction." The *Odes* says, "Your plans do not reach far,/And I therefore strongly admonish you."[18] This phrase applies well to her speech.

The Verse Summary says,

When Jiang Yi lost his position,
His mother took it to heart.
After he returned to live at home,
Eight yards of cloth were stolen.
She blamed the prime minister
In wisely measured words.
The king reinstated Yi,
And presented his mother with cloth and cash.

6.3 THE WIFE OF THE BOW MAKER OF JIN

The bow maker's wife was the daughter of an armor craftsman of Jin.[19] In the time of Duke Ping, the duke ordered her husband to make a bow.[20] After three years it was finished. When the duke drew the bow and shot, the arrow did not pierce even one layer of armor. The duke was angry and was about to execute the bow maker.

The bow maker's wife thereupon begged for an audience, saying, "I am the daughter of an armor craftsman and the wife of the bow maker. I would like to be granted an audience." When Duke Ping met with her she said, "Have you heard of Gong Liu's conduct in former times?[21] Whenever the sheep and oxen trampled their rushes and reeds, he felt great pity for the common people, and his concern even extended to plants and trees. Would he have countenanced the killing of an innocent person? Duke Mu of Qin encountered bandits who ate the meat of his fine steed, but he gave them wine to drink.[22] When an officer of King Zhuang of Chu tugged at his consort's robe, she tore off his hat tassel. But the king later drank with him quite happily.[23] As for these three rulers, their benevolence became known to the entire world. Eventually each one was requited [for their kindness], and their names have been passed down to present times.

"Formerly, Yao did not trim the thatch of his roof or carve its mottled beams. He had earthen steps of only three levels.[24] Even so, he felt that his workmen had toiled hard and that he was living in great comfort. Now, when my husband made this bow, his efforts were also laborious. The bow's shaft came from wood grown on the slopes of Mount Tai, and each day he would examine it three times in both the sunlight and the shade. It is decorated with the horn of oxen from Yan, bound with the tendons of deer from Jing, and glued together with adhesive derived from Yellow River fish. Since these four things are among the most select and extraordinary materials in the world, your inability to pierce even one layer of armor must be due to your inability to shoot. Yet you want to kill my husband. Isn't this mistaken?

"I have heard that in the Way of Archery, one's left hand should be held as firm as a rock, while the right hand should be held like a diagonal support beam. When the right hand releases the arrow, the left hand should not be aware of it. This is the Way of Archery."

When Duke Ping did what she said and shot, the arrow pierced seven layers of armor. The woman's husband was immediately set free and given three *yi* in cash.

A man of discernment would say, "The bow maker's wife was able to offer assistance in difficulty." The *Odes* says, "The ornamented bows are strong," and "They discharge the arrows and all hit."[25] This phrase describes the methods of archery.

The Verse Summary says,

Duke Ping of Jin commissioned a bow,
Which took three years to complete.
But he became angry with the bow maker

And was on the verge of punishing him.
The wife went and spoke to the duke,
And explained what materials were used in the bow.
She set forth the labor and difficulty involved,
And the duke thereupon released him.

6.4 THE WOMAN OF THE INJURED LOCUST TREE OF QI

The woman of the injured locust tree of Qi was the daughter of a man named Yan who damaged a locust tree.[26] Her name was Jing.

Duke Jing once had a locust tree that he loved.[27] He ordered someone to guard it and put up a wooden signpost with a proclamation that said, "Tampering with this locust will result in punishment. Damaging this locust will result in execution." After this had been done, Yan became intoxicated and damaged the tree. When the duke heard about it, he said, "He is the first to violate my proclamation." He then ordered an official to apprehend Yan and charge him with the crime.

Jing, in a state of alarm, went to the residence of the minister Yanzi and said, "Although your humble handmaiden is not worthy of this request, I wish to add myself to the ranks of your attendants."[28] When Yanzi heard this, he laughed and said, "Do I look like a lustful person? Why would she be offering herself to an old man like me? She probably has something she wants to tell me. Ask her to come in."

When she came through the gate, Yanzi saw her from afar and said, "That's odd! She looks deeply distressed." He then urged her to come forward and asked her to explain.

She responded, saying, "My father, Yan, has been fortunate enough to be counted as a resident of the city. He observed that the forces of yin and yang were out of balance, the wind and rain were not timely, and the five grains were not flourishing. For this reason he prayed and sacrificed to the great mountains and sacred rivers. But because he was no match for the sacrificial wine, he was the first to offend against the duke's proclamation. And because his intoxication had such serious implications, he is certain to be sentenced to death.

"I have heard that in governing the state, an enlightened ruler does not decrease salaries or increase punishments. He also does not tamper with public laws because of personal resentments, harm people for the sake of the six domestic animals, or damage sprouting grain in favor of [maintaining] wild pastureland.[29]

"Formerly, during the time of Duke Jing of Song, there was a great drought, and it did not rain for three years.[30] The Director of Divination was summoned and divined about it, saying, 'A sacrifice in the form of a person should be made.' Duke Jing descended from the hall, faced north, and kowtowed, saying, 'It is for the sake of my people that I request rain. Now, if I must sacrifice a person, then I beg to fulfill that role.' Before he could finish speaking, the heavens poured forth a great rain that covered an area of a thousand square *li*. Now, why did that happen? It was because he was able to subordinate himself to Heaven and to treat the people with kindness.

"Now, our ruler planted a locust tree and decreed that anyone who damages it will die. Further, because of this tree, he is going to kill my father and make me an orphan. I fear that this will damage his ability to govern and impair his reputation as an enlightened ruler. If neighboring states hear about it, they will say that he loves trees but abuses people. Can that be allowed to happen?"

Yanzi was alarmed and instantly understood. The next day he went to court and told Duke Jing, saying, "I have heard that exhausting the wealth and labor of the people is called tyranny. Worshipping trifles and playthings while imposing severe laws is called perversity. Decreeing punishments and executions that are unjust is called abuse. These three pose a great danger to the security of the state.

"At present, Your Majesty's exhausting the wealth and labor of the people in order to prepare lavish food and drink, increase musical performances of bells and drums, and maximize the number of palace buildings and structures is the most egregious form tyranny. Worshipping trifles and playthings while imposing severe laws is a flagrantly perverse way to treat the people. Punishing those who tamper with your locust tree, killing those who damage the tree, and exacting unjust punishments and executions are the most profound abuses of the people."

The duke said, "I will accept your directives." Yanzi left, and Duke Jing immediately dismissed the person guarding the locust tree, pulled up the wooden signpost, repealed the law against damaging the tree, and released the man who had been imprisoned for harming it.

A man of discernment would say, "Through her rhetorical skill, the woman of the injured locust tree was able to spare [her father] from punishment." The *Odes* says, "Examine this and study it;/Will you not find that it is truly so?"[31] These lines apply well to her actions.

The Verse Summary says,

Duke Jing loved his locust tree,
But a drunken man damaged it.
When Duke Jing was about to execute him,
His daughter trembled with fear.
She rushed to inform Yanzi,
And cited with praise the kings of former times.
Yanzi spoke in her favor,
And her father escaped calamity.

6.5 THE DISCRIMINATING WOMAN OF THE CHU COUNTRYSIDE

The discriminating woman from Chu's countryside was the wife of a Mr. Zhao.

Once, Duke Jian of Zheng sent a grandee to Jing on an official visit.[32] When he got to a narrow part of the road, he encountered a woman driving a cart. The hub of her wheel knocked against and snapped off the axle rod of the grandee's carriage. When the grandee became angry and was about to seize and whip her, the woman said, "I have heard that 'A gentleman does not misdirect anger nor does he shift blame.'[33] Just now, in this narrow road, I had already [moved over] as far as possible, but your driver didn't give way in the least. This is what damaged your carriage, but instead you seized on me. Isn't this a case of misdirected anger? Moreover, you were not mad at the driver but perversely vented your anger on me. Isn't this shifting the blame?

"The *Book of Zhou* says, 'Do not oppress widowers and widows; and hold in awe the illustrious.'[34] You hold the rank of grandee, yet your behavior is far from exemplary. Furthermore, you misdirected your anger and shifted the blame by letting off your driver and holding me responsible. You look down on those who are less important and weaker than you. Can that be called 'not oppressing widowers and widows'? If you are going to whip me, then whip me. What I will pity then is the loss of your decency."

The grandee was ashamed and unable to respond. He thereupon released her and asked her some questions, to which she replied, "I am a humble woman from Chu's countryside." The grandee said, "Why not follow me to Zheng?" She responded, saying, "I already have a humble husband, Mr. Zhao, back at home."[35] She then left.

A man of discernment would say, "The discriminating woman was able to use her rhetorical skills to escape difficulty." The *Odes* says, "For my freely expressing myself thus,/I have reason, I have good ground."[36] This phrase applies well to her.

The Verse Summary says,

The discriminating woman driving alone
Encountered an official from Zheng.
The official's axle was broken,
So he seized the woman in anger.
The grievance she set forth
Was so clearly arranged
That the official from Zheng was ashamed and left,
Not daring to say more.

6.6 THE MAIDEN OF THE MOUNTAIN VALLEY

The Maiden of the Mountain Valley was a woman [encountered while] washing her clothes alongside the road in a mountain valley.[37]

Once, when Confucius was traveling south and crossed a road running through a mountain valley, he saw a maiden wearing a jade girdle-pendant washing clothes. Confucius said to Zigong, "Do you think this washerwoman is someone we can converse with?"[38] He drew out a goblet [from his pack] and gave it to Zigong, saying, "Say something to her so we can observe her inclinations."

Zigong said, "I am a humble man of the north. I've been traveling from north to south, in hopes of reaching Chu. We're finding the summer weather we've encountered very hot. May I have a drink to refresh me?"

The maiden said, "The roads in this valley are isolated and full of twists and turns. Here, one current of the river runs clear, while the other is muddy, as it flows into the sea. If you want a drink, then drink. Why ask me for it?" But she accepted Zigong's goblet and filled it with water running against the current, then discarded it, pouring it out. Then she filled it to overflowing with water running with the current. She knelt and placed it on the sand, saying, "According to the rites, I must not hand [it to you]."[39]

Zigong returned and reported her words to Confucius, who said, "Just as I thought!" He then took out his lute, removed one of the pegs, and gave it to Zigong, saying, "Say something to her [about this]."

Zigong then approached her and said, "Earlier, when I heard your words, they were 'majestic like a fresh breeze,' neither harsh nor discourteous, with a restorative effect on my mind.[40] I have a lute, but a peg is missing. Can you tune it for me?"

The maiden said, "I am a humble person from the countryside, unrefined and ignorant. I know nothing about the five notes; how should I be capable of tuning your lute?"

Zigong reported this to Confucius, and Confucius said, "I knew it! When she encounters a worthy she treats him courteously."[41] He then took out five *liang* of fine and coarse cloth and gave it to Zigong, saying, "Say something to her [about this]!"[42]

Zigong then approached her, saying, "I am a humble man from the north. I am traveling from north to south in hopes of reaching Chu. I have five *liang* of both fine and coarse cloth. Though I would not dare to consider it sufficient for you, I would like to leave it here beside the water."

The maiden said, "Traveler, [you have lingered here] sighing for quite some time now and wish to divide up your wealth and throw it away on a humble country girl.[43] I am very young; how dare I accept [this from] you? [Though] you have not yet married, I have already learned the name of my betrothed."[44]

Zigong reported this to Confucius, who said, "I knew it! This woman understands human emotion and comprehends propriety as well."

The *Odes* says, "In the south rise the trees without branches,/Affording no shelter./By the Han are girls rambling about,/But it is vain to solicit them."[45] These words apply to her.

The Verse Summary says,

Confucius went out traveling
Through a mountain valley in the south.
He was intrigued by a maiden there,
And wanted to observe her customs.
When Zigong approached her three times,
Her words were discriminating and profound.
The Master said that she understood emotions,
Comprehended the rites, and was not depraved.

6.7 JUAN, THE WOMAN OF THE FERRY OF ZHAO

Juan, the woman of the Zhao ferry, was the daughter of a river ferry official of Zhao and the wife of Zhao Jianzi.[46] In the beginning, Jianzi went south to attack

Chu. He arranged a time with the ferry official, but when Jianzi arrived, the ferryman was collapsed in a drunken stupor, so he was not able to cross. Jianzi was angry and wanted to kill him.

Alarmed by the situation, Juan picked up the oar and fled. When Jianzi asked, "Why are you running away?" she replied, "I am the daughter of the ferryman. When my father heard that you were going east and making the crossing in unpredictable currents, he was afraid that winds and waves would arise and stir the water spirits. So he prayed and sacrificed to the spirits of the Nine Rivers and the Three Huai.[47] His offerings were complete and the rites were performed to perfection to bring forth blessings.[48] But he was no match for the last drops of the shaman's sacrificial wine, and that is how he became so intoxicated. If you wish to kill my father, I would like to offer myself to die in exchange for him."

Jianzi said, "But this is not your crime." Juan said, "You may wish to kill him because of his drunkenness. But I fear that [if] he is unable to feel any physical pain, he will not be aware that he has committed a crime. If you kill him while he is unaware of his crime, this will be tantamount to killing an innocent.[49] You should therefore wait until he wakes up to kill him so that you can make him aware of his crime." Jianzi said, "Well proposed!" He then released the ferryman and did not kill him.[50]

When Jianzi was about to ford the river, they were short one oarsman. So Juan rolled up her sleeves, took up an oar, and said, "I live between the Yellow and Ji rivers, and for generations we have worked with ferry boats, so I would like to fill in for the missing oarsman."[51] Jianzi said, "Just before I left, the officers and grandees I chose [for this mission] fasted, purified themselves, and bathed. It would not be right for them to ford the river in the same boat as a woman."

Juan replied, "I have heard that when Tang defeated the Xia, the horse on the left of his team of four was a black mare, and the one on the right was a *mi* mare, and he was thus able to expel Jie.[52] When King Wu defeated the Yin, the horse on the left of his team of four was a dappled gray mare, while the horse on the right was a brown piebald mare, and thus he was able to defeat Zhow all the way to the south of Mount Hua.[53] If you, sir, don't want to ford the river, then no more need be said. But what harm is there in sharing a boat with me?" Jianzi was pleased at this.

He thereupon forded the river with her, and midway Juan composed a song for him called "The Surging River." Its lyrics were:

Upon the boat, gazing west at the clear [river],[54]
The waves rose in the water, while in the distance, all was darkness.

He had prayed for blessings, but was overcome with wine.
The death sentence was about to be applied, and my heart filled with fear.
But now that he is free from harm, the river runs clear!
I take up the oar and grasp the moorings,
With the scaly dragons' help, my lord will indeed return.
With a call to the rowers, we move ahead free of doubt and fear!

Jianzi was greatly pleased. He said, "Earlier, I dreamed that I took a wife. Could it be this woman?" He then ordered someone to offer prayers so that she might become his wife. But Juan bowed to him twice and refused him, saying, "According to the rites for women, if there is no matchmaker there can be no marriage. Moreover, with very strict parents at home, I dare not entertain your request." She then made her apologies and left. When Jianzi returned, he presented gifts to her parents and had her established as his wife.[55]

A man of discernment would say, "The woman Juan was intelligent and articulate." The *Odes* says, "Rambling and singing,/I took occasion to give forth my notes."[56] These words apply well to this case.

The Verse Summary says,

When Zhao Jianzi wished to ford the river,
The ferry official was in his cups.
Jianzi planned to apply the death sentence,
And the woman Juan trembled with fear.
She took up an oar and set forth an explanation;
Her father was then spared misfortune.
Her worth could not be hidden for long,
And in the end became known to all.

6.8 THE MOTHER OF BI XI OF ZHAO

The mother of Bi Xi of Zhao was the mother of Bi Xi, the district magistrate of Zhongmou in Zhao.[57] Using Zhongmou as a stronghold, Bi Xi rebelled.[58] According to the laws of Zhao, all those who used a city to rebel would be executed and their families would be taken into custody.[59]

When Bi Xi's mother was about to be sentenced, she said to herself, "I should not be given the death sentence." When a senior official asked her about it, the mother replied, "Let me communicate with the ruler. If I can't speak to him directly, then this old lady will simply have to die." So the official spoke to Xiangzi on her behalf.[60] When Xiangzi had him question her about her reasons, the mother said, "If I can't see the ruler, then I have nothing to say."[61] Xiangzi thereupon agreed to see her, and asked, "Why should you not be given the death sentence?"

The mother said, "Why *should* I be given the death sentence?" Xiangzi said, "Your son rebelled." The mother said, "If a son rebels, why should the mother be punished with death?" Xiangzi said, "If a mother is unable to teach her son well, then it is she who has caused him to behave in a way that leads to rebellion. That being the case, why shouldn't a mother be subject to the death sentence?"

The mother said, "I thought you, sir, would have a good explanation for deciding to execute me. But instead, your reason is simply that I failed to educate my son? I finished doing that a long time ago. This matter is in fact your responsibility. I have heard that when a child is young and lazy, it is the fault of the mother. When he grows up and is of no use, then it is the father's responsibility. Now, when my son was young, he was not lazy. When he grew up, he was perfectly employable. So how is this situation my fault?

"I have heard that when a son is young, he acts as one's son. When he is grown, he acts as one's friend, and when one's husband dies, then one obeys one's son. I was able to make him into a grown man for you. You yourself selected him to serve as your minister. My son's role in this investigation is as your minister, not as my son. You have a violent minister. I don't have a violent son. That is why I say that I am innocent." Xiangzi said, "Well argued! Bi Xi's rebellion is indeed my fault." He then released her.

A man of discernment would say, "In the course of one conversation, Bi Xi's mother was able to make Xiangzi reconsider. She prompted him to refrain from shifting blame and thus obtained her own freedom." The *Odes* says, "Now that I have seen my lord,/My heart is entirely satisfied."[62] This phrase applies well to her case.

The Verse Summary says,

After Bi Xi rebelled,
His mother employed good logic.
When she was about to be sentenced,
She spoke to Xiangzi herself.
She set forth a mother's duties,
For her son, now grown, was the ruler's responsibility.
Xiangzi was pleased with her argument
And released her without charges.

6.9 LADY YU OF KING WEI OF QI

Lady Yu had the given name Juanzhi.[63] She was a high-ranking concubine of King Wei of Qi.[64] When King Wei assumed the throne, he did not rule for nine years but delegated governing to his senior ministers, so that the feudal lords began to encroach on [Qi].[65] One of his unscrupulous ministers, Zhou Pohu, monopolized power and began to act on his own authority. He was jealous of the worthy and envious of those with ability. In Jimo there was a worthy grandee whom he defamed day after day. While in E, there was an unprincipled grandee who, on the contrary, received his praises daily.[66]

Lady Yu told the king, "Pohu is a minister given to slander and flattery; you must send him away. In Qi there is a certain Mr. Beiguo, who is worthy, enlightened, and moral. He can join the ranks of your advisors." Pohu heard about this incident and then began to hate Lady Yu. He said, "In the village where she lived as a youth, she had an affair with Mr. Beiguo." The king then began to suspect her. So he shut her in a tower with nine stories and ordered an official immediately to begin a thorough investigation of her. Pohu bribed the official investigating her crime. So the official falsified her statement and sent it to the king.

When the king saw her statement, he felt that something was amiss, so he summoned Lady Yu and asked her about it himself.

Lady Yu said, "I have been fortunate to have received this body from my ancestors and to have been born here, between Heaven and earth. I left my humble thatched cottage and came to serve you, my enlightened sovereign, in his leisure moments. I waited upon you in your retiring room, laying out your bedroll and storing your mats.[67] I took care of sweeping and cleaning for you, and had the honor to superintend your bathing, all for more than ten years now. It was with great concern that I hoped to offer a word of advice to you. But I have been subjected to the maneuvering of a corrupt minister who has hidden me here a hundred layers deep. I never imagined that Your Majesty would see me again and speak with me.

"I have heard that jade that falls into mud is not considered polluted, and that when Liuxia Hui embraced a freezing woman, he was not regarded as debauched. This is because [a good reputation] accumulated [gradually] through consistent [behavior] is not subject to suspicion.[68] But 'a person passing through a melon field does not bend over to tie his shoes, and someone walking in a plum orchard does not adjust his hat.'[69] That I did not avoid these things was my first crime.

"After I fell into trouble, an official who received bribes allowed himself to be used by evildoers, so that I was falsely implicated but unable to set the record straight for myself. I have heard that once a widowed wife wept beside a wall and the wall collapsed in response.[70] There was also the fugitive officer whose sighs in the marketplace caused the market to close.[71] When sincerity develops within, it can move even walls and markets. My injustice is clearer than the sun, and though I cried out all alone, from within these nine stories, no one was the least bit moved. This is my second crime.[72] Because I have added these two crimes to my already sullied name, then naturally, it is not right that I should be allowed to live. But what keeps me alive is that I have not yet been able to clear my name.

"From ancient times onward there have been similar cases. Boqi was cast into the wilds.[73] Shensheng suffered calamity.[74] Though their filial piety and obedience were abundantly clear, they were nevertheless regarded as miscreants. Because I have already been sentenced to death, I will not repeat my case. But I would like to warn Your Majesty that your ministers are doing evil, and Pohu is the worst offender. If you do not assume your duty to govern, the state will be imperiled."

After this the king realized [his error]. He released Lady Yu, and honored her at court and in the market.[75] He enfeoffed the grandee of Jimo with ten thousand households, and boiled the grandee of E along with Zhou Pohu. He then raised troops and reclaimed the land that had been taken from him and awed all of Qi. Once people learned that he had boiled the grandee of E, no one dared to conceal wrongdoing but concentrated all efforts on fulfilling their responsibilities, so that the state of Qi became well governed.

A man of discernment would say, "Lady Yu was fond of goodness." The *Odes* says, "Let me see my husband,/And my heart will be at rest."[76] This phrase applies well to her case.

The Verse Summary says,

> The government of Qi had become lax,
> Bereft of rule for nine years.
> Lady Yu protested,
> But instead brought harm to herself.
> She set forth the situation,
> Pointing to august Heaven above.
> King Wei awakened to the truth
> And opposed the might of Qin.[77]

6.10 ZHONGLI CHUN OF QI

Zhongli Chun was a woman of the city of Wuyan in Qi and the queen of King Xuan.[78] She was peerless in her sheer ugliness. Her head was rounded like a bowl, and her eyes were deep set. She was tall, strong, and big-boned. She had an upturned nose and an Adam's apple. Her neck was stout and her hair was thin. She was stooped at the waist and had a protruding chest. Her skin appeared to be lacquered. She was already forty years old but had not been taken by anyone. She boasted of her marriageability but had found no mate. She wandered about but met only with rejection. So she brushed clean her short, rough robe and went to see King Xuan.

She told the herald, "I am a woman of Qi who cannot find a mate. I have heard of the king's sage virtue and would like to join the ranks of those who clean the rear palace.[79] I therefore prostrate myself before the Sima Gate with the hope that the king will allow it."[80]

When the herald made her request known, the king had just served wine on the Jian Terrace. When all assembled heard about it, they covered their mouths and laughed, saying, "She must be the world's most audacious woman! How peculiar!"

King Xuan then summoned her for an audience and told her, "Long ago our former sovereign made arrangements to find me marriage partners, and they now fill all the various ranks [designated for palace women].[81] Since you cannot presently find a match among the common people of the villages but seek the lord of ten thousand chariots, what extraordinary abilities do you possess?" Zhongli Chun said, "I have none. If I may say so, I simply admire Your Majesty's great righteousness."

The king said, "That may be the case, but what are you good at?"[82] After a long while, she said, "If I may be so bold, I am good at riddles."[83] The king said, "A riddle is exactly what I'd like to hear. Try one out on me!" But before [she] had even finished reciting it, [King Xuan] was quite lost.[84] Greatly flustered, the king got out *The Book of Riddles* and began reading it.[85] Then he withdrew and continued to analyze the riddle but was still unable to solve it.

The next day he summoned her again and questioned her, but she did not respond with a riddle. She merely opened her eyes wide, clenched her jaw, then raised her hand and slapped her knee, saying, "Danger, danger! It will come in four forms." King Xuan said, "I wish to hear your instructions."

Zhongli Chun replied, saying, "At present, in Your Majesty's administration of the state, in the west you face the problem of the overbearing Qin, and to the south you face the enmity of the mighty Chu. Externally you have the difficulties posed by these two states. Internally you have collected about you corrupt ministers, while the masses have no attachment to you. You are forty years old, yet you have not yet established an adult son to succeed you. You devote no attention to your sons, yet you concentrate on your wives, honoring those for whom you feel fondness and neglecting those whom you should trust. One day you will die, and the altars to the soil and grain will be unstable. This is the first danger.

"In your construction of the Jian Terrace, with its five levels, its gold and white jade embellishments, its ruby-studded mats and coverings, and its malachite, pearl, and gem adornments, you have exhausted your people.[86] This is the second danger.

"Worthies abscond to the mountains and forests, while flatterers dominate the ranks of your followers. The evil and deceptive populate your court, while those who admonish cannot gain admittance. This is the third evil.

"You drink to the point of drunkenness from night to dawn, and indulge yourself in the performances of female musicians and actors with great abandon and frivolity. Yet abroad you do not cultivate the rites of the feudal lords and at home you do not maintain authority in your state. This is the fourth danger. That is why I said, 'Danger, danger!'"

After this King Xuan sighed with regret, saying, "It pains me that I have only heard the words of the Lady of Wuyan today!"[87] Thereafter he tore down the Jian Terrace, discontinued the performances of his female musicians, sent away the flatterers, and removed the cut and polished gems [of his décor]. He then selected weapons and horses, filled his treasury, and opened up his four gates to summon and promote those who would speak honestly, with his invitation extending to the obscure and humble. He then divined to determine an auspicious day, established an heir apparent, appointed a Loving Matron [for the heir], and honored the Lady of Wuyan as his queen.[88] The great peace in the state of Qi was thus due to the efforts of this ugly woman.

A man of discernment would say, "Zhongli Chun was upright and possessed rhetorical skill." The *Odes* says, "Having seen our noble lord,/Our hearts are full of joy."[89] This phrase applies well to her.

The Verse Summary says,

> The woman of Wuyan
> Sought and addressed King Xuan of Qi.
> She distinguished the four dangers,
> And declared the state chaotic and troubled.

King Xuan followed her advice,
And opened his four gates.
He established an heir apparent,
And honored the Lady of Wuyan.

6.11 THE LUMP-NECKED WOMAN OF QI

The lump-necked woman was a mulberry picker of Dongguo in Qi.[90] She was also the queen of King Min of Qi.[91] There was a large lump on her neck, so she was called "Lump Neck."

Once, King Min went on an outing. When he came to Dongguo, all the people stared intently at him. Only Lump Neck went on picking mulberry leaves. The king was intrigued by this, so he summoned her and asked, "When I go for an outing, with a great array of carriages and horses, the common people old and young alike never fail to abandon their tasks and stare. But you went on picking mulberry leaves by the side of the road, never looking at me even once.[92] Why is that?"

She answered, saying, "I received instructions from my parents to pick mulberry leaves; I did not receive instructions to stare at Your Majesty." The king said, "What an extraordinary woman! And what a pity that you are lump-necked!" The woman said, "As for your handmaiden's occupation, I have only been charged with one task, and since I dare not forget it, what else would occupy my mind? And what harm is there in being lump-necked?" The king was greatly delighted with her, saying, "This woman is a worthy!"

He then ordered her to be put in one of the carriages in his entourage. The woman said, "I trust in the powers of Your Majesty. But [I must consider my] father and mother at home. If you order me to disobey their teachings and accompany Your Majesty, I will become a fallen woman.[93] Of what use would I be to you then?" The king was ashamed and said, "I am in error." The woman said, "For a pure maiden, if the rites are not complete, she would rather die than comply."

The king therefore sent her back and ordered an emissary with one hundred *yi* in cash to go ahead to arrange a betrothal and retrieve her. Her parents were very surprised and wanted to bathe and dress her. The woman said, "When I saw the king, this is how I looked. If I alter my appearance and change my clothes, he will not recognize me." After begging permission to die rather than go, she was eventually allowed to follow the emissary without changing a thing.

When King Min returned and saw all of his women, he told them, "Today when I went out, I acquired a female sage. She will arrive today to teach each and every one of you a thing or two." The women were all intrigued and assembled around the king in full dress. When she finally arrived, Lump-Neck took everyone by surprise. All of the women covered their mouths and laughed, while the attendants lost their composure and could not stop themselves [from laughing].

The king was greatly embarrassed and said, "Now don't laugh. At the moment she is simply not adorned [in court finery]. She will look a thousand times better when she is [appropriately] dressed." The woman said, "Even if you had said that by adorning myself there would be a *ten million*fold difference, this would still not describe it adequately. So why discuss it as nothing more than a thousandfold difference?"

The king said, "How can you say that?" She replied, "'People by nature are similar, it is in practice that they differ.'[94] Formerly, Yao, Shun, Jie, and Zhow were all Sons of Heaven.[95] Yao and Shun adorned themselves with benevolence and righteousness. Although they were Sons of Heaven, they were content with moderation and frugality. Their thatched roofs went untrimmed, and their oaken rafter beams were not carved. The women in their palaces did not favor sumptuous fabrics for their clothing, nor were they particular about food. And for the last thousand years down to the present, all under Heaven have ascribed goodness to them.

"Jie and Zhow did not adorn themselves with benevolence and righteousness. Their practice was to make harsh decrees and to construct high towers and deep pools. The women in their palaces minced about in fine silks and indulged themselves with pearls and jade. At no time were their desires sated. When they died, their states perished, and they became the laughingstock of all under Heaven. For more than a thousand years to the present, all under Heaven have ascribed wickedness to them. From this perspective, even if you said that there is a ten millionfold difference between adorning oneself and not adorning oneself, it would still be an inadequate comparison. So how can you say that the difference would merely be a thousandfold?"

After this, the ladies were all very ashamed. King Min was greatly moved and made the lump-necked woman his queen. He also issued a decree to lower the palace buildings, fill up the ponds and pools, restrict lavish meals, reduce musical performances, and cut off supplies of fine silk to the rear palace. In several months, the transformation spread to neighboring states, and all of the feudal lords came to Qi's court. [King Min] then invaded the three Jin, struck terror in Qin and Chu, and set himself up with the title "emperor."[96] That King Min was able to accomplish all of this was due to the efforts of the lump-necked woman. After she died, [the kingdom of Yan] destroyed Qi. King Min fled and was murdered abroad.[97]

A man of discernment would say, "The lump-necked woman was intelligent and acted with propriety." The *Odes* says, "Luxuriantly grows the aster-southernwood/In the midst of that large mound./Having seen our noble lord,/We rejoice and he shows us all courtesy."[98] These words apply well to this account.

The Verse Summary says,

> Qi's lump-necked woman
> Was picking mulberry leaves at Dongguo.
> When King Min ventured out on a leisure trip,
> She did not alter her behavior in the least.
> The king wanted to speak with her,
> And her words of advice were perceptive indeed.
> In the end she rose to the rank of queen,
> And her reputation was illustrious.

6.12 THE OUTCAST ORPHAN MAID OF QI

The outcast orphan maid was a woman from Jimo in Qi and the wife of the prime minister of Qi.[99] In the beginning, the outcast orphan maid, being without father or mother and having grown to be very ugly, was driven from her district three times and from her village five times. She had passed the marriageable age without finding anyone who would provide a home for her.

The prime minister of Qi's wife died, so the outcast maid went to the gate of King Xiang, and upon seeing the herald, said, "I have been driven from my district three times and from my village five times. I am an orphan without father or mother and have been rejected and cast into the wilds without any place to live. I hope to see His Majesty so that I may speak to him in my own foolish words."[100]

When the attendants reported this to the king, he stopped eating, spat out a mouthful of half-chewed food, and got up. The attendants said, "A person who has been expelled from her district three times must be disloyal. One who has been expelled from her village five times must be lacking in propriety. Why is Your Majesty so eager to meet someone who is disloyal and lacking in propriety?" The king said, "You don't understand.[101] When a cow lows and a horse does not respond, it is not because it doesn't hear the sound of the cow. It is because they are different species. This person must be different from other people." He then met with her and talked with her for three days.

On the first day she said, "Does Your Majesty know about the pillars of the state?" The king said, "I do not." The outcast maid said, "The pillar is the prime minister. If the pillar isn't straight, then the roof beams will not be secure. If the roof beams are not secure, the rafters will droop, so that the house will be in danger of collapsing. In the present case, the king is the roof beam and the people are the rafters, while the state is the house. The stability of the house depends upon the pillars, and the security of the state depends upon its prime minister. At present, Your Majesty is already greatly knowledgeable, but it is essential that you inquire into the matter of your prime minister." The king said, "I will do so."

On the second day, the king said, "What do you think of the prime minister?" The outcast maid said, "Your Majesty's prime minister is a paired-eye fish.[102] If he is well paired in office and at home, he will be able to accomplish things and make a contribution." The king said, "What do you mean?" The outcast maid said, "He should regard his colleagues as friends and his wife and children as worthies. This is what I mean by 'being well-paired in office and at home.'"

On the third day, the king said, "Is it possible to replace my prime minister?" The outcast maid said, "He is of middling talent, and if you seek another, you might not be able to find anyone who is appropriate. If there were someone who surpassed him, then why not [employ him]? But at present, there is no such person. But I have heard how an enlightened king employs people. He singles out [for special attention] one person and thereby makes use of him. In this way, Chu employed Yu Qiuzi and thereby obtained Sunshu Ao.[103] Yan employed Guo Wei and obtained Yue Yi.[104] If Your Majesty can truly encourage this man, then he can indeed be of use."

The king said, "How shall I employ him?" The outcast maid replied, "Formerly, Duke Huan of Qi honored a mathematician and thereby gained the allegiance of many accomplished officers.[105] When the King of Yue honored a praying mantis, brave officers were soon willing to die for him.[106] The Duke of She loved dragons, and a dragon suddenly descended before him.[107] Moreover, you will not need to wait long to elicit such responses."

The king said, "Excellent!" He then honored the prime minister, treated him with great respect, and gave him the outcast maid to wed. After three days, scholars from all four quarters came in multitudes to offer their allegiance to Qi, so that the state became well governed.

The *Odes* says, "I am granted an audience with my lord;/Side by side we sit and strum the zither."[108] These lines apply well to her account.

The Verse Summary says,

The outcast orphan maid of Qi
Went to King Xiang's gate.
Though she had been expelled five times,
The king still met with her.
She discussed governing the state
With refinement and aplomb.
They spoke for three days,
Till she was matched with the prime minister.

6.13 ZHUANG ZHI, THE MAIDEN OF CHU

Zhuang Zhi, the maiden of Chu, was the wife of King Qingxiang of Chu and came from a town in the district.[109] In the beginning, King Qingxiang was fond of towers and pavilions. He came and went at irregular times, and although he was forty years old, he had not established an heir to the throne. Those offering counsel were shut out, Qu Yuan was banished, and the state was imperiled.[110]

Qin wanted to invade [Chu] and therefore sent Zhang Yi there to sow discord.[111] He caused the king's courtiers to tell the king, "If you travel south five hundred *li* to Tang, there are pleasures to be enjoyed there."[112] So the king set out.

At this time Zhuang Zhi was twelve years old and told her mother, "The king is fond of immoderate pleasures and comes and goes at irregular times. He is already advanced in age, but he has not yet established an heir. Moreover, at present, Qin has sent people to bribe the king's courtiers to trick the king into traveling five hundred *li* away from [the capital] so that they can take measure of the situation. Because the king has already left, evil ministers are sure to lay plans with enemy states and prevent him from returning to his state. I would like to go advise him."

Her mother said, "You are a mere babe, what do you know about advising kings?" Her mother would not allow her to go, but Zhi slipped away. She made a flag with a pole and a bit of red silk. She took the flag and hid beside the road south of the city.

When the king's carriage arrived, Zhi raised the flag. The king saw it and stopped, ordering someone to go and inquire about it. The person he sent reported back, saying, "There is a young girl crouching there beneath a flag who requests an audience with Your Majesty." The king said, "Summon her."

When Zhi came forward, the king said, "What are you doing here?" Zhi replied, "I am a girl of the capital district. I'd like to discuss a riddle with Your Majesty, but I was afraid that I would be held back and prevented from seeing you. I heard that Your Majesty had set out on a five hundred-*li* journey, and so I used this flag, hoping to be seen."

The king said, "What is it that you wish to tell me?" Zhi replied, "The great fish has lost the water. There is a dragon without a tail. A wall is on the verge of collapsing inward, and Your Majesty does not see it."

The king said, "I don't understand." Zhi replied, "'The great fish has lost the water' refers to Your Majesty's traveling five hundred *li* outside of the kingdom, seeking pleasures ahead without any thought to the disasters emerging behind. The 'dragon without a tail' refers to your being forty years old but without an established heir to the throne, the kingdom's lack of a strong system of support while facing certain danger. The 'wall that is on the verge of collapsing inward' without Your Majesty's seeing it refers to disaster and chaos in the making, while Your Majesty refuses to change."

The king said, "How can this be the case?" Zhi said, "Your Majesty is fond of towers and pavilions, yet you have no pity for the common people. You come and go at irregular hours and seem to hear and see nothing. You are forty years old but have no heir apparent. The kingdom has no strong support, and conditions within the court and beyond are on the verge of collapse. The mighty Qin has sent people to sow discord among your courtiers to ensure that Your Majesty does not change his ways, so that the situation worsens daily. Now, while trouble is afoot, Your Majesty travels five hundred *li* outside the capital. If you insist on continuing on this course, your kingdom will no longer be your kingdom!"

The king said, "How can this be?" Zhi said, "You have brought forth these three difficulties because of five calamities."[113] The king said, "What are the five calamities?" Zhi said, "Palaces and buildings everywhere one looks, vast and extensive walls—this is the first calamity. All within the palace clothed in fine silk, while the common people lack even coarse clothing—this is the second calamity. Unrestrained luxury while the kingdom's resources are exhausted—this is the third calamity. The common people starve while your horses have more than enough grain—this is the fourth calamity. Wicked ministers at your side while the worthy cannot gain access—this is the fifth calamity. Your Majesty has begotten five calamities and therefore faces these three difficulties."

The king said, "Well argued!" He then ordered her to be taken in one of his carriages and immediately returned to his kingdom, but the gates were shut and the rebels had already established themselves there. The king then ordered troops from the Yan River and capital area to attack them, only barely overcoming them.[114] He then established Zhi as his wife and honored her with a position to the right of Zheng Xiu.[115] She brought to the king's attention matters concerning frugality and the welfare of the common people, and Chu became a strong kingdom again.

A man of discernment would say, "Although Zhuang Zhi violated the rites, in the end she embraced what was proper."[116] The *Odes* says, "The north wind whistles;/The snow falls and drifts about./Be kind to me, love me,/Take my hand and go home with me."[117] These lines apply well to this account.

The Verse Summary says,

> The maiden Zhuang Zhi of Chu
> Was but a young girl.
> Using a flag, she was able to meet the king.
> And lay out the perils and evils of the kingdom.
> She showed the king how the three difficulties
> Were compounded by the five calamities.
> The king took her back with him,
> And in the end met great success.

6.14 XU WU, A WOMAN OF QI

Xu Wu, a woman of Qi, was a poor wife who lived on the East Sea in Qi. She and her neighbor, Li Wu, belonged to an association that shared candles and met at night to spin.[118] Xu Wu was the poorest member of the group and often did not supply candles.

Li Wu told the group, "Xu Wu has repeatedly not contributed candles. I'd like to request that she not be allowed to work with us at night."[119]

Xu Wu said, "How can you say this? The reason I don't contribute candles is that I am poor. But I'm usually the first person to arrive and the last to leave. I sprinkle, sweep, and lay out the mats for those who attend.[120] I always take the thinnest and most threadbare mat and sit in the low part of the room. I do all of these things because I am poor and can't supply candles. If you add one person to the room, it doesn't make the light any darker. And if you subtract one person, it doesn't make the room any brighter. Would you begrudge the light that illuminates your walls and not allow this poor woman the favor of your mercy that she might continue her work?[121] Isn't it possible to let the group extend to me this kindness?" Li Wu was unable to respond, so [Xu Wu] once again joined them in the evening, and the matter was never discussed again.

A man of discernment would say, "If even this woman was able to use rhetoric to avoid being cast out by her neighbors, then how can rhetoric ever be neglected?" The *Odes* says, "If your words were gentle and kind,/The people would be settled."[122] These lines apply well to this case.

The Verse Summary says,

Xu Wu, the woman of Qi,
Was the only poor member of her spinning group.
At night she asked to share the candlelight,
But Li Wu refused her request.
When Xu Wu laid out her argument,
Her speech was clear indeed.
In the end she was allowed to return,
And the issue was never broached again.

6.15 THE DAUGHTER OF THE DIRECTOR OF THE GREAT GRANARY OF QI

The daughter of the director of the Great Granary of Qi was the youngest daughter of the Great Granary Director, Lord Chunyu, of the Han dynasty.[123] Her given name was Tiying. Lord Chunyu had no sons but five daughters. During the reign of Filial Emperor Wen, Lord Chunyu was convicted of a crime and faced punishment.[124] At the time, corporal punishment was still in use, and an imperial edict had been issued ordering judicial [officials] to detain Chunyu in Chang'an.[125] At the time of his arrest, Chunyu cursed his daughters, saying, "Though I have children, I have no sons, and in times of trouble you are utterly useless!" Tiying, for her part, wept bitterly and followed her father to Chang'an. She then memorialized the emperor, saying,

While your handmaiden's father served as an official, all the people of Qi praised him as upright and just. But now he has been tried in a court of law and faces punishment. I grieve that the dead cannot live again and that those who undergo mutilating punishment cannot be made whole again. Even if [those condemned] desire to reform and make a new beginning, they have no way to do so. Please allow me to enter service as a government slave to pay for my father's crime and to allow him to make a new beginning.[126]

The memorial was submitted to the Son of Heaven, who, moved by her intent, issued the following edict:

I have heard that in the time of Youyu, insignia on robes and hats and other kinds of markings on clothing were used to shame the people, so that they committed no crimes. Great indeed was his rule! Nowadays, however, the law prescribes the five forms of mutilating punishments, yet wrongdoing does not cease. With whom should the blame rest? It is due to my deficient virtue and failure to teach the people intelligently, for which I feel deeply ashamed. Indeed, when instruction is corrupt, the ignorant masses become ensnared. The *Odes* says, "Our kind and courteous ruler,/He is father and mother to his people." Nowadays, when a person has committed some fault, before any instruction is proffered, his punishment has already been meted out. If a person wants to reform and do good, the way is obstructed. I pity such people greatly! Now, when punishments extend to severing limbs or cutting flesh, the victims must suffer an entire lifetime. How utterly cruel and immoral! How indeed can I be called the father and mother of the people? Let the corporal punishments be abolished!

After this incident, those who had previously been punished by drilling into their skulls had their heads shaved instead, those whose ribs had been extracted were now caned, and those whose feet had been amputated were now shackled.[127] Lord Chunyu was thus spared punishment.

A man of discernment would say, "With one word Tiying inspired the mind of her sage ruler and brought about a most fitting conclusion to the affair." The *Odes* says, "If your words were gentle and kind,/The people would be settled."[128] These words apply well to her case.

The Verse Summary says,

Tiying pleaded her father's case
With great wisdom indeed.
Drawing upon her sincerity, she submitted a memorial
That was both eloquent and thorough.
Though they were the words of a mere girl,
They moved the sage [ruler's] thoughts.
In the end, corporal punishments were abolished,
And her father was spared.

7

THE DEPRAVED AND FAVORED

PREFACE

Only those such as the Depraved and Favored
Behave with contemptuous unconcern.
Dissolute, jealous, dazzling, and bewitching,
They turn their backs on principles and abandon what is right.
Regarding truth as falsehood,
They suffer misfortune and defeat.[1]

7.1 MO XI OF JIE OF THE XIA

Mo Xi was the consort of Jie of Xia.[2] She was beautiful in appearance, lacking in virtue, reckless, depraved, and immoral. Although her actions were those of a woman, she had the heart of a man and wore a sword and a man's cap.

Having abandoned propriety and morality, Jie indulged in lustful pastimes with his wives. He constantly sought beautiful women and housed them in the rear palace. He also gathered singers, actors, dwarves, and fools, and those who were able to perform amazing acrobatic feats, all of whom he kept at his side to create decadent entertainments.

Day and night he drank wine with Mo Xi and his palace ladies, never stopping for a moment.[3] He would place Mo Xi on his knee and do whatever she commanded. In the midst of this chaos, he lost his way entirely, growing ever more arrogant, extravagant, and self-indulgent. He made a lake of wine large enough to accommodate a boat. With one drumbeat, three thousand people drank from it like cattle. Their heads were fitted with halters to make them drink from the lake of wine. When those who became drunk drowned, Mo Xi found it amusing and laughed.

Long Feng remonstrated with him, saying, "A ruler without virtue will perish."[4] Jie said, "Will the sun perish? When the sun perishes, I will perish."[5] Jie paid no heed, and considering Long's words to be inauspicious, killed him.[6] He then built the Jade House and the Jasper Tower, which reached to the clouds. Although he had depleted his resources and exhausted all his wealth, he was still not satisfied. He summoned Tang and imprisoned him in the Xia Tower, but soon released him.[7] The feudal lords then staged a massive rebellion, whereupon Tang received the mandate and attacked Jie, doing battle with him at Mingtiao.[8] Jie's army did not fight. Tang therefore banished Jie, Mo Xi, and his favorite concubines, setting them adrift in a boat on the sea. They finally died in the mountains at Nanchao.[9]

The *Odes* says, "Admirable may be the wise woman,/But she is no better than an owl."[10] These words describe her well.[11]

The Verse Summary says,

> Mo Xi was wed to Jie;
> They were reckless, arrogant, and profligate.
> Jie was already without compunction,
> But then became twice as wild.
> Following the path of the dissolute,
> He had no sympathy for laws or rules.
> So the kingdom of Xiahou[12]
> Was overturned by the Shang.

7.2 DA JI OF ZHOW OF YIN[13]

Da Ji was the consort of Zhow of Yin and greatly favored by him.[14] Zhow surpassed others in his natural endowments and strength. He was able to fight wild beasts with his bare hands. His knowledge was sufficient to block criticism, and his rhetorical skills allowed him to cover up wrongdoing. He employed his abilities to aggrandize himself before his ministers and used his renown to elevate himself above the whole world. All other people he placed on a level beneath him.

He was fond of wine and depraved pleasures and was never apart from Da Ji. Whomever Da Ji recommended, he honored, and whomever she despised, he put to death. He [ordered] the creation of new forms of depraved music, the North District Dances, and other decadent musical forms.[15] He collected precious objects and stored them in the rear palace. His sycophants and women were granted whatever they desired. He also accumulated a hillock of distillery grains and sluiced wine into a lake. He created a forest of hanging meat in which he made nude people pursue each other so as to enliven drinking parties that lasted through the night.[16] Da Ji delighted in such things.

When the common people gazed on him with resentment and the feudal lords began to rebel, Zhow created the "roasting method." He forced felons to climb a bronze pillar that had been greased and heaped about with charcoal. Each time they fell down into the [burning] coals, Da Ji would laugh. Bi Gan remonstrated with him, saying, "If you do not cultivate the canons and laws of the former kings but instead employ a woman's words, then disaster will strike before the day is out!"[17] Zhow was angry and regarded his words as inauspicious. Then Da Ji said, "I have heard that the heart of a sage has seven apertures." So they cut open his heart to look at it. They proceeded to imprison the Viscount of Ji, while the Viscount of Wei fled.[18]

King Wu then received the mandate and raised troops to attack Zhow, doing battle with him at Muye.[19] [But] Zhow's troops [merely] inverted their lances.[20] Zhow then ascended the Lin Tower, donned a suit of precious jade, and killed himself.[21] After this, King Wu carried out Heavenly retribution, cutting off Da Ji's head and suspending it on a small white flag to indicate that the one who had destroyed Zhow was this woman.

The *Book of Documents* says, "The hen does not announce the morning. The crowing of the hen in the morning indicates the demise of the family."[22] The *Odes* says, "Our sovereign believes the scoundrels,/And the disorders thereby grow into oppression," and "They do not discharge their duties,/But only create distress to the king."[23] These words apply well to her.

The Verse Summary says,

When Da Ji was paired with Zhow,
It was delusion and chaos that she nurtured.
Zhow was already without morals,
And together they compounded each other's errors.
She pointed at the "roast" and laughed,
While dissenting officials were cut open or imprisoned.

But when defeated at Muye,
Shang was overturned and consigned to Zhou.

7.3 BAO SI OF YOU OF ZHOU

Bao Si was the daughter of a female slave and the queen of King You of Zhou.[24] Earlier, in the declining years of the Xia, spirits of the Bao people transformed themselves into two dragons.[25] Together they went to the king's court and said, "We are the two lords of Bao." The Xia ruler divined whether to kill them or allow them to go, but neither result was deemed auspicious.[26] When he divined, inquiring about storing their saliva, the [response] was auspicious.[27] He then set out sacrificial offerings of silk before them, whereupon the dragons suddenly disappeared. Then he stored their saliva in a box, which he placed on the altar of suburban sacrifices.[28] Down to the Zhou dynasty, nobody dared to open it. But at the end of King Li of Zhou's reign, when he opened [the box] to look at it, the saliva flowed throughout the court and could not be removed.[29] The king ordered women to strip [off their clothes] and curse it, whereupon it transformed into a dark lizard and entered the rear palace.[30] A slave girl in the palace who still had her baby teeth encountered it.[31] When she received the hairpin, she became pregnant.[32] At the time of King Xuan of Zhou she gave birth.[33] Because she had given birth without a husband, she was afraid and abandoned the child.

Before this, there was a folk song that went: "Reed quivers and mulberry bows/Will surely end the kingdom of Zhou."[34] King Xuan heard it, and later, when a man and his wife came to sell mulberry bows and reed quivers, the king ordered that they be seized and executed. The husband and wife then fled under cover of night.

Along the way, they heard the slave girl's abandoned [daughter] crying in the night.[35] Feeling pity for her, they picked her up and escaped to Bao, where she grew up to be a great beauty. A man of Bao named Xu, who was involved in a lawsuit, offered her [to the king] as recompense [for his crime].[36] King You accepted and favored her, whereupon he released Xu of Bao. She was therefore called Bao Si.

After Bao Si gave birth to Bofu, King You deposed the daughter of the Marquis of Shen and made Bao Si his queen. He then deposed the established heir apparent, Yijiu, and made Bofu his heir.[37]

King You was infatuated with Bao Si. Coming and going with her in the same carriage, he neglected matters of state, galloping forth with bows and arrows to hunt regardless of the season. All this he did to accord with Bao Si's wishes. They drank till intoxicated with actors and singers arrayed before them, using the night to continue the day's revels. Even so, Bao Si never laughed. King You wanted to make her laugh. But though he tried every method, she still would not laugh.

King You had prepared a warning beacon and large drums so that if raiders appeared he could deploy them. [Once] when the feudal lords had all come [in response to the beacon], but there were, in fact, no raiders, Bao Si laughed heartily. King You wanted to please her, so he raised the beacon fires again several times. But after this, no one trusted [these warnings], so the feudal lords no longer came [in response].

[At the time,] all those who provided loyal remonstration were punished, and only the words of Bao Si were heeded. Thus, superiors and inferiors flattered each other, and the common people became perverse and divisive. The Marquis of Shen thereupon joined forces with the state of Zeng, the Western Yi, and the Quan Rong, and attacked King You.[38] King You raised the beacon fires to summon troops, but no one came. [The Marquis of Shen's forces] then killed King You at the foot of Li Mountain, took Bao Si prisoner, confiscated the possessions of [the royal house of] Zhou, and left.[39] The feudal lords then went to meet with the Marquis of Shen, and together they enthroned the former heir apparent, Yijiu. He was known as King Ping.[40] From this time onward there was little to distinguish [the king of] Zhou from the other feudal lords.

The *Odes* says, "The majestic, honored capital of Zhou/Is being destroyed by Si of Bao."[41] These words refer to her.

The Verse Summary says,

The spirits of Bao transformed into dragons
And produced Bao Si.
She rose to be the consort of King You,
And deposed the queen and heir apparent.
When the beacon fires were raised to bring the troops,
She laughed when no raiders came.
The Marquis of Shen attacked Zhou
And destroyed his ancestral sacrifices.[42]

7.4 JIANG OF DUKE XUAN OF WEY

Xuan Jiang was the daughter of the Marquis of Qi and the wife of Duke Xuan of Wey.[43] In the beginning, Duke Xuan's wife, Yi Jiang, had given birth to Jizi. He was made heir apparent. The duke also married a woman of Qi, who was called Xuan Jiang. She gave birth to Shou and Shuo. Since Yi Jiang had died, Xuan Jiang wanted to establish Shou as heir apparent. So she plotted against Jizi with Shou's younger brother Shuo.

The duke sent Jizi to Qi, so Xuan Jiang secretly dispatched an assassin to wait for him at the border and kill him, saying, "When the one with a team of four horses and a white pennon arrives, you must kill him."[44] Shou heard about it and told the heir apparent, "Prince, you must flee!" Jizi said, "That is not possible. When a man abandons the orders of his father, how can he claim the name of 'son'?" Shou, thinking that it was crucial for the heir apparent to flee, began drinking with him, seized Jizi's pennon, and left. The brigand then killed Shou.

When Jizi revived, he looked for his pennon but couldn't find it. He then immediately went out searching for Shou, but found that he had already died. Jizi was pained that Shou had died for him. He therefore told the brigand, "I am the person you should have killed. What crime did *he* commit? Please kill me." The brigand then killed him.

Since the two sons had died, Shuo was then established as heir apparent. When Duke Xuan died, Shuo came to the throne and was known as Duke Hui.[45] To the end he had no progeny, and the disorder continued for five reigns. It was not until Duke Dai came to the throne that there was peace.[46]

The *Odes* says, "Here is this man,/With virtuous words, but not really good."[47] These words apply to her.

The Verse Summary says,

> Xuan Jiang of Wey
> Plotted against the heir apparent.
> Desirous of enthroning her son Shou,
> She secretly engaged an assassin.
> But Shou died as well,
> And Wey was therefore imperiled.
> Five reigns saw no peace;
> The chaos began with Jiang.

7.5 WEN JIANG OF DUKE HUAN OF LU

Wen Jiang was the daughter of the Marquis of Qi and the wife of Duke Huan of Lu.[48] While at home she had an incestuous relationship with her elder brother,

Duke Xiang of Qi.[49] [Later, it came to pass that] Duke Huan was preparing to attack Zheng in an effort to reinstate Duke Li.[50] When he set out, he planned to bring his wife along to Qi. Shen Xu said, "That won't do. Women have their [husbands'] homes and men have their own apartments [for their wives]. One sphere should not encroach upon the other. This is known as propriety, and tampering with this principle will lead to ruin. Thus, the rites dictate that unless there is an important reason, a married woman does not return home."[51] Duke Huan did not listen but went with her to Qi.

When Wen Jiang had a liaison with Duke Xiang, Duke Huan was enraged. He tried to stop her, but she would not desist. Wen Jiang reported this turn of events to Duke Xiang, who then feasted Duke Huan and offered him wine to make him drunk. He then sent Prince Pengsheng to pick him up and put him in his carriage.[52] But Pengsheng, taking advantage of the situation, fractured Duke Huan's ribcage and killed him, and the duke thus died in the carriage. The men of Lu sought redress for this shameful act, so the men of Qi killed Pengsheng.[53]

The *Odes* says, "Disorder does not come down from Heaven,/It is produced by women."[54] These words apply well to this case.

The Verse Summary says,

Wen Jiang was lascivious and reckless.
She was given in marriage to Duke Huan of Lu.
Together they returned to Qi,
Where she had an affair with Duke Xiang.
He dispatched Pengsheng,
Who injured Duke Huan, breaking his ribs.
This woman caused disorder,
Which led to misfortune and disaster.

7.6 AI JIANG OF DUKE ZHUANG OF LU

Ai Jiang was the daughter of the Marquis of Qi and the wife of Duke Zhuang.[55] In the beginning, before Ai Jiang entered [Lu as a bride], the duke had several times gone to Qi and had illicit relations with her.[56] When she entered [Lu], she came with her younger sister Shu Jiang.[57] The duke had ordered the wives of the grandees of the ducal clan to present her with gifts of silk.

The grandee Xiafu Buji said, "The gifts of wives should not exceed dates and nuts to fulfill the rite.[58] The gifts of men should not exceed jade, silk, beasts, and birds as a sign of respect. At present, the women's use of silk obliterates the distinction between men and women. The distinction between men and women is one of the great principles of the state. Is this not, then, inappropriate?"

But the duke paid no heed. He also painted the pillars of Duke Huan's ancestral temple red and carved its rafters in order to impress Ai Jiang.[59]

Ai Jiang was arrogant and lustful and had affairs with two of the duke's younger brothers, Prince Qingfu and Prince Ya.[60] Ai Jiang wanted to enthrone Qingfu. But when the duke died, Ziban succeeded him.[61] Qingfu and Ai Jiang then plotted together and killed Ziban at the home of the Zhang family. Shu Jiang's son was then enthroned, and he was known as Duke Min.[62]

After Duke Min came to the throne, the excesses of Qingfu and Ai Jiang grew greater still. Ai Jiang also plotted with Qingfu to kill Duke Min and set up Qingfu as duke.[63] They commissioned Bu Yi to ambush and murder Duke Min at the Wuwei [gate].[64] [Qingfu] was then about to set himself up as duke, but the men of Lu plotted against him. Qingfu became alarmed and fled to Ju, while Ai Jiang fled to Zhu.[65] Duke Huan of Qi then enthroned Duke Xi.[66] When he heard that Ai Jiang and Qingfu had endangered Lu through their illicit behavior, he summoned Ai Jiang and had her killed with poison.[67] [The state of] Lu then executed Qingfu.

The *Odes* says, "Ever flow her tears!/But of what avail is her lament?"[68] These words apply well to her.

The Verse Summary says,

> Ai Jiang was fond of evil.
> And had illicit relations with Duke Zhuang.
> She extended her involvement to include his two brothers,
> For she was arrogant, envious, and perverse.
> It was Qingfu upon whom she relied,
> So the state fell into ruin.
> Duke Huan of Qi moved in with troops,
> And killed Ai Jiang with poison.

7.7 LI JI OF DUKE XIAN OF JIN

Li Ji was a woman of the Li Rong and the wife of Duke Xian of Jin.[69] In the beginning, Duke Xian married a woman of Qi, who was mother to the wife of Duke Mu of Qin and to the heir apparent Shensheng.[70] The duke also married two Rong women, who gave birth to the Princes Chonger and Yiwu.[71] When Duke Xian attacked and conquered the Li Rong, he obtained Li Ji and brought her home. She gave birth to Xiqi and Zhuozi.[72] Li Ji was a favorite of Duke Xian. After [his wife], Jiang of Qi, died, he established Li Ji as his wife.

Li Ji wanted Xiqi established as heir to the throne, so she plotted with her sister, saying, "If the [princes] were absent from court for one day, in that space of time we could 'apply the knife' and thereby create an opening to oust the heir apparent and the two princes."

Therefore, Li Ji made a proposal to the duke, saying, "Quwo is your ancestral city and Pu and Erqu form your borders.[73] They cannot be without their lords. If your ancestral city is without its lord, the people will not feel a sense of awe, and the border area, absent of its lords, will incite the ambitions of insurgents. When insurgents entertain ambitions, the people will regard your government with contempt, and the state will be endangered. If the heir apparent is sent to Quwo and the two princes are sent to reside in Pu and Erqu, then the people can be made to feel a sense of awe and insurgents will become fearful."[74] Thereafter, the duke sent the heir apparent to reside in Quwo, Chonger to reside in Pu, and Yiwu to reside in Erqu.

One night, after Duke Xian of Jin and Li Ji had sent the heir apparent far away, Li Ji began to weep. The duke asked her what was wrong, and she replied, "I have heard that Shensheng is by nature fond of benevolence but strong-willed, and that he is very generous and loving toward the people. And now he is saying that you are infatuated with me, and that this will bring disorder to the state. Will it not then be for the sake of the state and the people that he will take a strong stand against you?[75] And since you are not yet ready to die, what can you do? Why not kill me? You wouldn't want to bring disorder to the people because of one concubine."

The duke said, "How can one be kind to the people but unkind to one's father?" Li Ji said, "Serving one's father and serving the people are not the same. Now, if a man slays his ruler to benefit the people, would the people not support him? If a man confers benefits and gains favor, removes disorder and pleases the masses—who would not desire such a turn of events?[76] Although he loves you, his ambitions can't be suppressed. If Zhow had had a virtuous son who had first killed Zhow without publicizing his evil, Zhow would have died all the same, but without resorting to the helping hand of King Wu in the obliteration of Zhow's ancestral sacrifices.[77] When our former lord, Duke Wu, annexed Yi, and King Mu of Chu murdered [his father, King] Cheng, both acted on behalf of the people without considering their own kin.[78] If you do not plan for this early on, disaster is sure to befall you."

144 • THE DEPRAVED AND FAVORED

The duke was frightened and said, "What should I do?" Li Ji said, "Why not retire, claiming old age, and hand the government over to him? Once he obtains power and governs, isn't he likely to set you aside as an object of concern?" The duke said, "That won't do. I'll have to think about this." From this time onward he began to be suspicious of his heir apparent.

Li Ji then sent someone bearing the duke's orders to tell the heir apparent, "The duke dreamt that he saw Jiang of Qi. Go as quickly as possible to offer sacrifices to her."[79] Shensheng therefore sacrificed at Quwo and returned to Jiang with some of the offerings.[80] The duke was out hunting and not present at the time, so Li Ji received the offerings. She then placed poison in the wine and put a toxic substance in the meat offerings. When the duke arrived, he summoned Shensheng, who offered him the meat.

Li Ji said, "Any food from outside should be tested first." She poured some of the wine on the ground and the ground [foamed] into a mound. Shensheng was alarmed and went out. When Li Ji gave the wine to the dog, the dog died. She then proceeded to give wine to the attendant, and the attendant died. Li Ji then looked up to Heaven, beat her breast, and wept. When she saw Shensheng she cried, "Alas! The state, *your* state—why were you so impatient to become ruler? Considering your father's kindness, if you could bear to do this, how much less will you consider the people of the state? And to *kill* one's own father in pursuit of gain—how could anyone stand to gain from such a thing?"[81]

The duke sent someone to tell the heir apparent, "You'd better consider this well." The Grand Tutor Li Ke said, "If you go to him and explain yourself, you will be spared. Otherwise, you will not be spared." The heir apparent said, "My father is old now. If I go and explain myself, then Li Ji will die, and he would never be able to bear it." He therefore hanged himself in the temple at Xincheng.[82]

The duke then killed [the heir apparent's] Lesser Tutor, Du Yuankuan, and sent the eunuch Chu to assassinate Chonger.[83] Chonger therefore fled to the Di.[84] The duke then sent Jia Hua to assassinate Yiwu, and Yiwu fled to Liang.[85] He then expelled all of the ducal sons and established Xiqi as his heir.

When Duke Xian died, Xiqi came to the throne, but Li Ke killed him. Then Zhuozi came to the throne, and Li Ke killed him as well.[86] He then proceeded to humiliate Li Ji, whipping and then killing her.[87] [The state] of Qin then placed Yiwu on the throne; this was Duke Hui.[88] When Duke Hui died, his son, Ziyu, succeeded him; this was Duke Huai.[89] The people of Jin killed Duke Huai at Gaoliang and enthroned Chonger; this was Duke Wen.[90] The disorder extended to five reigns before peace was restored.[91]

The *Odes* says, "A woman with a long tongue/Is like a stepping-stone to disorder"; and "A clever woman topples walls."[92] These words describe her well.

The Verse Summary says,

The stepmother, Li Ji,
Misled and confused Duke Xian of Jin.
She plotted against and slandered the heir apparent,
Poisoning the wine in her bid for power.
As a result, Shensheng died,
And the princes fled.
While she herself paid for her crime,
Five reigns were plunged into chaos.

7.8 MU JIANG OF DUKE XUAN OF LU

Mu Jiang was a daughter of the Marquis of Qi, the wife of Duke Xuan of Lu, and the mother of Duke Cheng.[93] She was highly intelligent but wanton in her conduct; therefore, her posthumous name was Mu (Contrary).[94]

Early on, when Duke Cheng was still a youth, Mu Jiang had an affair with Shusun Xuanbo, whose given name was Qiaoru.[95] Qiaoru and Mu Jiang planned to oust the Ji and Meng lineages and usurp power in the state of Lu.[96]

Jin and Chu were at the time battling at Yanling, and the duke was leaving to assist Jin.[97] When he was about to leave, Jiang told him, "You must expel the Ji and Meng [lineages]. They are working against you." But the duke declined her request because of the difficulties in Jin, begging to take orders from her when he returned. [Qiaoru] also bribed a grandee of Jin, bidding him to detain Jisun Hangfu, and telling him that if he agreed to the murder of Zhongsun Mie, Lu would then be willing to serve Jin as [loyally] as Jin's own officers.[98] [Ultimately] the men of Lu would not comply with Qiaoru and agreed by covenant to expel him. Qiaoru then fled to Qi, and Lu removed Mu Jiang to the Eastern Palace.[99]

When she first left, Mu Jiang ordered a milfoil divination to be made. The result was the second line of the [hexagram] "Stopping."[100] The diviner said, "This is known as deriving 'Accord,' from 'Stopping.' 'Accord' refers to getting out, so you will soon get out."

Jiang said, "No. In the *Zhou Yi*, it says, '"Accord" indicates greatness, success, benefit, and rectitude without blame.'[101] 'Greatness' is the height of goodness; 'success' is the confluence of [all] excellence; 'benefit' is the harmonizing of duty;

and 'rectitude' is the trunk of all affairs.[102] Ultimately, these cannot be false. Thus it is only through the [qualities associated with] 'Accord' that one can be without blame. Now, I am a woman who has helped to create disorder. Moreover, because I already occupy an inferior position, but have furthermore failed to be compassionate, I cannot be called 'great.' To destabilize the state and one's family cannot be called 'success.' To act in a way that brings harm to my person cannot be called 'benefit.' And to abandon my position to indulge myself cannot be called 'rectitude.'[103] One who possesses these four virtues is in 'accord' and without blame. I have none of these, so how can the augury be 'Accord'? Because I chose wickedness, can I avoid blame? I will die here and I will never get out." In the end she died in the Eastern Palace.[104]

A man of discernment would say, "What a pity! Though Mu Jiang had the gift of intelligence, in the end she could not suppress her debauchery and insubordination." The *Odes* says, "When a gentleman indulges in such pleasure,/Something may still be said for him./When a lady does so,/Nothing can be said for her."[105] These words apply well to this case.

The Verse Summary says,

> Mu Jiang was licentious,
> And Xuanbo was arrogant indeed.
> They schemed to oust the Ji and Meng
> In their desire to control Lu.
> Abandoned and rejected,
> She was broken and downcast.
> Later, though her words proved good,
> She could never amend these wrongs.

7.9 XIA JI, A WOMAN OF CHEN

Xia Ji, a woman of Chen, was the mother of the Chen grandee Xia Zhengshu and the wife of Yushu.[106] She was a peerless beauty. She practiced the techniques of inner cultivation that enabled her to conceal her age and replenish her youth.[107] Three times she served as queen and seven times as wife.[108] Dukes and marquises competed for her, and each one of them became infatuated and lost all sense of purpose. Xia Ji's son, Zhengshu, was a grandee.[109] Gongsun Ning, Yi Hangfu, and Duke Ling of Chen were all engaged in illicit relations with Xia Ji.[110] Sometimes, as a joke, they appeared at court wearing bits of her clothing or with her intimate garments draped inside their robes.

Xie Ye saw this and told them, "If the ruler has committed some indiscretion, you should conceal it.[111] At present you yourselves are prompting the ruler to do these things, not waiting for a private moment of leisure at court, but making a game of it in the presence of officials and commoners. What do you mean by this?"

The two men informed Duke Ling, who said, "That everyone knows about my indiscretion is harmless. But Xie Ye knowing about it makes me feel ashamed." He then ordered someone to ambush Xie Ye and kill him.[112]

Duke Ling and the two ministers were once drinking at the Xia residence and summoned Zhengshu. The duke joked with the two gentlemen, saying, "Zhengshu looks like you." The two gentlemen retorted, "Not as much as he resembles you." Zhengshu was stung by these words. When Duke Ling finished his wine and went out, Zhengshu, concealing himself behind the stable gate with a crossbow, shot and killed Duke Ling. Gongsun Ning and Yi Hangfu then both fled to Chu, while Wu, Duke Ling's heir apparent, fled to Jin.[113] The next year, King Zhuang of Chu raised troops and executed Zhengshu.[114] He brought stability to the state of Chen and made Wu the ruler. This was Duke Cheng.

When King Zhuang saw how beautiful Xia Ji was, he wanted to take her into his harem.[115] Wuchen, the Duke of Shen, remonstrated with him, saying, "This won't do.[116] Your Majesty has punished an act of wrongdoing. But if you take Xia Ji, it will be seen as a matter of lust for this woman. Lusting after women is licentiousness, and licentiousness is a serious offense. I hope Your Majesty will think this over."

The king followed his advice. He ordered that an opening should be made in the rear wall [of the harem], through which she was released.[117] General Zifan then saw her beauty and also wanted to take her.[118] Wuchen admonished him, saying, "She is a person of evil omen [responsible for] the killing of Yushu, the murder of Duke Ling, the execution of Xia Nan, the flight of Kong and Yi, and the destruction of the state of Chen.[119] There are many beautiful women in the world. Why must you choose her?"

Zifan therefore desisted. King Zhuang then married Xia Ji to the court deputy Xiang Lao.[120] But Xiang Lao died at Bi, and his corpse had not been recovered.[121] His son, Heiyao, then began to have illicit relations with Xia Ji. Wuchen then met with Xia Ji and told her, "Return home. I will make a formal petition of betrothal to you [there]."[122]

King Gong [of Chu] came to the throne, and Wuchen was sent on a diplomatic mission to Qi. [When he left,] he took with him all of his household possessions and [instead] went to Zheng.[123] [Upon his arrival] he asked someone to summon Xia Ji with the message, "The corpse can be recovered."[124] Xia Ji then went to join him. Wuchen ordered his assistant to return to Chu the gifts [he had been given to present to Qi], and fled with Xia Ji to Jin. The grandee Zifan was infuriated with him and joined with Zichong to annihilate Wuchen's clan and divide his property.[125]

The *Odes* says, "A person like this,/Bent on marriage alone,/Utterly lacking in faith,/And ignorant of destiny."[126] This ode shows how the allure of favorites leads to destruction.

The Verse Summary says,

> Xia Ji was a great beauty
> Who annihilated states and destroyed Chen.
> She caused the flight of two grandees
> And the murder of her own son.
> She nearly misled King Zhuang of Chu,
> But brought destruction to Wuchen.
> Zifan, vexed and alarmed,
> Annihilated the Duke of Shen's family and seized his wealth.

7.10 SHENG JI OF DUKE LING OF QI

Sheng Ji was the daughter of the Marquis of Lu, the wife of Duke Ling, and the mother of the heir apparent Guang.[127] She was also called Meng Zi.[128] She had illicit relations with the grandee Qing Ke.[129] Once, he was brought into a side gate of the palace in a carriage with her, wearing concealing clothing.[130] Bao Qian saw them and reported the incident to Guo Zuo.[131] Guo Zuo then summoned Qing Ke for questioning. For a long time afterward, Qing Ke did not venture out, but told Meng Zi, "Guo Zuo reproved me." This infuriated Meng Zi.

At the time, Guo Zuo was serving as an assistant to Duke Ling in a meeting with the feudal lords in Keling, while Gaozi and Baozi were put in charge of domestic security [and hence remained in the capital].[132] Upon the return of [Duke Ling and Guo Zuo], Bao and Gao closed the city gates before their arrival and began to question all travelers. Meng Zi then slandered them, saying, "Gao and Bao were going to refuse you entry because they planned to enthrone Prince Jiao, and Guo Zuo was privy to the plan."[133]

The duke was angry and had Bao Qian's foot amputated and expelled Gaozi and Guo Zuo, who both fled to Ju.[134] He made Cui Zhu a grandee and ordered Qing Ke to assist him.[135] He then led an army to surround Ju but was not victorious. Guo Zuo meanwhile sent someone to kill Qing Ke.[136] Duke Ling then made a covenant with Zuo and restored him [to his original position]. But Meng Zi once again slandered him and had him killed. When Duke Ling died, Gao and Bao were reinstated and had Meng Zi killed.[137] The disorder in Qi then ceased.

The *Odes* says, "Those from whom come no lessons, no instruction,/Are women and eunuchs."[138] These words apply well to this case.

The Verse Summary says,

Sheng Ji, consort of Duke Ling of Qi,
How dissipated her conduct.
She behaved wantonly with Qing Ke,
And because of this, Bao Qian suffered.
She slandered Gao and Bao
Till they fled from Qi.
She employed deceptions, sowing treachery and disaster,
Which in the end destroyed her as well.[139]

7.11 DONGGUO JIANG OF QI

Dongguo Jiang of Qi was the wife of the Duke of Tang and the elder sister of Cui Zhu's charioteer, Dongguo Yan.[140] She was beautiful and alluring. When the Duke of Tang died, Cuizi came to pay his condolences and found her most pleasing, so after discussing the matter with Yan, he married her.

After she had gone to live at Cui's home, which was next to the duke's palace, Duke Zhuang began an illicit affair with her and frequently went to the Cui residence.[141] Cuizi was aware of the situation.

One day the duke gave Cuizi's cap to an attendant.[142] Cuizi was angry and, claiming to be sick, stayed at home. The duke climbed his tower to get a view of the Cui residence, and from the top of the tower joked with Dongguo Jiang. The duke then climbed down to join her, at which point, Dongguo Jiang darted inside and shut the door. The duke tried to push his way through, saying, "Open the door. It's me."

Dongguo Jiang said, "My husband is here and has not yet bound his hair."[143] The duke said, "I've come to inquire about Cuizi's illness. Won't you open the door?" Cuizi and Jiang then went out of a side door and shut the gate, while an assemblage of men sounded the drums. The duke was afraid. He then grasped a pillar and began to sing.[144] The duke pleaded with Cuizi, saying, "I know that I have done wrong. Please allow me to reform myself. I will be at your service, my lord. If you don't believe me, allow me to make a covenant with you."

Cuizi said, "I dare not obey your orders." He then left. The duke also pleaded with the Cui family's steward, saying, "Please allow me to go to the temple of my ancestors and die there." The Cuis' steward said, "Your servant [Cui] Zhu is ill and not here. I therefore do not dare to obey your orders." The duke then tried to get over the wall and escape, but Cui shot him, hitting him in the heel. The duke then fell backward, whereupon [Cui] murdered the duke.

Before this, Dongguo Jiang had gone to live with [Cui] along with Tang Wujiu, the son of her former husband. Cuizi was fond of him and made him his chief minister. Cuizi's former wife had two sons. The eldest was called Cheng, and the youngest was called Qiang. After Jiang entered the Cui household, she gave birth to two sons named Ming and Cheng.[145]

Because Cheng was ill, Cuizi demoted him and made Ming his successor. Cheng asked someone to request the Cui fief for him, where he could retire. Cuizi pitied him and granted him this request. But Tang Wujiu and Dongguo Yan disagreed and would not allow it. In a rage, Cheng and Qiang decided to murder them and informed Qing Feng about their plan.[146]

Qing Feng was a grandee of Qi. He was secretly planning to wrest power from the Cui lineage and hoped that they would annihilate one another, so he told the two sons, "Kill them." Thereupon the two sons returned and killed Tang Wujiu and Dongguo Yan in the courtyard of the Cui residence. Cuizi was furious and told Qing, "I am worthless. I have sons whom I have failed to instruct, so it has come to this. That I serve you is known to all in the capital populace. And though it is humiliating to send [another to deal with Cheng and Qiang], there is no other way to stop them."[147]

Qing Feng thus ordered Lupu Pie to lead a band of men along with the capital populace to burn Cui's granaries and stables and kill Cheng and Qiang.[148] Cui's wife said, "It is better to die than to live like this." She then hanged herself and died. When Cuizi returned and found his granary and stables burned and his wife and sons dead, he too hanged himself and died.

A man of discernment would say, "Dongguo Jiang killed one ruler of a state and annihilated three families.[149] She also destroyed herself. She can indeed be called inauspicious." The *Odes* says, "Though branches and leaves remain unharmed,/The roots were long ago damaged."[150] These words describe the situation well.

The Verse Summary says,

Dongguo Jiang of Qi
Was the wife of Cui Zhu.
She led Duke Zhuang astray,
And placed her trust in Wujiu.
The disaster encompassed Ming and Cheng,[151]
Who in contention for the fief committed murder.
Father and mother, with no one to depend on,
Then witnessed the Cui lineage's final end.

7.12 THE TWO DEPRAVED WOMEN OF WEY

The two depraved women of Wey were Nan Zi and Bo Ji of Wey.[152] Nan Zi was a woman of Song and the wife of Duke Ling of Wey.[153] She had illicit relations with Zichao of Song.[154] When Kuaikui, the heir apparent, learned of it, he became enraged with them. Nan Zi then slandered the heir apparent to Duke Ling, saying, "The crown prince wishes to kill me."[155] Duke Ling became furious with Kuaikui, and so Kuaikui fled to Song. When Duke Ling died, Kuaikui's son Zhe was placed on the throne and became Duke Chu.[156]

Bo Ji of Wey was the elder sister of Kuaikui, the wife of Kong Wenzi, and the mother of Kong Kui.[157] Kong Kui served as prime minister to Duke Chu. After [Kong] Wenzi's death, Bo Ji and a page of the Kong family, Hun Liangfu, engaged in licentious relations.[158] Bo Ji sent Liangfu to see Kuaikui. Kuaikui told him, "If you can help me return to my state, I shall reward you with a grandee's carriage and pardon you three times the death penalty." They made a covenant, and Kuaikui promised to give Bo Ji to Liangfu as a wife. Liangfu was delighted and told Bo Ji, who was greatly pleased.

Thereafter, Liangfu and Kuaikui stopped in an orchard of the Kong family. At dusk, the two men, wearing concealing clothing, rode forth in a carriage and entered Bo Ji's apartments.[159] After they had eaten their meal, Bo Ji, carrying a spear and positioned in front of Kuaikui and five armored soldiers, drove her son Kong Kui into a privy, where she forced him to enter into a covenant.[160] Duke Chu then fled to Lu, and Zilu died [in the fray].[161] Kuaikui afterward ascended the throne and became Duke Zhuang.[162] He killed the lady Nan Zi and also killed Hun Liangfu.[163]

Because of disorder in Rongzhou, Duke Zhuang again fled to another state.[164] After four years, Duke Chu again entered Wey. When he was about to return, a grandee killed [Bo Ji], the mother of Kong Kui, and welcomed the duke.[165]

These two women caused the disorder of five generations, and not until the time of Duke Dao was peace restored.[166]

The *Odes* says, "Look at the rat; it has its skin./But a man without dignity/A man without dignity/Why doesn't he just die!"[167] These words describe them well.

The Verse Summary says,

Nan Zi was deluded and lustful.
It was Song Zichao with whom she had intimate relations;
The one she slandered was Kuaikui,
And she caused him to flee.
Kong Kui's mother was also favored.
She caused the flight and reentry of two rulers.
The two disorders were intertwined
And worked together to destroy lives.

7.13 LING OF ZHAO'S WOMAN OF THE WU FAMILY

Ling of Zhao's woman of the Wu family was called Meng Yao.[168] She was the daughter of Wu Guang and [became] the queen of King Wuling of Zhao.[169] Earlier, King Wuling had taken as a wife the daughter of the King of Hann.[170] When she gave birth to a son named Zhang, she was made queen, and Zhang was made heir apparent.

The king once dreamed that he saw a maiden playing the zither, who sang:

A beauty, so dazzling;
A face like a flowering begonia.
'Tis fate, 'tis fate,
To be born at this heaven-appointed time,
When no one knows my splendor!

Another day, when the king was happily drinking wine, he mentioned the dream several times and expressed his wish to see the maiden. When Wu Guang heard this, he made arrangements with the queen to present to the king his daughter Meng Yao.

She was very attractive. The king loved and favored her and never left her side. After several years she gave birth to a son named He. Meng Yao frequently hinted that the queen was contemplating adultery and that the heir apparent had behaved in an unfilial manner. The king then proceeded to depose his queen and heir apparent and appointed Meng Yao as Queen Hui and made He king. He was known as King Huiwen.[171] King Wuling then called himself the Lord's Father and enfeoffed Zhang with Dai, calling him the Lord of Anyang.[172]

In his fourth year [King Huiwen] brought all of his ministers to court, and the Lord of Anyang [also] came. From the side of the hall the Lord's Father observed the assembled ministers and members of the royal house, and noticed that Zhang looked dispirited. Contrary to expectations, he was now his younger brother's vassal, and [his father] pitied him. At the time, Queen Hui had long since died and those loyalties had faded, so he thought about dividing Zhao and making Zhang King of Dai. But nothing was ever decided, and the matter was put to rest.

Then, one day, when the Lord's Father had gone to the Shaqiu palace, Zhang marshaled his soldiers to rebel.[173] Li Dui then raised troops from the four settlements and attacked Zhang.[174] Zhang's troops then fled to the Lord's Father, who gave them asylum. Dui therefore surrounded the palace of the Lord's Father.

After killing Zhang, he consulted with his men, saying, "We surrounded the Lord's Father because of Zhang. But as soon as we lay down our weapons, we will be exterminated." They therefore maintained their siege. The Lord's Father wanted to escape but could find no way out. He was also without food, finding only a baby bird, which he ate. After more than three months, he starved to death at the Shaqiu palace.

The *Odes* says, "They respond to you with baseless stories,/And thus robbers and thieves are in your court."[175] This means that evil emerges from the inner [chambers].

The Verse Summary says,

The daughter of Wu with a face like a begonia,
In spirit form roused King Ling of Zhao in a dream.
After she became his favored intimate,
His mind became deluded.
He cast off his queen and incited war;
His son He brought this about.
The Lord's [Father] was barricaded at Shaqiu,
And the disorder toppled the state.[176]

7.14 QUEEN LI OF KING KAO OF CHU

Queen Li of King Kao of Chu was the younger sister of Li Yuan, a man of Zhao, and the queen of King Kaolie of Chu.[177] In the beginning, King Kaolie had no sons, which troubled the Lord of Chunshen.[178] It so happened that Li Yuan, who served as Lord Chunshen's attendant, had given his younger sister to Lord Chunshen. When she knew she was pregnant, Yuan's younger sister, taking advantage of a leisure moment, told Lord Chunshen, "The King of Chu has honored and favored you more than his own brothers. You have now served as Chu's prime minister for more than thirty years. But because the king has no sons, after he [completes] his hundred years, his elder and younger brothers will be enthroned.[179] After Chu establishes a new ruler, each one will honor those closest to him. So how much longer can you expect to be favored? What is more, you have long served in your position and have frequently failed to treat the king's brothers with courtesy. If one of the king's brothers does in fact come to the throne, you will be visited with disaster. How then will you preserve your ministerial seal of office and your fief in Jiangdong?[180]

"I now know that I am pregnant, though no one else knows about it. I have not received your favor for long. If you were to use your prominence to present me to the King of Chu, the King of Chu is sure to favor me. If, Heaven willing, the child is a boy, then it will be your son who will be king, and Chu will be yours for the taking. How does this compare with facing unimaginable criminal charges?"

Lord Chunshen enthusiastically endorsed her plan. He then sent Yuan's sister to guarded quarters and told King Kaolie about her. King Kaolie summoned and favored her, whereupon she gave birth to Dao, who was established as heir apparent. Yuan's sister was made queen, while Li Yuan was honored with important responsibilities. He then gathered about him a [band] of officers for the purpose of killing Lord Chunshen in order to silence him.

When King Kaolie died, Yuan killed Lord Chunshen and exterminated his family. Dao was then enthroned as King You.[181] [After King You's death] the queen enthroned King Kaolie's posthumous son Youu as King Ai.[182] The henchmen of the younger brother of King Kaolie, Prince Fuchu, had heard that King You was not the son of King Kaolie and had similar suspicions about King Ai.[183] So they attacked and killed King Ai and the Queen Dowager, annihilated the family of Li Yuan, and set up Fuchu as king.[184] In five years [Chu] was destroyed by Qin.

THE DEPRAVED AND FAVORED • 155

The *Odes* says, "Their words are very sweet,/And the disorders thereby increase."[185] These words apply well to her actions.

The Verse Summary says,

The younger sister of Li Yuan
Made use of Lord Chunshen.
King Kaolie had no sons,
So she was presented to him.
She knew she was with child upon entering the harem,
And that the child would be made heir.
But having established the roots of rebellion,
Her clan was exterminated.

7.15 THE SONGSTRESS QUEEN OF KING DAO OF ZHAO

The Songstress Queen was a singer from Handan and the queen of King Dao-xiang of Zhao.[186] At an earlier time, she had brought disorder to an entire clan. When she became widowed, King Daoxiang was struck by her beauty and married her. Li Mu remonstrated with him, saying, "This won't do. A woman's impropriety is the means by which state and family are turned upside down and made unstable. This woman has brought disorder to her clan. Shouldn't Your Majesty be alarmed?"[187] The king said, "Whether there is disorder or not depends on how I govern." He then proceeded to marry her.

Earlier, King Daoxiang's queen had given birth to a son named Jia who became heir apparent. After the Songstress Queen entered the court at the rank of consort, she gave birth to a son named Qian. The Songstress Queen then became a great favorite of the king and secretly slandered the queen and the heir apparent to the king. She [also] arranged for someone to offend the heir apparent and thus provoke him into committing a crime. The king thereupon dismissed Jia and set up Qian [in his place], and deposed the queen and established the songstress as queen. When King Daoxiang died, Qian was enthroned as King Youmin.[188]

The Songstress Queen was dissolute and immoral. She developed an illicit connection with the Lord of Chunping and frequently received bribes from Qin.[189] She made the king execute his great general, the Lord of Wuan, Li Mu. Afterward, when Qin troops marched in, no one could stop them. Qian was then taken prisoner by Qin, and Zhao was destroyed. The grandees, resentful that the

Songstress Queen had slandered the heir apparent and killed Li Mu, had her killed and exterminated her family. Together they enthroned Jia at Dai.[190] After seven years they could not defeat Qin. Zhao was then annihilated and became a commandery [of Qin].

The *Odes* says, "If a man have not dignity of demeanor,/What should he do but die?"[191] These words apply well to her.

The Verse Summary says,

> The Songstress Queen of King Daoxiang of Zhao
> Was insatiably covetous.
> She destroyed the true queen and heir,
> Working her deceit with guile.
> She was debauched with Lord Chunping,
> And ruthlessly pursued what she desired.
> She received bribes, ravaged Zhao,
> And died in the kingdom she destroyed.

8

SUPPLEMENTARY BIOGRAPHIES

8.1 THE WOMAN OF THE SUBURBS OF ZHOU

The woman of the suburbs of Zhou was a woman who had once encountered the Zhou grandee Yin Gu in the suburbs.[1]

In the time of King Jing of Zhou, Prince Zhao, presuming upon his favored position, caused disorder, struggling with King Jing over the succession so that King Jing could not enter [the capital].[2] Yin Gu, along with Ying, the Earl of Shao, and Lu, the Earl of Yuan, sided with Prince Zhao.[3] According to the *Spring and Autumn Annals,* in the second year of Duke Zhao in the sixth month, when Jin troops installed King [Jing], Yin Gu and Prince Zhao left, taking with them the archives of Zhou, and fled to Chu.[4]

Several days later, when [Yin Gu] was on the road returning [to the capital], the woman of the suburbs of Zhou came upon him and reproached him, saying, "When you are here, you encourage others to bring about calamity. When you depart, you return again after a few days. This being the case, is it possible that you can survive more than three years?" In the twenty-ninth year of Duke Zhao, forces from the capital did in fact kill Yin Gu.[5]

A man of discernment would say, "The woman of the suburbs of Zhou abhorred the manner in which Yin contributed to disorder. She knew that Heaven would not assist him and revealed the time of his demise. In the end, it was just as she said." The *Odes* says, "My illustrations are not taken from things remote;/Great Heaven makes no mistakes."[6] These words apply well to this case.

8.2 THE WOMAN ORATOR FROM THE STATE OF CHEN

The woman orator was a mulberry picker from the state of Chen.[7] Once a grandee of Jin named Xie Jufu was serving on a diplomatic mission in Song and passed through Chen. He happened upon the woman picking mulberries and stopped to tease her, saying, "Sing for me, then I'll leave you alone." The mulberry picker thus made for him the following song:

> At the gate to the tombs there are thorny brambles;
> They should be cut away with an axe.
> That man is not good,
> And the people of the State know it.
> They know it, but he will not desist;
> Long it has been thus with him.[8]

The grandee said, "Sing another stanza." The woman sang,

> At the gate to the tombs there are plum trees;
> Owls roost there.
> That man is not good,
> And I sing to admonish him.
> I admonish him, but he pays me no heed;—
> When he is overthrown, he will think of me.

The grandee said, "There are indeed plum trees here, but where are the owls?" The woman said, "Chen is a small state wedged between two large states. You control it with starvation and besiege it with troops. If even people flee, how much more the owls?" The grandee then relented and let her go.

A man of discernment would say, "The woman orator was chaste, upright, and rhetorically skilled. She was accommodating and compliant yet maintained her principles." The *Odes* says, "Having seen my noble lord,/He was pleased and showed us all courtesy."[9] These words describe this case well.

8.3 THE ELDER SISTER OF NIE ZHENG

[The elder sister of Nie Zheng] was the elder sister of the courageous man-at-arms of Qi, Nie Zheng.[10]

After the death of Nie Zheng's mother, his elder sister was his only surviving [family member]. At the behest of Yan Zhongzi of Puyang, Nie Zheng had assassinated the prime minister of Hann, Xia Lei.[11] The men he had killed numbered in the dozens, and fearing that disastrous consequences would be visited upon his sister, Nie flayed the skin from his face, gouged out his eyes, and slashed his flesh before he died.[12] Hann exposed his corpse in the marketplace and posted a reward of one thousand cash for information, but no one knew who he was.

His sister said, "My younger brother was worthy indeed. To cherish my own life and thus obliterate my brother's name is not what he would have wished." So she went to Hann, wept over Nie Zheng's corpse, and told the officials, "The one who killed Hann's prime minister was my younger brother, Nie Zheng of Deepwell Village in Zhi."[13] She then killed herself beside his corpse.

When her act became known throughout the states of Jin, Chu, Qi, and Wey, they all said, "Not only was Nie Zheng brave, his elder sister was also a heroic woman!"

A man of discernment would say, "Nie Zheng's elder sister was empathetic and courageous. She refused to forgo death so that [her brother's] name would not be forgotten." The *Odes* says, "On the dreaded occasion of death and burial,/ It is brothers who greatly sympathize."[14] This means that during the trials of death and mourning, only brothers can truly sympathize with each other. These words apply to her as well.

8.4 THE MOTHER OF THE WANGSUN LINEAGE

The mother of the Wangsun lineage was the mother of the Qi grandee Wangsun Jia.[15] When Jia was fifteen, he went to serve King Min of Qi.[16] [At the time], the country was in great disorder. King Min fled and was killed, but the people of his kingdom did not seek out the culprit.[17]

Wangsun's mother told him, "If you go out in the morning and come back late, I stand by the door and watch for you. In the evening, if you go out and don't return, I stand by the village gate and watch for you. At present, you serve the king, and the king has fled, but you don't know where he is. Why then did you still return home?"

Wangsun Jia then went to the marketplace and issued an order to the common people, saying, "Nao Chi has brought disorder to the state of Qi and killed King Min.[18] Those of you who wish to join me in punishing him, bare your right shoulder!"[19] Four hundred men from the market followed him, and together they punished Nao Chi, stabbing and killing him.

A man of discernment would say, "Wangsun's mother was dutiful and able in instruction." The *Odes* says, "Teach and train your sons,/And they will become as good as you are."[20] These words apply well to this case.

8.5 THE MOTHER OF CHEN YING

[Chen Ying's mother] was the mother of Chen Ying, the Marquis of Tangyi of the Han dynasty.[21] Earlier, Ying had served as the Scrivener of Dongyang.[22] He had long been a trusted resident of the district and was esteemed as an elder. It so happened that during the time of the Second Emperor of Qin, the youths of Dongyang murdered the district magistrate.[23] Several thousands of them gathered together to establish a new leader, but they had no appropriate candidate. So they approached Chen Ying.

Chen Ying declined, saying that he was unable, but they forced him to be their leader. When his followers in the district reached twenty thousand men, they wanted to make Ying king.

Ying's mother said, "As a woman married into this family, I have heard that its ancestors have never received any particularly great honor. Now suddenly to acquire great fame would be inauspicious. It would be better to place your troops under the command of another. If you are successful, then you might be enfeoffed as a marquis. If you fail, then it will be easy to escape without anyone identifying you."

Ying followed her advice and placed his troops under the command of Xiang Liang.[24] Liang gave him the title "Pillar of the State." Later, when the Xiang lineage was defeated, Ying gave his allegiance to the Han, and in recognition of his contributions was enfeoffed as the Marquis of Tangyi.

A man of discernment would say, "Ying's mother understood Heaven's decrees. She was also able to maintain the ancestral legacy so that blessings were transmitted to later generations. Her deliberations were profound indeed." The *Odes* says, "He would leave his plans to his descendants,/And secure comfort and support to his son."[25] These words apply well to her.

8.6 THE MOTHER OF WANG LING

[The mother of Wang Ling was] the mother of the Han Chancellor, the Marquis of Anguo, Wang Ling.[26] In the beginning, Ling was regarded as one of the district's most dashing figures. Before Gaozu had become eminent, he looked up to Ling as an elder brother.[27] When Gaozu began his uprising in Pei, Ling gathered about him several thousand followers and placed his troops under the command of the King of Han.[28]

Xiang Yu, who was by now an enemy of the Han, captured Wang Ling's mother and held her in his camp.[29] When Ling's messenger arrived, [Xiang Yu] seated Ling's mother facing east, hoping to win over Ling.[30] Ling's mother, while privately seeing off the messenger, wept, saying, "For this old lady's sake, please tell Ling to serve the King of Han well. The King of Han is a great man. Do not on my account be of two minds. Tell him that I am already dead." Then, to incite Ling, she fell on a sword and died.

Xiang Yu was furious and had her boiled. Ling, for his part, became even more determined, and in the end assisted Gaozu in bringing stability to all under Heaven. His rank reached that of chancellor and he was made a marquis, a rank he passed down for five generations.

A man of discernment would say, "Wang Ling's mother was able to cast aside her own life for the sake of duty, and it was by this means that she established her son." The *Odes* says, "My person is rejected;/What avails it to care for what may come after?"[31] [These words describe] an empathy that endures to the end of one's life.[32] The empathy of Ling's mother continued to exert an influence for five generations.

8.7 THE MOTHER OF ZHANG TANG

[The mother of Zhang Tang] was the mother of the Han Imperial Counselor Zhang Tang.[33] On the basis of his knowledge of legal writings, Tang served the Filial Emperor Wu of the Han as Imperial Counselor.[34] He was contentious and fond of humiliating others, for which his mother often angrily criticized him. By nature he was unable to repent and reform. Inevitably, he provoked the resentment of the Chancellor Yan Qingdi and his three chief clerks.[35] When the King of Zhao memorialized the throne about one of Zhang Tang's crimes, Zhang was detained in prison by the Superintendent of Trials.[36] Meanwhile, the chancellor and the three chief clerks forwarded more evidence of his crimes, whereupon Zhang committed suicide. When Zhang's brothers and sons wanted to give him a lavish burial, his mother said, "Tang was an eminent minister of the Son of Heaven, but he died in disgrace. Why then should we give him a lavish burial?"

His body was therefore conveyed on an oxcart, and he was buried with an inner but no outer coffin. When the Son of Heaven heard about it, he said, "A mother of this sort will produce the same kind of son!" He then made a thorough investigation of the case and executed the three chief clerks. Chancellor Yan Qingdi committed suicide.

A man of discernment would say, "Zhang Tang's mother was able to restrain herself and enlighten the ruler of the time." The *Odes* says, "Of that splendid eldest Jiang,/Her virtuous fame will not be forgotten."[37] These words apply well to her.

8.8 THE MOTHER OF JUAN BUYI

[The mother of Juan Buyi] was the mother of the Han Governor of the Capital, Juan Buyi.[38] She was empathetic and skilled at teaching. When Buyi became governor of the capital, he would travel to the various districts to review the records of prisoners.[39] When he returned, his mother would always immediately ask if he had overturned any convictions and inquire how many people had been spared the death penalty. When Buyi had overturned the convictions of many people, his mother would smile, drink, eat, and talk with a great joy that was markedly different from her usual behavior. But if no one had been released, his mother would become angry and refuse to eat. Because of this, Buyi was strict but not cruel in the administration of his official duties.

A man of discernment would say, "Buyi's mother was able to teach with empathy." The *Odes* says, "The angry terrors of Compassionate Heaven/Extend through the world below."[40] This means that the Way of Heaven cherishes life and deplores cruelty in the world.

8.9 THE WIFE OF YANG

The wife of Yang was the wife of the Han Chancellor, the Marquis of Anping, Yang Chang.[41]

Upon the death of Emperor Zhao, He, the King of Changyi, came to the throne. But he behaved disgracefully.[42] General-in-Chief Huo Guang and General of Chariots and Cavalry Zhang Anshi deliberated and wanted to depose He and enthrone a new emperor.[43]

After they completed their discussions, they asked the Superintendent of Agriculture, Tian Yannian, to report the matter to Chang.[44] Chang was alarmed and didn't know what to say. With perspiration drenching the back of his robe, he could only say, "I see."

When Yannian left to adjust his robe, Chang's wife immediately emerged from the eastern chamber and told him, "This is a critical matter of state.[45] The General-in-Chief has already made a decision and has asked the Nine Ministers of State to come and report the matter to you.[46] If you don't quickly respond and demonstrate solidarity with the General-in-Chief but hesitate and make no decision, their first order of business will be to put you to death."

When Yannian returned, Chang, his wife, and Yannian discussed the matter and agreed to implement the General-in-Chief's proposal. They joined together to depose the King of Changyi and enthrone Emperor Xuan.[47] A little more than a month later, Chang died, whereupon his fief was increased by 3,500 households.

A man of discernment would say, "Chang's wife can indeed be said to have understood how events are triggered." The *Odes* says, "Truly that worthy lady,/ With her admirable virtue, is come to instruct me."[48] These words apply well to her deeds.

8.10 XIAN, WIFE OF HUO GUANG

Xian, the wife of Huo [Guang], was the wife of the Han General-in-Chief and Bolu Marquis, Huo Guang.[49] She was extravagant, dissolute, and cruel, and disregarded laws and regulations.

As a loyal and cautious man, Guang had received the dying command of Filial Emperor Wu to support and assist the young ruler.[50] Furthermore, during the reign of Filial Emperor Xuan, because of Huo's efforts to enthrone the emperor, he was greatly honored and favored to a degree that no other official enjoyed.

Xian had a young daughter whose style name was Chengjun and had hoped that this daughter would obtain noble rank. But no opportunity presented itself until Emperor Xuan's consort, Empress Xu, fell ill just as she was about to give birth.

At the time, Xian told the female physician, Chunyu Yan, "Childbirth is one of the most momentous events in a woman's life, and ten die for each one that survives.[51] Since the empress is just about to give birth, it would be possible to use this occasion to slip something into her medicine to do away with her. If you can help my daughter to become empress, wealth and honor will come to us all."

Yan agreed to her plan and added ground aconite seeds to the large pill made by the grand physician and gave it to the empress. She was thus able to kill Empress Xu by poisoning.

When the affair came to a critical pass, Xian told Guang what had happened.[52] Huo Guang was shocked and horrified, and since Yan had already been punished, he sent a report to the throne asking the emperor to make a note that Yan should not receive further punishment. Xian then set about preparing Chengjun's wardrobe and other items that she would need in the palace. Thus it came to pass that she was made empress.

At this time, the son of Empress Xu, as son of the primary wife, was established as heir apparent. Xian became so angry that she spit blood and refused to eat, saying, "This child was born to the emperor when he was still a commoner.[53] How is it that he has been made heir apparent? If my daughter has a son, will he be made a mere king?" She then instructed the empress to poison the heir apparent. The empress summoned the heir apparent to dine with her several times, but each time his governess tasted the food first.

After Guang died, his son Yu inherited the rank of Marquis of Bolu. Xian made arrangements to change the burial grounds created while Guang was alive by enlarging them and making them very lavish. She had a "spirit path" constructed and made a covered walkway, where concubines and female slaves were confined.[54] She also built mansions and commissioned a grand carriage appointed with embroidered cushions and armrests, painted with gold, and equipped with padded wheels. It was drawn by female slaves who donned colorful silk clothing for Xian's leisure excursions. Xian also developed an illicit relationship with the Supervisory Slave, Feng Zidu.[55] Meanwhile, [her son] Yu and his cronies became more self-indulgent with each passing day.

When Emperor Xuan heard about their immoral behavior, and when details about the murder of Empress Xu began to circulate, Xian became alarmed. She began laying plans for a rebellion whereby the heir apparent would be deposed and Yu established in his place. When the plot came to light, all members of the Huo family, including their maternal and paternal cousins, were cut in two at the waist, and Xian's corpse was exposed in the marketplace.[56] The empress was deposed and sent to live in the Palace of the Shining Tower.

The *Odes* says, "The great destruction they cause/Is unknown to themselves."[57] This refers to becoming so habituated to evil that one is no longer aware of one's own wrongdoing. This can be said of Xian, the wife of Huo.

8.11 THE MOTHER OF YAN YANNIAN

[The mother of Yan Yannian] was the mother of the Governor of Henan, Yan Yannian of Donghai.[58] She had given birth to five sons, all of whom possessed the qualities required of officials and had reached the rank of two thousand piculs.[59] The people of Donghai referred to her as "Madam Yan of the Ten Thousand Piculs."

When Yannian served as Governor of Henan, wherever he went he had a reputation for being severe. During the winter, when prisoners from the districts were transferred to his office for prosecution, blood flowed for several *li*. The people of Henan called him the "Butcher-in-Chief."

Once his mother came from Donghai, wishing to spend the La festival with Yannian.[60] When she arrived in Luoyang and encountered the prisoners who had undergone punishment, she was greatly alarmed. She then stopped at a lodge in the city and refused to enter Yannian's quarters. When Yannian went to the lodge to visit her, his mother closed her door and wouldn't see him. When Yannian took off his cap and prostrated himself before her [door], she finally agreed to see him.

She then berated Yannian, saying, "You have been fortunate to serve as this commandery's governor with sole authority over a territory of one thousand [square] *li*. But I have heard nothing of your benevolence, righteousness, or use of education as a means to bring peace and security to the ignorant masses. Instead, you have relied on exacting punishments and executing large numbers of people in order to assert your authority. Is this what is meant by 'serving as father and mother to the people'?" Yannian admitted his error, bowing with his head touching the ground, and apologizing until his mother agreed to be taken in a carriage to his residence.

When his mother had seen the completion of the La rituals, she told Yannian, "The Way of Heaven is numinously perspicacious; you cannot kill others on your authority alone.[61] I do not intend to spend my old age watching my grown son suffer execution.[62] I will take leave of you and return east to prepare a place for a grave."[63]

She then left and returned home, recounting to his brothers and kinsmen what she had told Yan. After a little more than a year, a document drawn up by one of Yannian's assistants implicated Yannian on ten charges. The investigation was passed on to the Secretary to the Imperial Counselor, who then executed Yannian in the marketplace.[64] All of Donghai praised his mother as worthy and wise.

A man of discernment would say, "Yan's mother possessed empathetic wisdom and trusted in the Way." The *Odes* says, "The sorrow of my heart,/Can it only be of the moment?"[65] These words apply well to Yan's mother.

8.12 BRILLIANT COMPANION FENG OF THE HAN

Brilliant Companion Feng of the Han was the Brilliant Companion of Filial Emperor Yuan and the daughter of General of the Right and Superintendent of the Palace Feng Fengshi.[66]

In the second year of Emperor Yuan's reign, the Brilliant Companion was selected to enter the rear palace, starting at the rank of Superior Attendant.[67] After several months she was given the rank of Comely One. When she gave birth to a son who would later become King Xiao of Zhongshan, her rank was changed from Comely One to Favorite Beauty.[68]

Once during the *jianzhao* period, the emperor, followed by all of the palace women, visited the Tiger Enclosure to watch a spectacle of fighting beasts.[69] A bear escaped from the enclosure, climbed over the railings, and headed for their pavilion. The assembled ladies and the Brilliant Companion Fu all fled in terror. But Favorite Beauty Feng directly confronted the bear and stood fast. The attendants were thus able to attack and kill the bear.

The Son of Heaven questioned the Favorite Beauty about it, saying, "It is human nature to be terrified under such circumstances, so how is it that you were able to confront the bear?" She replied, "I have heard that wild beasts stop once they obtain human prey. I was afraid that it was going to reach the place where you were seated, so I placed myself in front of it." Emperor Yuan sighed, and from this time forward he felt profound respect for her. The Brilliant Companion Fu and the others all felt ashamed.

In the following year, the King of Zhongshan was enfeoffed, and Feng was promoted from Favorite Beauty to Brilliant Companion. She followed the king to his kingdom and was then called the Queen Dowager of Zhongshan.[70]

A man of discernment would say, "The Brilliant Companion was brave and strove to fulfill her duty." The *Odes* says, "The ruler's favorites/Follow him to the hunt."[71] The *Analects* says, "To see what is right and not to do it is want of courage."[72] The Brilliant Companion exemplifies both sayings.

8.13 THE WIFE AND DAUGHTER OF WANG ZHANG

The wife and daughter of Wang Zhang were [respectively] the wife and the daughter of the Han Governor of the Capital, Wang Zhongqing.[73]

As a student, Zhongqing studied in Chang'an, living alone with his wife. Once, he fell ill, and lacking a quilt, he slept under cattle-warming blankets. When he began to utter his dying words, weeping profusely, his wife snorted and became angry, saying, "You are honored and valued at court. Indeed, who is more honored than you? But now that you have become ill and fallen on hard times, you don't rouse yourself to action but instead weep and snivel. How pathetic!" Afterward, Zhang's official rank reached that of Governor of the Capital.

Emperor Cheng's maternal uncle, the General-in-Chief Wang Feng, controlled the government and monopolized power.[74] Although [Wang] Zhang had been promoted by Feng, he was unwilling to become his adherent. When a solar eclipse occurred, Zhang sent a sealed confidential report to the throne concerning the event, stating that Feng should be removed from his post.[75]

When he had completed the report and was about to submit it to the throne, his wife stopped him, saying, "People ought to know when enough is enough. Have you already forgotten about the time when you were reduced to weeping under the cattle blanket?" Zhang said, "This is not something that women and children understand!"

When his report reached the emperor, the Son of Heaven could not bear to remove Feng from his post. After this incident, Zhang was targeted by Feng and eventually charged with the crime of being "greatly refractory," after which he was detained and imprisoned.[76]

Zhang had a young daughter who was twelve years old. One night, she called out in tears, saying, "Earlier, when we were at the jail and heard the prisoners being counted, there were nine.[77] Just now they stopped at eight. My father was always resolute. The first to die must have been my father." The next day when they made inquiries, they discovered that he had in fact died.[78] Zhang's wife and child were then transferred to Hepu.[79]

After Feng died, the Marquis of Chengdu, Wang Shang, became the General-in-Chief.[80] He was grieved over Zhang's innocence and petitioned for the return of Zhang's wife and child and the restoration of their property, land, houses, and staff.[81]

A man of discernment would say, "Wang Zhang's wife understood the principle of 'contracting and expanding.'"[82] The *Odes* says, "The terrors of great Heaven are excessive,/But indeed I have committed no crime."[83] This means that when the king governs with cruelty, the innocent will meet with disaster.

8.14 FAVORITE BEAUTY BAN[84]

Favorite Beauty Ban was the daughter of Bureau Head of the Left and [Colonel] of the Picked Cavalry, Ban Kuang, and the Favorite Beauty of Filial Emperor Cheng of the Han.[85] She was endowed with extraordinary ability and skilled in rhetoric. When she first entered the rear palace, she was selected to serve as Junior Attendant. But in a very short time she was greatly favored and made Favorite Beauty.

Once, when Emperor Cheng was at leisure in the rear court, he wanted to take the Favorite Beauty for a drive in his carriage. But she refused, saying, "When I look at ancient paintings and illustrations, the worthy and sage rulers are always depicted with their renowned ministers at their sides. It is only the last rulers of the Three Epochs who are shown with their women.[86] If I ride with you, won't that make you look like one of them?"

The emperor was impressed with her response and dropped the plan. When the Empress Dowager heard about it, she was pleased and said, "In antiquity there was Fan Ji, and now we have the Favorite Beauty Ban."[87]

Whenever Ban recited from the *Odes, The Modest and Retiring, Emblems of Virtue,* or *The Instructress,* she always repeated the words three times.[88] Whenever she came before the emperor or presented a memorial to him, she always followed ancient ritual.

From the *hongjia* period onward, Emperor Cheng began to favor other women of his harem, so the Favorite Beauty presented him with her attendant Li Ping.[89] Ping received the emperor's favor and was established as Favorite Beauty. He said, "Earlier, Empress Wey also arose from humble beginnings."[90] He then bestowed upon Ping the surname Wey so that she was called Favorite Beauty Wey.

Later, Zhao Feiyan and her sister were favored. Arrogant and jealous, they slandered the Favorite Beauty, stating that she harbored malicious intentions and had uttered imprecations.[91] When the Favorite Beauty was questioned on this charge, she said, "I have heard that 'Death and life are fated, and wealth and honor are decided by Heaven.' If even one who makes an effort to behave honorably cannot count on good fortune, then what can one who does evil expect? If ghosts and spirits have consciousness, they would not accept the pleas of the disloyal. If they have no consciousness, then what benefit could I expect by making such a plea?[92] I would therefore never have done such a thing." The emperor was pleased with her response and, pitying her, presented her with one hundred *jin* of gold.[93]

As Zhao Feiyan became more arrogant and possessive, the Favorite Beauty feared that it would not be long before she herself became endangered. She therefore asked to care for the Empress Dowager in the Palace of Eternal Trust. The emperor agreed to this plan. The Favorite Beauty therefore withdrew to the Eastern Palace, where she composed the following rhapsody to express her sorrow.[94]

From my ancestors I received an inheritance of virtue,
And through this blessed endowment,
I, though a humble person, advanced to the palace
And took my place among the lower ranks in the inner courtyard.[95]
I have received my sage ruler's nurturing kindness,
Which rivals the resplendent brilliance of sun and moon.
Extending his radiant luster,
I received his abundant favor at Zengcheng manor.[96]
Having been favored beyond my worth,
I presume to savor those moments of joy.
Waking or sleeping, I repeatedly sigh.
I smooth my nuptial sash as a reminder,
Lay out my portraits of women and make them my mirror.[97]
I turn to the Women's Counselor and query her on the *Odes*.
I am moved by warnings about the wife who "announces the dawn,"[98]
And lament the evil deeds of the voluptuous Bao [Si].[99]
I admire Huang and Ying, the two wives of Shun,[100]
And glorify Ren and Si, the matriarchs of the Zhou.[101]
Though I am ignorant and cannot aspire to their examples,
How could I put them out of mind and forget them?
As the years pass, I grieve and brood,
Mourning the decline of once-resplendent beauty.
I ache for the [children born to me] in the Yanglu and Zhe Hall,[102]
Who all met with misfortune while still in swaddling clothes.
Was it due to some misdeed of mine,
For which Heaven could not be entreated?
The bright sun quickly shifts its rays;
Evening falls, and it becomes dark.

Still, I am supported above and below by munificent virtue,
And not cast aside for my transgressions.
I offer [the Empress Dowager] reverent care in the Eastern Palace,
Requesting to serve her in her final days in the Palace of Lasting Trust.[103]
I will sprinkle and sweep her canopied room
Till death ends my own appointed days.
May my bones be buried at the foot of the mountain,
Resting in the abundant shade of pines and cypresses.
Recapitulation:
Hidden deep in the palace, where seclusion breeds quiet,
The main gate is shut, and the smaller one, locked.
The ornamented halls are dusty, and the jade steps are covered in moss.
The central courtyard is overgrown, covered in green grasses;
The broad halls are dim, and the curtains are drawn.
Through gaps in the slatted windows, the wind soughs,
Ruffling my robe and wafting the red silk gauze,
Rustling, swishing, making the fine silks sound.
My spirit roves into the distance from these serene surroundings:
If my lord never visits, how can I receive his favor?
Looking down at the red tiles,
I think of my lord's ornamented slippers;
Looking up at the Cloud-Patterned Chamber,
Two streams of tears begin to flow.[104]
I gaze about me with a resigned expression,
And fill my winged goblet, hoping to dispel my cares.
People are born into this world but once,
And pass quickly like drifting clouds.
I have enjoyed exceptional honor and fame,
And dwelt in the greatest splendor one born into this world could know.
So I rouse myself to enjoy all pleasures to the fullest—
Future blessings cannot be counted on.
"Green Robe," "White Flower,"
As in ancient times, hold true now.[105]

When Emperor Cheng died, the Favorite Beauty served in his funerary park.[106] When she died, she was buried there.

A man of discernment would say, "Favorite Beauty Ban's refusal to ride with the emperor in his carriage matched the integrity of Queen Xuan. Her recommendation to rank Li Ping as her peer made her an equal of the virtuous Fan Ji. The explanation she offered when she had been accused of laying curses rivaled the wisdom of Ding Jiang. Her willingness to provide reverent care in the Eastern Palace were comparable to the good works of the [Filial] Widow [of Chen].[107] When she composed rhapsodies, she was sorrowful without being self-lacerating and submitted herself to fate without resentment." The *Odes* says,

> There is our elegant and accomplished prince,
> As from the knife and the file,
> As from the chisel and the polisher!
> How grave is he and dignified!
> How commanding and distinguished!
> Our elegant and accomplished prince,
> Never can he be forgotten.[108]

These words describe Favorite Beauty Ban well.

8.15 ZHAO FEIYAN OF THE HAN

Zhao Feiyan and her younger sister were the daughters of Zhao Lin, the Marquis of Chengyang, and the favored consorts of Filial Emperor Cheng.[109] When Feiyan was first born, her parents did not lift her up. But when she had not died after three days, they took her up and raised her.[110]

Once, when Emperor Cheng was traveling incognito, he stopped at the residence of Princess Hengyang, where a musical performance was being held.[111] When the emperor saw Feiyan, he was delighted with her. He summoned her to enter the palace and she was greatly favored. She had a younger sister who was also summoned. Both of them were made Favorite Beauties. When their eminence eclipsed all other women in the rear palace, their father, Lin, was enfeoffed as the Marquis of Chengyang. Soon, Feiyan was established as empress, and her younger sister was made Brilliant Companion.

After Feiyan was made empress and [the emperor's] affections began to fade, the Brilliant Companion became favored above all others. She resided in the Zhaoyang Lodge. Its court was vermilion, the upper hall was lacquered with a threshold of gilded bronze, and the stairs were made of white jade. All along the walls the exposed beams were decorated with gold rings inlaid with Lantian jade and adorned with bright pearls and kingfisher feathers. Such things had never before been seen in the rear palace.

The sisters were the sole objects of the emperor's devotion. Still, neither of them had borne a child. They were arrogant, seductive, unyielding, and regarded all in the rear palace with jealous suspicion.

Eventually, the emperor began to favor Fair Lady Xu, and she gave birth to a child.[112] When the Brilliant Companion heard about it, she told the emperor, "You have been deceiving me about spending time in the central palace.[113] Otherwise, how is it that Fair Lady Xu has given birth?"[114] She then flew into a rage, striking herself with her own hands and dashing her head against a pillar. She then flung herself from the bed to the floor, weeping and refusing to eat, saying, "Now what are you going to do with me? Just let me die!"

The emperor said, "I made a point of telling you about this, so why are you angry?" He too refused to eat. The Brilliant Companion said, "If it is as Your Majesty suggests, then why are you refusing to eat? You have always said, 'I promise that I will never turn my back on you.' But now Fair Lady Xu has given birth to a child, so you have indeed gone back on your promise. Why is that?" The emperor said, "I promise the Zhao family that I will never enthrone Lady Xu as empress, and in the whole world there will never be anyone who surpasses the Zhaos. There is nothing to worry about."

The emperor then summoned Lady Xu and ordered her to kill the child she had given birth to and to place it inside a leather case and bind it shut.[115] After the emperor and the Brilliant Companion both looked at [the child], it was bound up again, affixed with the seal of the Assistant to the Imperial Counselor, and taken out and buried beneath the wall of the prison.

Cao Gong, a woman employed as a scribe in the empress's palace whose courtesy name was Weineng, had [also] been favored by the emperor and given birth.[116] Once again the emperor complied with the wishes of the Brilliant Companion and ordered the child killed without asking whether it was male or female. When Gong had still not killed the child, the Brilliant Companion was infuriated.

Ji Wu, the Assistant Warden of the Prison of the Lateral Courts, asked the Palace Attendant at the Yellow Gates to submit a memorial to the emperor, which said, "Your Majesty has no heir. When it comes to sons, there is neither highborn nor humble.[117] Please consider this well." The emperor disregarded him. When the child was eight or nine days old, he was taken away and killed. The Brilliant Companion then gave Weineng a letter and some medicine, with orders to kill herself.[118] When Weineng received the letter, she said, "As expected, the two sisters will soon control all under Heaven! Indeed, my son has a widow's peak, just like Emperor Yuan![119] Where is my child now? Have they already killed him?" She then drank the medicine and died.

After this, all women who [conceived or] bore children after being favored by the emperor died immediately afterward, or were made to drink medicines that induced abortions. For this reason, Emperor Cheng was without an heir. After Emperor Cheng died, a successor was found among the imperial relatives outside of the emperor's direct line of descent, but he too was without issue.[120]

A man of discernment would say, "The Brilliant Companion Zhao was identical to Bao Si in her cruel depravity, while Emperor Cheng's delusion and recklessness were the same as those of King You."[121] The *Odes* says, "The pond is parched,/ Nothing will come from its banks./The spring is spent,/Nothing comes from within."[122] In the time of Emperor Cheng, his uncles dominated the outer court, while the Zhaos controlled the inner court.[123] In bringing about his own depletion, he indeed came to resemble the pool and the spring.[124]

8.16 EMPRESS WANG, CONSORT OF FILIAL EMPEROR PING OF THE HAN

Empress Wang of Filial Emperor Ping of the Han was the daughter of the An Han Duke, Senior Tutor, and Marshal of State Wang Mang and the empress of Filial Emperor Ping.[125] She was of gentle character and principled in her behavior. When Emperor Ping came to the throne, she was nine years old, and Wang Mang controlled the government. Wishing to emulate the earlier example of Huo Guang, he betrothed his daughter to the emperor.[126]

In a hypocritical display that was in fact designed to bring the [marriage] rituals to completion, he protested against the Empress Dowager's commissioning the Superintendent of the Lesser Treasury of the Changle Palace, the Superintendent of the Imperial Clan, and the Director of the Secretariat to present the betrothal gifts.[127] The Senior Tutor, the Chancellor, and the Imperial Counselor, along with forty of their subordinates, donning deerskin caps and white robes, then announced the betrothal in the ancestral temple.

The next year in spring, the Chancellor, the Imperial Counselor, and the Generals of the Right and Left were commissioned to escort the emperor's carriage to fetch the empress at the residence of the Duke Giving Tranquility to the Han. The Chancellor conferred upon [the empress] a corded imperial seal of office, mounted her carriage, and ordered the roads to be cleared for her procession.

Going through the Yanshou Gate of Shanglin Park, she entered the front hall of the Weiyang Palace. After the assembled ministers took their places and completed the ceremonies, an amnesty was declared for all under Heaven.[128] Rewards were given to all dukes, ministers, guards, and those who had performed various services according to their ranks.

A little more than a year after the empress had been installed, Emperor Ping died. Several years later, Wang Mang usurped the Han throne. The empress was eighteen years old at the time.

After the Liu family had been ousted, the empress refused to attend court, claiming to be ill. Wang Mang, feeling both respect and pity for her, decided to arrange a marriage for her. He ordered the heir of the General of State Sun Jian to array himself in finery and take a physician to go and inquire about her illness.[129] But the empress was furious and had his attendants caned. Because of this incident, she became ill and was unwilling to rise [from her bed]. Afterward, Wang Mang did not dare force the issue. When Han troops finally killed Wang Mang and set fire to the Weiyang Palace, the empress said, "How can I ever face the house of Han?" She then threw herself into the fire and died.[130]

A man of discernment would say, "Emperor Ping's consort exemplified a natural purity in her actions. Faced with survival or destruction, she did not alter her convictions. She can indeed be called a woman whose principles could not be sullied." The *Odes* says, "With his two tufts of hair falling over his forehead,/ He was my mate;/And I swear that till death, I will have no other."[131] These words describe her well.

8.17 LADY HANN OF THE GENGSHI EMPEROR

Lady Hann of Gengshi of the Han was the wife of Emperor Gengshi, Liu Shenggong.[132] She was fawning, depraved, seductive, fond of drink, and indecorous.

Earlier, at the end of Wang Mang's reign, Gengshi had made use of popular uprisings in Xinshi, Pinglin, and the Lower Yangze to make himself the Gengshi General.[133] His troops grew in might each day, until he named himself emperor and reestablished Han rule.

Shentu Jian attacked Wang Mang and sent his head to Yuan.[134] The Gengshi Emperor looked at it and said, "He would not have ended this way if he had been more like Huo Guang."[135] Lady Hann said, "If he hadn't ended this way, how could you have become emperor?" It was this sort of clever talk that emboldened the Gengshi Emperor.

The emperor began to neglect his official duties, and since Lady Hann was fond of drink and sensual pleasures, they spent each day together gorging themselves in drunken disarray. Finally, the emperor ordered one of his attendants to station himself behind a screen where he would pretend to be the emperor and address the assembled ministers. Knowing that the voice was not that of the emperor, the ministers became filled with resentment. When the ministers of the secretariat reported to the throne, Lady Hann would say, "The emperor was just now enjoying a drink with me. Must you use this particular moment to make a report?" Because of these incidents he could not maintain control, and the nobles deserted and rebelled.[136]

When the Red Eyebrows entered the pass, he could not stop them.[137] He then took his wife and children, handed over his imperial seal of office, and surrendered to the Red Eyebrows. He was then killed by the Red Eyebrows.

The *Odes* says, "Those who are benighted and ignorant/Are devoted to drink, and more so daily."[138] These words epitomize the Gengshi Emperor and Lady Hann.

8.18 THE WIFE OF LIANG HONG

The wife of Liang Hong was the wife of Liang Bochun of Youfufeng and a daughter of the Meng family who came from the same commandery as Liang.[139] She was very ugly in appearance but most refined in the practice of virtue. Many [men] from her village sought her, but in each case the girl would not agree to a match. When she reached the age of thirty, her parents demanded that she explain just what it was that she desired [in a husband]. She said, "I want someone with the principles and integrity of Liang Hong."

At the time, Liang was still unmarried. Many of the old distinguished families of Fufeng wanted to marry their daughters to him, but he too would not agree to a match with any of them. When he heard about the worthy conduct of the daughter of the Meng family, he sought to marry her.

Miss Meng entered his home arrayed in splendor. But after seven days, the ceremonies had still not been completed. The wife knelt and asked, "I have heard of my master's lofty righteousness and how has he rejected scores of women. I too have disappointed many men. Now that I have been selected to come here, I would like to know why."

Hong said, "I wanted someone who wore coarse clothes, with whom I could withdraw from the world and escape the times. Your fine silk attire and blackened brows are not what I desire."

The wife said, "I was afraid that you would not be able to stand me otherwise! Fortunately, I am prepared for a life of reclusion!" She then changed back into coarse clothing, and with her hair coiffed in a mallet-shaped chignon, came before him again. Hong said delightedly, "A woman like this is indeed the wife for me!" He then gave her the courtesy name Deyao and the name Mengguang, and himself the name Yunqi and the courtesy name Siguang. Together they went into seclusion in the mountains of Baling.[140]

At this time, Wang Mang's Xin dynasty had just been defeated.[141] Hong and his wife went into deep seclusion, engaging in plowing, weeding, and weaving to provide food and clothing for themselves. Reciting texts and playing the zither, they forgot about the joys of wealth and honor.

Later, Hong took his wife to Kuaiji, where he hired himself out as a grain pounder.[142] Although he worked among common laborers, each time [Liang's] wife brought him his meals, she raised the dish to eye level, not daring to gaze on him directly. She cultivated herself through ritual observances so that all present respected and admired her.[143]

A man of discernment would say, "Liang Hong's wife was fond of the Way and content in poverty. She was not anxious about honors and pleasure." The *Analects* says, "Riches and honors acquired by unrighteousness are to me as a floating cloud."[144] These words may well be applied to her.

8.19 EMPRESS MINGDE, NÉE MA

Empress Mingde, née Ma, was the consort of Emperor Ming of the Han and the daughter of the General Who Calms the Waves and Zhongcheng Marquis of Xinxi, Ma Yuan.[145]

As a child, she was precocious. At thirteen she was selected to enter the household of the heir apparent.[146] In her relations with her peers, she took care to ensure that all of them would have the opportunity to meet with her lord. Her efforts to place the interests of others ahead of her own were invariably motivated by utter sincerity, and because of this she was favored. When she [discussed] governmental affairs, her responses were always compassionate and principled. If there was something she was uneasy about, she would clearly lay out her reasons.

At this time, there were no women who were with child or who had given birth in the rear palace. [The future empress] often remarked that the time had come to establish an heir apparent.[147] She recommended and promoted her peers as if she feared she would never make up for lost time. When a woman of the rear palace had met with the emperor, she immediately took special pains to care for her. If a woman was especially favored, then she became even more solicitous.

At the time, there were few palace attendants, so that the empress took on many tasks herself. Once, after she finished sewing a dancer's upper robe, her hands had become chapped and chafed. But she never discussed such personal affairs with her attendants. This she did in an effort to prevent servants from misspeaking and for fear that they might, through a mere look, reveal something she had complained about. Thus, she took precautions to prevent the spread [of idle chatter]. And in this way she was cautious about small [but potentially troublesome] events.

In the third year of the *yongping* era, officials memorialized the throne about establishing an empress in the Palace of Prolonged Autumn to lead the eight concubines.[148] Though the emperor had not yet mentioned the matter, the Empress Dowager said, "Since the virtue of Honorable Lady Ma outshines that of all of the other women in the rear palace, then it is she [who should be selected]."[149] She was therefore elevated to the status of empress.

The empress herself wore coarse silk, while her attendants wore unembellished skirts with no decorative borders. Her entourage consisted of women of the Qiang, Hu, Wo, and Yue peoples, and none of her former staff were asked to serve.[150] When the kings and maternal kin came to court and saw her from afar wearing her robe of coarse silk, they thought it was fashioned of the finest fabric. But when they came closer and saw it, they laughed. The empress said, "This silk dyes well. That's the only reason I use it!" Elders who heard about this incident all sighed with admiration.

She did not enjoy travel and sightseeing and had never as much as looked out of the palace windows. She was also not fond of musical performances. Occasionally, the emperor would stay in the palaces in his imperial parks, but because of her predilections, she would rarely accompany him. But she would always warn him about rising with the birds at dawn because of the dangers posed by noxious vapors and humid conditions. She was always thoughtful in her exhortations, and so the emperor accepted her advice.

She was able to recite the *Book of Changes* and had studied the *Odes, Analects*, and the *Spring and Autumn Annals* and was able to explain their general significance. She had read the *Songs of Chu* and especially admired rhapsodies and hymns, but disliked anything too frivolous or florid.[151] When she listened to what others had to say and observed debates, she was always adept at abstracting the essential points. When she read the "Basic Annals of Emperor Guangwu," she never failed to sigh with admiration when she came to the passage that said,

"When he was presented with a Thousand-League Horse and a precious sword, the emperor had the horse yoked to his drummer's cart and gave the sword to a mounted guard, since he did not like to handle precious items."[152]

At the time, there was a trial concerning Chu, in which those who had been imprisoned all testified against each other.[153] A great number of people were implicated.[154] The empress feared that such biased evidence would cloud [the truth]. So when the opportunity presented itself, she explained the situation to the emperor, who was deeply pained by this turn of events. In a state of agitation, he rose in the middle of the night, dressed, and continued thinking over and discussing what she had told him without bringing in any of his ministers or subordinates.

The empress's ambitions were all directed toward self-mastery and assisting [the ruler].[155] She did not interfere at court on behalf of her own family. Her elder brother served as the Rapid-as-a-Tiger [General] of the Household.[156] Her younger brothers served as Gentlemen of the Yellow Gates.[157] Up to the *yongping* era their positions remained the same.[158]

When Emperor Ming was in poor health, he once summoned the Gentleman of the Yellow Gate [Ma] Fang, who went to visit him with a physician and medicines, tending him day and night with great solicitude. When the emperor died, the empress compiled his *Diary of Activity and Repose*, but omitted mention of Fang's visiting the emperor with medicine and a doctor.[159]

It came to pass that the dukes, ministers, and marquises submitted a memorial stating that it would be appropriate to honor the old ordinances and enfeoff the maternal relatives.[160] The Empress Dowager proclaimed, "That maternal relatives tend to become overbearing and unrestrained is a fact that has been transmitted across generations. Throughout the *yongping* era, I personally reviewed the situation, and, determined that my own kin must not indulge in unrestrained behavior, I did not allow them positions of power. At present, there has been a drought for several years so that displaced people fill the streets. Some of them are at the point of starvation. Bestowing fiefs at this time would be highly inappropriate and must not be done.

"Furthermore, our late emperor declared that the [territory] allotted to the kings should be half of that given to the King of Chu and the King of Huaiyang, and [specifically] that 'My sons should not be placed on par with the sons of Emperor Guangwu.'[161] How can one even think of comparing the Ma family to the Yin family?[162]

"I have cultivated myself, hoping to uphold my obligation to our late emperor above, and to prevent the deterioration of his virtue here below. For my clothing,

I have worn robes of coarse cloth, and for my meals, I have not requested to be served only those things that I particularly enjoy eating. As for my attendants, none of them wear scented garments but plain silk, and nothing more.[163] In this way I had hoped to serve as a leader to all, thinking that when the maternal kin observed me, they would be moved and practice self-restraint. But on the contrary, they all claimed that it is my nature to love frugality.

"Earlier, when we once passed through the gate of the Glittering Dragon [Park] to meet with and inquire after the maternal kin, their carriages flowed like water, their steeds were like dragons, and their slaves were dressed in green arm guards with neat white collars and sleeves.[164] When I looked back at the attendants at my side, they paled by comparison. I did not reprimand them but simply cut their annual expenditures, hoping to silence and put an end to this sort of clamor. No wise subject would ever attempt to be like his ruler, so how much more the case for family members?

"The reason people want to be enfeoffed as marquises is simply that they desire to use the emolument to nourish and care for their kin, to offer and maintain their sacrifices, and to see that they themselves are warm and well-fed. At present, when sacrifices are made, they receive the victims from eminent officials, precious items from the commanderies and kingdoms, grain from the Minister of Agriculture, and for personal use, clothing made from remnants of silk from the imperial palace.[165] Could this still not be enough? Must they also be the recipients of fiefs by imperial fiat? It is the duty of the Palace of Eternal Joy to address such issues. Shouldn't the inner court after all be ashamed before the world?"[166]

Before this, when the Colonel of the City Gates and the Colonel of the Elite Cavalry arranged for their mother's funeral, they erected a mound that was somewhat larger [than what was deemed appropriate].[167] Afterward, when the Empress Dowager commented on it, they were alarmed and immediately reduced the size of the mound. Those ranked both above and below them took note and proceeded to observe all the laws and regulations, while no one among the families of the kings and marquises dared to violate the prohibitions.

When the King of Guangping, the King of Julu, and the King of Lecheng came to court to inquire after [the emperor], she saw that their carriages, saddles, and bridles were all pure black without any decorations in gold, silver, or other colors, and that the horses were no more than six feet high.[168] Emperor Zhang, in accord with the wishes of the Empress Dowager, presented them with five million cash. But the Princess of Xinping, who was wearing a purple silk robe with a straight white lapel, was reprimanded and did not receive so generous a gift.[169] After this the imperial kin became uniform in their dress. Having been instructed without severity, they all complied. This was because [the Empress Dowager] had relied on her personal example to lead them.

She also set up a weaving room and a room for rearing silkworms in the Glittering Dragon Park, which the Empress Dowager would personally visit to observe its operations. She took great pleasure in this activity. She also taught the young princes, testing them on their ability to recite and discuss [texts] joyfully and harmoniously. Day and night, to the very end of her life, she discussed the Way. She cared for Emperor Zhang more fervently than if she had actually given birth to him, and Emperor Zhang's treatment of her plumbed the depths of filial piety.

A man of discernment would say, "At home, the Virtuous Empress served as a model for all of the women, and throughout the realm she was regarded as an exemplary Mother Empress." The *Odes* says, "Here is a good and righteous ruler,/ Who is looked up to by the people and by all;/He keeps his heart, and his plans are formed on mature deliberation,/Searching carefully for helpers."[170] These words describe her well.

8.20 LADY LIANG YI

Lady Liang Yi was the daughter of Liang Song, the wife of Fan Diao, the aunt of Filial Emperor He of the Han, and the twin sister of Empress Gonghuai.[171]

In the beginning, when Empress Gonghuai was selected to enter the lateral courts, she served Filial Emperor Zhang, was favored by him, and gave birth to Emperor He.[172] He was made heir apparent, and Empress Dou raised him as her own child.[173]

Upon Emperor He's birth, the Liang family was delighted and congratulated each other, which was brought to the attention of Empress Dou. Empress Dou was arrogant and overbearing, and in an effort to monopolize power and harm other distaff kin, she slandered the Liang family. At the time, while [Liang] Song was in his native commandery of Anding, an order was issued to seize and kill him and to move his dependants to Jiuzhen.[174]

Later, when Emperor He came to the throne and Empress Dou had died, all of the Dous were either put to death or banished for their crimes.[175] [Liang] Yi, who was living among the common people, submitted a memorial to the throne demanding justice. It said, "Formerly, when my twin sister, the Honorable Lady, entered the rear palace, she received most generous kindness from our late emperor and was favored by him.[176] August Heaven transmitted its mandate, and she gave birth to the enlightened and sage [ruler] that is Your Majesty. Because of the false accusations of Dou Xian and his brothers, she was harassed to the point of death.[177] My father, [Liang] Song, suffered injustice and died in prison, and his bones remain unburied.[178] My elderly mother and orphaned brothers were banished to distant lands ten thousand *li* away. I alone escaped, hiding in the wilds, fearing for my life and without any means to make my plight known.[179]

"Now, through your divine and sage virtue and control of the subtle triggers of all events, the evils committed by Dou Xian and his brothers have been punished, so that boundlessly, throughout the whole world, all things find their proper place. Because I have been fortunate to live and breathe again, to wipe my eyes and once again see, I brave death to make my plea.

"My father has already perished and cannot be made to live again. My mother is now seventy years old. My younger brother, [Liang] Tang, and others were sent far away to the ends of the earth, and I don't know whether they are dead or alive.[180] I therefore beg that my mother and brothers be allowed to return to their native commandery and that I be allowed to collect the bones of my father [Liang] Song for burial.

"I have heard that when Emperor Wen ascended the throne, the Bo family received generous treatment, and upon Emperor Xuan's succession, the Shi family flourished again.[181] I grieve that though our own family can claim bonds like that of the Bo and Shi, as maternal kin we alone have received no special mercy."

When this memorial was presented to the throne, the Son of Heaven was moved and astonished.[182] He ordered the Regular Attendant and the Prefect of the Lateral Courts to investigate the case. After the facts of the case had been made clear, they summoned [Yi] for an audience.

When she came face to face with the emperor, she wept. He then rewarded her for her loyalty to her sister. Because Yi had always exhibited principled behavior, and because she had taken the lead in this affair, the emperor was very pleased with her and gave her the title Lady Liang. He also promoted Yi's husband, Fan Diao, to the post of Gentleman of the Palace, and later made him Commander of the Feathered Forest Guards.[183]

[Ritual observances] for Empress Gonghuai's reinterment were held at the Chengguang Palace, and she was buried in the Western Tombs. Liang Song was posthumously made the Marquis of Kin Deserving Mercy. The emperor also ordered the return of Liang's mother and brothers. When they arrived, he conferred on her brothers marquisates and fiefs of five thousand households.

A man of discernment would say, "Lady Yi's tragic account brought to light her family's suffering, enlightened the ruler of her time, brought honor to the spirit of her father, called home her mother from afar, elicited the blessing of three kingdoms for her family, and allowed the Son of Heaven to complete the rituals appropriate to mother and son."[184] The *Odes* says, "They shall be illustrious from age to age,/Zealously and reverently pursuing their plans./Admirable are the many officers/Born in this royal kingdom."[185] These words describe her case well.

NOTES

INTRODUCTION

1. See, for example, Joan Judge and Hu Ying, eds., *Beyond Exemplar Tales: Women's Biography in Chinese History* (Berkeley: University of California Press, 2011).

2. For discussion of these two contrasting sets of governing principles, see Michael Loewe, *Crisis and Conflict in Han China* (London: George Allen and Unwin, 1974), 140–153.

3. A thorough study of Liu Xiang can be found in Qian Mu, *Han Liu Xiang Xin fuzi nianpu* (Taipei: Taiwan shangwu shuju, 1987). Also see Bret Hinsch, "Reading the *Lienüzhuan* (Biographies of Women) through the life of Liu Xiang," *Journal of Asian History*, 39, no. 2 (2005): 129–157.

4. See Ban Gu, *Hanshu* (Beijing: Zhonghua shuju, 1962), 36, 1921–1922. Liu Jiao and his younger son, Liu Yingke, were affiliated with Shen Gong and the Lu School of the *Odes*. Future references to the *Hanshu* of Ban Gu will be cited as *Hanshu*. The first number cited designates the *juan* number and those that follow are page numbers. References to multiple *juan* are separated by semicolons.

5. See *Hanshu* 36, 1926, 1927, 1929.

6. See *Hanshu* 36, 1928–1929.

7. See *Hanshu* 36, 1929; 88, 3618. Liu Xiang is also associated with the rival *Gongyang Commentary*. See Xu Yan's (ca. ninth to tenth century) notes to He Xiu's preface to the *Gongyang zhuan* in Ruan Yuan, ed., *Shisanjing zhushu* (SSJZS), (Beijing: Zhonghua shuju, 1979), vol. 2, 2190.

8. See *Hanshu* 36, 1929–1930. His rivals were on the one hand, the two consort families, Shi, the family of Yuandi's great-great-grandmother, Shi Liangdi, and the family of his mother, Xu Pingjun; and on the other, the eunuchs Hong Gong and Shi Xian. Emperor Yuan had delegated much of his power to Shi Xian. In response, Liu Xiang, Xiao Wangzhi, and Zhou Kan sought to remove eunuchs from positions of power.

9. See *Hanshu* 36, 1949.

10. See *Hanshu* 30, 1701; for translation and analysis, see Mark Edward Lewis, *Writing and Authority in Early China* (Albany: State University of New York Press, 1999), 325–332. Also see Edward L. Shaughnessy, *Rewriting Early Chinese Texts* (Albany: State University of New York Press, 2006), 2–3; and Zeng Yifen and Cui Wenyin, *Zhongguo lishi wenxianxue shi shuyao* (Beijing: Shangwu yinshuguan, 2000), 28–68.

11. See *Hanshu* 30, 1727. The term *pian* refers to bound documents written on bamboo or wooden strips that formed one literary unit, such as a chapter. See Tsuen-hsuin Tsien, *Written on Bamboo and Silk: The Beginnings of Chinese Books and Inscriptions,* 2nd ed. (Chicago: University of Chicago Press, 2004), 99, 120–121.

12. See *Hanshu* 36, 1957–1958.

13. The name Zhao refers to Chengdi's empress Zhao Feiyan. According to Yan Shigu's note, Wei refers to one of Chengdi's Favorite Beauties, Li Ping, who had been renamed Wei because her rise from obscurity to high position resembled that of Wudi's empress Wei Zifu. Wei is mentioned in LNZ 8.14. Hereafter, *Lienü zhuan* biographies will be cited as LNZ followed by the chapter number and then the number of the biography in that chapter (e.g., LNZ 8.14). This form of citation is based not on a particular edition but on the standard numbering scheme of most editions, such as that found in the *Sibu beiyao*. In contrast, both the *Sibu congkan* edition and that of D. C. Lau follow a slightly different order for the placement of three biographies in chapter one: 1.9, 1.10, and 1.11.

14. *Hanshu* 36, 1957–1958.

15. Sima Qian, *Shiji* (Beijing: Zhonghua shuju, 1959), 49, 1981. Future references to Sima Qian's *Shiji* will be simply cited as *Shiji*. The first number cited designates the *juan* number and those that follow are page numbers. References to multiple *juan* are separated by semicolons.

16. *Shiji* 49, 1967. These views are consonant with those expressed in the "Hun Yi" chapter of the *Liji*. See SSJZS, vol. 2, 61/453–454. See translation in James Legge, trans., *Li Chi: Book of Rites,* 2 vols. (1885; reprint, New Hyde Park: University Books, 1967), vol. 2, 433.

17. See discussion in Anne Behnke Kinney, *Representations of Childhood and Youth in Early China* (Stanford: Stanford University Press, 2004), 119–131.

18. See discussion in Kinney, *Representations of Childhood,* 72–74. Her death, according to *Shiji* 9, 405, stemmed from supernatural rather than natural causes. She died of a dog bite, which diviners identified as retribution for her murder of her son's half-brother, Ruyi.

19. *Shiji* 9, 411.

20. See *Shiji* 112, 2961.

21. See Michael Loewe and Denis Twitchett, eds., *The Cambridge History of China* (Cambridge, England: Cambridge University Press, 1986), vol. 1, 174–175, for a genealogical table of Wei Zifu's family. On Huo Guang, see *Hanshu* 68.

22. See *Hanshu* 97B, 3966, and LNZ 8.10.

23. See discussion in Kinney, *Representations of Childhood*, 80–82, 143–144.

24. See, for example, *Hanshu* 93, 3726–3727, and *Hanshu* 78.

25. At the time Xiao Wangzhi served as General of the Van and Superintendent of the Palace.

26. *Hanshu* 36, 1949.

27. *Hanshu* 81, 3338–3340.

28. See *Hanshu* 97B, 3984.

29. See *Hanshu* 60, 2667–2674; 77, 3251–3254; 81, 3341–3342; 85, 3443–3453.

30. *Hanshu* 10, 306–307; 27C.a, 1474–1475.

31. See discussion in Homer Dubs, *The History of the Former Han Dynasty*, 3 vols. (Baltimore: Waverly Press, 1944–1955), vol. 2, 358–359.

32. See discussion in Kinney, *Representations of Childhood,* 142–143.

33. See *Hanshu* 97B, 3973.

34. Favoring one's relatives is praised in the "Yaodian" chapter of the *Shangshu*. See James Legge, trans., *The Chinese Classics,* 5 vols. (Hong Kong: University of Hong Kong Press, 1960), vol. 3, 17. Also see *Mencius* 6B.3.2 in Legge, *The Chinese Classics*, vol. 2, 427; *Zhongyong*, 20: 14 in Legge, *The Chinese Classics*, vol. 1, 410; and Dubs, *History of the Former Han Dynasty*, vol. 2, 292–294.

35. *Hanshu* 97B, 3974.

36. For Empress Xu's enthronement, see *Hanshu* 10, 306. Empress Xu had given birth to a daughter and a son, but both died in infancy. See *Hanshu* 97B, 3973.

37. See, for example, *Hanshu* 85, 3443–3450; 97B, 3974–3975.

38. *Hanshu* 97B, 3983.

39. *Hanshu* 100A, 4203.

40. *Hanshu* 97B, 3983–3984 and LNZ 8.14.

41. *Hanshu* 97B, 3984–3985.

42. See LNZ 8.15.

43. These events are all narrated in *Hanshu* 97B, 3973–3999.

44. *Hanshu* 11, 333. Emperor Ai was the grandson of Emperor Yuan and the son of King Gong of Dingtao.

45. *Hanshu* 97B, 4004.

46. See Cao Zhaolan, *Jinwen yu Yin Zhou nüxing wenhua* (Beijing: Beijing daxue chubanshe, 2004).

47. *Zhouli*, in SSJZS, vol. 1, 7/419B. The *Liji* does, however, supply a fair amount of material concerning women's roles in various rituals, but less on moral and ethical behavior. See, for example, "Nei Ze," in *Liji*, SSJZS, vol. 2, 28/243A–B: "A girl at the age of ten ceased to go out (from the women's apartments). Her governess taught her (the arts of) pleasing speech and manners, to be docile and obedient, to handle the hempen fibers, to deal with the cocoons, to weave silks and form fillets, to learn (all) woman's work, how to furnish garments, to watch the sacrifices, to supply the liquors and sauces, to fill the various stands and dishes with pickles and brine, and to assist in setting forth the appurtenances for the ceremonies." Translated by Legge, *Li Chi*, vol. 1, 479.

48. See, for example, *Zuo zhuan,* Xiang, year 30 in Legge, *The Chinese Classics,* vol. 5, 556.

49. See Martin Kern, *The Stele Inscriptions of Ch'in-shih-huang: Text and Ritual in Early Chinese Imperial Representation* (New Haven: American Oriental Society, 2000), 164–182.

50. The *Shiji* states that Empress Dowager Dou (d. 135 BCE), consort of Wendi and mother of Jingdi, was fond of Huang-Lao philosophy, which she required the men in her family to read. The biographical account of Dou's childhood does not mention education of any sort; furthermore, her brothers are described as humble and requiring teachers to facilitate their new connections with the imperial court. See *Shiji* 49, 1974. The empress dowager therefore probably acquired her learning later in life. That she was literate at the end of her life is suggested by the grandee secretary Zhao Wan's request in 140 BCE that Emperor Wu forbid the practice of memorializing the grand empress dowager concerning government affairs (*Hanshu* 6, 157). Zhao was imprisoned for his suggestion and finally committed suicide. Another possibility, however, is that the empress dowager had someone read government documents to her. Still, there is plausible evidence of court women's literacy in the song lyrics and memorials composed by the Han princesses who, during Wudi's reign, were sent to non-Chinese states in the west to foster diplomatic relations with the peoples who lived on China's borders. See, for example, *Hanshu* 96B, 3903–3904.

51. *Hanshu* 97B, 3985–3987; also see "Favorite Beauty Ban," LNZ 8.14.

52. *Hanshu* 97B, 3984; Burton Watson, trans., *Courtier and Commoner in Ancient China: Selections from the* History of the Former Han *by Pan Ku* (New York: Columbia University Press, 1974), 262. The *Modest Maiden* is a book whose title is derived from the first poem in the *Book of Odes*—"Guan Ju."

53. Liu Xiang mentions *taiping* in several of his writings collected in the *Hanshu*; see *Hanshu* 36, 1932, 1942, 1946. For Dong Zhongshu's views on *taiping*, see *Hanshu* 56, 2506; and more generally, Chen Chi-yun, *Hsün Yüeh and the Mind of Late Han China* (Princeton: Princeton University Press, 1980), 19–25.

54. *Hanshu* 8, 257; 74, 3144–3145. See discussion in Kinney, *Chinese Views of Childhood,* 77–78.

55. *Hanshu* 8, 264.

56. *Hanshu* 12, 351, 356.

57. *Hanshu* 72, 3066.

58. For other examples of the ways officials' wives and men's conduct in the inner chambers were scrutinized, see Huan Kuan, *Yantie lun,* in Wang Yunwu, ed., *Sibu congkan zhengbian,* 100 vols. (Taipei: Taiwan Shangwu yinshuguan, 1979), vol. 17, 2/9B (chap. 9); 4/6A, 4/13A (chaps. 17, 19), and 5/14B (chap. 24). Future references to the *Sibu congkan zhengbian* will be cited as SBCK.

59. See Keith Knapp, "The *Ru* Interpretation of *Xiao*," *Early China* 20 (1995): 195–222.

60. See LNZ 2.3.

61. See, for example, LNZ 1.9 and 7.8.

62. See LNZ 6.14.

63. In Liu Xiang's *Xinxu,* item 1.3 in SBCK, vol. 17, 1/2B, where he also cites this story, Fan Ji claims to have refrained from monopolizing the ruler's affections so as to not harm his "righteousness" (義 *yi*) or "sense of duty." This story is also found in *Hanshi waizhuan* in SBCK, vol. 3, 2/3A–4A; translated in James Hightower, trans., *Han Shih Wai Chuan: Han Ying's Illustrations of the Didactic Application of the "Classic of Songs"* (Cambridge, Mass.: Harvard University Press, 1952), 41–43. In this account, Fan Ji's motive is frivolous by comparison: "I would not dare to keep other beauties in obscurity for private motives. I want you to see more of them that you may be happy."

64. See LNZ 6.12.

65. See, for example, LNZ 6.1, 6.4, 6.15.

66. Eric Henry, trans., *The Garden of Eloquence* (Seattle: University of Washington Press, forthcoming).

67. On textual sources of the *Lienü zhuan,* see Ho Che Wah, Chu Kwok Fan, and Fan Siu Piu, *The Gu Lienü Zhuan with Parallel Passages from Other Pre-Han and Han Texts, The Da Dai Liji with Parallel Passages from Other Pre-Han and Han Texts* (Hong Kong: The Chinese University of Hong Kong, 2004). Their study provides a general sense of textual parallels but is not exhaustive.

68. Shimomi Takao, *Ryū kō Retsujoden no kenkyū* (Tokyo: Tōkaidō daigaku shuppankai, 1989), 42–43. The primary connections between a biography and earlier sources are summarized in a table on 886–899. I have collapsed his categories 4–5, as the distinction he makes between the two seems negligible.

69. In the notes to my translation, I have tried to point out textual parallels between a given biography and earlier sources.

70. See, for example, Shimomi, *Ryū kō Retsujoden no kenkyū,* 58–59. Also see Bret Hinsch, "The Composition of *Lienüzhuan*: Was Liu Xiang the Author or Editor?" *Asia Major,* 3rd series, 20, no. 1 (2007): 1–23; and on a related topic, Eric Henry, "Anachronisms in *Lüshi Chunqiu* and *Shuo Yuan,*" *Early Medieval China* 9 (2003): 127–138.

71. See *Hanshu* 30, 1727.

72. *Hanshu* 36, 1957–1958.

73. See Xu Jian, "Ping Feng" in *Chuxue ji,* 2 vols. (Taipei: Dingwen shuju, 1972), 25/3, vol. 2, 599. The *Bielu,* compiled by Liu Xiang ca. 26 BCE, represents the first known bibliography of Chinese texts. It was an annotated catalog of books that had been collected as part of an imperial campaign to reconstitute the imperial library that had been destroyed in the civil wars prior to the establishment of the Han empire.

74. See Zheng Xiaoxia and Lin Jianyu, eds., *Lienü zhuan huibian,* 10 vols. (Beijing: Beijing tushuguan, 2007), vol. 7, 283, 291. Future references to this work will be cited as LNZHB.

75. Zhangsun Wuji, (d. 659), *Suishu jingji zhi* (Shanghai: Shangwu yinshuguan, 1955), 58–59. Zhangsun's annotations simply note a 15-*juan* edition annotated by Cao Dagu.

76. Zhangsun Wuji, *Suishu jingji zhi,* 58–59.

77. Guoli zhongyang tushuguan, *Guoli zhongyang tushuguan shanben xu, ba, jilu* (Beijing: Guoli zhongyang tushuguan, 1992–1994), vol. 2, 1. This text provides a convenient collection of prefaces to the *Lienü zhuan*.

78. Some of her commentary can be found in Li Shan's commentary to the *Wenxuan* and elsewhere. References to Ban Zhao's interlinear notes as well as her discussion of the preface can be found in Wang Yaochen's ca. 1034–1038 *Chongwen zongmu*, recollected and re-edited by Qian Tong (fl. 1799) et al., in *Guoxue jiben congshu* ([China]: Shangwu shuju, n.d.). Also, the *Siku quanshu zongmu* makes reference to the *Chongwen zongmu* editions that included her commentary. See Yong Rong (1744–1790), *Siku quanshu zongmu*, 2 vols. (Beijing: Zhonghua shuju, 1965), vol. 1, 85/728.

79. These two biographies are LNZ 8.1 and 8.20 respectively.

80. For Cai Ji's "Postscript," see LNZHB, vol. 7, 314.

81. See discussion in Chen Liping, *Liu Xiang Lienü zhuan yanjiu* (Beijing: Zhongguo shehui kexue yuan, 2010), 39–43.

82. For example, this edition appears in Ruan Yuan's *Wenxuanlou congshu*, compiled in the Daoguang reign period (1821–1850). See Zhang Tao, "Liu Xiang *Lienü zhuan* de banben wenti," *Wenxian* (1989): 250–253.

83. For an overview of the textual history of the *Lienü zhuan*, see Chen Liping, *Liu Xiang Lienü zhuan yanjiu*.

84. Teng Zhaozong, "Yinwan Hanmu jiandu gaishu," *Wenwu* 7 (1996): 32–36.

85. See Lin Meicun and Li Junming, eds., *Shule heliuhuo chutu Han jian* (Beijing: Wenwu chubanshe, 1984), 83, 142. The title is shown on strip no. 789, which corresponds to Stein no. T.XXVIII.10. Also see a study in Ma Zhiquan, "Dunhuang xuanquanzhi *Lienüzhuan* jian kaolun" in *Ludong daxue xuebao* 28, no. 6 (2011): 26–29, 65.

86. Fragments can also be found in the *Yiwen leiju, Chuxue ji, Shi zhengyi* (詩正義), *Shiji zhengyi* (史記正義), *Shiji suoyin* (史記索隱), and *Taiping yulan*.

87. LNZHB, vol. 7, 294.

88. See Yuan Ke, *Shenhua lunwen ji* (Shanghai: Shanghai guji chubanshe, 1982), 139–152. I am grateful to Eric Henry for alerting me to this reference.

89. I am grateful to Keith Knapp for pointing out relevant art historical materials discussed in his book, *Selfless Offspring: Filial Children and Social Order in Medieval China* (Honolulu: University of Hawai'i Press, 2005), 99–100.

90. See Mencius' famous account of this myth in *Mencius* 5A.2; translated in Legge, *The Chinese Classics*, vol. 2, 346–347.

91. It is possible, however, that Zeng Gong also altered biography 1.5 in order to align it with the *Mencius*. See notes in translation.

92. See Xu, *Chuxue ji*, vol. 2, 599. Also see discussion in Wu Hung, *The Double Screen: Medium and Representation in Chinese Painting* (Chicago: University of Chicago Press, 1996), 84–92.

93. See *Hanshu* 100A, 4200–4201. Da Ji's biography appears in LNZ 7.2. A screen depicting exemplary women is also mentioned as a feature of the court of the Later Han Emperor

Guangwu (r. 25–57). See Fan Ye et al., comp., *Hou Hanshu* (Beijing: Zhonghua shuju, 1965), 26, 904–905. Future references to this work will be cited as *Hou Hanshu*.

94. Wu Hung, *The Double Screen*, 86.

95. For early illustrations, see Wu Hung, *The Double Screen*, 84–92; *The Wu Liang Shrine: The Ideology of Early Chinese Pictorial Art* (Stanford: Stanford University Press, 1989), 172–173, 252–272; Julia K. Murray, *Mirror of Morality: Chinese Narrative Illustration and Confucian Ideology* (Honolulu: University of Hawai'i Press, 2007), 28–31; and Kuroda Akira, "Retsujoden zu no kenkyū," *Kyoto gobun* 15 (2008), and "Retsujoden zu no keifu," *Guoji Hanxue yanjiu tongxun* 4 (2011): 69–133; and Chen, *Liu Xiang* Lienü zhuan *yanjiu*, 52–80. For examples of illustrated editions of the text, see www2.iath. virginia.edu/xwomen/.

96. The *Kongzi jiayu* of Wang Su (195–256) contains a passage describing Confucius' visit to the Hall of Illumination, the walls of which were decorated with portraits of both good and evil rulers. See *Kongzi jiayu*, SBCK, vol. 17, 3/2B–3A. *Huainanzi* also includes a reference to didactic murals from the Western Zhou. See D. C. Lau, ed., *A Concordance to the* Huainanzi (Hong Kong: The Commercial Press, 1992), 9/80/19.

97. *Hanshu* 68, 2960. Also see didactic murals mentioned in the biography of Yang Yun (fl. 56 BCE) in *Hanshu* 66, 2891.

98. See Xiao Tong, *Wenxuan*, 3 vols. (Beijing: Zhonghua shuju, 1981), 11/19B–20A; David Knechtges, trans., *Wen xuan*, 3 vols. (Princeton: Princeton University Press, 1987), vol. 2, 262–277.

99. See *Hou Hanshu* 10B, 438; 26, 904–905. Another, possibly earlier example is in *Hanshu* 10, 301, which refers to the "Painted Hall of the First Lodge" in which Emperor Cheng was born. Ying Shao's note says that the lodge was reserved for giving birth and suckling and that it was decorated with a painting of "The Mother with Nine Sons." The painting may thus depict LNZ 1.12.

100. For Cai Yong's paintings, see Zhang Yanyuan, *Lidai minghua ji*, in *Huashi congshu*, ed. Yu Anlan, 4 vols. (Shanghai: Shanghai renmin chubanshe, 1963), vol. 1, 60–61.

101. See Wu Hung, *The Wu Liang Shrine*, 172–173, 252–272. The murals on Li Gang's temple depicted LNZ 6.10 (Zhongli Chun), LNZ 4.14 (Widow of Liang), and LNZ 2.5 (Ji, wife of King Zhuang of Chu). The Xinjin coffin depicts the story of Qiu Hu's wife (LNZ 5.9); see Wu Hong, "Myths and Legends in Han Funerary Art," in *Stories from China's Past: Han Dynasty Pictorial Tomb Reliefs and Archaeological Objects from Sichuan Province, People's Republic of China*, ed. Lucy Lim (San Francisco: The Chinese Culture Foundation of San Francisco, 1987), 152, plate 55; and Zhang Xunliao, "Sichuan Dong Han mu Qiu Hu xi qi huaxiang zhuan, huaxiang shi yu changqu huayang Lienü zhuan," in *Xihua daxue xuebao* 5 (2006): 1–10. For the Helinger murals, see Gai Shanlin, *Helinger Han mu bihua* (Huhehot: Neimenggu renmin chubanshe, 1978), 8; and Kuroda Akira, "Retsujoden zu no kenkyū," *Kyoto gobun* 15 (2008).

102. See discussion of this term in William Nienhauser's *The Grand Scribe's Records*, 6 vols. (Bloomington: Indiana University Press, 1994), vol. 7, v–vii; James Hightower, "Ch'ü

Yuan Studies," *Silver Jubilee Volume of Zinbun Kagaku Kenkyusyo* (Kyoto, 1954), 197; Burton Watson, *Ssu-ma Ch'ien, Grand Historian of China* (New York: Columbia University Press, 1958), 122.

103. See Nienhauser, *The Grand Scribe's Records*, vol. 7, vii (parentheses my own).

104. See *Hanshu* 62, 2738.

105. See Xu Shen, *Shuowen jiezi jinshi*, 3 vols., ed. Tang Kejing (Changsha: Yulu shushe, 1997), vol. 1, 595.

106. See, for example, *Xunzi*, "Wang Ba," in D. C. Lau, ed., *A Concordance to the* Xunzi (Hong Kong: Commercial Press, 1996), 11/55/17; *Lüshi chunqiu*, "Lülan: xiaoxing," in D. C. Lau, *A Concordance to the* Lüshi chunqiu (Hong Kong: Commercial Press, 1994), 14.1/70/9; and Huang Huaixin, annotator, *Xiao erya huijiao ji shi* (Xi'an: San Qin chubanshe, 2003), 69.

107. See *Shiji* 61, 2121.

108. Others construe the term as the verb "to set forth." I follow Nienhauser, *The Grand Scribe's Records*, vol. 7, vii.

109. Also, see Zhang Xuecheng's (1738–1801) discussion of the distinction between the terms 列女 and 烈女 in *Wenshi tongyi* in *Sibu beiyao*, 610 vols. (Taipei: Taiwan zhonghua shuju, 1965), vol. 108, 7/26A.

110. *Hanshu* 36, 1957–1958.

111. See Xu, *Chuxue ji*, 25/3 ("Ping Feng"), vol. 2, 599.

112. Grant Hardy translates Sima Qian's term *liezhuan* as "categorized biography." See his *Worlds of Bronze and Bamboo: Sima Qian's Conquest of History* (New York: Columbia University Press, 1999), 38.

113. See *Shiji* 130, 3301–3302.

114. See my discussion of the Han interest in the impact of mothers on a child's moral development in *Representations of Childhood*, chapter 1.

115. See punctuated text of Emperor Chengzu's preface in Guoli zhongyang tushuguan, *Guoli zhongyang tushuguan shanben xu, ba, jilu*, vol. 2, 38. *Mencius* 5A.4 makes it clear that Shun did have a son, though he was considered unworthy. See translation in Legge, *The Chinese Classics*, vol. 2, 358–359.

116. For Yao's mother, see, for example, *Shiji* 1, 14–15. Her life may have been devoid of the sort of moral lessons necessary to construct an opening biography.

117. See Mark Edward Lewis, *Sanctioned Violence in Early China* (Albany: State University of New York Press, 1990), 168, 171. We can also speculate that Liu Xiang chose not to discuss Shun's mother in this context because she was notably bad.

118. On the Liu imperial family's descent from Yao, see Ban Biao's (3–54 CE) "Wang Ming Lun," in *Hanshu* 100A, 4208; translated in William Theodore de Bary, ed., *Sources of Chinese Tradition* (New York: Columbia University Press, 1960), vol. 1, 176.

119. Liang Duan, *Lienü zhuan jiaozhu*, in LNZHB, vol. 7, 1/21A, 355.

120. See "Ji Ming," Mao no. 96, in SSJZS, vol. 1, *Maoshi zhengyi*, 5.1/81A, 349.

121. See LNZ 2.2, 2.4. In LNZ 2.4, "Ji, Wife of Duke Mu of Qin," Ji prevents her husband, the duke, from killing her brother, first by blaming herself for having neglected to instruct her brother properly, and second, by threatening to set herself and her children afire if the duke refuses to release her brother.

122. See LNZ 2.2.

123. See LNZ 2.13, 2.14, 2.15.

124. See 2.7.

125. See LNZ 2.9, 2.12, 2.14.

126. Lau, *Huainanzi*, 9//81/9–10; translation based on John S. Major, Sarah A. Queen, Andrew Seth Meyer, and Harold D. Roth, trans., *The Huainanzi: A Guide to the Theory and Practice of Government in Early Han China* (New York: Columbia University Press, 2010), 337. I am grateful to Eric Henry for alerting me to this passage.

127. See LNZ 3.10.

128. See LNZ 3.6.

129. See 3.13.

130. See discussion of the concept of "Great Peace" in Chi-yun Chen, *Hsün Yüeh: The Life and Reflections of an Early Medieval Confucian* (Cambridge, England: Cambridge University Press, 1975), 31.

131. See LNZ 4.2.

132. See extensive notes on this incident in the translation of LNZ 4.2.

133. See *Gongyang zhuan* in SSJZS, vol. 2, 21/120A–B., 2314; *Guliang zhuan* in SSJZS, vol. 2, 16/68A–B, 2432; and my essay, "Death by Fire," www2.iath.virginia.edu/xwomen/boji_essay.html.

134. *Guliang zhuan* in SSJZS, vol. 2, 16/68B, 2432.

135. See LNZ 8.16.

136. For early views opposing these practices, see, for example, *Mencius* 4A:27; Legge, trans., *The Chinese Classics*, vol. 2, 307; and *Zhuangzi*, SBCK, vol. 27, "Robber Zhi," 9/39A; Burton Watson, trans., *The Complete Works of Chuang Tzu* (New York: Columbia University Press, 1968), 329–330.

137. For a look at the impact of ritual neglect on the fate of a family, see Kinney, "A Spring and Autumn Family," *Chinese Historical Review* 20, no. 2 (2013): 113–137.

138. For a study of suicide in early China, see Kristinia Lindell, "Stories of Suicide in Ancient China: An Essay on Chinese Morals," *Acta Orientalia* 35 (1973): 167–239.

139. See *Hanshu* 8, 257; 74, 3144–3145.

140. *Analects* XV:8; translation based on Legge, *The Chinese Classics*, vol. 1, 297.

141. This view is summarized in the *Classic of Filial Piety* as follows: "Perfect filial piety and fraternal duty reach to (and move) the spiritual intelligences, and diffuse their light on all within the four seas—they penetrate everywhere." See *Xiaojing*, chapter XVI; translation by Legge, *The Sacred Books of China: The Texts of Confucianism*, vol. 3, 486.

142. See LNZ 6.15.

143. See, for example, *Odes, Xiao Ya*, "Zheng Yue," Mao no. 192, *The Chinese Classics*, vol. 4, 318; *Guoyu*, 2 vols. (Shanghai guji chubanshe, 1978), "Jinyu," Part 1, item 2.

144. See LNZ 7. 9. For a discussion of Xia Ji, see Wai-yee Li, *The Readability of the Past in Early Chinese Historiography* (Cambridge, Mass.: Harvard University Asia Center, 2007), 152–160.

145. See table of contents in the Liang Duan edition followed by Cai Ji's postface in LNZHB, vol. 7, 312–314.

146. See LNZ 1.9.

147. Instances of missing "man of discernment" comments are particularly concentrated in LNZ 7.

148. See Eric Henry, "'Junzi yue' versus 'Zhongni yue' in *Zuo zhuan*," *Harvard Journal of Asiatic Studies* 59, no. 1 (1999): 125–161.

149. See, for example, Zheng Liangshu, "Lun *Zuo zhuan* 'junzi yue' fei houren suo fuyi," in Zheng Liangshu, *Zhujian boshu lunwenji* (Beijing: Zhonghua shuju, 1982), 342–357.

150. For example, in LNZ 1.9, the comments are attributed to Zhongni, that is, Confucius.

151. Examples of more specific content can be found at LNZ 1.13, 2.1.

152. This is how Henry characterizes the comments found in the *Zuo zhuan*. See "'Junzi yue' versus 'Zhongni yue' in *Zuo zhuan*," 148.

153. See the "Preface to the Mao Version of the *Book of Odes*," in Xiao Tong, *Wenxuan*, vol. 2, 45/21A; translated in Knechtges, *Wen xuan*, vol. 1, 75, 79. The same six terms also appear in the *Zhouli* as techniques used by singers. See *Zhouli*, SSJZS, vol. 1, 23/158A, 796.

154. For more on these terms, see James J.Y. Liu, *Chinese Theories of Literature* (Chicago: University of Chicago Press, 1975), 64, 108–110.

155. See Wenxuan, vol. 1, 17/4B; translation by Knechtges, *Wen xuan*, vol. 3, 219.

156. See Ouyang Xun, ed., *Yiwen leiju*, 2 vols. (Shanghai: Shanghai guji chubanshe, 1999), vol. 1, 56/1018; translation by Knechtges, *Wen xuan*, vol. 1, 2, 75.

157. See Liu Xie, *Wenxin diaolong zhu* (Taipei: Minglun chubanshe, 1970), 2/158; translation in Vincent Yu-chung Shih, *The Literary Mind and the Carving of Dragons* (New York: Columbia University Press, 1957), 50.

158. See Liu Xie, *Wenxin diaolong zhu*, 2/158; translation in Shih, *The Literary Mind*, 52.

159. See Liu Xie, *Wenxin diaolong zhu*, 2/158–159; translation in Shih, *The Literary Mind*, 53.

160. See Liu Xie, *Wenxin diaolong zhu*, 2/158–159; translation in Shih, *The Literary Mind*, 53.

161. For Zeng Gong, see LNZHB, vol. 7, 291.

162. Zhangsun Wuji (d. 659), et al., *Suishu jingji zhi* (Shanghai: Shangwu yinshuguan, 1955), 58.

163. See Chen Liping, *Liu Xiang Lienü zhuan yanjiu* (Beijing: Zhongguo shehui kexue yuan, 2010), 81–102; Zhangsun Wuji, *Suishu jingji zhi*, 58–59; for Yan Zhitui, see *Yanshi jiaxun*, SBCK, vol. 22, Part II, 26A; and Xu Jian, "Ping Feng," in *Chuxue ji*, 25/3,

vol. 2, 599. The *Bielu*, compiled by Liu Xiang ca. 26 BCE, represents the first known bibliography of Chinese texts.

164. See Zheng Xiaoxia, *Lienü zhuan huibian*.

165. See www2.iath.virginia.edu/xwomen/intro.html.

166. See Liang Duan (梁端), *Lienü zhuan jiaozhu* in LNZHB, vol. 7; Xiao Daoguan (蕭道管), *Lienü zhuan jizhu*, in LNZHB, vol. 8; and Wang Zhaoyuan (王照圓), *Lienü zhuan buzhu*, in LNZHB, vol. 5.

167. According to *Hou Hanshu* 84, 2792, Ban's daughter-in-law, a Lady Ding, compiled Ban's writings after her death. The commentary is not specifically mentioned, although the collection is said to have contained *zhu* (注) "notes." For an English-language study of Ban Zhao, see Nancy Lee Swann, *Pan Chao, foremost woman scholar of China, first century A.D.; background, ancestry, life, and writings of the most celebrated Chinese woman of letters* (New York: Russell & Russell, 1968). *Hou Hanshu* 60, 1972, states that Ban Zhao's colleague, Ma Rong (79–166), also annotated the *Lienü zhuan*, but this work is no longer extant.

168. See Liu Xiaobiao's annotations to Liu Yiqing's *Shishuo xinyu*, "Xian Yuan," item 5 in *Shishuo xinyu jiaojian* (Taipei: Letian chubanshe, 1973), 510, note 1.

169. His surname is also sometimes written as Qimu (綦母).

170. Shimomi Takao, *Ryū kō Retsujoden no kenkyū*; Huang Qingquan, annotator and Chen Manming, editor, *Xinyi Lienü zhuan* (Taipei: Sanmin shuju, 1996); Zhang Tao, Lienü zhuan *yizhu* (Ji'nan: Shandong daxue chubanshe, 1990).

171. D. C. Lau, ed., *A Concordance to the* Gu Lienü zhuan (Hong Kong: The Commercial Press, 1993).

172. See www2.iath.virginia.edu/xwomen/intro.html.

173. In the Spring and Autumn period, the hierarchy of aristocratic titles in descending order beneath the Zhou king (王 *wang*) can be generally summarized as marquis (侯 *hou*), earl (伯 *bo*), viscount (子 *zi*), and baron (男 *nan*). Western scholars vary greatly in their translations of these titles. For a complete study of titles in China, see Charles O. Hucker, *A Dictionary of Official Titles in Imperial China* (Stanford: Stanford University Press, 1985).

1. THE MATERNAL MODELS

In her *Lienü zhuan jiaozhu*, found in the *Sibu beiyao*, 610 vols. (Taipei: Taiwan zhonghua shuju, 1965), vol. 104, 1/13B–14A, and in the LNZHB, vol. 7, 355, Liang Duan (d. 1825) cites Wang Hui's (ca. 1063 CE) comment that there are fifteen biographies in all of the *Lienü zhuan* chapters apart from the first, which has only fourteen biographies. See details in my introduction.

1. Youyu is another name for Shun derived from the name of his fief: the place called Yu. As is the case for a number of early place names, here the name of the fief is preceded

by the word *"you,"* which functioned either as an article or as the word "to possess."
For an early account of Shun's family and his relation to the place called Yu, see James
Legge's translation of the *Shangshu,* in *The Chinese Classics,* 5 vols. (Hong Kong: Uni-
versity of Hong Kong Press, 1960), vol. 3, 26–30. See Mencius's account of this myth
in *Mencius* 5A.2; translated in Legge, *The Chinese Classics,* vol. 2, 346–347. Also see
an account in *Shiji* 1, 21–35; translated in Nienhauser et al., trans., *The Grand Scribe's
Records,* 6 vols. (Bloomington: Indiana University Press, 1994–2006), vol. 1, 8–13.
According to one scheme, Yao is the first of the legendary rulers of predynastic times.

2. Gusou means "blind old man."

3. Pei Yin's (fl. 438 CE) *Jijie* commentary to the *Shiji* records Zheng Xuan's (127–200
CE) definition of the Chiefs of the Four Sacred Mountains as officials in charge of the
areas in the four cardinal directions where the four sacred mountains are located. See
Shiji 1, 21, note 6. Also see *Shangshu,* "Yao dian," 11; translated in Legge, *The Chinese
Classics,* vol. 3, 22.

4. The "Way of Wives" (婦道 *fudao*) signifies the true or orthodox way to fulfill this
social role.

5. The term "feelings of affection" (思慕 *simu*) is often specifically associated with filial
piety. See *Xunzi,* SBCK, vol. 17, 13.24A, in John Knoblock, trans., *Xunzi: A Translation and Study of the Complete Works,* 3 vols. (Stanford: Stanford University Press,
1982), vol. 3, 72; and *Liji,* "Wen Zang," in James Legge, trans., *Li Chi: Book of Rites,* 2
vols. (1885; reprint, New York: University Books, 1967), vol. 2, 377.

6. In Spring and Autumn times a ruler could take more than one principal wife, but they
were ranked as "primary" (*yuanfei*) and "secondary" (*erfei*), etc., and only the primary
principal wife held the title of queen. See Melvin Thatcher, "Marriages of the Ruling
Elite in the Spring and Autumn Period," in *Marriage and Inequality in Chinese Society,*
ed. Rubie S. Watson and Patricia Buckley Ebrey (Berkeley: University of California
Press, 1991), 25–57. Here I translate the highest rank as "queen" and the secondary rank
as "consort."

7. Youbei was located in present-day Hunan, north of Dao county.

8. Cangwu is a mountain in present-day Ningyuan county in Hunan province.

9. Chonghua means "Double Splendor" but can also be interpreted as meaning "double
pupils," a peculiar feature of Shun's appearance, according to some early sources.

10. They were worshipped as river goddesses. Songs associated with their cult survive in
the "Nine Songs" section of the *Chuci.* See D. C. Lau, ed., *A Concordance to the* Chuci
(Hong Kong: The Commercial Press, 2000), 5; and David Hawkes, *The Songs of the
South: An Ancient Chinese Anthology of Poems by Qu Yuan and Other Poets Translated,
Annotated and Introduced by David Hawkes* (Harmonsworth: Penguin Books, 1985),
104–109.

11. *Book of Odes, Song,* "Lie Wen," Mao 269, translated in Legge, *The Chinese Classics,*
vol. 4, 573.

12. The name Jiang Yuan means "Jiang, the Progenitor." Her clan name, according to Pei
Yin's *Jijie,* is Jiang. See *Shiji* 4, 111, note 2. This passage of the *Shiji* also states that

Jiang Yuan was a daughter of the Youtai lineage and the wife of the emperor Ku, in contrast to the *Lienü zhuan* account, which makes her the daughter of the Marquis of Tai but does not connect her to any husband. See *Shiji* 4, 111–112; translated in Nienhauser, *The Grand Scribe's Records*, vol. 1, 55. For an account of Jiang Yuan (as well as the mother of Xie mentioned in LNZ 1.3) based on the Warring States period bamboo manuscript, *Zigao*, see Sarah Allan, "Not the *Lun yu*: The Chu Script Bamboo Manuscript, *Zigao*, and the Nature of Early Confucianism," *Bulletin of the School of African and Oriental Studies* 72, no. 1 (2009): 115–151. Modern scholars have identified Tai as being west of the intersection of the Qiju and Wei rivers, about 50 miles west of modern-day Xi'an. See Tan Qixiang, *Zhongguo lishi ditu ji*, 5 vols. (Shanghai: Ditu chubanshe, 1982), vol. 1, map 17. One of the earliest sources for Jiang Yuan is the *Book of Odes, Da Ya*, "Sheng Min," Mao no. 245; SSJZS, 17.1/260–62. Opinions concerning the date of this ode vary. Fu Sinian, *Fu Sinian quanji*, 7 vols. (Taipei: Lianjing chuban gongsi, 1980), vol. 1, 235–239; and C. H. Wang, *From Ritual to Allegory: Seven Essays in Early Chinese Poetry* (Hong Kong: Chinese University Press of Hong Kong, 1988), 76 suggests that the *Da Ya*, the section of the *Odes* to which "Sheng Min" belongs, was composed circa ninth to eighth century BCE. W.A.C.H. Dobson, "Linguistic Evidence and the Dating of the *Book of Songs*," *T'oung Pao* 51, no. 4–5 (1964): 322–334, suggests a date of the tenth to ninth century BCE. Also see Joseph Roe Allen, "The End and the Beginning of Narrative Poetry in China," *Asia Major* 2, no. 1 (1989): 1–24.

13. According to traditional chronology, Yao reigned from 2145 to 2045 BCE. On the significance of supernatural footprints, see Bernhard Karlgren, "Some Fecundity Symbols in Ancient China," *Bulletin of the Museum of Far Eastern Antiquities* 2 (1930):1–54.

14. The *yin* and *si* sacrifices are those made to Heaven, the Lord on High, or other Heavenly spirits.

15. The name Hou Ji can be translated "Prince Millet." The *Odes* and the *Shiji* both mention that Hou Ji was enfeoffed with the territory of Tai. See *Book of Odes, Da Ya*, "Sheng Min," Mao no. 245; translated in Legge, *The Chinese Classics*, vol. 4, 465–472; and *Shiji* 4, 113.

16. This injunction comes from *Shangshu*, "Shundian," translated by Legge, *The Chinese Classics*, vol. 3, 40–44; SSJZS, vol. 1, *Shangshu*, 3/17C–18C.

17. *Book of Odes, Lu Song*, "Bi Gong," Mao no. 300; translated in Legge, *The Chinese Classics*, vol. 4, 620–621. According to the *Mao Commentary*, a temple dedicated to Jiang Yuan was restored during the reign of Duke Xi of Lu (r. 659–627 BCE). The rulers of Lu traced their descent to Jiang Yuan's son, Hou Ji. See *Maoshi zhengyi*, SSJZS, vol. 1, 20.2/346C, 614. By Han times, only its foundations survived and became the site for the Hall of Numinous Brilliance constructed by Liu Yu (d. 128 BCE), King Gong of Lu. See *Wenxuan* 11/19B–20A; translation by David Knechtges, *Wen xuan*, 3 vols. (Princeton: Princeton University Press, 1987–1996), vol. 2, 262–277.

18. *Book of Odes, Lu Song*, "Si Wen," Mao no. 275. Translated by Legge, *The Chinese Classics*, vol. 4, 580.

19. Like the "Way of Wives," the Way of Mothers" (母道 *mudao*) signifies the true or orthodox way to fulfill this social role.

20. On the place called Song or Yousong, see Guo Moruo, *Zhongguo shigao ditu ji* (Shanghai: Ditu chubanshe, 1979), vol. 1, map no. 9, B5. According to Ma Chiying, *Shiji jinzhu*, vol. 1, 41, note 4, Yousong is a clan name associated with the area located in present-day Yongji county, Shanxi.

21. The location of Xuanqiu is unknown.

22. Xie was the progenitor of the line that founded the Shang dynasty. For a similar account see *Shiji* 3, 91; translated in Nienhauser, *The Grand Scribe's Records*, vol. 1, 41.

23. On the relation between Bo and the area around present-day Yanshi city in Henan, see Robert Thorp, *China in the Early Bronze Age: Shang Civilization* (Philadelphia: University of Pennsylvania Press, 2006), 67; David Keightley, ed., *The Origins of Chinese Civilization* (Berkeley: University of California Press, 1983), 505, 508, 525; and Louisa Huber, "The Bo Capital and Questions Concerning Xia and Early Shang," *Early China* 13 (1988): 46–77.

24. This statement is drawn from the *Shangshu*, "Shundian"; see translation by Legge, *The Chinese Classics*, vol. 3, 44. The five orders of human relationships refer to the bonds between father and child, husband and wife, ruler and subject, elder brother and younger brother, and friend and friend. See Mencius' understanding of this statement in *Mencius* 3A.8; translation by Legge, *The Chinese Classics*, vol. 2, 250–252.

25. Mencius understood the five teachings as follows: "Between father and son, there should be affection; between sovereign and minister, righteousness; between husband and wife, attention to their separate functions; between old and young, a proper order; and between friends, fidelity." *Mencius* 3A.8; translation by Legge, *The Chinese Classics*, vol. 2, 251–252.

26. The first year of Tang of Yin (Cheng Tang) would have been 1554 BCE. Yin is another name for the Shang dynasty, but there is no evidence that the Shang referred to itself by this name. See Michael Loewe and Edward L. Shaughnessy, eds., *The Cambridge History of Ancient China: From the Origins of the Civilization to 221 B.C.* (Cambridge, England: Cambridge University Press, 1999), 232–233, 248.

27. The *Book of Odes*, *Shang Song*, "Chang Fa," Mao no. 304. Translation based on Bernhard Karlgren, trans., *The Book of Odes* (Goteborg: Elanders Boktryckeri Aktiebolag, 1950), 265. The text of *Lienü zhuan* omits the word "God" (*di*).

28. The *Book of Odes*, *Shang Song*, "Xuan Niao," Mao no. 303. Translation based on Legge, *The Chinese Classics*, vol. 4, 636–638.

29. Here I follow Liang Duan's reading of *shi* (飾) as *chi* (飭) "to instruct." See LNZHB, vol. 7, 321.

30. See another account in *Shiji* 2, 80; translated in Nienhauser, *The Grand Scribe's Records*, vol. 1, 35; and *Mencius* 3A.4, translated in Legge, *The Chinese Classics*, vol. 2, 251. Yu of Xia ascended the throne after the death of Shun, though Yu was not a lineal descendant of Shun. Ultimately, Yu's son Qi succeeded his father and thus consolidated the Xia dynasty. There is no historical evidence for a dynasty called Xia.

31. This phrase is drawn from the "Yi Ji" chapter of the *Shangshu*. Translation based on Legge, *The Chinese Classics*, vol. 3, 85.

32. *Book of Odes*, Da Ya, "Ji Zui," Mao no. 247; translation based on Legge, *The Chinese Classics*, vol. 4, 475–478.

33. The term "to divide the land" (敷土 *futu*) is found in conjunction with the labors of Yu in the "Yu Gong" chapter of the *Shangshu*. See Legge translation, *The Chinese Classics*, vol. 3, 93.

34. The lines in this summary may be disordered, so that Qi wept and wailed before Yu went out to labor. See Xiao Daoguan's comments in LNZHB, vol. 8, 52. I have rendered the term *lunxu* as "ordered their affairs" rather than "discoursed on precedence" to accord with the current order of the text.

35. Tang, the first ruler of the Shang dynasty, is also called Cheng Tang or Tang of Yin. Yin is another name for the Shang dynasty. On Youshen's marriage, see *Shiji* 3, 93–94; translated in Nienhauser, *The Grand Scribe's Records*, vol. 1, 42–43. Using astronomical events as absolute dates, Keightley surmises that the first year of Tang of Yin would have been 1554 BCE. See Loewe and Shaughnessy, *The Cambridge History of Ancient China*, 248. On Tang's sons and successors, see *Mencius* VA.6–7; translated in Legge, *The Chinese Classics*, vol. 2, 360–364. On the location of the Youshen homeland as located southeast of modern Kaifeng in Henan, see Nienhauser, *The Grand Scribe's Records*, vol. l, 43, note 29. Tan, *Zhongguo gujin diming dacidian*, vol. 3, 2389, locates Shen northwest of Cao county in present-day Shandong.

36. According to *Shiji* 3, 98, Cheng Tang's eldest son, Taiding, predeceased his father, so Waibing ascended the throne. Only three years later, Waibing died and his younger brother, Zhongren, became king.

37. While there are no extant historical records for the ranking of women in the opening years of the Shang, Warring States and Han texts describe how women were formally ranked in aristocratic households during the Spring and Autumn and somewhat later periods of Chinese history. See Thatcher, "Marriages of the Ruling Elite," 33–35.

38. *Book of Odes*, Zhou Nan, "Guan Ju," Mao no. 1; translation based on Legge, *The Chinese Classics*, vol. 4, 1–5. Some early commentaries suggest that the lady who is the subject of this ode is Tai Si, bride of King Wen of the Zhou dynasty, who also hailed from the Youshen clan and married a dynastic founder. For discussion see Steven Van Zoeren, *Poetry and Personality: Reading, Exegesis, and Hermeneutics in Traditional China* (Stanford: Stanford University Press, 1991), 89–90, 136–139, 268, note 25, 275, note 45; Jeffrey Riegel, "Eros, Introversion, and the Beginnings of *Shijing* Commentary," *Harvard Journal of Asiatic Studies* vol. 57, no. 1 (June 1997):143–177.

39. Yi Yin, who is the subject of numerous legends, is also mentioned in Shang oracle-bone inscriptions. See Loewe and Shaughnessy, *The Cambridge History of Ancient China*, 254, and Kwang-chih Chang, *Shang Civilization* (New Haven: Yale University Press, 1980), 10, 177, 192. For an early textual reference to Yi Yin, see *Lüshi chunqiu*, "Ben Wei," in D. C. Lau, *A Concordance to the* Lüshi chunqiu (Hong Kong: The Commercial Press, 1994), 14.2/70–71/29–4; translated in John Knoblock and Jeffrey

Riegel, *The Annals of Lü Buwei* (Stanford: Stanford University Press, 2000), 307. It is curious that he is mentioned in the Verse Summary but not in the body of the biography. A note to the *Hou Hanshu* biography of Cui Qi (fl. mid-second century CE), which quotes this biography, suggests that Yi Yin was originally mentioned in the body of the biography. See Fan Ye, *Hou Hanshu* 80A, 2619. The term *ying*, "bridal party," is subject to several interpretations. In general, it refers to a marriage practice of the ruling elite in which a group of women not only accompany a bride on the occasion of her marriage to a ruler from another state but also wed the ruler and assume ranks in the harem beneath that of the principal bride. According to one account, Yi Yin is said to have served as a cook in Youshen's bridal entourage as a means to gain access to Tang. See, *Shiji* 3, 94; translated in Nienhauser, *The Grand Scribe's Records*, vol. 1, 43. On the term *ying*, see Thatcher, "Marriages of the Ruling Elite," 31.

40. For a study of early illustrations of these women, see Kuroda Akira, "Retsujoden zu no keifu," *Kyoto gobun* 15 (2008): 1–30

41. Jiang is Tai Jiang's clan name. Her place of origin, Youtai, is written as 有台 or 有邰. Some editions say that she was from the Youlü (有吕) lineage. See LNZHB, vol. 7, 324; vol. 8, 602–603. Modern scholars have identified Youtai (or simply Tai) as being west of the intersection of the Qiju and Wei rivers, about 50 miles west of modern-day Xi'an. See Tan, *Zhongguo lishi ditu ji*, 5 vols. (Shanghai: Ditu chubanshe, 1982), vol. 1, map 17. According to this assignment of lineage, Tai Jiang hails from the same clan as Jiang Yuan (LNZ 1.2). Wang Ji, Tai Jiang's son, is also known as Jili or Gong Ji.

42. Tai Wang is also known as Gugong Danfu, on which, see *Shiji* 4, 113–116; translated in Nienhauser, *The Grand Scribe's Records*, vol. 1, 56–57.

43. The list of offspring mentioned in the *Shiji* account cited above differs from this list.

44. Liang Duan cites sources that identify those who were guided by Tai Jiang as her sons. See LNZHB, vol. 7, 324. Also, see for example, the Tang dynasty commentary of Li Xian to the biography of Cui Qi (fl. 140 CE) in *Hou Hanshu* 80A, 2619, note 2, which quotes a slightly different text for this account but also notes that she guided her sons.

45. On this enterprise, see *Book of Odes*, *Da Ya*, "Mian," Mao no. 237; translated in Legge, *The Chinese Classics*, vol. 4, 438. The commentaries make a special point of noting Tai Jiang's contribution to the establishment of a new kingdom. See SSJZS, vol. 1, 16.2, 242A–B. Tai Wang is said to have led his people from the midst of the Rong and Di "barbarians" to settle at the foot of Mount Qi in the central Wei River valley in Shaanxi. For current views on this legend of the origins of the Zhou people, see Loewe and Shaughnessy, *The Cambridge History of Ancient China*, 292–351.

46. The SBCK edition interpolates a sentence here, which is included in D. C. Lau's edition but which I have omitted.

47. Her clan name was Ren. This line and the next are loosely based on the description of Tai Ren found in the ode "Da Ming," Mao no. 236; translated in Legge, *The Chinese Classics*, vol. 4, 433. Zhi was a feudal territory of the Shang dynasty associated with the area southeast of present-day Runan in Henan province.

48. Latrines in houses were often located over pigpens. See Qinghua Guo, *The Minqqi Pottery Buildings of Han Dynasty China 206 BC–AD 220: Architectural Representations and Represented Architecture* (Eastbourne, Sussex, UK: Sussex Academic Press, 2010), 125–137.

49. Here the mother's deportment mirrors the correct attitudes prescribed in the *Book of Rites* as well as those that purportedly distinguished Confucius. The *Analects*, for example, provides a similar account of the master's deportment: "He did not eat meat that was not properly cut up. . . . If his mat was not straight, he did not sit on it. . . . In bed he did not lie like a corpse." See *Analects* X:8–16, translation by Legge, *The Chinese Classics*, vol. 1, 232–235.; and "Qu Li," part 1, *Liji*, SSJZS, vol. 1, 2/12. The prohibition against standing on one foot is reminiscent of one of the apotropaic postures mentioned in the Shuihudi text, "Jie." See Donald Harper, "Chinese Demonography of the Third Century B.C.," *HJAS* 45, no. 2 (1985): 459–498. This posture may also be offensive in that it resembles the stance of a mutilated (and thus impure) convict. On the latter see Robin Yates, "Purity and Pollution in Early China," *Integrated Studies of Chinese Archaeology and Historiography* 4 (July 1997): 479–536. Also see Harold Roth, *Original Tao* (New York: Columbia University Press, 1999), 109–113 on the significance of "aligning" (*zheng*) the body in meditative practice. Further, in virtually the same words once used to describe Xunzi's true gentleman or man of discernment, the ideal expectant mother was said to see, speak, and hear no evil. See "Yue Lun" (Discourse on Music), *Xunzi*, SBCK, vol. 17, 14/4a.

50. The blind musicians (瞽 *gu*) are associated with the court rituals of the Western Zhou. See *Book of Odes, Zhou Song,* "You Gu," Mao no. 280, translated in Legge, *The Chinese Classics*, vol. 4, 586–587.

51. The D. C. Lau edition has emended "various things" (萬物 *wanwu*) to "parents" (父母 *fumu*). See D. C. Lau, *A Concordance to the* Gu Lienü zhuan (Hong Kong: The Commercial Press, 1993), 1.6/4/9. See discussion of how unborn children take on the characteristics of the sensory stimuli experienced by their mothers in Anne Behnke Kinney, *Representations of Childhood and Youth in Early China* (Stanford: Stanford University Press, 2004), 16–21.

52. She is mentioned in *Shiji* 35, 1563; translated in Nienhauser, *The Grand Scribe's Records*, vol. 5.1, 191.

53. See the ode, "Da Ming," Mao 236, cited above.

54. This list of Tai Si's sons differs somewhat from the list found in *Shiji* 35, 1563; translated in Nienhauser, *The Grand Scribe's Records*, vol. 5.1, 191–192. Some scholars suggest that Boyi Kao predeceased King Wen, see Loewe and Shaughnessy, *The Cambridge History of Ancient China*, 309, note 38. A number of textual references, however, state that Fa "set aside" Boyi Kao. See Sarah Allan, *Heir and Sage: Dynastic Legend in Early China* (San Francisco: Chinese Materials Center, 1981), 112, note 12.

55. This narrative conveniently omits mention of the intense conflict among these brothers, specifically, the coup staged by Guan Shu Xian, Cai Shu Du, and Huo Shu Wu in

collaboration with Wu Geng, nominal ruler of the Shang people against Dan, Duke of Zhou, who had declared himself regent to King Cheng, son of the recently deceased King Wu. See *Shiji* 4, 131–132; translated in Nienhauser, *The Grand Scribe's Records*, vol. 1, 64–65.

56. Lau's *A Concordance to the* Gu Lienü zhuan includes in this biography a paragraph (1.6/4/17–24) that is generally regarded as a later interpolation. See Liang Duan's comments in LNZHB, vol. 7, 327.

57. *Book of Odes, Da Ya*, "Da Ming," Mao no. 236; translation based on Legge, *The Chinese Classics*, vol. 4, 434–435. The Wei River rises in the mountains of southeastern Gansu province and flows east though Shaanxi province to join the Yellow River. It is 537 miles long, and its valley was an early center of Chinese civilization.

58. *Book of Odes, Da Ya*, "Si Qi," Mao no. 240. Translation based on Legge, *The Chinese Classics*, vol. 4, 446.

59. Her name combines the posthumous name of her husband—Ding—and her clan name, Jiang. Duke Ding reigned from 588 to 576 BCE. His son's name is unknown. I transliterate his state as Wey (衛) to distinguish it from Wei (魏).

60. *Book of Odes, Bei Feng*, "Yan Yan," Mao 28, translation based on Legge, *The Chinese Classics*, vol. 4, 42–44. The Mao commentary associates this ode not with Ding Jiang, but Zhuang Jiang. See Anne Behnke Kinney, "The *Book of Odes* as a Source of Women's History" in *Overt and Covert Treasures: Essays on the Sources for Chinese Women's History*, ed. Clara Wing-chung Ho (Hong Kong: Chinese University of Hong Kong Press, 2012), 61–111. In her commentary to the *Lienü zhuan*, Liang Duan also mentions that this interpretation of the ode is derived from the now lost Lu school commentary. For discussion of Liu Xiang's use of this ode, see also Bret Hinsch, "The Composition of *Lienüzhuan*: Was Liu Xiang the Author or Editor?" *Asia Major*, 3rd series, 20, no. 1 (2007): 15–16. Also see Chen Zhi's historical analysis of the ode in "A New Reading of 'Yen-Yen,'" *T'oung Pao*, 2nd series, vol. 85, fasc. 1/3 (1999), 1–28; and Riegel, "Eros," 143–177.

61. This line is also found in "Yan Yan," Mao no. 28. Liang Duan suggests that the couplet is cited with reference to a passage in the "Fang Ji" chapter of the *Liji*, which, according to Zheng Xuan's commentary to the *Liji*, attributes this line to Ding Jiang as a criticism of her stepson, Duke Xian, who mistreated her after he came to the throne. See SSJZS, vol. 2, 51/391B–C; and Legge, trans., *Li Chi*, vol. 2, 288.

62. The *Mao Commentary* says little about the moral implications of Ding Jiang's decision to go afar when she saw off her daughter-in-law. Zheng Xuan, however, makes it clear that Ding Jiang "exceeded" the rites in the negative sense of the phrase by going beyond the gate of her home. See *Mao Shi* in SSJZS, vol. 1, 2.1/30B, 298. The ritual limitation on the movement of women is also mentioned in *Zuo zhuan*, Xi 22; translated in Legge, *The Chinese Classics*, vol. 5, 183.

63. See *Zuo zhuan*, Wen 1 (626 BCE); Cheng 7 (584 BCE); and Cheng 14 (577 BCE), especially Cheng 7, in Legge, *The Chinese Classics*, vol. 5, 364. The city of Qi 戚 (north

of present-day Puyang in Henan) was the feudal territory of the Sun family and a strategic location in the interstate politics of Jin, Zheng, Wu, and Chu. Sun Linfu may have offered Qi to Jin when he fled to Jin, but Jin later returned the territory to Wey. See Yang Bojun, *Chunqiu Zuozhuan zhu,* 4 vols. (Beijing: Zhonghua shuju, 1981), vol. 2, 509, 835.

64. Xi Chou was a powerful grandee of Jin who served as Jin's diplomat to foreign states. He is also mentioned in LNZ 3.6.

65. *Book of Odes, Cao Feng,* "Shi Jiu," Mao no. 152; translation based on Legge, *The Chinese Classics,* vol. 4, 223.

66. See *Zuo zhuan,* Cheng 14; translated in Legge, *The Chinese Classics,* vol. 5, 385. Jing Si was a concubine of Duke Ding.

67. As Liang Duan points out, this passage resembles but does not replicate the text in the *Zuo zhuan.* She also suggests that "good people" (善人 *shanren*) is probably an error for "me" (寡人 *guaren*). The *Zuo zhuan* has "the one who is not yet dead" (未亡人 *wei wangren*), that is, the duke's widow, Ding Jiang.

68. Zhuan, Duke Xian's younger brother, was also referred to as Xian 鮮 (not to be confused with Duke Xian 獻).

69. Sun Linfu is also called Sun Wenzi. The implication here is that Ding Jiang's prognostication concerning Duke Xian's future impact on the state of Wey is sufficiently alarming to cause Sun to ready himself for a precipitous departure from the state.

70. Here I follow the Liang Duan commentary, which adds the word *zui* ("fault") in the first clause. The meaning here differs substantially from the *Zuo* text and appears to be a scrambled version of it. The *Zuo* says: "If there be no Spirits, what is the use of such an announcement? If there be, they are not to be imposed upon;—guilty as he is, how can he announce that he is free from guilt?" (無神何告, 若有不可誣也, 有罪若何 告無); translation by Legge, *The Chinese Classics,* vol. 5, 465.

71. See *Zuo zhuan,* Xiang 10, 26, 27.

72. *Book of Odes, Da Ya,* "Ban," Mao no. 254, translation based on Legge, *The Chinese Classics,* vol. 4, 499–504

73. Huang Er was a grandee of the state of Zheng. The events described here are recorded in *Zuo zhuan,* Xiang 10. Essentially, Wey went to the aid of Song. In response, Zheng wanted to invade Wey to help Chu. Wey resisted Zheng and in the process captured Huang Er at Quanqiu, a place in the state of Song northwest of present-day Yongcheng in Henan.

74. In keeping with the text of the *Zuo zhuan,* I follow Liang Duan in reading "forest" (林 *lin*) as "hill" (陵 *ling*). The method of divination was either plastromancy or scapulomancy, whereby turtle plastrons or ox scapulas were heated in fire. The cracks that appeared were then interpreted as omens.

75. *Book of Odes, Xiao Ya,* "Chang Chang Zhe Hua," Mao no. 214; translation based on Legge, *The Chinese Classics,* vol. 4, 385. The poem expresses how the worthy can adapt to all circumstances (whether going left or right).

76. On *wenci*, "cultivated speech," see David Schaberg, *A Patterned Past: Form and Thought in Early Chinese Historiography* (Cambridge, Mass.: Harvard University Asia Center, 2001), 81–86.

77. Duke Zhuang of Wey reigned from 757 to 735 BCE. Note that there are two different rulers called Duke Zhuang of Wey. This biography concerns the first. The second reigned for one year in 478 BCE. The Duke Zhuang of this biography lived in pre-Spring and Autumn times, so he is mentioned only once in the *Zuo zhuan* under Yin 3.

78. Her name means Jiang of Duke Zhuang, that is, her clan name is Jiang and Zhuang is the posthumous name of her husband.

79. The interpretation of the ode as found in the *Zhongyong* suggests that the plain outer robe represents the virtuous man's humility and eschewal of outward display and his determination to cultivate his inner qualities: "It is said in the *Book of Poetry*, 'Over her embroidered robe she wears a [plain] garment,' expressing how the wearer disliked the display of the beauty [of the robe]. Just so, it is the way of the superior man to prefer concealment [of his virtue], while it daily becomes more illustrious, and it is the way of the small man to seek notoriety, while he daily goes more and more to ruin"; translated by Legge, *The Chinese Classics*, vol. 1, 430–432.

80. *Book of Odes*, Wey Feng, "Shuo Ren," Mao 57; translation based on Legge, *The Chinese Classics*, vol. 4, 94–95.

81. As in the ode quoted above, the heir apparent is here indicated by the term "eastern palace" (東宮 *donggong*). This sentence seems to be out of context.

82. Duke Zhuang of Wey also married a woman of Chen, Li Gui, whose only son died. Dai Gui had accompanied Li Gui upon her marriage to Duke Zhuang. Duke Huan of Wey reigned from 734 to 719 BCE.

83. These events, including a speech on the dangers of bad parenting, are recounted in *Zuo zhuan*, Yin 3; see Legge, *The Chinese Classics*, vol. 5, 13–14.

84. The line suggests that one should not encourage people in their bad habits. *Book of Odes*, Xiao Ya, "Jiao Gong," Mao no. 223; translated by Legge, *The Chinese Classics*, vol. 4, 406.

85. Wang Zhaoyuan suggests that the word *mei* (妹) is possibly an error for *huan* (桓). See LNZHB, vol. 5, 322.

86. In some editions, the order of biographies 1.9–1.11 differs. I follow the order found in Liang Duan, LNZHB, vol. 7, and in *Sibu beiyao*.

87. Jing is a posthumous name (*shi* 謚) meaning "respectfully attentive." Jiang is her clan name and Ji is her husband's lineage name. On posthumous names for women, see Yang, *Chunqiu Zuozhuan zhu*, vol. 1, 2; vol. 2, 562, note 7.6. It is important to note that the terminology of naming is used inconsistently so that the term for "posthumous name" sometimes designates a descriptive sobriquet used during a person's life. Jing Jiang was born ca. 540 BCE. Ju was a small state located in present-day Shandong province. Although the rulers of Ju held the clan name Si, the name Dai Si is not consistent with the other clan name she is given here: Jiang. The Qing commentator, Gu Guangqi (1766–1835), plausibly argues that the reference to Dai Si is incorrect and is

due to a confusion between Gongsun Ao (also called Mubo) on the one hand, who according to *Zuo zhuan,* Wen 7, had married a Dai Si from Ju, and the Gongfu Mubo of the present story, who married a woman from Ju with the clan name Jiang, on the other hand. See Gu Guangqi, *Lienü zhuan gaizheng,* in LNZHB, vol. 3, 283. The name Ji here refers to the Jisun lineage of Spring and Autumn times, of which Jing Jiang's husband (Gongfu Mubo) was a member. Along with the Shunsun and Mengsun lineage, the Jisun was one of the three great ministerial families that controlled of the state of Lu. They were also known as the "Three Huan," namely, the three younger sons of Duke Huan of Lu (r. 711–694 BCE) and their descendants. They headed the "three ministries" (*sanqing*) of state by hereditary privilege. See Loewe and Shaughnessy, *The Cambridge History of Ancient China,* 598. They are also mentioned in LNZ 3.9.

88. Gongfu Mubo was a grandee of the state of Lu, as was his son, Gongfu Wenbo (b. ca 520 BCE), who was also known as Gongfu Chu. Mubo's nephew, Ji Kangzi, held a more important position in Lu, that of *qing,* or "minister." All three of these men were members of the Jisun lineage.

89. I follow Liang Duan's annotation, which suggests that the word *yang* (養) in the phrase *shouyang* (守養) is an error for *yi* (義) and should therefore be read as *shouyi* (守義), "to maintain righteousness," which in turn means "to maintain chastity." See LNZHB, vol. 7, 333.

90. King Wu of Zhou reigned ca. 1045–1043 BCE.

91. The king could not ask them to help him in so menial a task because he regarded them as his peers.

92. Duke Huan of Qi (r. 685–643 BCE), an important figure in Spring and Autumn China, presided over all of the other feudal lords as leader, or "hegemon."

93. The Duke of Zhou was the younger brother of King Wu of Zhou. He served as regent to King Wu's son, King Cheng (r. 1042/35–1006 BCE).

94. *Book of Odes, Da Ya,* "Wen Wang," Mao no. 235, translated by Legge, *The Chinese Classics,* vol. 4, 429.

95. The warp threads are the strong lengthwise threads held in tension on the loom, while the weft threads are inserted alternately over and under the warp threads as filler. The Chinese term for warp, *jing,* also means "a constant rule" or "a standard," and came to be used to describe a "classic" text.

96. I am grateful to Dieter Kuhn for his assistance in the understanding and translation of these terms in a personal communication of July 2009. Kuhn discusses the loom of Lu in detail in *Zur Entwicklung der Webstuhltechnologie im alten China* (Heidelberg: Edition Forum, 1990), 46–52. The term *fu* (幅) refers to a "temple," that is, an adjustable bar with sharp points placed on the woven web of fabric to maintain a constant width.

97. According to Kuhn, the function of the "batten" is not entirely clear. "Maintaining the connection" can be understood as the process of beating the weft into the warp. The "pushing and sending forth" of threads might refer to either the weft or the weft

and the warp ends on either side of the batten. I also direct readers to general images and descriptions of loom technology at http://en.wikipedia.org/wiki/Loom. Here, the batten is described as follows: "As the shuttle moves across the loom laying down the fill yarn, it also passes through openings in another frame called a reed (which resembles a comb). With each picking operation, the reed presses or battens each filling yarn against the portion of the fabric that has already been formed."

98. According to Kuhn (in personal communication), "The heddle arrangement which is referred to here may have been a rod with string loops attached. When such a rod with heddles is lifted up it has to be pushed and pulled several times so as to prevent the unlooped warp threads from coming up with the looped ones."

99. A "reed comb," as part of a loom, is a toothed, comblike device that holds the longitudinal strands of the warp in alignment between its teeth and pushes each lateral or weft thread against the rest as the cloth is woven.

100. The "cloth-beam" (軸 *zhou*) is a round beam that maintained the density of warp threads.

101. According to Dieter Kuhn, the "warp-beam" (摘 *di*) is "a revolving cylindrical axis fitted into a frame. Onto this beam the warp threads were rolled to the requisite length. A revolving warp-beam of this kind not only paid out the warp threads as needed, but also helped regulate the tension of the weave in the direction of the warp and thus maintained an even density. That was important in keeping to the standards laid down for size and weight of silk fabric intended as tax payments, remuneration, gifts or tributes." See his "Silk Weaving in Ancient China: From Geometric Figures to Patterns of Pictorial Likeness," *Chinese Science* 12 (1995): 79, 99. Also see Angela Sheng, "The Disappearance of Silk Weaves with Weft Effects in Early China," *Chinese Science* 12 (1995): 41–76, for discussion and illustrations.

102. The Three Excellencies (also translated as the "Three Ducal Ministers") according to one definition found in the *Book of Documents*, served advisory roles in the highest level of government. See Legge, *The Chinese Classics,* vol. 3, 527. Also see LNZ 6.1, note 7.

103. This anecdote is found in *Guoyu*, "Luyu," part 2, item 13.

104. Jisun, that is, Ji Kangzi, was a powerful minister to Duke Ai of Lu and an associate of Confucius.

105. The "greater-colored robes" refer to ceremonial garments of five colors worn on this occasion. See *Zhouli*, in SSJZS, 20/138C. Some editions of LNZ have *shide* (施 德) for *dide* (地 德) and *zuzhi* (組 織) for *zushi* (祖 識). I follow the latter readings, which reflect the text of the *Guoyu*. The phrase "virtues of earth" refers to natural resources that bring benefit to the people. See *Guoyu*, vol. 1, 206, note 8.

106. The "lesser-colored robes" refer to ceremonial garments of three colors worn on this occasion. See *Zhouli*, in SSJZS, 20/139A.

107. The text reads "the hundred craftsmen," but the annotations in the *Guoyu* gloss the terms as "the hundred officials" (百官 *bai guan*). See *Guoyu*, vol. 1, 207, note 15.

108. Here I follow the text as it appears in *Guoyu*, "Luyu," part 2, item 13.

109. For a diagram of the official regalia mentioned in this passage, see Zhou Xibao, *Zhong-guo gudai fushi shi* (Beijing: Zhongguo xiju chubanshe, 1996), 34–35.

110. Zhongni was the style name of Confucius (551–479 BCE).

111. *Book of Odes, Da Ya*, "Zhan Yang," Mao no. 264; translation based on Legge, *The Chinese Classics*, vol. 4, 562; and Karlgren, *The Book of Odes*, 237.

112. This story corresponds to *Guoyu*, "Luyu," part 2, item 11. Nangong and Lu were both grandees of the state of Lu.

113. I follow the annotations in the corresponding *Guoyu* passage, vol. 1, 203, note 9, which suggest that the *Guoyu* text is a condensed version of a sentence that can be rendered, "By way of which ritual did you serve this person turtle?" (猶何禮有黿 *you he li you bie*).

114. "Taking care over minutiae" means that one is vigilant about untoward events at their inception, when it is still possible to control and contain them. See Kinney, *Representations of Childhood*, 21–22.

115. *Book of Odes, Xiao Ya*, "Lu Ming," Mao no. 161; translation by Legge, *The Chinese Classics*, vol. 4, 247.

116. See *Guoyu*, "Luyu," part 2, item 16. Also see alternative accounts of this event in *Han-shi waizhuan*, in SBCK, vol. 3, 1/8B; translated in James Hightower, *Han Shih Wai Chuan*, 26–27; and in *Zhanguo ce*, in SBCK, vol. 14, 6/58B; translated in James Irving Crump, *Chan-kuo Ts'e* (San Francisco: Chinese Materials Center, 1979), 338.

117. *Odes, Lu Song*, "You Bi," Mao no. 298; translation by Legge, *The Chinese Classics*, vol. 4, 615.

118. For a variation on this story, see *Liji*, "Tan Gong," SSJZS, vol. 1, 9/76B; translated in Legge, *Li Chi*, vol. 1, 176: "At the mourning for Mubo [her husband], Jing Jiang wailed for him in the daytime, and at that for Wenbo [her son], she wailed for him both in the daytime and the night. Confucius said, 'She knows the rules of propriety.'"

119. This story corresponds to *Guoyu*, "Luyu," part 2, item 12. The action takes place in the household of Ji Kangzi, Jing Jiang's nephew. As a hereditary noble, Ji was entitled to possess land and an attached population who paid taxes to him. The residence was thus a political unit, where he held court, as well as a dwelling that housed his family and other dependents. See Mark Edward Lewis for a discussion of the household as a political unit in *The Construction of Space in Early China* (Albany: State University of New York Press, 2006), 78–82.

120. I translate this sentence as it appears in the *Guoyu*, "Luyu," part 2, item 12.

121. This story corresponds to *Guoyu*, "Luyu," part 2, item 14. Ritual dictated that women should not cross the threshold when greeting guests.

122. Daozi was Jing Jiang's father-in-law.

123. The implication here is that she would not accept the offerings directly with her own hand, as ritual forbade the direct exchange of items between men and women in order to avoid physical contact.

124. I translate this sentence as it appears in the *Guoyu*, that is, without the second negative. The idea is that she was careful to avoid both drinking too much and sitting down to feast with male kin.

125. *Odes, Wey Feng*, "Mang," Mao no. 58; see Legge's translation in *The Chinese Classics*, vol. 4, 99, and glosses on the word *shuang* (爽) in Karlgren, *Glosses on the Book of Odes*, 158.

126. The first part of the opening sentence is missing; I have followed Liang Duan's reading, which incorporates the title as the first line of the biography. Zifa is mentioned in *Xunzi*, "Qiang Guo." In the "Dao Ying Xun" chapter of the *Huainanzi*, he is identified as a general who served King Xuan of Chu (r. 369–339 BCE). He is also mentioned in the "Xiu Wu" chapter of that text.

127. These were regarded as poor rations. See *Hanshu* 31, 1802.

128. King Goujian of Yue reigned from 496 to 465 BCE.

129. *Odes, Tang Feng*, "Xi Shuo," Mao no. 114; translated by Legge, *The Chinese Classics*, vol. 4, 175.

130. *Odes, Xiao Ya*, "Xiao Yuan," Mao no. 196; translated by Legge, *The Chinese Classics*, vol. 4, 334.

131. Meng Ke of Zou, the great Confucian philosopher, is better known in the West by his Latinized name Mencius (372–289 BCE). Zou was a small state located in present-day Shandong province directly south of Qufu. For another early account of Mencius's mother, see *Hanshi waizhuan* in SBCK, vol. 3, 9/1 and 9/9; translated in Hightower, *Han Shih Wai Chuan*, 290, 305–306.

132. The Six Arts are ritual, music, archery, charioteering, writing, and mathematics. An alternative explanation defines them as the six classics: the *Odes*, the *Spring and Autumn Annals*, the *Book of Documents*, the *Book of Changes*, and the *Rites*.

133. "Gradual transformation" refers to both a child-rearing technique, whereby a child is morally formed through daily exposure to correct models of behavior, and a more general principle for moral transformation. See Kinney, *Representations of Childhood*, 16–25.

134. *Book of Odes, Yong Feng*, "Gan Mao," Mao no. 53. Translation based on Legge, *The Chinese Classics*, vol. 4, 86. Also see Karlgren, trans., *The Book of Odes*, 34–35. Karlgren understands the ode as follows: "A fine gentlemen comes in grand state to pay court to his lady. Seeing him approach, she meditates on how she ought to receive him." Here this quotation may be interpreted as the thoughts of Mencius's mother contemplating what she could do for her son.

135. Zi Si, a renowned Confucian philosopher, is said to be the grandson of Confucius.

136. *Book of Odes, Yong Feng*, "Gan Mao," Mao no. 53; translation based on Legge, *The Chinese Classics*, vol. 4, 86.

137. See "Quli," *Liji*, in SSJZS, vol. 1, 2/10A; translated in Legge, *Li Chi*, vol. 1, 70–71.

138. Based on what follows, the word *mian* (敏) appears to be an error for *ye* (也). See LNZHB, vol. 7, 347.

139. *Book of Changes*, hexagram no. 37, "Jia Ren"; translated in Z. D. Sung, *The Text of Yi King*, 160.

140. *Book of Odes, Xiao Ya*, "Si Gan," Mao no. 189. Translation based on Karlgren, *Glosses on the Book of Odes*, 70. Also see Legge, *The Chinese Classics*, vol. 4, 303.

141. See *Guliang zhuan*, Yin 2; see SSJZS, 1/3B, vol. 2, 2367B; and *Liji*, "Jiao Te Sheng," in SSJZS, vol. 2, 26/228C, 1456C; translated in Legge, *Li Chi*, vol. 1, 441.

142. *Odes, Lu Song*, "Pan Shui," Mao no. 299. Also see Legge, *The Chinese Classics*, vol. 4, 617.

143. The La sacrifice occurred at the very end of the year to welcome the new year with religious observances and secular feasting. See Derk Bodde, *Festivals in Classical China: New Year and Other Annual Observances during the Han Dynasty 206 B.C.–A.D. 220* (Princeton: Princeton University Press, 1975), 49–75. Also See William Boltz, "Philological Footnotes to the Han New Year Rites," *Journal of the American Oriental Society*, vol. 99, no. 3 (July–September, 1979):423–439; Mark Edward Lewis, *Sanctioned Violence in Early China* (Albany: State University of New York Press, 1990), 185–190; and Legge, trans., *Li Chi*, vol. 1, 298–310.

144. This principle is enunciated in *Guliang zhuan*, Yin 2. See SSJZS, 1/3B, vol. 2, 2367B.

145. Duke Mu of Lu reigned 409–376 BCE.

146. See "Sang Fu Si Zhi," in *Liji*, SSJZS, vol. 2, 1695A; Legge, *Li Chi*, vol. 2, 467.

147. *Odes, Bei Feng*, "Quan Shui," Mao no. 39. Translation based on Legge, *The Chinese Classics*, vol. 4, 63.

148. Wei was created through the partition of the Spring and Autumn state of Jin ca. 453 BCE. It occupied land in the present-day provinces of Shanxi and Henan. Mang Mao is called Meng Mao (孟卯) in the "Fan Lun" chapter of the *Huainanzi*, where he is identified as a man of Qi who served Wei. He is also mentioned in the *Zhanguo ce*. Among its several meanings, the term "Kind Mother" (慈母 *cimu*) was a complimentary name for a stepmother. It was also an official title for a nurse who assisted in the raising of a child. For this second usage I translate the term "Loving Matron." See further notes at LNZ 6.10.

149. One *chi* was roughly equivalent to one foot.

150. I follow Liang Duan's annotation, which suggests that *fanmu* (凡母) be read as *fanren* (凡人).

151. King Anxi of Wei reigned from 276 to 243 BCE.

152. *Odes, Cao Feng*, "Shi Jiu," Mao no. 152. Translation based on Legge, *The Chinese Classics*, vol. 4, 222–223.

153. This story closely follows *Hanshi waizhuan* 9/1B, translated in Hightower, *Han Shih Wai Chuan*, 291.

154. The bribe was one hundred *yi* (鎰), that is, approximately 68 pounds or 31 kilograms of *jin* (金), "cash," which in pre-Qin times were coins cast in any one of several precious metals such as gold, bronze, copper, or silver, but based on a standard of weight in gold. Some scholars speculate that at the time, money was used not so much as a

vehicle of exchange for goods but to pay taxes or fines to the government. See Loewe and Shaughnessy, *The Cambridge History of Ancient China*, 606–607; and Anna Seidel, "Buying One's Way to Heaven: The Celestial Treasury in Chinese Religion," *History of Religions* 17, no. 3–4 (1978): 419–431. On the gold standard, see D. C. Lau, ed., *Guanzizhuzi suoyin* (Hong Kong: The Commercial Press, 2001), 1.5/11/16, 1.5/12/7; translated in W. Allyn Rickett, *Guanzi: Political, Economic, and Philosophical Essays from Early China* (Princeton: Princeton University Press, 1985), 118–121; and Walter Scheidel, "The Monetary Systems of the Han and Roman Empires," in *Rome and China: Comparative Perspectives on Ancient World Empires,* ed. Walter Scheidel (Oxford: Oxford University Press, 2009), 137–207.

155. King Xuan of Qi reigned from 319 to 301 BCE.
156. *Odes, Wei Feng,* "Fa Tan," Mao no. 112. Translation based on Legge, *The Chinese Classics,* vol. 4, 170.

2. THE WORTHY AND ENLIGHTENED

1. The term "worthy" (賢 *xian*) refers to one who is morally and intellectually capable.
2. Here I follow Wang Niansun's (1744–1832) reading of "worthy" (賢 *xian*) as a mistake for "to attend to" (覽 *lan*). See LNZHB, vol. 7, 301.
3. King Xuan of Zhou reigned from 827/25 to 782 BCE. The Lu interpretation of the *Odes* associates this story with the ode "Guan Ju" (Mao no. 1). See discussion in Wang Xianqian, *Shi sanjia yi ji shu,* 2 vols. (Beijing: Zhonghua shuju, 1987), vol. 1, 4–7. On King Xuan's reign in traditional and bronze sources, see Michael Loewe and Edward L. Shaughnessy, eds., *The Cambridge History of Ancient China: From the Origins of the Civilization to 221 B.C.* (Cambridge, England: Cambridge University Press, 1999), 345–348. For a discussion of the status, wealth, and archaeological remains of women of Qi from this period, see Ying Yong, "Gender, Status, Ritual Regulations and Mortuary Practice," in *Gender and Chinese Archaeology,* ed. Katheryn Linduff and Yan Sun (Walnut Creek, Calif.: Altamira Press, 2004), 194–197.
4. LNZHB, vol. 7, 357 supplies words that are missing from the present-day text and which I have included in my translation. In Han sources, the "Lanes of Perpetuity" (*yongxiang* 永巷) was another name for the "Lateral Courts" (*yiting* 掖庭), which designated the side apartments of the palace where the women of the harem lived and which housed the administrative offices of the harem that were staffed by eunuchs. There was also a special prison in the Lanes of Perpetuity for palace women. See Hans Bielenstein, *The Bureaucracy of Han Times* (Cambridge, England: Cambridge University Press, 1980), 53. In earlier sources, the term *xiang* (lane) is mentioned in connection with the women's quarters in *The Book of Odes, Xiao Ya,* "Xiang Bo," Mao no. 200; see *Mao Shi,* SSJZS, 12.3/188A.
5. For rites that are similar to these injunctions, see *Liji,* "Nei Ze," in SSJZS, vol. 2, 1462C; translated in James Legge, *Li Chi: Book of Rites,* 2 vols. (1885; reprint, New

York: University Books, 1967), vol. 1, 455; "Yu Zao," in SSJZS, vol. 2, 30/254B, 1482B; translated in Legge, *Li Chi*, vol. 2, 18.

6. *Odes, Da Ya,* "Jia Le," Mao no. 249. Translation based on James Legge, trans., *The Chinese Classics,* 5 vols. (1893; reprint, Hong Kong: University of Hong Kong Press, 1960), vol. 4, 482.

7. *Odes, Xiao Ya,* "Xi Sang," Mao no. 228. Translation based on Legge, *The Chinese Classics,* vol. 4, 415; and Bernhard Karlgren, *The Book of Odes* (Goteborg: Elanders Boktryckeri Aktiebolag, 1950), 181.

8. See Bernhard Karlgren, *Glosses on the Book of Odes* (Goteborg: Elanders Boktrykeri Aktiebolag, 1964), "Glosses on the Siao Ya Odes," 161.

9. Her name means "the lady of the Ji clan of Wey." Duke Huan of Qi (r. 685–643 BCE) had six concubines who were treated as wives (夫人 *furen*). Two were called Ji of Wey, but were distinguished by the designations "elder" and "younger." Both of these women gave birth to sons who were later made dukes. It is not clear from this narrative which Ji of Wey this biography addresses. See *Zuo zhuan,* Xi 17; translated in Legge, *The Chinese Classics,* vol. 5, 173. Also see Melvin Thatcher, "Marriages of the Ruling Elite in the Spring and Autumn Period," in *Marriage and Inequality in Chinese Society,* ed. Rubie S. Watson and Patricia Buckley Ebrey (Berkeley: University of California Press, 1991), 33. This story was included in the "Admonitions Scroll" of Gu Kaizhi (c. 345–406 CE), but only the caption remains and the illustration has been lost. For this painting and other illustrations of this story, see Shane McCausland, ed., *Gu Kaizhi and the Admonitions Scroll* (London: The British Museum Press, 2003), 57, 89–90, 126, 154–155, 162.

10. The music of Zheng and Wey was regarded as particularly dissolute. See Cao Dagu's (Ban Zhao's) annotation to this line preserved in *Wenxuan* 56, 2B. For discussion of the music of Zheng and Wey, see Kenneth DeWoskin, *A Song for One of Two: Music and the Concept of Art in Early China* (Ann Arbor: The University of Michigan Center for Chinese Studies, 1982), 92–98; and Wong Siu-kit and Lee Kar-shui, "Poems of Depravity: A Twelfth-Century Dispute on the Moral Character of the *Book of Songs*," *T'oung Pao* 75, no. 4–5 (1989): 209–225.

11. In the Spring and Autumn period, the Zhou king, though nominally in charge of all of the feudal states, was a mere cipher who held no real power or authority. A hegemon (霸 *ba*) was a ruler of one of the feudal states who lacked the legitimacy of the Zhou king but through his political and military power was recognized by all of the feudal lords as first among equals. See Loewe and Shaughnessy, *The Cambridge History of Ancient China,* 551–562.

12. Compare this account to a similar tale found in *Hanshi wai zhuan,* SBCK, vol. 3, 4/2B; translated in James Hightower, *Han Shih Wai Chuan: Han Ying's Illustrations of the Didactic Application of the Classic of Songs* (Cambridge, Mass.: Harvard University Press, 1952),128–129. Here it is not Ji but a sage named Dongguo Ya who makes predictions based on the ruler's behavior, and it is the state of Ju rather than Wey that is being considered for attack.

13. He acceded to her wish to spare Wey. Also see a similar account in D. C. Lau, *A Concordance to the* Lüshi chunqiu (Hong Kong: Commercial Press, 1994), "Chong Yan," 18.2/110/13; translated in John Knoblock, and Jeffrey Riegel, *The Annals of Lü Buwei* (Stanford: Stanford University Press, 2000), 446–447.

14. *Odes, Yong Feng,* "Junzi Jie Lao," Mao no. 47. Translation based on Legge, *The Chinese Classics*, vol. 4, 78.

15. Jiang is her clan name and Qi is her state of origin; her name thus means "the lady of the Jiang clan of Qi." Both Duke Huan of Qi (r. 685–643 BCE) and Duke Wen of Jin (r. 636–628 BCE) were known as "hegemons." See note at LNZ 2.2. Accounts of this story appear in the *Zuo zhuan*, Xi 23, translated in Legge, *The Chinese Classics*, vol. 5, 187; *Guoyu*, "Jinyu," part 4, item 2; and *Shiji* 39, 1658, translated in William Nienhauser et al., *The Grand Scribe's Records*, 6 vols. (Bloomington: Indiana University Press, 1994–2006), vol. 5.1, 326–327.

16. Duke Xian (r. 676–651 BCE) wanted to demote his heir apparent Shensheng and appoint as his successor his younger son, Xiqi, the child of his concubine Li Ji, whom the duke had elevated to the position of wife. To rid the court of contenders and consolidate her own son's place on the throne, Li Ji falsely accused Shensheng of attempting to poison his father. Rather than trying to prove his innocence (and her culpability) to his father, and convinced that his father would perish without the love of Li Ji, Shensheng committed suicide. See *Zuo zhuan*, Xi 4–5, and discussion in Anne Behnke Kinney, *Representations of Childhood and Youth in Early China* (Stanford: Stanford University Press, 2004), 86–88.

17. Chonger is known by a variety of names and titles in this biography. He is called Duke Wen of Jin, which did not become his official title until after he assumed the throne of Jin. Prior to this time he was known by the title *gongzi* (公子), which I translate here as "prince." Strictly speaking, this term should be translated as "the duke's son," but "prince" seems less awkward.

18. Duke Wen and his uncle Fan (who served as an official in Qi and who was also known as Zifan or Hu Yan 狐偃) fled after the death of Duke Xian and the ensuing struggle over who should succeed the duke. Chonger remained in exile for some nineteen years before returning to his state. See *Guoyu*, "Jinyu," part 4, items 1–2. The Di people were culturally distinct from the Chinese of the period and regarded by them as "barbarians." See Loewe and Shaughnessy, *The Cambridge History of Ancient China*, 944–947.

19. This is a paraphrase of *Odes, Da Ya,* "Da Ming," Mao no. 236.

20. *Odes, Xiao Ya,* "Huang Huang Zhe Hua," Mao no. 163. Translation based on Legge, *The Chinese Classics*, vol. 4, 249.

21. Duke Mu of Qin reigned 659–621 BCE. *Odes, Qin Feng,* "Wei Yang," Mao no. 134, according to Mao, was written on the occasions of Chonger's return to Jin with the help of Duke Mu of Qin's son and heir, Duke Kang. Duke Kang of Qin was also the nephew of Chonger, as Duke Mu was married to Chonger's half-sister. Duke Kang is the boy called Ying mentioned in LNZ 2.4.

22. Duke Huai of Jin reigned from 636 to 635 BCE.
23. The master of covenants (盟主 *mengzhu*) was employed to create cooperation between states under the direction of a hegemon. The institution arose when the Zhou king was too weak to maintain order among the feudal lords. See Mark Edward Lewis, *Sanctioned Violence in Early China* (Albany: State University of New York Press, 1990), 43–52; and *Guoyu*, "Jinyu," part 4, items 2–3.
24. *Odes, Chen Feng*, "Dong Men Zhi Chi," Mao no. 139. Translation based on Legge, *The Chinese Classics*, vol. 4, 209. The standard edition of the *Odes* has "virtuous lady" (淑姬 *shuji*) rather than the phrase "eldest Jiang" (孟姜 *mengjiang*) quoted here.
25. Mu is her husband's posthumous name and Ji is her clan name. Her name thus means "the lady of the Ji clan, consort of Duke Mu." Duke Mu of Qin reigned 659–621 BCE and Duke Xian reigned 676–651 BCE. The mother of Mu Ji and Shensheng was a Jiang of Qi, who had first served as concubine to Duke Wu of Jin (r. 678–677) and then was taken as a wife by Duke Wu's son, Duke Xian. The mother of Duke Hui (r. 650–637 BCE) was a woman of the Lesser Rong tribe. See *Zuo zhuan*, Zhuang 28; Xi 14, 15.
26. For the story of Shensheng and Duke Xian, see LNZ 7.7. According to *Zuo zhuan*, Xi 4, after engineering the death of Shensheng in order to place her own son on the throne, Duke Xian's concubine Li Ji slandered two of the duke's other sons, saying that they had colluded with Shensheng to kill Duke Xian. Chonger and Yiwu therefore fled. Duke Xian had many sons who were also expelled at this time. Eventually Yiwu, and then, some nineteen years later, Chonger, requested and received aid from Qin to return to Jin to rule.
27. Liang is located south of Hancheng city in present-day Shaanxi province.
28. Duke Hui (Yiwu) reigned from 650 to 637 BCE.
29. *Zuo zhuan*, Xi 15, shows Mu Ji making a similar suggestion.
30. The gift was the ceding of land to Qin, according to the *Zuo zhuan*, Xi 15: "To the earl of Qin he had promised five cities beyond the He, with all the country on the east which had formed the territory of Guo, as far as mount Hua on the south, and to the city of Xieliang on the north of the He; but he did not surrender any of this territory, any of these cities." Translated by Legge, *The Chinese Classics*, vol. 5, 167.
31. According to *Shiji* 5, in 646 BCE, Jin not only refused to give grain to Qin but also initiated the conflict after deciding that, in its weakened state, Qin would be an easy target.
32. *Shiji* 5 is more explicit: "Fast and be abstinent! I am going to offer the Lord of Jin as a sacrifice to the Supreme Deity." Nienhauser, *The Grand Scribe's Records*, vol. 1, 97.
33. This section of the biography is a paraphrase of *Zuo zhuan*, Xi 15. Legge translates the phrase *lixin* (履薪) as "treading on faggots (which she caused to be placed on the ground and steps)." See *The Chinese Classics*, vol. 5, 168. The idea here seems to be that Ji brought her children to the tower prepared for immolation. Legge translates the name of the daughter as two names of two individuals, but I follow Yang Bojun, *Chunqiu Zuozhuan cidian* (Beijing: Zhonghua shuju, 1985), 968.

34. The Ling Tower was located in a suburb of the Qin capital.

35. A *lao* sacrifice consisted of a bull, a ram, and a boar.

36. *Odes, Qin Feng,* "Wei Yang," Mao no. 134. Translation based on Legge, *The Chinese Classics,* vol. 4, 203. Mao also attributes this ode to Ying, Mu Ji's son and the heir apparent of Qin.

37. *Odes, Da Ya,* "Yi," Mao no. 256. Translation based on Legge, *The Chinese Classics,* vol. 4, 511.

38. Fan is both a place name and a family name associated with a descendant of King Wen of the Zhou dynasty who was enfeoffed by King Xuan of Zhou (r. 827/25–782 BCE) with the territory of Fan, now associated with the area around present-day Qiyuan in Henan. Fan was absorbed by Chu in 622 BCE. See Xu Shaohua, *Zhoudai nanwang lishi dili yu wenhua* (Wuhan: Wuhan University Press, 1994), 131–136. This woman's name could therefore be understood as "the lady of the clan of Ji who came from Fan." According to Zheng Qiao's (c. 1161) "Yi yi wei shi," *Shizu lüe,* part 3 in *Tongzhi,* Fan was indeed a state that held the Ji surname. See Zheng Qiao, *Tongzhi* (Taipei: Xinxing shuju, 1959), vol. 4, 27/1. The LNZ text describes Fan Ji as King Zhuang's "wife" (夫人 *furen*), but as she shares her rank with seven other women and is outranked by two, she was almost certainly not a primary wife. It is thus possible that the word *ji* (姬) could also be translated as referring to the rank of "Lady," a term for a high-ranking concubine. In this case, her name would mean "the concubine named Fan," or "the concubine from Fan." For further discussion of this term, see notes at LNZ 5.4, and *Hanshu* 4, 105, note 2. King Zhuang of Chu reigned from 613 to 591 BCE. He was one of the five great hegemons of the Spring and Autumn period, who, according to Han Feizi, absorbed 26 states into his own territory. See *Han Feizi,* "Youdu," in SBCK, vol. 18, 2/1A, translated in Burton Watson, *Han Fei Tzu: Basic Writings* (New York: Columbia University Press, 1964), 21. Also see *Shiji* 40, 1700–1703, translated in Nienhauser, *The Grand Scribe's Records,* vol. 5.1, 393–399. On the hegemony of Chu, see Frank Kierman, trans., *China in Antiquity,* by Henri Maspero (University of Massachusetts Press, 1978), 204–208.

39. In early China, hunting was considered to be part of a set of activities related to sacrifice and warfare. See Lewis, *Sanctioned Violence in Early China,* 15–25. Hunting for mere pleasure was frowned upon as a pastime that undermined the serious business of governance. Also see Kinney, *Representations of Childhood,* 56–58.

40. This story is illustrated in the Song copy of the "Admonitions Scroll" of Beijing's Palace Museum. See McCausland, ed., *Gu Kaizhi,* 89, 93–94, 126, 146, 148, 155, 162, 185.

41. An early version of this story is found in *Hanshi waizhuan* in SBCK, vol. 3, 2/3A–4A; translated in Hightower, *Han Shih Wai Chuan,* 41–43. In this account, Fan's motive is frivolous by comparison: "I would not dare for private motives to keep other beauties in obscurity, and I want you to see more of them that you may be happy" (不敢私願蔽眾美,欲王之多見則娛). In Liu Xiang's *Xinxu,* in SBCK, vol. 17, 1/2B, where he also cites this story, Fan claims to have refrained from monopolizing the ruler's affections so as to not harm his "righteousness" or "sense of duty" (義 *yi*).

42. Chairs were not introduced into China until the Tang dynasty. People typically sat on the floor on mats. When speaking with a superior during a meeting or banquet, it was considered polite to move backward on one's mat.

43. Sunshu Ao was the chief counselor of Chu, a rank equivalent to prime minister. For more information, see notes to biography 3.5 in chapter 3, and note 44 below.

44. Barry Blakeley argues that the term "chief counselor" (令尹 lingyin) was "A title unique to Chu and ... originally may have been the field commander, but by the seventh century it had assumed the function of prime minister, in charge of both civil and military administration." See Barry Blakeley, "Chu Society and State: Image versus Reality," in *Defining Chu: Image and Reality,* ed. Constance Cook and John Major (Honolulu: University of Hawai'i Press, 1999), 60–61.

45. *Odes, Wey Feng,* "Shuo Ren," Mao no. 57. Translation based on Legge, *The Chinese Classics,* vol. 4, 96. Like the Han and Lu schools of the *Odes,* the *Lienü zhuan* interprets this line as referring to the ruler's wife rather than the ruler himself. See Wang Xianqian, *Shi sanjia yi ji shu,* vol. 1, 286. The idea is that the ruler should not be so consumed with court business that he has only the late hours of the night to spend with his consort.

46. *Odes, Shang Song,* "Na," Mao no. 301. Translation based on Legge, *The Chinese Classics,* vol. 4, 633.

47. The subject of this biography, according to Liu Xiang, is the author of the ode "Ru Fen," found in the *Zhounan* section of the *Odes,* Mao no. 10, translated in Legge, *The Chinese Classics,* vol. 4, 17–18. The *Mao Commentary* to the *Book of Odes* ascribes "Ru Fen" to the wife of an official during the waning years of the Shang, when the future Zhou King Wen (r. 1099/56–1050 BCE) was beginning to attract the loyalty of the people. In the ode, according to Mao's reading, she walks along the raised banks of the Ru River, collecting firewood, at first missing, and then later being reunited with her husband. In the last stanza she exhorts her husband to think of his parents and maintain his virtue in spite of the tyranny of the last rulers of Shang. For an interpretive overview of this ode, see Edward Shaughnessy, *Before Confucius: Studies in the Creation of the Chinese Classics* (Albany: State University of New York Press, 1997), 221–238. In the beginning of the Zhou dynasty, Zhou was divided into two areas, Shaonan and Zhounan. Zhounan was the area located in modern Henan province, encompassing portions of the Luo and Yellow rivers and the area that lay to the south. The River Ru is in Henan, and the banks were like dykes, raised high to keep the water from flooding. The Zhounan official seems to have been involved in flood control.

48. The idea seems to be that she feared that he had failed in his mission and fled rather than returning home and facing punishment. The remainder of the story seems to argue that as long as his parents were alive, he would never entertain such a dangerous plan, since his wife and parents might be punished in his stead. The dilemma here is that of a worthy man who must serve a tyrannical ruler.

49. Shun is also featured in LNZ 1.1. Descriptions of Shun's various occupations are also found in *Shiji* 1, 32; see Nienhauser, trans., *The Grand Scribe's Records,* vol. 1, 11.

50. This phrase is used to describe Confucius' disciple Zengzi (see LNZ 1.11) in *Hanshi waizhaun* in SBCK, vol. 3, 1/1; translated in Hightower, *Han Shih Wai Chuan*, 11. To assume an official position to nourish parents was considered a filial duty. Mencius said, 'There are three things which are unfilial, and to have no posterity is the greatest of them." See *Mencius*, 4A.26; *Mengzi zhushu* in SSJZS, vol. 2, 7B/59B, 2723B. Translation based on Legge, *The Chinese Classics*, vol. 2, 313. Mencius does not state what the other two unfilial acts are, but Zhao Qi supplies them in his commentary: "By flattering assent to encourage parents in unrighteousness; and secondly, not to succor their poverty and old age by engaging in official service. The third is to not marry and lack heirs, thereby cutting off sacrifices to the ancestors."

51. To avoid violating the law and thus corporal or capital punishments was also considered a filial duty. See *Xiaojing*, chapter 2; translation by Legge, *The Sacred Books of China*, vol. 3, 434.

52. The phoenix, dragon, and *qilin* are all mythical beasts of good omen.

53. *Odes, Zhounan*, "Ru Fen," Mao no. 10. Translation based on Legge, *The Chinese Classics*, vol. 4, 18. The bream's red tail indicates that the fish is in danger, perhaps injured. The fire is the danger posed by the ruler, one the husband must brave to protect his parents.

54. Reading *zhou* (周) as *hai* (害).

55. The "Woman of Distinction" was an honorary title. The word *zong* means "honored," but also "head," "leader," or "elder." See definition in, for example, Ying Shao, *Fengsu tongyi*, "Zhengshi," in *Fengsu tongyi jiaozhu*, 2 vols., ed. Wang Liqi (Beijing: Zhonghua shuju, 1981), vol. 1, 68.

56. The ritual employing the "marriage cup" (醮 *jiao*) is described in the *Liji*, "Hun Yi," chapter: "The father gave himself [sic] the special cup to his son, and ordered him to go and meet the bride; it being proper that the male should take the first step [in all the arrangements]. The son, having received the order, proceeded to meet his bride. Her father, who had been resting on his mat and leaning-stool in the temple, met him outside the gate and received him with a bow, and then the son-in-law entered, carrying a wild goose. After the [customary] bows and yieldings of precedence, they went up to the hall, when the bridegroom bowed twice and put down the wild goose. Then and in this way he received the bride from her parents. After this they went down, and he went out and took the reins of the horses of her carriage, which he drove for three revolutions of the wheels, having handed the strap to assist her in mounting. He then went before, and waited outside his gate. When she arrived, he bowed to her as she entered. They ate together of the same animal, and joined in sipping from the cups made of the same melon; thus showing that they now formed one body, were of equal rank, and pledged to mutual affection." Translated by Legge, *Li Chi*, vol. 2, 428. The cup was not specific to marriage and was also used in the capping ceremony.

57. See *Liji*, "Nei Ze," in SSJZS, vol. 2, 28/243B, 1471B; translated in Legge, *Li Chi*, vol. 1, 479.

58. This sentence was restored to the text. See Liang Duan, LNZHB, vol. 7, 370.

59. *Odes, Da Ya,* "Zheng Min," Mao no. 260. Translation based on Legge, *The Chinese Classics,* vol. 4, 542.

60. Zhao Cui (d. 622 BCE) was a member of the most powerful ministerial lineage in the state of Jin. This story is told in *Zuo zhuan,* Xi 24, translated in Legge, *The Chinese Classics,* vol. 5, 191 and *Shiji* 43, 1781–1782. Duke Wen of Jin (r. 636–628 BCE), Chonger, is also mentioned in LNZ 2.3, 2.4.

61. Her clan name was Ji. Her name means "the Ji clan wife of Zhao [Cui]."

62. The Di people were culturally distinct from the Chinese of the period, who regarded them as "barbarians." See Loewe and Shaughnessy, *The Cambridge History of Ancient China,* 944–947. See *Zuo zhuan,* Xi 23.

63. Their clan name is Wei, while Shu means "third daughter" and Ji means "fourth/youngest daughter." These women were captives from the Qianggaoru tribe. See *Zuo zhuan,* Xi 23; translated in Legge, *The Chinese Classics,* vol. 5, 186.

64. Yuan, Ping, and Lou are the names of fiefs held by the three brothers. See Yang, *Chunqiu zuozhuan zhu,* 417.

65. "To serve with towel and comb" means to perform wifely duties.

66. *Odes, Bei Feng,* "Gu Feng," Mao no. 35. Translation based on Legge, *The Chinese Classics,* vol. 4, 55.

67. *Odes, Bei Feng,* "Gu Feng," Mao no. 35. Translation based on Legge, *The Chinese Classics,* vol. 4, 56.

68. See *Zuo zhuan,* Xi 24.

69. See *Zuo zhuan,* Xuan 2; translated in Legge, *The Chinese Classics,* vol. 5, 291.

70. The wording of this phrase differs slightly from that recorded in *Zuo zhuan,* Xuan 2. Duke Cheng of Jin, named Heitun (meaning "Black Buttocks," perhaps a reference to a genetic trait known as the "Mongol spot"), reigned from 606 to 600 BCE. The mark is explained in *Guoyu,* "Zhouyu," part 3, item 2.

71. For an account of the reorganization of Jin's government, see *Zuo zhuan,* Xuan 2, translated in Legge, *The Chinese Classics,* vol. 5, 291.

72. *Odes, Da Ya,* "Yi," Mao no. 256. Translation based on Legge, *The Chinese Classics,* vol. 4, 516.

73. Tao may refer to Taoqiu (陶丘), which was northwest of the present-day county of Dingtao (定陶) in Shandong province. Taoqiu was the capital of Cao, one of the major states of the Spring and Autumn period. But by the seventh century BCE, Cao had become a satellite of Chu. Dazi was probably given Tao as a fief, where he ruled and received income from taxes.

74. Dou Ziwen (d. 625 BCE), a renowned leader of Chu, is also called Dou Guwutu. He is also mentioned in LNZ 2.5 and 3.5. See more on this figure in Blakeley, "Chu Society," 60–61.

75. See alternative reading of this sentence in Li Fang, *Taiping yulan,* 7 vols. (Tainan: Pingping chubanshe, 1965), vol. 4, 472/5A.

76. The implication here seems to be that as a form of camouflage, spots would serve the leopard better than black fur.

77. The term used for Dazi's crime, *dao* (盗), is generally translated as "robbery," but according to Liu Shao (fl. ca. 234 CE), it encompasses accepting gifts from subordinates, accepting bribes, and illegal profit obtained by extortion. I have translated the term as "graft," but given the meaning of the original term (i.e., *dao*), one suspects that there was some pressure exerted on the subordinates from whom gifts were "accepted." See A.F.P. Hulsewe, *Remnants of Han Law* (Leiden: E. J. Brill, 1955), 32–33.

78. *Odes, Yong Feng,* "Zai Chi," Mao no. 54. Translation based on Legge, *The Chinese Classics,* vol. 4, 89.

79. Liuxia Hui's name was actually Zhan Huo. He was given the name "Liuxia," which means "beneath the willows," either because he received revenue from a town called Liuxia or because a willow grew overhanging his house. He once served as a criminal judge (士師 *shishi*). See Legge, *The Chinese Classics,* vol. 1, 298– 299, where Liuxia Hui is cited in *Analects* XV:13. Also see *Analects* XVIII:8. According to the *Guoyu,* he served under Duke Xi of Lu (r. 659–627 BCE). See *Guoyu,* "Luyu," part 1, items 6, 9.

80. This sentence is a paraphrase of *Analects* XVIII:2.

81. This sentence is a paraphrase of *Mencius* 2A.9 and 5B.1.

82. *Odes, Xiao Ya,* "Xiao Min," Mao no. 195. Translation based on Legge, *The Chinese Classics,* vol. 4, 333. Presumably these words describe the disciple's limited knowledge of her husband.

83. Chen Hanzhang reads *bi* (必) as *bi* (畢) and *cun* (存) as *zai* (在), rendering the line, "The disciples were all present." See LNZHB, vol. 8, 620.

84. Qian Lou is mentioned in the bibliographic section of the *Hanshu* as the author of the *Qian Louzi,* a Daoist text that is no longer extant. See *Hanshu* 30, 1730. Qian Lou's biography is also included in Huangfu Mi's (215–282 CE) *Gaoshi zhuan,* where he is identified as a man of Qi noted for his purity and integrity. See *Gaoshi zhuan* in SBBY, vol. 104, part B, 5.

85. Zengzi was an eminent disciple of Confucius.

86. D. C. Lau's edition of the *Lienü zhuan* interpolates eight characters here that I have not included in my translation. Wang Zhaoyuan's commentary on this passage states that although the rites prohibited women from going outside their doors to either welcome someone in or send someone off, the present case was a matter of accepting condolences and by necessity required her presence. See LNZHB, vol. 5, 376.

87. On the dressing and laying out of the deceased, see *Liji,* "Sang Fu Da Ji," in SSJZS, vol. 2, 1571–1587, and Legge, trans., *Li Chi,* vol. 2, 173–200.

88. Officials' salaries were often paid, at least in part, in grain. Judging by Han calculations, the grain given to Qian Lou might have been equivalent to more than one month of an official's salary. See Michael Loewe, "The Measurement of Grain During the Han Period," *T'oung Pao,* 2nd series, 49, no. 1–2 (1961): 64–95.

89. *Odes, Chen Feng,* "Dong Men Zhi Chi," Mao no. 139. Translation based on Legge, *The Chinese Classics,* vol. 4, 209.

90. Yanzi, also known as Yan Ying, first served Duke Ling of Qi in 556 BCE and continued service through the reign of Duke Jing of Qi until his death in 500 BCE. His biography is found in *Shiji* 62, 2134–2137; translated in Neinhauser, *The Grand Scribe's Records*, vol. 7, 14–19. Liu Xiang's portrayal of him in the current *Lienü zhuan* biography draws heavily from the *Shiji* account. He is also mentioned in LNZ 6.4.

91. The title "Commissioned Wife" was conferred on the wives of grandees. See *Yili*, SSJZS, vol. 1, 31/1109C. According to the *Liji*, the duty of the commissioned wife was to assist the wife of the ruler. See *Liji* in SSJZS, vol. 2, "Ming Tang," 31/1489C; translated in Legge, *Li Chi*, vol. 2, 33.

92. At this time there were several systems of measurement in use, which makes it difficult to gauge accurately the heights of the two men in this story. One *chi* was roughly equivalent to 23 cm. We know from other texts that Yanzi was unusually short, so it is likely that he was not quite five feet tall, while his driver was probably six feet or more in height. For references concerning weights and measures in early China, see Nienhauser, *The Grand Scribe's Records*, vol. 1, xxxi–xxxiv.

93. Duke Jing reigned from 547 to 490 BCE.

94. *Odes, Xiao Ya,* "Ju Xia," Mao no. 218. Translated by Karlgren, *The Book of Odes* 172. Also see, Legge, *The Chinese Classics*, vol. 4, 393.

95. Jieyu was a contemporary of Confucius. He is said to have once met with Confucius when he approached the philosopher in his carriage around 489 BCE. See *Lunyu* XVIII:5. It is quite likely that the name Jieyu is simply a sobriquet that means "approaching the carriage," referring to his meeting with Confucius. His real name, according to Huangfu Mi, was Lu Tong. See Huangfu Mi, *Gaoshi zhuan*, in SBCK, vol. 104, 1/9A–9B. He is also known as the "Madman of Chu," on which, see Laurence Schneider, *A Madman of Ch'u: The Chinese Myth of Loyalty and Dissent* (Berkeley: University of California Press, 1980); and Alan J. Berkowitz, *Patterns of Disengagement: The Practice and Portrayal of Reclusion in Early Medieval China* (Stanford: Stanford University Press, 2000), 43.

96. On the significance of this gift, see notes to LNZ 1.14. Huainan, literally, "south of the Huai River," refers to the eastern portion of the state of Chu that lay north of the Yangzi River in present-day Anhui and Jiangsu provinces. See Barry Blakeley, "The Geography of Chu," in *Defining Chu: Image and Reality*, ed. John S. Major and Constance Cook (Honolulu: University of Hawai'i Press, 1999), 9–20.

97. Evidently, Jieyu considered his earlier silence in the presence of the king's messenger as a form of consent. Compare with *Hanshi waizhuan*, in SBCK, vol. 3, 2/12B; translated in Hightower, *Han Shih Wai Chuan*, 59–60.

98. *Odes, Zhou Nan,* "Tu Ju," Mao no. 7. Translation based on Legge, *The Chinese Classics*, vol. 4, 13.

99. Sima Qian notes a contemporary opinion that the Daoist philosopher Laozi and Lao Laizi were the same person. He also lists Lao Laizi as a teacher of Confucius. See *Shiji* 63, 2141; 67, 2186. The *Hanshu* bibliography lists a Daoist text called the *Lao Laizi* in sixteen sections. See *Hanshu* 30, 1730. Liang Duan suggests that a section of the extant

biography may have been lost, as the *Yiwen leiju* cites the *Lienü zhuan* as the source of the famous story of how Lao Laizi dressed as an infant to make his elderly parents feel young again. The current biography, however, includes no such anecdote. See Ouyang Xun, "Ren Bu: Xiao," *Yiwen leiju*, 2 vols. (Shanghai: Shanghai guji chubanshe, 1999), vol. 1, 369.

100. Meng Mountain is located in central Shandong.

101. The king's gifts were meant to induce Laizi to come to court to serve in his government.

102. "The orphaned one" is a humble and filial term used by the ruler to refer to himself.

103. *Odes, Chen Fen,* "Heng Men," Mao no. 138. Translation based on Karlgren, *The Book of Odes,* 89; and Arthur Waley, *The Book of Songs* (New York: Grove Press, 1960), 27.

104. Wuling was a place located in present-day Shandong province. Zizhong, a man of Warring States times, is noted under a variety of names in an array of early Chinese texts. In *Mencius* 3B.10, he is also called Chen Zhongzi (陳仲子), where he is described as a man of Qi and the younger brother of a minister of Qi, named Dai (戴). He is also mentioned in *Gaoshi zhuan.* The present story is also told involving different people in *Hanshi waizhuan,* in SBCK, vol. 3, 9/12; translated in Hightower, *Han Shih Wai Chuan,* 311–312.

105. This term is a humble way to refer to one's own wife.

106. This sentence admits a number of interpretations. I follow Shimomi here. See discussion in Shimomi Takao, *Ryū kō Retsujoden no kenkyū* (Tokyo: Tōkaidō daigaku shuppankai, 1989), 351, note 5. Liang Duan notes that the parallel passage in *Hanshi wai zhuan* omits the initial negative. Other interpretations include: "If it were not for [the lure of these] things, you would not be considering governing."

107. *Odes, Qin Feng,* "Xiao Rong," Mao no. 128. Translation based on Legge, *The Chinese Classics,* vol. 4, 195. The LNZ uses slightly different language than appears in the *Odes* but with the same general meaning.

3. THE SYMPATHETIC AND WISE

"Sympathetic wisdom" refers not so much to feelings of sympathy but to the ability to intuitively and empathetically understand others through close observation of the minute details of their behavior, and then predict correctly how they will behave or what fates they will meet. For further discussion, see the introduction. I am grateful to Eric Henry for alerting me to and offering a slightly different rendering of this title. In a personal communication of September 2012, Henry suggests as an alternate translation of the title of this chapter "Those with a Deep Grasp of Character and Events." I agree with this interpretation but have tried to adhere more closely to the title's literal meaning.

1. This story is based on an account found in the *Guoyu,* "Zhouyu," part 1, item 2; it is also found in *Shiji* 4, 140–141. The name of Duke Kang's mother, Wei, is not mentioned in

either of those sources. Mi was a state located in the southeastern portion of present-day Gansu province. It is mentioned in the *Bamboo Annals,* Di Xin 32, as an independent kingdom, which, before the founding of the Zhou dynasty, surrendered to King Wen of Zhou (r. 1099/56–1050 BCE). See James Legge's translation of the relevant passage in *The Chinese Classics,* 5 vols. (1893; reprint, Hong Kong: University of Hong Kong Press, 1960), vol. 3, 140. The *Odes* also contains a poem about King Wen's battle with Mi. See Legge, *Da Ya,* "Huang Yi," Mao no. 241; *The Chinese Classics,* vol. 4, 448–455. The rulers of the state of Mi shared the clan name Ji (姬) with the house of Zhou. The exact dates of Duke Kang are unknown.

2. King Gong of Zhou reigned from 917/15 to 900 BCE. The source of the Jing River is in present-day Gansu province south of Guyuan county. Eventually, it forms a confluence with the Wei (渭) River. In this account, the duke becomes attached to the three women without observing any of the proper marriage rites. On these rites, see Melvin Thatcher, "Marriages of the Ruling Elite in the Spring and Autumn Period," in *Marriage and Inequality in Chinese Society,* ed. Rubie S. Watson and Patricia Buckley Ebrey (Berkeley: University of California Press, 1991), 35–36. In the present story, Duke Kang's behavior is made all the more egregious by the fact that he acquired these women while he was simply a guest in the king's entourage.

3. *Shiji* 4, 140–141, states that "When a duke moves about, he does not cause the crowd to dismount"; translation based on William Nienhauser, trans., *The Grand Scribe's Records,* 6 vols. (Bloomington: Indiana University Press, 1994–2006), vol. 1, 70. The *Lienü zhuan* casts this sentence in the positive. I follow Ban Zhao's interpretation of this line, noted in the *Zhengyi* commentary to the *Shiji.* See *Shiji* 4, 141, note 5. Ban explains that dukes or feudal lords, as an act of courtesy, dismounted to consult or converse with groups of people. The implication is that the feudal lords deferred to the group. Liang Duan (LNZHB, vol. 7, 389) also follows Ban, based on a comparison with *Shuo yuan,* "Jing Shen"; see D. C. Lau, ed., *A Concordance to the Shuoyuan* (Hong Kong: Commercial Press, 1992), 10.3/77/15.

4. Here, according to Wei Zhao's commentary to the parallel passage in *Guoyu,* "Zhouyu," part 1, item 2, the three women were of the same clan name and born of one father. See *Guoyu,* vol. 1, 9, note 8. For further discussion of royal marriage practices, see *Zhouli,* in SSJZS, vol. 1, 7/46C, 684.

5. An early account of King Gong's annihilation of Mi is found in the *Bamboo Annals,* King Gong 4. See Legge translation, *The Chinese Classics,* vol. 3, 151.

6. *Odes, Tang Feng,* "Xi Shuo," Mao no. 114. Translation based on Legge, *The Chinese Classics,* vol. 4, 174.

7. Man was her clan name; Deng refers to her state of origin. Her name thus means, "the lady of the clan of Man who came from Deng." Deng was an ancient state that may have been situated north of Xiangfan (襄樊) in present-day Hubei. See Li Xueqin, *Eastern Zhou and Qin Civilizations* (New Haven: Yale University Press, 1985), 154–188. King Wu of Chu reigned from 740 to 689 BCE.

8. Luo was a small state west or northwest of Yicheng in present-day Hubei. This story appears in *Zuo zhuan,* Huan 13; translated in Legge, *The Chinese Classics,* vol. 5, 60–61.

9. The title *moao* originally alluded to a ritual responsibility but later designated a high military position. For discussion of the term *moao*, see Barry B. Blakeley, "Chu Society and State Image versus Reality," in *Defining Chu: Image and Reality,* ed. Constance Cook and John S. Major (Honolulu: University of Hawai'i Press, 1999), 56, 58.

10. Dou Bobi was the uncle of King Wu.

11. The "grandee" refers to Dou Bobi.

12. Pusao is the site of a battle where Qu Xia attacked and defeated the state of Yun (鄖) in 701 BCE. See *Zuo zhuan,* Huan 11; translated in Legge, *The Chinese Classics,* vol. 5, 56–57.

13. Lai was a small state located north or northeast of Sui county in present-day Hubei.

14. The River Yan flowed from southwest Baokang County in Hubei through Nanzhang and Yicheng before entering the Han River.

15. Lurong was an ancient state northeast of Nanzhang County in present-day Hubei.

16. The officers of the expedition regarded their failure as a punishable crime. Huanggu and Yefu were located somewhere near Jiangling in present-day Hubei.

17. *Book of Odes, Ta Ya,* "Dang," Mao no. 255; translation by Legge, *The Chinese Classics,* vol. 4, 509.

18. Sui was a small state northwest of Sui county in present-day Hubei. This event occurred in 690 BCE and is narrated in *Zuo zhuan,* Zhuang, year 4, translated in Legge, *The Chinese Classics,* vol. 5, 77.

19. According to the account in the *Zuo zhuan*, before the battle, the king had gone to fast in the ancestral temple. The king's agitation might thus be understood as prompted by the ancestors.

20. *Manmu* may refer to a kind of pine tree, but it may also be a place. It is associated with Manmu Mountain in present-day Hubei, east of Zhongxiang county, but its exact location cannot be determined. The campaign ended successfully for Chu, and concluded when Sui swore a covenant with Chu.

21. *Yijing,* "Feng Gua: Duan Ci," hexagram no. 55; translation based on James Legge, in Z. D. Sung, *The Text of Yi King* (Taipei: Wenhua tushu gongsi, 1975), 259.

22. Duke Yi of Wey reigned from 668 to 661 BCE; Duke Mu of Xu reigned from 697 to 656 BCE. Xu was located east of Xuchang in present-day Henan province. Xu was relatively small but still considered to be one of the fifteen major states of the Spring and Autumn period. *Zuo zhuan,* Min 2, gives the wife of Duke Mu of Xu a very different ancestry. It claims that she was the daughter of the notorious Xuan Jiang (see LNZ 7.4) by Xuan Jiang's own stepson, Gongzi Wan (also called Zhaobo). He was the son of Duke Xuan of Wey (718–699 BCE) by a concubine. In this account, Xuan Jiang was forced to marry Gongzi Wan, thereby positioning him to serve as Duke Hui's regent. See LNZ 7.4 and Anne Behnke Kinney, "The Mao Commentary to the *Book of Odes,*"

in *Overt and Covert Treasures: Essays on the Sources for Chinese Women's History*, ed. Clara Wing-chung Ho (Hong Kong: Chinese University of Hong Kong Press, 2012), 61–111.

23. The phrase "chariots and swift horses" also foreshadows the ode cited below that is attributed to the wife of Duke Mu of Xu, called "Zai Chi," or "Galloping My Horses," in which she describes her desire to race back to Wey after its near destruction by enemy invasion.

24. This story is told in *Zuo zhuan*, Duke Min, 2; Legge, *The Chinese Classics*, vol. 5, 129–130. Also see *Hanshi waizhuan*, SBCK, vol. 3, 2/2B; trans. by James Hightower, *Han Shih Wai Chuan: Han Ying's Illustrations of the Didactic Application of the Classic of Songs* (Cambridge, Mass.: Harvard University Press, 1952), 40.

25. According to Nicola Di Cosmo, "Whether 'Di' was a generic word for 'northern foreigners,' or a specific ethnonym, or even a political unit or a state, cannot be determined." See Nicola Di Cosmo, *Ancient China and Its Enemies: The Rise of Nomadic Power in East Asian History* (Cambridge, England: Cambridge University Press, 2002), 109.

26. Chuqiu is located east of present-day Hua county in Henan province.

27. Cao was the capital of Wey.

28. The identity of the great officer is uncertain. Zhu Xi speculates that he was an officer of Xu sent to make the duchess of Xu return in accordance with ritual restrictions on women traveling beyond the households of their husbands. See Hattori Unokichi, *Kanbun Taikei* (Taipei: Xinwenfeng chubanshe, 1978), vol. 12, 3/13. Also see Wang Xianqian, *Shi sanjia yi ji shu*, 2 vols. (Beijing: Zhonghua shuju, 2009), vol. 1, 259.

29. *Odes, Yong Feng*, "Zai Chi," Mao no. 54. Translation based on Legge, *The Chinese Classics*, vol. 4, 87.

30. Cao was located southwest of Dingtao of Shandong province. This story is found in *Zuo zhuan*, Xi 23; translated by Legge, *The Chinese Classics*, vol. 5, 187; and *Guoyu*, "Jinyu" 4, item 5.

31. Prince Chonger of Jin assumed the throne as Duke Wen of Jin and reigned from 636 to 628 BCE. He is also mentioned in LNZ 2.3, 2.4, 2.8.

32. Duke Gong of Cao reigned from 652 to 618 BCE. His name is usually written as 共.

33. The configuration of Chonger's ribs may be apocryphal. Many heroes and sages of antiquity are described as possessing bizarre physical characteristics as an outward sign of their unique qualities. It is also possible that Chonger suffered from Jarcho–Levin syndrome.

34. *Odes, Da Ya*, "Zheng Min," Mao no. 260. Translation based on Legge, *The Chinese Classics*, vol. 4, 543.

35. Sunshu Ao (fl. c. 597 BCE) is also mentioned in biography 2.5. The chief counselor was a rank equivalent to that of prime minister. There is much controversy surrounding his name, which is also transliterated as Sun Shuao. He is also known as Wei Ailie (蒍艾獵) (Wei also sometimes transliterated as Kui) or Wei Ao (蒍敖). See William

Nienhauser, "A Reexamination of 'The Biographies of the Reasonable Officials' in the *Records of the Grand Historian*," *Early China* 16 (1991): 218–222. He is mentioned in *Zuo zhuan*, Xuan 11, 12; translated in Legge, *The Chinese Classics*, vol. 5, 310, 318. Also see a brief biography in *Shiji* 119 translated in Burton Watson, *Records of the Grand Historian of China*, 2 vols. (New York: Columbia University Press, 1958), vol. 2, 413–415. Barry Blakeley briefly discusses his legend and its historical basis in "Chu Society and State," 60–61, and in "King, Clan and Courtier in Ch'u Court Politics," *Asia Major*, series III, no. 2 (1992): 1–39.

36. *Shangshu*, "Cai Zhong Zhi Ming," translated in Legge, *The Chinese Classics*, vol. 3, 490.

37. *Odes, Bei Feng*, "Kai Feng," Mao no. 32. Translation based on Legge, *The Chinese Classics*, vol. 4, 50.

38. Bo Zong (d. 576 BCE) was a virtuous official of Jin who advised both Duke Jing of Jin (r. 599–581 BCE) and Duke Li of Jin (r. 580–573 BCE). Liu Xiang's story is based on an account found in *Guoyu*, "Jinyu," part 5, item 14; and *Zuo zhuan*, Cheng 15; translated in Legge, *The Chinese Classics*, vol. 5, 389. Bo Zong is also mentioned in *Zuo zhuan*, Xuan 15, Cheng 5.

39. I follow the wording of this saying as found in *Zuo zhuan*, Cheng 15, which replaces the word "to love" (愛 *ai*) with "to hate" (惡 *wu*).

40. Yangzi here refers to Yang Chufu (陽處父), an influential minister of Jin who served in a military and diplomatic capacity. He was murdered in 621 BCE by a disgruntled officer whom Yang had replaced with a more worthy man. See *Zuo zhuan*, Wen 6; Legge, *The Chinese Classics*, vol. 5, 243–245.

41. Bi Yang's name in LNZ is written 畢羊; in the *Guoyu* it appears as 畢陽. Bi Yang, a grandee of Jin, is mentioned in the *Guoyu* version of this story but not in the account found in the *Zuo zhuan*. The last words in this phrase can also be construed as "and handed over [his son] to him."

42. Luan Buji's name appears as Luan Fuji in the *Zuo zhuan*. He was an officer of Jin and is mentioned only once in the *Zuo zhuan* (Cheng 15), when he and Bo Zong are both killed by the Xi family. The Three Xi included Xi Zhi, Xi Chou, and Xi Qi. They were a powerful ministerial family of Jin who filled important military and diplomatic roles in that state. They are mentioned in *Zuo zhuan*, Cheng 8, 11, 12, 13, 15, 17.

43. Jing was another name for the state of Chu.

44. *Odes, Da Ya*, "Ban," Mao no. 254. Translation based on Legge, *The Chinese Classics*, vol. 4, 501.

45. Duke Ling of Wey reigned from 534 to 493 BCE. He is also mentioned in LNZ 7.12, where his wife is identified as the notorious Nan Zi. It is unlikely, however, that the wife mentioned in this biography is Nan Zi. For discussion, see Shimomi, *Ryū kō Retsujoden no kenkyū*, 390–391.

46. Towers (闕 *que*) or "pillar gates" were erected at the entry to walled cities and palace complexes and were thus emblems of authority. See Mark Edward Lewis, *The*

Construction of Space in Early China (Albany: State University of New York Press, 2006), 153–155; Wu Hung, *Monumentality in Early Chinese Art and Architecture* (Stanford: Stanford University Press, 1995), 102–110.

47. Qu Boyu, also called Qu Yuan (瑗), was an upright official from the state of Wey. He is mentioned in *Zuo zhuan*, Xiang 14, 26, 29.

48. See *Liji*, "Qu Li," in SSJZS, vol. 1, 3/24B; translated in James Legge, *Li Chi: Book of Rites*, 2 vols. (1885; reprint, New York: University Books, 1967), vol. 1, 97.

49. *Liji*, "Qu Li," part 1, SSJZS, vol. 1, 1253B; translated in Legge, *Li Chi*, vol. 1, 97.

50. *Odes, Xiao Ya*, "He Ren Si," Mao no. 199. Translation based on Legge, *The Chinese Classics*, vol. 4, 344.

51. The title "marquis" is a mistake for "duke." See Liang Duan, LNZHB, vol. 7, 400. Duke Ling of Qi reigned from 581 to 554 BCE. This biography is based on *Zuo zhuan*, Xiang 19 (554 BCE); translated in Legge, *The Chinese Classics*, vol. 5, 483. Also see *Shiji* 32, 1499–1500; trans. in Nienhauser, *The Grand Scribe's Records*, vol. V.1, 97–98. As she is a daughter of a ruler of Song, her clan name is Zi; the name Zhong signifies her birth order as second among daughters.

52. *Zuo zhuan*, Xiang 19 says, "The marquis of Qi had married Yan Yi Ji (顏懿姬), a daughter of Lu, but she bore him no son. Her niece, Zong Sheng Ji (鬷聲姬), however, bore him Guang, who was declared his eldest son and successor." Legge, *The Chinese Classics*, vol. 5, 483. Both of these women held the Ji clan name. Yan is Yan Yi Ji's mother's clan name. Yi is Yan Yi Ji's posthumous name. Zong is Zong Sheng Ji's mother's clan name. Sheng here designates Zong Sheng Ji's posthumous name. See Yang Bojun, *Chunqiu zuozhuan zhu*, 4 vols. (Beijing: Zhonghua shuju, 1981), vol. 3, 1048, n. 19.5.

53. The *Zuo zhuan* says that these two women were ranked among the concubines (諸子 zhuzi) and that only Rong Zi was favored. See *Zuo zhuan*, Xiang 19; Legge, trans., *The Chinese Classics*, vol. 5, 483. On the term *zhuzi*, see Yang, *Chunqiu Zuozhuan zhu*, 1048.

54. The *Zuo zhuan* says that Ya was given to Rong Zi. See *Zuo zhuan*, Xiang 19; Legge, trans., *The Chinese Classics*, vol. 5, 483.

55. I follow the reading of the *Zuo zhuan*, which has *jian* (間) rather than *wen* (聞).

56. Gao Hou was a member of one of the powerful ministerial families of Qi who struggled with the Cui family for power. Cui Zhu (see note 58 below) killed him in 554 BCE. See *Zuo zhuan*, Xiang 19; Legge, trans., *The Chinese Classics*, vol. 5, 483.

57. Here, LNZ has the name Gao Hou, while both *Zuo zhuan*, Xiang 19, and *Shiji* 32, 1499–1500, state that it was Cui Zhu who welcomed Guang. I have emended the translation to correct for this error. See commentary in LNZHB, vol. 5, 405. Cui Zhu, a favorite of Duke Hui of Qi (r. 608–599 BCE), was the head of the powerful Cui clan. He had been driven out of Qi when his patron died. See *Zuo zhuan*, Xuan 10; translated in Legge, *The Chinese Classics*, vol. 5, 307. He is also mentioned in LNZ 7.11.

58. Guang was enthroned as Duke Zhuang of Qi (r. 553–548 BCE).

59. The *Lienü zhuan* here mentions only the death of Gao and not that of Rong Zi. According to *Zuo zhuan*, Xiang 19, she was murdered by Guang in a particularly vicious manner. According to *Shiji* 32, 1499–1500, after Guang came to the throne, he proceeded to kill Rong Zi and arrest Ya.

60. *Odes, Da Ya*, "Yi," Mao no. 256. Translation based on Legge, *The Chinese Classics*, vol. 4, 518.

61. Zangsun, also called Zang Wenzhong (臧文仲) and Zangsun Chen (臧孫辰), was a highly regarded though often controversial official in the state of Lu who served Dukes Zhuang, Xi, Min, Xi, and Wen (ca. 683–621 BCE). He is criticized in the *Confucian Analects*; see V:17, XV:13.

62. Gaozi (fl. 685 BCE) was an official of the state of Qi. He is also called Gao Xi (高傒). See *Zuo zhuan*, Min 2, Zhuang 9, 22. Guozi might refer to an officer of Qi named Guo Zhuangzi (國莊子), also called Guo Guifu (歸父), or another Guo in his father's generation. Guozi is mentioned in *Zuo zhuan*, Xi 33.

63. The Shunsun, Mengsun, and Jisun lineages composed the three great ministerial families that controlled the state of Lu. They were also known as the "Three Huan," namely, the three younger sons of Duke Huan of Lu (r.711–694 BCE) and their descendants. They are also mentioned in LNZ 1.9.

64. The *qin* was a musical instrument consisting of an oblong wooden boxlike body with strings stretched horizontally over the top surface. The "harmony of the *qin*" is a metaphor for conjugal harmony.

65. The commentaries interpret the phrase "*tong* fish" (同魚) in a variety of ways. The annotations attributed to Cao Dagu (Ban Zhao) gloss *tong* (同) as "the jagged/interlocking pattern of fish scales" (銅 *tong*). See LNZHB, vol. 8, 629.

66. *Odes, Wei Feng*, "Zhi Hu," Mao no. 110. Translation based on Legge, *The Chinese Classics*, vol. 4, 168.

67. Shu Ji's clan name is Ji, while her first name, Shu, indicates that she was third-born among daughters. Yangshezi, also called Yangshe Zhi (職), was a grandee of the state of Jin. Shuxiang (d. ca. 520 BCE) was also called Yangshe Xi. He served as grand tutor of Jin and played a prominent role in international diplomacy. The Yangshe lineage, a collateral branch of the ruling lineage in the state of Jin, flourished under Shuxiang's leadership during the mid-sixth century BCE but was annihilated soon after his death. Yang was not the original family name but a name derived from Shuxiang's fief, which was located southeast of present-day Hongdong county in Shanxi.

68. *Odes, Da Ya*, "Yi," Mao no. 256. Translation based on Legge, *The Chinese Classics*, vol. 4, 515.

69. This tale is recounted in *Zuo zhuan*, Zhao 28; see translation in Legge, *The Chinese Classics*, vol. 5, 726–727. Wuchen of the Shen dependency in Chu (fl. ca. 590–570 BCE) served as a high-ranking official in the court of King Zhuang of Chu (r. 613–591 BCE). He is also known as Qu Wuchen and by his polite name Ziling. His wife, the notorious Xia Ji, is the subject of LNZ 7.9. Zheng was located in the vicinity of present-day Zhengzhou in Henan.

70. The wording here differs from that of *Zuo zhuan*, Zhao 28, and omits the final clause that I here cite: "Formerly Shuxiang had wished to marry a daughter of Wuchen, duke of Shen, but his mother wanted him to take one of her own kindred instead." Translated by Legge, *The Chinese Classics*, vol. 5, 726. Shuxiang worried that his mother's ambitious brothers had promoted Shu Ji's interests at court at the expense of other ducal consorts, which in turn had limited the number of the duke's progeny. Thus, Shuxiang may be suggesting that he does not want to be under the thumb of his uncles and other maternal kin. Also see *Zuo zhuan*, Xiang 21, for a reference to Shu Ji's jealousy; translated in Legge, *The Chinese Classics*, vol. 5, 491. See discussion in Li, *The Readability of the Past*, 153–160.

71. Ziling is the polite name of Wuchen. See LNZ 7.9 for a slightly different account of these deaths.

72. Duke Mu of Zheng reigned from 627 to 606 BCE; his son, Duke Ling of Zheng, Zihe (also transliterated as Zimo), succeeded him in 605 BCE, reigning for only one year. Wei Zhao's (204–273 CE) note says that Xia Ji was the daughter of Duke Mu's lesser concubine, a woman named Yao Zi. See *Guoyu*, "Chuyu," part 1, item 4, vol. 2, 539, note 1.

73. Kui was a legendary figure associated with music and mentioned in the "Shun Dian" and "Yi Ji" chapters of the *Book of Documents*; see translation in Legge, *The Chinese Classics*, vol. 3, 47–49, 87–89.

74. In early Chinese legend, Yi is described as a prince with prodigious abilities in archery. According to the *Zuo zhuan*, Xiang 4, Yi usurped the throne of the Xia dynasty and was subsequently murdered. See translation in Legge, *The Chinese Classics*, vol. 5, 424.

75. The three dynasties were the Xia, the Shang, and the Western Zhou, destroyed, according to a number of traditional accounts, by the beauties Mo Xi, Da Ji, and Bao Si, respectively. For their biographies, see LNZ 7.1–3. Prince Gong (恭) probably refers to Prince Gong (共) of Jin, also known by the name Shensheng. He was the heir apparent of Duke Xian of Jin (r. 676–651). He was deposed and eventually forced by his father's concubine, Li Ji, to take his own life. See LNZ 7.7 for her biography.

76. Here and elsewhere I give full force of meaning to the initial particle *fu* (夫) as introducing a statement of some kind of truth or generally applicable principle. For discussion of the rhetorical use of this word, see Eric Henry, trans., *Garden of Eloquence* (Seattle: University of Washington Press, forthcoming).

77. Duke Ping of Jin reigned from 557 to 532 BCE.

78. The *Zuo zhuan* reports that Shiwo in collaboration with Qi Ying perpetrated a number of lawless acts and was, on account of them, put to death in 514 BCE. See *Zuo zhuan*, Zhao 28, Legge, *The Chinese Classics*, vol. 5, 726.

79. *Odes*, *Xiao Ya*, "Xiao Min," Mao no. 195. Translation based on Legge, *The Chinese Classics*, vol. 4, 332.

80. Shuyu is also known as Yangshe Fu. *Guoyu*, "Jinyu," part 8, item 3, also recounts the auguries of Shuyu's birth. Shuyu was killed in 528 BCE while serving in place of his absent colleague, Shi Jingbo, to adjudicate a dispute. He accepted a bribe from the

guilty litigant, Yongzi, and ruled against the other, namely Xing Hou. Xing Hou, who was outraged by the outcome of the case, murdered both Shuyu and Yongzi while still at court. See *Zuo zhuan*, Zhao 14, translated in Legge, *The Chinese Classics*, vol. 5, 656, and *Guoyu*, "Jinyu" part 9, item 1.

81. Xing Hou (d. ca. 528 BCE) was the son of Qu Wuchen of Shen (one of Xia Ji's husbands and the father of the woman that Shuyu's brother, Shuxiang, married). His name was Qu Huyong. Xing had received his fief (called Xing and from which his name is derived) from his father, Wuchen. Yongzi was a man of the state of Chu who left that state to become an officer of Jin. He was given a fief called Chu (郜), near present-day Wen county (溫) in Henan, which bordered on Xing's fief. See *Zuo zhuan*, Xiang 26, translated in Legge, *The Chinese Classics*, vol. 5, 526–527.

82. Han Xuanzi (d. 514 BCE) served as prime minister in Jin from 540 to 514 BCE. The above incident is recounted in *Zuo zhuan*, Zhao 14, translated in Legge, *The Chinese Classics*, vol. 5, 656.

83. *Odes*, *Da Ya*, "Sang Rou," Mao no. 257. Translation based on Legge, *The Chinese Classics*, vol. 4, 526.

84. Fan Xianzi, a grandee in the state of Jin, held the lineage name Fan and was also called Shi Yang. He served as prime minister in Jin from 510 to 503 BCE. The Fan lineage, named for their holdings in Fan, was one of the six most powerful ministerial lineages in the state of Jin, but it was annihilated in the civil wars of 497–490 BCE.

85. Zhao Jianzi was also called Zhao Yang and Zhao Meng. He was the chief of the Zhao lineage of Jin who, from 497 BCE onward, headed the state of Jin. He was responsible for ousting the Fan and Zhonghang lineages. A number of scholars have identified Zhao Jianzi as the initiator of the covenant texts excavated at Houma between 1965 and 1966 and dated to the decade following 496 BCE. See Susan Weld, "The Covenant Texts from Houma and Wenxian," in *New Sources of Early Chinese History: An Introduction to the Reading of Inscriptions and Manuscripts*, ed. Edward Shaughnessy (Berkeley: The Society for the Study of Early China and the Institute of East Asian Studies, University of California, 1997), 125–160. He is also mentioned in LNZ 6.7.

86. According to Wang Zhaoyuan, the word "horse," which I have omitted in the translation, is an error here, though it is conceivable that the sentence can be rendered as follows: "Issue an order to clear the stumps on the mountain, and then you will be able to accomplish what needs to be done for the horses." See LNZHB, vol. 5, 416.

87. The meaning here is either that the *task* of clearing the mountainous area of stumps had been completed or following Shimomi Takao, *Ryū kō Restujoden no kenkyū* (Tokyo: Tōkaidō daigaku shuppankai, 1989), 420, that only the *order* to clear stumps on the mountains was completed but not enacted, so that the task of clearing stumps in the orchard would seem easier by comparison.

88. Reading the initial 夫 as 去, according to Wang Zhaoyuan, LNZHB, vol. 5, 416.

89. Zhi Bo was also known by the names Xun Yao and Zhi Yao. The Zhi and the Zhonghang lineages were collateral branches of the Xun lineage. His lineage name was Zhi

and his posthumous name was Xiangzi. He headed the Zhi lineage in the mid-fifth century and was one of the most powerful and aggressive figures in Jin at the time. He tried to eliminate the Zhao lineage. He died in 453 BCE. See *Zuo zhuan*, Dao 4.

90. *Odes, Da Ya*, "Zhan Yang," Mao no. 264. Translation based on Legge, *The Chinese Classics*, vol. 4, 564. The LNZ text has the word *e* (訛) instead of *hou* (後).

91. This phrase is probably meant to bring to mind *Analects* I.3: "Fine words and an insinuating appearance are seldom associated with true virtue." Translation by Legge, *The Chinese Classics*, vol. 1, 139.

92. Gongcheng was a name derived from an official title. Gongcheng Zipi is not mentioned in earlier sources.

93. This interpolation is suggested by Gu Guangqi in LNZHB, vol. 3, 295.

94. She may also be referring to the passing of the time in which she should have been married. According to the *Book of Rites*, women should be engaged at age fifteen and married at twenty, but under special circumstances could wait until age twenty-three to marry. See "Nei Ze," *Liji*, SSJZS, vol. 2, 1471B; translated by Legge, *Li Chi*, vol. 1, 479.

95. "To sing the first note" also means "to take the lead." Here she is paraphrasing *Odes, Zheng Feng*, "Cuo Xi," Mao no. 85.

96. *Odes, Zheng Feng*, "Cuo Xi," Mao no. 85. Translation based on Legge, *The Chinese Classics*, vol. 4, 138.

97. *Odes, Yong Feng*, "Zai Chi," Mao no. 54, Legge, *The Chinese Classics*, vol. 4, 87.

98. A similar tale is told in *Hanshi waizhuan*; see SBCK, vol. 3, 2/2A; translated in Hightower, *Han Shih Wai Chuan*, 41–42. This city is associated with Cishi (次室), a town west of present-day Zou county in Shandong.

99. See note 95 above.

100. Duke Mu of Lu came to the throne in 407 BCE. *Shiji* 46, 1885–1886, states that Qi repeatedly attacked Lu at this time, taking the city of Cheng. *Mencius* 6B.6 also suggests that during this reign, Lu lost its independence. Also see Yang Kuan, *Zhanguo shi* (Shanghai: Shanghai Renmin chubanshe 1981), 270.

101. In the *Hanshi waizhuan* telling of a similar tale, the events suffered by the woman are closely connected to the actions of the ruler. Here the speaker seems to be providing an example of how a seemingly random event can lead to disaster.

102. *Odes, Wang Feng*, "Shu Li," Mao no. 65. Translation based on Legge, *The Chinese Classics*, vol. 4, 111.

103. Quwo was located northeast of present-day Lingbao in Henan. Ru Er is mentioned as a key figure in a diplomatic mission in 295 BCE from Wei to Wey mentioned in *Shiji* 44, 1850–1851. Ru Er is also mentioned in *Zhanguo ce*, in SBCK, vol. 14, 3/51A, 3/62A; translated in James Irving Crump, *Chan-kuo Ts'e*, 2nd ed., revised (San Francisco: Chinese Materials Center, 1979), 110, 123.

104. King Ai of Wei was the son of King Xiang of Wei (r. 318–296). There is debate concerning King Ai's reign because it does not appear in some chronologies. See *Shiji* 44, 1848–1850.

105. This rule is also enunciated in *Zuo zhuan*, Zhuang 24 (670 BCE) and here refers to ritual differences in the kinds of gifts presented by men and women to a new bride. See translation in Legge, *The Chinese Classics*, vol. 5, 108. For a discussion of the separation of the sexes in early China, see Lisa Raphals, *Sharing the Light: Representations of Women and Virtue in Early China* (Albany: State University of New York Press, 1998), 207–213.

106. To "receive the hairpin" meant to be betrothed. Liang Duan notes that the term *hao shi* refers to the style name given to a woman when she is betrothed. The idea here seems to be that the name is both a summary of her good points and a reminder to live up to them. See LNZHB, vol. 7, 416. Also see *Liji*, "Nei Ze," in SSJZS, vol. 2, 1471; translated in Legge, *Li Chi*, vol. 1, 477–479; and *Yili*, "Shi Hun Li," in SSJZS, vol. 1, 6/26C. The *Bohu tong* says, "Why must a person have a name? It is to reveal his nature and to serve as a representation of himself in the reverential service of others. The *Lun yü* says: 'If names are not correct the words will not conform [with reality].'" It also claims that a person is given a style name as "a crowning touch to a person's virtue, to show a person's merits and to honor the [new] adult." See *Bohu tong* in SBCK, vol. 22, 8/8B–12B. Translation based on Tjan Tjoe Som, trans., *Po Hu T'ung: The Comprehensive Discussions in the White Tiger Hall*, 2 vols. (Leiden: Brill, 1952), vol. 2, 579, 588; and *Lunyu* XIII:3.

107. The status of a man's official wife is signaled by a formal betrothal proposal from the groom's side and followed by an elaborate series of rituals. A crucial aspect of the marriage ritual was the presentation of gifts from both the bride's and the groom's families. See Thatcher, "Marriages of the Ruling Elite," 35–37. Also see *Yili*, "Shi Hun Li," in SSJZS, vol. 1, 4/17B, 6/30.

108. According to some ritualists, the groom was required personally to fetch the bride at her residence. See *Liji*, "Fang Ji," in SSJZS, vol. 2, 51/394C; translated in Legge, *Li Chi*, vol. 2, 299; also *Mencius* 6B.1; translated in Legge, *The Chinese Classics*, vol. 2, 422. In some cases, a representative of the groom went to the bride's home and escorted her to her new home.

109. For Tushan, see LNZ 1.4; for Mo Xi, see LNZ 7.1.

110. For Youshen, see LNZ 1.5; for Da Ji, see LNZ 7.2.

111. For Tai Si, see LNZ 1.6; for Bao Si, see LNZ 7.3.

112. King Kang reigned from 1005/3 to 978 BCE. Liang Duan omits the word "court" (朝) from the end of this sentence. See LNZHB, vol. 7, 417. Wang Zhaoyuan, in contrast, omits the word "wife" (夫人), according to the text as preserved in Li Shan's commentary to *Wenxuan* 49/19B, making the king the one who rose late. See LNZHB, vol. 5, 425. Liang Duan's reading is more consistent with the annotations of Yu Zhenjie, also included in the *Wenxuan* passage cited above, which faults the wife. A similar story but involving a different royal couple is found in LNZ 2.1.

113. "Guan, Guan Cry the Ospreys," is the title of the first poem in the *Book of Odes*; see *Zhou Nan*, "Guan Ju," Mao no. 1; translated in Legge, *The Chinese Classics*, vol. 4,

1–5. According to the Mao commentary, it celebrates the bride of King Wen of Zhou (r. 1099/56–1050 BCE). In contrast, King Kang's moral transformation, purportedly incited by this ode, is mentioned in *Hou Hanshu* 10A, 397; 54, 1776, and appears to represent the Lu School interpretation of this ode. For other comments on the transformative influence of Mao no. 1, see *Hanshu* 60, 2669.

114. A similar phrase (乘居匹游 *chengju piyou*) is also used in Zhang Hua's "Rhapsody on the Wren," and is translated by Knechtges as "dwells is twos and travels in pairs." See *Wenxuan* 13, 202, and translation in David Knechtges, *Wen xuan*, 3 vols. (Princeton: Princeton University Press, 1987–1996), vol. 3, 57. Xiao Daoguan argues that the phrase 乘居 *chengju* (to live in groups) is a mistake for 乖居 *guaiju* (to couple indiscriminately), which makes better sense in this context. See LNZHB, vol. 8, 178.

115. The "Three Bonds and the Six Ties" refer to the major and minor human relationships, respectively. The "Three Bonds" are the ones listed in this passage. The "Six Ties" generally include paternal and maternal uncles, brothers, lineage members, teachers, and friends. For a discussion c. 79 CE, see *Bohu tong* in SBCK, vol. 22, 7/11–13; translation in Som, *Po Hu T'ung*, vol. 2, 559–561.

116. From 350 to 250 BCE, two alliances formed, the "Vertical Alliance," which was composed of states linked from north to south, and the "Horizontal Alliance," which was formed among states ranging east to west and dominated by the state of Qin. Although these alliances were in a constant state of flux, each was defined by either a forced subservience or hostile opposition to Qin.

117. One *zhong* of grain was roughly equivalent to sixteen pounds. In Warring States times, grain was beginning to be used for official salaries and as a reward for devoted service. See Michael Loewe and Edward L. Shaughnessy, eds., *The Cambridge History of Ancient China: From the Origins of the Civilization to 221 B.C.* (Cambridge, England: Cambridge University Press, 1999), 606–607.

118. In 298 BCE, the state of Qi allied with Hann and Wei to attack Qin in a war that lasted three years. In 295 BCE, the allied forces defeated Qin and were able to reclaim land Qin had taken from them. See Yang, *Zhanguo shi*, 334; Loewe and Shaughnessy, *The Cambridge History of Ancient China*, 636–637. Also see Maspero, translated in Frank Kierman, *China in Antiquity* (University of Massachusetts Press, 1978), 259.

119. *Odes, Zhou Song*, "Jing Zhi," Mao no. 288. Translation based on Legge, *The Chinese Classics*, vol. 4, 598.

120. Liang Duan suggests that the words 子 and 納 are reversed. See LNZHB, vol. 7, 418.

121. Zhao She was a highly regarded general who served King Huiwen of Zhao (r. 298–266 BCE). Accounts of his life and that of his son, Zhao Kuo, appear in *Shiji* 81, 2444–2452; translated in Hsien-yi Yang and Gladys Yang, *Selections from Records of the Historian* (Beijing: Foreign Language Press, 1979), 139–151; and in Nienhauser, *The Grand Scribe's Records*, vol. 7, 267–273. Liu Xiang's account follows this *Shiji* biography. Mafu was a mountain northwest of Handan in present-day Hebei. King Huiwen granted this fief to Zhao She for his victory over Qin in 269 BCE. In addition to Hann

and Wei, Zhao was one of three successor states created by the partition of the earlier state of Jin and officially recognized as such in 403 BCE. Zhao spread across the northern half of present-day Shanxi province, the southern portion of modern Hebei, and a portion of modern Henan.

122. King Xiaocheng of Zhao (r. 265–245 BCE) was impatient with Lian Po's decision to bide his time rather than engage Qin troops directly. He was also swayed by what may have been disinformation on the part of a Qin agent who told him that Kuo was the only general Qin truly feared. The biography of Lian Po, one of Zhao's most illustrious generals, appears alongside that of General Zhao in *Shiji* 81.

123. Personally serving meals to others was a sign of great respect.

124. In early China, punishment for a serious offense, such as failure to achieve a military objective, was extended to the offender's family.

125. That is, she had an empathetic grasp of her son's character and could predict how events would unfold.

126. *Odes, Da Ya*, "Ban," Mao no. 254. Translation based on Legge, *The Chinese Classics*, vol. 4, 501.

4. THE CHASTE AND COMPLIANT

1. Shaonan was the area located in the western portion of present-day Henan province and included parts of present-day Shaanxi and Hubei. Shen, apparently considered part of the area of Shaonan, was an ancient state located in present-day Nanyang in Henan. See a similar account in *Hanshi waizhuan* in SBCK, vol. 3, 1/1B; translated in James Hightower, *Han Shih Wai Chuan: Han Ying's Illustrations of the Didactic Application of the Classic of Songs* (Cambridge, Mass.: Harvard University Press, 1952), 12. This story shares features with an account found in the Mao commentary on the *Book of Odes* for the ode "Xing Lu" (Mao no. 17). This ode is also cited at the end of this biography. Mao claims that the ode represents a legal case brought before the Duke of Shao concerning the daughter of Shen's refusal to go to the home of her husband until the proper ceremonies were performed. See SSJZS, vol. 1, *Maoshi zhengyi*, 1.4/20A; translation of Mao's comments in "The Little Preface," found in James Legge, *The Chinese Classics*, 5 vols. (1893; reprint, Hong Kong: University of Hong Kong Press, 1960), vol. 4, 39. The Duke of Shao, also known as Grand Protector Shi, is mentioned in early Western Zhou bronze inscriptions. See Edward L. Shaughnessy, *Before Confucius: Studies in the Creation of the Chinese Classics* (Albany: State University of New York Press, 1997), 101–136. He served as an instructor to his nephew, the young King Cheng (r. 1042/35–1006), who is said to have come to the throne as a minor.

2. Feng was an ancient state located east of present-day Hu county in Shaanxi.

3. The phrase I have translated as "bring her to their home" (迎之 *yingzhi*) generally refers to the ritual (sometimes expressed by the term "to receive" 逆 *ni*) whereby the

groom or his representative is sent to fetch the bride at her parent's home and escort her back to the home of her new husband. See Legge's description of this custom in his translation of *Zuo zhuan,* Xuan 5, in *The Chinese Classics,* vol. 5, 298.

4. In this story as it appears in the *Taiping yulan,* annotators explain the term 其人 *qiren* as referring to a go-between. See Li Fang, *Taiping yulan,* 7 vols. (Tainan: Pingping chubanshe, 1965), vol. 4, 541/20/6A.

5. It is not clear which commentary is being cited here, but a similar phrase, cited as coming from the *Yijing,* though not found in the traditionally transmitted text, can be found in *Liji,* "Jing Jie," in SSJZS, vol. 2, 50/383A; translated in James Legge, *Li Chi: Book of Rites,* 2 vols. (1885; reprint, New York: University Books, 1967), vol. 2, 260. Liu Xiang does, however, cite similar text in *Shuoyuan* 3.1/18/23 and attributes it to the *Yijing.*

6. Compare with *Liji,* "Ai Gong Wen," in SSJZS, vol. 2, 50/383C; translated in Legge, *Li Chi,* vol. 2, 264–265, which also includes a substantial discussion of the necessity of the rite whereby the groom fetches the bride.

7. According to the commentaries, defendants were held in detention during the course of the lawsuit. See SSJZS, vol. 1, *Maoshi zhengyi,* 1.4/20B.

8. *Odes, Shao Nan,* "Xing Lu," Mao no. 17; translation based on Legge, *The Chinese Classics,* vol. 4, 27.

9. Here, as in the case of several stories connected to the composition of odes (e.g., LNZ 4.3), the "man of discernment" probably refers to Confucius in his capacity as editor of the *Odes.*

10. *Odes, Shao Nan,* "Xing Lu," Mao no. 17; translation based on Legge, *The Chinese Classics,* vol. 4, 28.

11. Bo Ji's clan name is Ji, while Bo means "eldest daughter." Duke Xuan of Lu reigned from 608 to 591 BCE and Duke Cheng from 590 to 573 BCE. This account of Bo Ji's life is drawn in part from both the *Chunqiu* and the *Zuo zhuan,* Cheng 9, Xiang 30. See translations in Legge, *The Chinese Classics,* vol. 5, 370–371, 555–558. Its interpretation of the event, however, is more in keeping with the Guliang commentary to the *Chunqiu,* the school of interpretation most closely aligned with Liu Xiang's views. For a study of the various interpretations of this tale, see Sarah Queen, "The Many Faces of Song Bo Ji," forthcoming. Also see Anne Behnke Kinney, "A Spring and Autumn Family," *Chinese Historical Review* 20, no. 2 (2013): 113–137.

12. Mu Jiang's biography is found in LNZ 7.8 along with accounts of other notorious women. Duke Gong of Song reigned from 588 to 576 BCE. Song, one of the major states of the Spring and Autumn period, was a small state located on the southern edge of the central plain in the area of the present-day provinces of Henan and southwestern Shandong. The *Chunqiu* records this marriage as occurring in 582 BCE, in the second month of the ninth year of Duke Cheng of Lu's reign (590–572 BCE).

13. Strictly speaking, only her mother bade her go, as Bo Ji's father was no longer alive. According to some ritualists, the practice of "welcoming" or "fetching" the bride

was an important step in the marriage ritual. See notes in LNZ 4.1. The *Zuo zhuan* (Cheng 9) criticized the handling of Bo Ji's marriage for different reasons. See Kinney, "A Spring and Autumn Family." Also see Zheng Xuan's comment in *Gongyang zhuan,* Cheng 9, in SSJZS, vol. 2, 17/99C; and the perspective of the *Guliang zhuan* in SSJZS, vol. 2, 14/57A.

14. On this rite, see *Bohu tong,* in SBCK, vol. 22, 9/4B; translated in Tjan Tjoe Som, *The Po Hu T'ung: The Comprehensive Discussions in the White Tiger Hall,* 2 vols. (Leiden: Brill, 1952), vol. 1, 250. According to some ritualists, the marriage was regarded as finalized only after the completion of this ceremony. See *Liji,* "Zengzi Wen," in SSJZS, vol. 2, 18/164B–C; translated in Legge, *Li Chi,* vol. 1, 322.

15. Ji Wenzi (d. 568 BCE) was also known as Jisun Xingfu. He headed the government of Lu from 601 to 568 BCE and served as the lineage chief of the Jisun.

16. The duke here is Bo Ji's brother, Duke Cheng of Lu (r. 590–573 BCE).

17. The "departed" refers to Bo Ji's father, Duke Xuan of Lu. Liang Duan surmises that the word *di* (地) is missing before the word *xia* (下). See LNZHB, vol. 7, 423.

18. The text incorrectly dates the fire to the reign of Duke Jing of Song (r. 515–451 BCE). According to the *Spring and Autumn Annals,* it occurred in 543 BCE, during the reign of Bo Ji's son, Duke Ping (r. 574–529 BCE). See *Chunqiu Zuo zhuan,* SSJZS, vol. 2, 40/390B (Xiang 30).

19. The terms I have translated as "governess" (保 *bao*) and "tutor" (傅 *fu*) referred not simply to those assigned to take care of and instruct the young but also, as in this case, to those who served as personal advisors to aristocrats through adulthood. The names are almost certainly related to the ancient "three excellencies," that is, the *taibao, taifu,* and *taishi,* who were advisors to the Zhou kings. See *Da Dai Liji,* in SBCK, vol. 3, 3/1A–B.

20. The fire was likely not confined to the palace and was regarded as a major disaster in the state of Song. See *Chunqiu,* Xiang 30. Chanyuan was located northwest of Puyang in present-day Henan province.

21. Compare with *Liji,* "Nei Ze," in Legge, *Li Chi,* vol. 1, 454–455; SSJZS, vol. 2, 1462C.

22. *Odes, Da Ya,* "Yi," Mao no. 256. Translation based on Legge, *The Chinese Classics,* vol. 4, 515.

23. The identity of the wife is unclear. I follow Liang Duan's correction of the title to conform to the *Taiping yulan* reading, in which the word *xuan* (宣) in the title is not the name of the woman's husband (Duke Xuan of Wey) but an error for "widow" (寡 *gua*). See *Taiping yulan,* "Renshi," part 82, "Zhen Nü," 441/3A, vol. 4, 2350. Some annotators have tried to identify this woman as the wife of Duke Xuan of Wey (see LNZ 7.4), but no earlier text corroborates this story.

24. Well before a bride's arrival at her husband's home, marriage agreements between states were made, and a series of rites connected with marriage were carried out. The exact point in the ritual timeline at which a woman was considered to be married was a matter of opinion based on individual ritual practices. Some women, such as the subject of this biography, regarded themselves as married as soon as they had been

betrothed. See discussion in *Liji*, "Zeng Zi Wen," in SSJZS, vol. 2, 18/164A–B; translated in Legge, *Li Chi*, vol. 1, 320–321.

25. The duke's request to "share a kitchen" is a self-deprecating proposal of marriage.

26. *Odes, Bei Feng*, "Bo Zhou," Mao no. 26. Translation based on Legge, *The Chinese Classics*, vol. 4, 39.

27. Here I follow the correction of *ye* (也) to *ji* (己); see Liang Duan's commentary in LNZHB, vol. 74/3B, 426; and that of Chen Hanzhang, LNZHB, vol. 8, 639.

28. *Odes, Bei Feng*, "Bo Zhou," Mao no. 26. Translation based on Legge, *The Chinese Classics*, vol. 4, 39; and Bernhard Karlgren, *The Book of Odes* (Goteborg: Elanders Boktryckeri Aktiebolag, 1950), 15.

29. The "man of discernment" here most likely refers to Confucius in his role as editor of the *Odes*.

30. Cai and Song, though relatively small in territory, were both numbered among the fifteen major states of the Spring and Autumn period. Cai was located in present-day Henan and Anhui provinces, and Song lay to its northeast separated from Cai by the state of Chen.

31. On the rite called *jiao* (醮), see *Liji*, "Hun Yi," in SSJZS, vol. 2, 61/452C; translated in Legge, *Li Chi*, vol. 2, 429. Also see *Yili*, "Shi Hun Li," in SSJZS, vol. 1, 6/ 971B–973A; John Steele, trans., *The I-li* (London: Probsthain, 1917), vol. 1, 18–41.

32. *Odes, Zhounan*, "Fou Yi," Mao no. 8. Translation based on Legge, *The Chinese Classics*, vol. 4, 14–15. According to a note found in Xiao Tong, *Wenxuan*, "Bien Ming Lun," 54/13B (Beijing: Zhonghua shuju, 1981), the ode is a wife's lament on her husband's fatal illness. Mao's "Minor Preface" provides a different context for this poem.

33. Reading *yuan* (願) as *qing* (傾). See LNZHB, vol. 7, 427.

34. Li was a small state located next to Wey and southwest of Changzhi in present-day Shanxi province. See notes 36 and 37 below for possible historical contexts for this story. The Lu School of the *Odes* makes this story the background for the ode "Shi Wei," Mao no. 36. See Wang Xianqian, *Shi sanjia yi ji shu*, 2 vols. (Beijing: Zhonghua shuju, 2009), vol. 1, 180.

35. An opportune time would be when a woman had not yet consummated the marriage or had not become too old to preclude remarriage.

36. *Odes, Bei Feng*, "Shi Wei," Mao no. 36. Translation based on Karlgren, *The Book of Odes*, 23. The Mao commentary reads this ode as dating to the time of Duke Xuan of Wey (718–700 BCE) and written to the Marquis of Li by officers of Li, who had become refugees in Wey after being driven from their state by the Di. For another incident involving Li and Wey, which occurred around 594 BCE, see *Zuo zhuan*, Xuan 15; trans. in Legge, *The Chinese Classics*, vol. 5, 328.

37. *Odes, Bei Feng*, "Shi Wei," Mao no. 36. Translation based on Legge, *The Chinese Classics*, vol. 4, 59. The text here has "road" rather than Mao's "dew." The idea seems to be that if it were not for the duke's attitude, she would not be stranded in this unsatisfactory situation.

38. Here the "man of discernment" refers to Confucius.

39. Her clan name was Ji, while Meng indicates that she was the eldest daughter. Within the sequence *bo* (伯) "eldest," *zhong* (仲) "second" or "middle," *shu* (叔) "third," *ji* (季) "youngest," the term *meng* is not a synonym for *bo*. While the term *bo* denoted the eldest offspring of a principal wife or consort, *meng* denoted the eldest offspring of a concubine or secondary consort. See Kong Yingda's commentary to *Zuo zhuan*, Yin 1 in SSJZS, vol. 2, 2/10C. Also see *Bohu tong*, SBCK, vol. 22, 8/12A; translated in Som, *Po Hu T'ung*, vol. 2, 589. Duke Xiao of Qi reigned from 642 to 633 BCE. *Zuo zhuan*, Cheng 18 and Xiang 23, mention the Hua lineage but not Meng Ji or of any of the events in this story.

40. The rule for when a girl was to marry according to the "Nei Ze" chapter of the *Liji* is as follows: "At fifteen, she assumed the hairpin; at twenty, she was married, or, if there were occasion (for the delay), at twenty-three." Translation by Legge, *Li Chi*, vol. 1, 479; SSJZS, vol. 2, 1471.

41. I follow Liang Duan's suggestion that the word "not" was erroneously dropped from this sentence. See LNZHB, vol. 7, 429. For these injunctions, see *Liji*, "Nei Ze," SSJZS, vol. 2, 1462C; translated in Legge, *Li Chi*, vol. 1, 454–455.

42. The rituals described in this section can be found in the *Liji*, "Hun Yi," SSJZS, vol. 2, 1680C; Legge, trans., *Li Chi*, vol. 2, 428–434. Also see *Yili*, "Shi Hun Li," in SSJZS, vol. 1, 6/ 971B–973A; Steele, trans., *The I-li*, vol. 1, 18–41; *Bohu tong* in SBCK, vol. 22, 9/3–4; translated in Som, *Po Hu T'ung*, vol. 1, 247–249. Also see *Zuo zhuan*, Huan 3; translated in Legge, *The Chinese Classics*, vol. 5, 42–43.

43. The mother's tying of the bridal sash is mentioned in *Odes, Bin Feng*, "Dong Shan," Mao no. 156; translated by Legge, *The Chinese Classics*, vol. 4, 238. A similar exhortation is quoted in *Mencius* 3B.2.2; see translation in Legge, *The Chinese Classics*, vol. 2, 264–265.

44. Reading *er* (尔) as *shi* (示).

45. The ritual whereby the groom fetches the bride and drives her back to his home is described in *Liji*, "Hun Yi," SSJZS, vol. 2, 1680C; Legge, trans., *Li Chi*, vol. 2, 429.

46. I have, according to Liang Duan's annotations, omitted the two words *san gu* (三顧), which appear to be errors. The word *san* ("three") may also be an error for the word *qu* (曲 "to avert"). See LNZHB, vol. 7, 429. According to the *Yili*, "Shi Hun Li," there are two carriages, one for the bride and one for the groom. At this point in the ritual, the groom briefly drives the bride's carriage. Then a driver takes over and the groom goes back to his own carriage.

47. Liang Duan reads *yu* (與) as *yu* (輿), "carriage floorboard." The *Bohu tong* explains this rite as follows: "The husband meets her in person, [he drives the carriage for] three revolutions of the wheels, descends, and glances at her indirectly; this is to avoid [feelings of] uncontrolled passion." See *Bohu tong* in SBCK, vol. 22, 9/3; translated based on Som, *Po Hu T'ung*, vol. 1, 248.

48. Langye was a fief in Qi located in present-day Shandong.

49. Chariots that required riders to stand rather than sit were considered to be inappropriate vehicles for women. See *Liji*, "Qu Li," SSJZS, vol. 1, 1252C; translated in Legge, *Li Chi*, vol. 1, 96.

50. Zheng Xuan states that this sort of carriage was for the use of women. See *Zhouli*, "Chun Guan: Jin Che," in SSJZS, vol. 1, 27/185C, 823C.

51. The terminology for the two kinds of attendants here is similar to that found in the descriptions of women assigned to care for newborn sons in *Liji*, "Nei Ze," SSJZS, vol. 2, 1469B; Legge, trans., *Li Chi*, vol. 1, 472–473.

52. The practice of a woman sounding her sash pendants when she leaves a room is mentioned in LNZ 2.1 and in Fu Sheng's *Shangshu dazhuan*, as cited in Li Shan's commentary to the "Lament" of Yan Yannian, in *Wenxuan*, vol. 3, 58/2A.

53. Her speech is nearly identical to that delivered by Zhang Chang (fl. 61 BCE) to the Empress Dowager Wang in response to her participation in hunting expeditions. See Ban Gu, *Hanshu* (Beijing: Zhonghua shuju, 1962), 76, 3220.

54. See *Liji*, "Qu Li," SSJZS, vol. 1, 2/12C; translated in Legge, *Li Chi*, vol. 1, 77.

55. *Odes, Xiao Ya*, "Du Ren Shi," Mao no. 225. Translation based on Legge, *The Chinese Classics*, vol. 4, 409.

56. A similar sentiment is found in *Yijing*, "Great Appendix," part 1, chapter 8, in SSJZS, vol. 1, 7/68A; translated in Z. D. Sung, *The Text of Yi King* (Taipei: Wenhua tushu gongsi, 1975), 290: "Careless laying up of things excites robbery, as a woman's adorning herself excites lust."

57. Xi was a small state located on the north bank of the Upper Huai River in Henan province, southwest of present-day Xia county. It was one among a series of states that fell to Chu in the period 688–656 BCE, when Chu extended its territory into the Nanyang Basin. See Barry B. Blakeley, "The Geography of Chu," in *Defining Chu: Image and Reality*, ed. Constance Cook and John S. Major (Honolulu: University of Hawai'i Press, 1999), 15. This story, with a very different ending, is found in *Zuo zhuan*, Zhuang 10, 14; translated in Legge, *The Chinese Classics*, vol. 5, 87, 92–93. The *Zuo zhuan* version of the story is also used by Wang Wei in a poem on Lady Xi. See translation in Burton Watson, *The Columbia Book of Chinese Poetry: From Early Times to the Thirteenth Century* (New York: Columbia University Press, 1984), 200. The wife of Xi, according to the *Zuo zhuan*, was named Gui (媯).

58. This was King Wen of Chu, who reigned from 689 to 677 BCE.

59. She means that she will never remarry.

60. *Odes, Wang Feng*, "Da Ju," Mao no. 73. Translation based on Legge, *The Chinese Classics*, vol. 4, 121. The Mao commentary regards this ode as a diatribe against the degenerate morals of the age. See Legge, "The Little Preface," in *The Chinese Classics*, vol. 4, 48. Legge also summarizes the ode as being "spoken by some lady of the eastern Zhou that would fain have gone with her lover, but was restrained by her fear of some great officer, who amid the degeneracy of the times, retained his purity and integrity." See Legge, *The Chinese Classics*, vol. 4, 121.

61. *Odes, Bei Feng*, "Gu Feng," Mao no. 35. Translation based on Legge, *The Chinese Classics*, vol. 4, 55.

62. Qi Liang's given name (bestowed in childhood) was Zhi, and his polite (or "style") name, the one bestowed upon coming of age, was Liang. This story is based on an

earlier account found in *Zuo zhuan*, Xiang, 23, 25; translated in Legge, *The Chinese Classics*, vol. 5, 503–504, 514. For a complete study, see Kinney, "The Significance of the Commoner Woman of Qi in the 'Lanming' Chapter of the *Huainanzi*," in *Text in Context: New Perspectives on the Huainanzi*, ed. Sarah Queen and Michael Puett (Leiden: Brill, forthcoming).

63. Duke Zhuang of Qi reigned from 553 to 548 BCE. Ju was a small state located east of the Si River in present-day Juxian in Shandong province.

64. Even ordinary statements made by rulers were politely referred to as "decrees." Qi Liang's wife had encountered on the road the group transporting her husband's body back home.

65. Another ritual indiscretion of this sort is mentioned in the "Tan Gong" chapter of the *Liji*. See SSJZS, vol. 1, 10/84B, 1312; translated in Legge, *Li Chi*, vol. 1, 188: "The duke sent a message of condolence to Kui Shang, and the messenger met him [on the way to the grave]. They withdrew to the wayside, where Kui drew the figure of his house, [with the coffin in it], and there received the condolences. Zengzi said, 'Kui Shang's knowledge of the rules of ceremony was not equal to that of the wife of Qi Liang. When Duke Zhuang fell on Ju by surprise at Duo, Qi Liang met his death. His wife met his bier on the way and wailed for him bitterly. Duke Zhuang sent a person to convey his condolences to her; but she said, "If his lordship's officer had been guilty of any offense, then his body should have been exposed in the court or the marketplace, and his wife and concubines apprehended. If he were not chargeable with any offense, there is the poor cottage of his father. This is not the place where the ruler should demean himself to send me a message."'" Also see the "Tan Gong" chapter of the *Liji* in SSJZS, vol. 1, 7/54B, 1282; translated in Legge, *Li Chi*, vol. 1, 134.

66. She means that she has neither close nor distant relatives. The "five categories" refers to the degrees of mourning based on the relationship of the mourner to the deceased (parent, spouse, etc.) and expressed through the use of graded mourning garments to be worn for a specific period of time in each case. See *Liji*, "Sang Fu Xiao Ji," in SSJZS, vol. 2, 1495A; translated in Legge, *Li Chi*, vol. 2, 42.

67. I interpret the word "establish" in the sense in which it is used in *Zuo zhuan*, Xiang 24; translated in Legge, *The Chinese Classics*, vol. 5, 507. Here it refers to establishing an imperishable legacy of virtue.

68. The Zi River flows north in Shandong province east of Zibo into the sea.

69. *Odes, Gui Feng*, "Su Guan," Mao no. 147. Translation based on Legge, *The Chinese Classics*, vol. 4, 216.

70. As a daughter of the ruler of Qin, her clan name was Ying, while Bo indicates that she was the eldest daughter. As Liang Duan points out (see LNZHB, 434–435), King Mu of Qin reigned from 659 to 621 BCE, yet the battle described in this story, according to *Zuo zhuan*, Ding 4, occurred in 506 BCE, some 115 years after King Mu's death. See translation in Legge, *The Chinese Classics*, vol. 5, 753. The text's identification of Bo Ying's father is therefore problematic. Bo Ying's husband, King Ping of Chu, reigned from 528 to 516 BCE and her son, King Zhao, reigned from 515 to 489 BCE. While

the *Zuo zhuan* does not mention Bo Ying, a similar incident is noted in both *Guliang zhuan*, Ding 4, in SSJZS, vol. 2, 19/80, 2444C, and *Gongyang zhuan*, Ding 4, in SSJZS, vol. 2, 25/143, 2337C. For more speculation on the identity of this woman, see Takao Shimomi, *Ryū kō Retsujōden no kenkyū* (Tokyo: Tōkaidō daigaku shuppankai, 1989), 493–494.

71. Boju, a city in Chu, was located northeast of Macheng in present-day Hubei.

72. Ying was Chu's capital, but its exact location is controversial. There is a growing consensus that it was located north of the city of Jingzhou (a Yangzi River city in Hubei), south of the Jinan mountains. Also see Blakeley, "The Geography of Chu," 1–20. Blakeley places Ying south of the bend of the Han River, in Hubei's Yicheng county.

73. He Lü (r. 514–496 BCE) was the ruler of Wu.

74. These prohibitions are mentioned in *Liji*, "Nei Ze," in SSJZS, vol. 2, 28/240, 1466C; translated by Legge, *Li Chi*, vol. 1, 470; and "Qu Li," SSJZS, vol. 1, 2/12C, 1240C; translated in Legge, *Li Chi*, vol. 1, 77.

75. Annotators suggest a number of variant readings for *shi* (施), which I have here translated as "transform." Also see Shimomi, *Ryū kō Retsujōden no kenkyū*, 495, note 7.

76. For early textual references to such punishments, see *Zhouli*, "Da Sima" (on bestial behavior within or outside of the family punished with death), in SSJZS, vol. 1, 29/29B, 835B; *Gongyang zhuan*, Zhao 31 (on Duke Yan of Zhulou's illicit relations with nine palace women of Lu and subsequent execution ca. 511 BCE), in SSJZS, vol. 2, 24/137B; *Zuo zhuan*, Cheng 4; and Legge, *The Chinese Classics*, vol. 5, 355, 357 (on Zhao Ying of Jin's banishment after having illicit relations with his brother's widow ca. 586 BCE).

77. Liang Duan suggests reading *sang* (喪) as *shi* (失). See LNZHB, vol. 7, 435–436. The phrase might therefore be construed as "When men and women err."

78. The "Lanes of Perpetuity" were the women's quarters of the palace.

79. See *Zuo zhuan*, Ding 5, translated in Legge, *The Chinese Classics*, 760–761.

80. *Odes, Da Ya*, "Han Lu," Mao no. 239. Translation based on Legge, *The Chinese Classics*, vol. 4, 446.

81. Jiang is her clan name. King Zhao of Chu reigned from 515 to 489 BCE. A tomb tentatively identified as that of King Zhao was unearthed in 2008 in Zhangyangcun village, Chuandianzhen town, in Jingzhou, Hubei province. Although Jiang was the wife of the king, King Zhao's successor, King Hui (r. 488–432 BCE), was not the son of Chaste Jiang but of a Lady Zhao, a concubine of King Zhao from the state of Yue. See *Shiji* 66, 2182–2183; translated in William Nienhauser et al., *The Grand Scribe's Records*, 6 vols. (Bloomington: Indiana University Press, 1994–2006), vol. 7, 59–60.

82. The term used for the "pavilion on the water" (漸臺 *jiantai*) can refer to a terrace, tower, or pavilion built on the water's edge or, according to Yan Shigu's note to *Hanshu* 25B, 1245, one situated in the middle of a lake or pond.

83. A tally was a document, usually made of bamboo, divided into two halves and used for official identification or verification of orders. See Tsuen-hsuin Tsien, *Written on Bamboo and Silk: The Beginnings of Chinese Books and Inscriptions*, 2nd ed. (Chicago:

University of Chicago Press, 2004), 121. Also see *Zhouli,* "Di Guan: Zhang Jie," in SSJZS, vol. 1, 15/102A, for a description of the use of tallies in maintaining the security of the state.

84. *Odes, Cao Feng,* "Shi Jiu," Mao no. 152. Translation based on Legge, *The Chinese Classics,* vol. 4, 223.

85. Bo Ji's biography can be found in LNZ 4.2.

86. Strictly speaking, Bai was not a duke. The title here, as was common practice, was a courtesy title posthumously conferred on royal princes. Duke Bai's personal name was Sheng. Also known as Wangsun (or "Prince") Sheng (王孫勝), he was the son of Jian, King Ping of Chu's (r. 528–516 BCE) deceased heir apparent, and thus King Ping's grandson. He died in the course of mounting a dangerous and bloody rebellion against the Chu throne. For the story of Duke Bai's demise, see *Zuo zhuan,* Ai 16 (481 BCE); translation in Legge, *The Chinese Classics,* vol. 5, 846–848. Also see his biography in *Shiji* 66, 2173, 2182–2183; translated in Nienhauser, *The Grand Scribe's Records,* vol. 7, 51, 59–60.

87. As recounted in LNZ 4.9, the states of Wu and Chu were enemies, and Chaste Ji, of the present biography, was the granddaughter-in-law of Bo Ying (LNZ 4.9), another woman who was harassed by a King of Wu. Duke Bai of Chu died in 479 BCE, so it is likely that her unwelcome suitor was King Fu Chai of Wu (r. 495–477 BCE). In early China, the prospective groom was required to make a formal petition for betrothal, called *pin* (聘), in order to establish a woman as his primary wife. The absence of a formal petition meant that the woman would marry him as a concubine. See, for example, *Zuo zhuan,* Cheng 11, Zhao 25, Ai 11, translated in Legge, *The Chinese Classics,* vol. 5, 376, 708, 826; and *Bohu tong* in SBCK, vol. 22, 9/6a; translation in Som, *Po Hu T'ung,* vol. 1, 252–253.

88. The rear palace (後宮 *hougong*) was where the ruler's women resided.

89. *Analects* VIII:7: "The philosopher Zeng said, "The officer may not be without breadth of mind and vigorous endurance. His burden is heavy and his course is long. Perfect virtue is the burden which he considers it is his to sustain;—is it not heavy? Only with death does his course stop;—is it not long?" Translation based on Legge, *The Chinese Classics,* vol. 1, 210. A similar saying can be found in *Liji,* "Biao Ji," in SSJZS, vol. 2, 54/412A; translated in Legge, *Li Chi,* vol. 2, 334; and in the *Odes,* Mao 260.

90. *Odes, Zheng Feng,* "You Nü Tong Ju," Mao no. 83. Translation based on Legge, *The Chinese Classics,* vol. 4, 137.

91. Commentators note that in Warring States times, there was no king of Wey and suggest that "King Ling" is an error for "Ling Shi" (靈氏), which is how this name appears later in the text, and which I translate as "Lord Ling." An "attendant concubine" (傅妾 *fuqie*) was most likely a concubine who also functioned as a personal maid.

92. The *Shiji,* however, states that when the Second Emperor of Qin came to the throne (ca. 209 BCE), the last ruler of Wey, Lord Jiao (君角), was demoted to the rank of commoner, and the sacrifices to Wey were extinguished. See *Shiji* 37, 1605.

93. The phrase "reverent care" (供養 *gong yang*) elevates the act of merely providing for the physical needs of superiors to doing so with reverence and respect. On the history of this concept, see Keith Nathaniel Knapp, *Selfless Offspring: Filial Children and Social Order in Medieval China* (Honolulu: University of Hawai'i Press, 2005), 113–136.

94. The term I have translated as "you," *ruzi* (孺子), was a term used to refer to a concubine who served in an aristocratic household. See Yan Shigu's note in *Hanshu* 15A, 445.

95. While it was the duty of the wife to serve her husband's parents, the concubine's duty was to serve the wife. See, for example, *Yili*, "Sang Fu," in SSJZS, vol. 1, 31/165B, 1109; trans. in Steele, *The I-li*, vol. 2, 22.

96. The seven grounds for divorcing a wife, including the failure to produce offspring, are mentioned in LNZ 2.7. Still, expelling a barren wife when a family could afford a concubine was an unusual and somewhat drastic measure. The earliest reference to divorce on the grounds of barrenness appears to be in *Da Dai liji* in SBCK, vol. 3, 13/6A. Also see Jack L. Dull, "Marriage and Divorce in Traditional China: A Glimpse at 'Pre-Confucian' Society," and Tai Yen-hui, "Divorce in Traditional Chinese Law," in *Chinese Family Law and Social Change in Historical and Comparative Perspective,* ed. David C. Buxbaum (Seattle: University of Washington Press, 1978), 52–64, 75–106. Nevertheless, if it accorded with the wishes of the husband, barren wives could claim the children of concubines. Likewise, a concubine could not claim a biological child as her own and her child could not claim her as mother, unless the father ordered it. See *Yili*, "Sang Fu," in SSJZS, vol. 1, 31/159C, 1103; trans. in Steele, *The I-li*, vol. 2, 14. The dilemma here is that normally, a concubine cannot be elevated to the status of wife, but at the same time, a woman can receive her rank through her son. In this case, as mother of the heir, the concubine was eligible for a more elevated status in the household.

97. I translate the term *junzi* (君子) as "persons of distinction."

98. *Odes, Bei Feng,* "Bo Zhou," Mao no. 26. Translation based on Legge, *The Chinese Classics*, vol. 4, 39.

99. A textual variant of the phrase "ashamed to concede" (慚讓 *canran*) is "to be mortified and refuse" (慚辭 *canci*).

100. A textual variant of the phrase "undaunted" (閒眼 *xianxia*) is "in good measure" (有度 *youdu*). For similar usage of the term *xianxia*, see *Hanshu* 48, 2226, and *Shuoyuan*, SBCK, vol. 17, 9/8A.

101. On the yellow swan, see Homer Dubs, *History of the Former Han Dynasty* (Baltimore: Waverly Press, 1944), vol. 2, 153–154.

102. *Odes, Wei Feng,* "Yuan You Tao," Mao no. 109. Translation based on Legge, *The Chinese Classics*, vol. 4, 165.

103. The Liang mentioned in this story is most likely the capital of the kingdom of Wei (one of the three successor states of Jin, established ca. 376 BCE), which lay south of

the Yellow River. The location of Liang's territory was roughly equivalent to that of modern-day Kaifeng in eastern Henan province. One commentator, Chen Hanzhang, has suggested that this story refers to the Former Han dynasty King of Liang, Liu Hui, who was appointed king in 196 BCE. See LNZHB, vol. 8, 646.

104. A less compacted version of this sentiment can be found in the notes to *Wenxuan*, 38/27B, written by an early commentator of *Lienü zhuan*, Mother Zhao (d. 243 CE; also called Zhao Yi, "Imperial Concubine Zhao," and Yu Zhenjie). Her paraphrase of this line is as follows: "Human beings receive their lives from Heaven and their lives are long. Dogs and horses receive their lives from Heaven and their lives are short. Yet my husband, on the contrary, has died before his dogs and horses."

105. The statement concerning her desire to follow her husband in death (literally, "to stay close to his coffin") is deleted in a number of early editions. See Shimomi, *Ryū kō Retsujōden no kenkyū*, 517, note 6.

106. The widow of Liang is here mutilating herself to prevent further attention from suitors. Punishments in early China often involved various forms of bodily mutilation, including amputation of the nose. Thus, she is perhaps preempting the king by punishing herself for refusing his proposal.

107. Generally speaking, the obligations were to pay taxes and, in the case of men, to perform military or labor service. See, for example, *Shiji* 68, 2230; translated in Nienhauser, *The Grand Scribe's Records*, vol. 7, 89–90.

108. *Odes, Wang Feng*, "Da Ju," Mao no. 73. Translation based on Legge, *The Chinese Classics*, vol. 4, 121.

109. Chen was a state in Spring and Autumn times and was later made into a prefecture in the Qin dynasty. In the Han, under Emperor Gaozu, it became the kingdom of Huaiyang, located in present-day Huaiyang, Henan province. During the reign of Emperor Wen (r. 180–157 BCE), it was divided into the three commanderies of Huaiyang, Yingchuan, and Runan.

110. Liang Duan notes that the word "earth" seems to be an error but offers no alternative reading. See LNZHB, vol. 7, 447. I translate it as "the world."

111. This sentence has been restored to the text from the *Taiping yulan*.

112. The title of the Governor of Huaiyang has been emended from "grand administrator" (太守 *taishou*) to "governor" (*shou*). At this time, Shentu Jia (申屠嘉) served as governor. In 164 BCE, he was appointed Imperial Counselor, and then Chancellor in 162 BCE. He died in 155 BCE. He was known for his uncompromising honesty and integrity and was given the posthumous title "Virtuous." *See Shiji* 96, 2682–2685; translated in Burton Watson, *Records of the Grand Historian: Han Dynasty I* (Hong Kong: Columbia University Press, 1993), 214–217.

113. One catty (*jin*) was equivalent to approximately 245 grams. Forty catties would be equivalent to 9.8 kilograms.

114. *Odes, Yong Feng*, "Ding Zhi Fang Zhong," Mao no. 50. Translation based on Legge, *The Chinese Classics*, vol. 4, 83, following the translation in the notes.

5. THE PRINCIPLED AND RIGHTEOUS

In the chapter, "righteousness," one possible translation of the word *yi* (義), refers to acts of bravery and moral courage. Eric Henry (personal communication, October 2012) associates the word *yi* with the phrase "on seeing an opportunity to do a noble deed, to boldly step forth and do it" (見義勇為 *jian yi yong wei*); hence, in many contexts, "gallantry." He states that, "Of all the classical Chinese virtues, *yi* is the most closely aligned with action; it cannot in fact *exist* until somebody does something."

1. Duke Xiao of Lu reigned from 796 to 769 BCE.

2. Duke Wu of Lu reigned from 825 to 816 BCE, and King Xuan of Zhou reigned from 827/25 to 782 BCE. This story is related in *Gongyang zhuan*, Zhao 31, in SSJZS, vol. 2, 24/137–138, 2331–2332. The story, minus the righteous nurse, is recounted in *Guoyu*, 2 vols. (Shanghai: Guji chubanshe, 1978), "Zhouyu," part 1, item 7; and *Shiji* 33, 1527–1528, trans. in William Nienhauser, et al., *The Grand Scribe's Records*, 6 vols. (Bloomington: Indiana University Press, 1994–2006), vol. 5.1, 142. On this period of Western Zhou history and this specific incident, see Li Feng, *Landscape and Power in Early China: The Crisis and Fall of the Western Zhou, 1045–771 BC* (Cambridge, England: Cambridge University Press, 2006), 134–140.

3. Naming the younger son as heir violated the basic rules of succession. The *Shiji* version of this tale includes a long critique of the king's decision.

4. Duke Yi reigned from 815 to 807 BCE.

5. The literal meaning of the title "prince" (公子 *gongzi*) is "the duke's son." Some translators prefer simply to transliterate the title as part of the name: for example, Gongzi Cheng.

6. In contrast to this narrative and that of the *Shiji*, Wei Zhao indicates that Boyu was another name for Kuo himself, not his son. See *Guoyu*, "Zhouyu," part 1, item 7.

7. The eleventh year of Boyu's reign was 796 BCE.

8. *Lunyu* VIII:6. Translation based on James Legge, trans., *The Chinese Classics*, 5 vols. (1893; reprint, Hong Kong: University of Hong Kong Press, 1960), vol. 1, 210.

9. The name Zheng Mao means "Mao of the state of Zheng." In this account, Mao, serving in the capacity of a secondary bride, accompanied a woman from the state of Qin with the clan name Ying, who was married as principal bride to the King of Chu. The term *ying* (媵) refers to the custom by which several states sent secondary brides to accompany a principal bride in her marriage to a ruler. On this practice, see *Gongyang zhuan*, Zhuang 19, in SSJZS, vol. 2, 8/41C, 223; Melvin Thatcher, "Marriages of the Ruling Elite in the Spring and Autumn Period," in *Marriage and Inequality in Chinese Society*, ed. Rubie S. Watson and Patricia Buckley Ebrey (Berkeley: University of California Press, 1991), 31–32. Although Mao does occur as a surname (see *Zuo zhuan*, Zhao 1; Yang, *Chunqiu Zuozhuan zhu*, 1217), as a secondary bride in a royal wedding, Mao of Zheng most likely belonged to the Ji clan, the clan name of the rulers of Zheng. She is also referred to in this story as Zimao, which appears to be a polite form of her first name.

10. King Cheng of Chu reigned from 671 to 625 BCE.

11. The "rear palace" was where the royal women were housed. See *Liji*, "Hun Yi," in SSJZS, vol. 2, 61/453–454, 1681C–1682A; translated in James Legge, *Li Chi: Book of Rites*, 2 vols. (1885; reprint, New York: University Books, 1967), vol. 2, 432. In this section of the *Liji*, the queen is shown organizing the royal women into six palaces. According to Zheng Xuan, these dwellings were located behind the palace structures used for official business.

12. Wang Zhaoyuan understands the phrase "a woman comports herself with propriety and dignity" as meaning that a woman should move straight ahead and not lean or look from side to side. See Wang Zhaoyuan (1763–1851), *Lienü zhuan buzhu*, in LNZHB, vol. 5, 470.

13. Rulers of the Spring and Autumn period could have more than one primary wife at a time. See Thatcher, "Marriages of the Ruling Elite," 29.

14. This story is told in *Zuo zhuan*, Wen 1; Legge, *The Chinese Classics*, vol. 5, 230; and *Shiji* 40, 1698–1699, though in both cases Zheng Mao is not mentioned.

15. Zishang is also called Dou Bo.

16. These observations are based on physiognomic interpretations of Shang Chen's appearance and voice. For similar tales, see LNZ 3.10, and *Zuo zhuan*, Xuan 4, Zhao 28.

17. See *Zuo zhuan*, Xi 33; translated in Legge, *The Chinese Classics*, vol. 5, 226.

18. The text here says "heir apparent" but is clearly referring to Zhi. Below, "heir apparent" refers to Shangchen.

19. Bear's paw was a delicacy requested by the duke as his last meal. Or, as suggested in Schaberg, Li, and Durrant's forthcoming translation of the *Zuo zhuan*, he may have chosen it because it was difficult to obtain and thus would delay the inevitable.

20. *Odes, Zheng Feng*, "Gao Qiu," Mao no. 80. Translation based on Bernhard Karlgren, trans., *The Book of Odes* (Goteborg: Elanders Boktryckeri Aktiebolag, 1950), 54. Compare Arthur Waley, "That great gentleman,/Would give his life rather than fail his lord," in *The Book of Songs* (New York: Grove Press, 1960), 111; and Legge, "That officer rests on his lot and will not change," in *The Chinese Classics*, vol. 4, 132.

21. Duke Mu of Qin reigned from 659 to 621 BCE. Ying was the clan name of the ruling family of Qin. Huai was the posthumous name of Ying's husband, so her name means "lady of the Ying clan, [consort of Duke] Huai." Duke Huai's given name was Yu (he is also called "Ziyu" in this story). He was the eldest son of Duke Hui of Jin (r. 650–637 BCE). He reigned briefly after his father's death until he was murdered by his paternal uncle, Chonger. Chonger became Duke Wen of Jin (r. 636–628 BCE). See *Zuo zhuan*, Xi 24; translated in Legge, *The Chinese Classics*, vol. 5, 190–191; and *Shiji* 39, 1655. Ying was later married to Chonger. See *Zuo zhuan*, Xi 23; translated in Legge, *The Chinese Classics*, vol. 5, 187; also see *Shiji* 39, 1660; and *Guoyu*, "Jinyu," part 4, item 9.

22. During the Spring and Autumn period, the rulers of states exchanged their sons in a system of hostages. If one state threatened another, the state under attack could counter with a threat to kill the attacker's son who resided as hostage in that state.

23. He served as hostage from 643 to 638 BCE.

24. Here he is quoting lines that appear in several extant texts from the third century BCE; for example, "Ai Ying," the third of the *Nine Declarations* (*Jiu Zhang*) of the *Chuci*. See D. C. Lau, ed., *A Concordance to the* Chuci, 4.3/12/11; translation in David Hawkes, *The Songs of the South: An Ancient Chinese Anthology of Poems by Qu Yuan and Other Poets Translated, Annotated and Introduced by David Hawkes* (Harmondsworth: Penguin, 1985), 166.

25. In Chinese texts of the Spring and Autumn period onward (see, e.g., *Zuo zhuan,* Xiang 14), we see a wife's duties to her husband described as "serving him with towel and comb." In *Hanshi waizhuan* (ca 150 BCE), one woman describes these duties as follows: "For eleven years I have been privileged to wait on Your Highness when you were bathing and washing your hair by holding your towel and comb and by spreading your coverlet and mat." See *Hanshi waizhuan,* SBCK, vol. 3, 2/3A; translated by James Hightower, *Han Shih Wai Chuan: Han Ying's Illustrations of the Didactic Application of the Classic of Songs* (Cambridge, Mass.: Harvard University Press, 1952), 42.

26. This biography does not include a quotation from the *Odes*.

27. The subject of this biography is the woman of Yue mentioned in *Zuo zhuan,* Ai 6, 16 and *Shiji* 40, 1717–1718. King Goujian reigned from 496 to 465 BCE. Yue, located in the fertile Yangzi delta, emerged as a powerful state in the late sixth century BCE, and by 473 BCE, under the leadership of Goujian, the concubine's father, was the most powerful state in China at the time. Cho-yun Hsu describes the people of Yue as being of non–Hua Xia ethnic and cultural origin. See Michael Loewe and Edward L. Shaughnessy, eds., *The Cambridge History of Ancient China: From the Origins of the Civilization to 221 B.C.* (Cambridge, England: Cambridge University Press, 1999), 565. King Zhao of Chu reigned from 516 to 489 BCE.

Ji (姬), the title of the person who is the subject of this biography, refers to a high-ranking concubine; I translate this word as "Lady" when used as a title in a name and "consort" when used as rank. Her counterpart in the story, the Lady of Cai, describes herself as one of the king's "wives and concubines" (妃嬪 *feibin*). The rank of "lady" therefore may have referred to *bin*, a special category of concubines who were treated like wives. The term *bin* seems to be distinguished from the more ordinary concubines (*qie*妾) in *Guoyu* 6, "Qiyu," item 1, which states that Duke Huan of Qi had nine *fei* (wives) and six *bin*, as well as several hundred concubines. *Zuo zhuan,* Xi 17, states that Duke Huan had three wives (夫人 *furen*), who were all barren, and six favorite concubines who were treated as wives. Also see Thatcher, "Marriages of the Ruling Elite," 50, note 10. The word *ji* (姬) is also a complimentary term for a woman. This meaning, according to Yan Shigu, is derived from the fact that in early times, women from the Ji clan, because of their affiliation to the house of Zhou, were considered to be the most distinguished among all the states. See *Hanshu* 4, 105, note 2, where Ru Chun (ca. 220–265 CE) suggests that when used to refer to a woman, the term is pronounced *yi,* though Yan Shigu disagrees with him on this score.

While the word *ji* most often refers to the clan name (姓 *xing*) Ji, as a daughter of the royal family of Yue, her clan name would have been Si 姒, not Ji. Understanding this woman's status is also complicated by the mention of what appear to be betrothal gifts presented by the king when he went to fetch her. Furthermore, based on the fact that her palace is mentioned in the *Zuo zhuan* ten years after the king's death, with the implication that she was then still alive, Yang Bojun concludes that the LNZ story is a fabrication, which may explain some of the more puzzling elements of this tale. See Yang Bojun, *Chunqiu Zuo zhuan zhu,* 4 vols. (Beijing: Zhonghua shuju, 1981), 1703.

28. This was a large hunting park located in present-day Hubei.

29. King Zhuang reigned from 613 to 591 BCE. Technically, the rulers of Chu were "viscounts" (子 *zi*), but they referred to themselves as kings. For this incident, see *Lüshi chunqiu,* "Zhong Yan," in SBCK, vol. 22, 18/4A–5B; translated in John Knoblock and Jeffrey Riegel, *The Annals of Lü Buwei* (Stanford: Stanford University Press, 2000), 445–446; and *Shiji* 40, 1700. Duke Zhuang is also mentioned in LNZ 2.5, 7.9.

30. "To increase devotion toward him" might also be construed as "to increase his devotion toward her."

31. What follows is related in *Zuo zhuan,* Ai 6, and *Shiji* 40, 1717, but in both of these cases, the Lady of Yue is mentioned only as the mother of the king's successor and does not elucidate her relationship to King Zhao. In *Zuo zhuan,* Ai 16, however, reference is made to the palace of the consort of Zhao, that is, the consort of King Zhao of Chu, and the mother of his successor, King Hui (r. 488–432 BCE). Chen was one of the fifteen major states of the Spring and Autumn period. It bordered on Chu in present-day Huaiyang of Henan province.

32. The diviner mentioned in the *Zuo zhuan* account is called the "Scribe of Zhou" (周史 *zhoushi*), whereas Liu Xiang's *Shuoyuan* records the name as Zhou Li (州黎). See *Shuoyuan* in SBCK, vol. 17, 1/17.

33. See *Shiji* 40, 1717–1718.

34. This incident is related in *Zuo zhuan,* Ai 6. King Hui of Chu reigned from 488 to 432 BCE. On his reign and that of his father, King Zhao, see Barry B. Blakeley, "King, Clan and Courtier in Ancient Ch'u," *Asia Major,* 3rd series, 5, no. 2 (1992): 1–39.

35. *Odes, Bei Feng,* "Gu Feng," Mao no. 35. Translation based on Legge, *The Chinese Classics,* vol. 4, 55; and Karlgren, *Book of Odes,* 22.

36. Ge was a small city in the state of Qi, located in the vicinity of Yishui county in present-day Shandong province. It is mentioned in *Mencius* IIIB.10.5 as belonging to a noble family of the state of Qi. The *Zhushu jinian* records a Rong attack on Ge in the sixth year of Zhou King You (776 BCE) as a prelude to the fall of the Western Zhou five years later. See *Zhushu jinian* in SBCK, vol. 5, 17A; translation by Legge in *The Chinese Classics,* vol. 3, 157. For further speculation on this connection, see Chen Hanzhong's note in *Lienü zhuan jiaozhu,* LNZHB, vol. 8, 649.

37. According to Nicola Di Cosmo, "The term 'Rong' was used in Chinese sources as a blanket word that included many alien peoples around and within the territory occupied by the Zhou, without a specific ethnic connotation." See Loewe and Shaughnessy, *The Cambridge History of Ancient China,* 921–922.

38. No such quotation can be found in the extant *Zhoushu* chapter of the *Shangshu*.
39. A *tailao* sacrifice included offerings of an ox, a sheep, and a pig and was a mark of great distinction to its recipient.
40. One hundred *yi* of cash represented about 31 kilograms of coins, usually cast in copper or bronze in the pre-Qin period. Presumably, the Rong ruler was moved by the death of the general's wife and ceded the land back to the Zhou.
41. *Odes, Xiao Ya,* "Gu Zhong," Mao no. 208. Translation based on Legge, *The Chinese Classics,* vol. 4, 367.
42. The "Five Glories" most likely refers to the five virtues that are mentioned in this biography: benevolence, righteousness, filial piety, loyalty, and worthiness.
43. Here I follow Liang Duan's reading of the second xing (幸) in the phrase *xing er de xing* (幸而得幸) as "to escape."
44. Liang Duan notes that the phrase, "A man of discernment would say, 'The Righteous Aunt...'" should be restored here.
45. *Odes, Da Ya,* "Yi," Mao no. 256. Translation based on Legge, *The Chinese Classics,* vol. 4, 511.
46. Zhao Jianzi was the chief of the Zhao lineage and an official in Jin who, from 497 BCE onward, headed the state. He is also mentioned in LNZ 3.11. Xiangzi (r. 475–425) succeeded him. Dai was a small state located in present-day Wei county in Hebei province. Zhao Xiangzi annexed it in 475 BCE. This story, with some variations, is found in *Zhanguo ce* in SBCK, vol. 14, 9/14b–15a, translated in James Irving Crump, *Chan-kuo Ts'e,* 2nd ed., revised (San Francisco: Chinese Materials Center, 1979), 521–522; *Lüshi chunqiu* in SBCK, vol. 22, 14/15, translated in Knoblock and Riegel, *The Annals of Lü Buwei,* 322–323; and *Shiji* 43, 1793–1794.
47. According to the account in the *Lüshi chunqiu,* he had been directed by his dying father to climb the mountain upon his father's death so that he would catch a glimpse of Dai and thus understand that he should annex it.
48. Here, and in the *Lüshi chunqiu,* Zhao Xiangzi "fetches" (迎 *ying*) his sister, a term traditionally but not exclusively used to indicate the practice whereby a prospective husband (or some other designated individual) fetches a woman and escorts her to her marital home. In the *Shiji* account of this tale, the Lady of Dai merely kills herself when she learns that her brother has annexed her husband's state, and no mention is made of Xiangzi's plans for her. Early texts suggest that Spring and Autumn period aristocrats presented women to others as a means of establishing bonds but also as a form of bribery; see Kinney, "A Spring and Autumn Family."
49. According to the *Lüshi chunqiu,* she sharpened a hairpin and stabbed herself with it, and the site was later named after this incident.
50. *Odes, Da Ya,* "Yi," Mao no. 256. Translation based on Legge, *The Chinese Classics,* vol. 4, 515; and Karlgren, *The Book of Odes,* 218.
51. King Xuan of Qi reigned from 319 to 301 BCE.
52. Reading *xing* (行) as *yi* (義); see LNZHB, vol. 7, 468.

53. *Odes, Da Ya,* "Quan E," Mao no. 252. Translation based on Legge, *The Chinese Classics,* vol. 4, 493.

54. The words "a man who is unfilial and unprincipled" (不孝不義之人) have been restored from the *Taiping yulan.* See LNZHB, vol. 7, 471.

55. This comment is similar to a passage in the *Xiao jing,* "Sheng Zhi" chapter. See SSJZS, vol. 2, 5/16, 2554A; translated in Henry Rosemont and Roger Ames, *The Chinese Classic of Family Reverence* (Honolulu: University of Hawai'i Press, 2009), 110.

56. This is a quotation from *Analects* XVI:11, translation based on Legge, *The Chinese Classics,* vol. 1, 314.

57. *Odes, Wei Feng,* "Ge Ju," Mao no. 107. Translation based on Legge, *The Chinese Classics,* vol. 4, 164.

58. The term for this relationship is *yingqie* (媵妾) and generally denoted a woman who accompanied a bride to the groom's household and served as his concubine. In this tale, the concubine is also referred to as a *yingbi* (媵婢), which would point to her being a particularly low-status concubine, as *bi* means "servant" or "slave." This story is also told in *Zhanguo ce,* in SBCK, vol. 14, 9/22B–23A; translation in Crump, *Chankuo Ts'e,* 531. Here, and in *Shiji* 69, she is merely referred to as a concubine (妾 *qie*). See *Shiji* 69, 2265; translated in Nienhauser, *The Grand Scribe's Records,* vol. 7, 111.

59. *Odes, Da Ya,* "Yi," Mao no. 256. Translation based on Legge, *The Chinese Classics,* vol. 4, 514.

60. According to the *Shiji,* the king's name was Jia (假); see *Shiji* 44, 1864. He reigned from 227 to 225 BCE. This story also appears in *Hanshi waizhuan,* SBCK, vol. 3, 9/3B–4A; translated in Hightower, *Han Shih Wai Chuan,* 294–295. On wet nurses, see Jen-der Lee, "Wet Nurses in Early Imperial China," *Nan Nü* 2, no.1 (2000): 1–39.

61. See *Shiji* 44, 1864. Wei was defeated by Qin and made a commandery in 225 BCE.

62. On the extermination of relatives as a form of punishment, see A.F.P. Hulsewe, *Remnants of Han Law* (Leiden: E. J. Brill, 1955), 112–132.

63. The *tailao* sacrifices consisted of offering an ox, a sheep, and a pig.

64. This description of the caretakers assigned to aristocratic children is based on *Liji,* "Nei Ze," in SSJZS, vol. 2, 1469B; translation based on Legge, *Li Chi,* vol. 1, 472–473.

65. Phrases similar to this one can be found in the *Xunzi,* "Rong Ru," in SBCK, vol. 17, 2/12A; translated in John Knoblock, *Xunzi: A Translation and Study of the Complete Works* (3 vols. Stanford: Stanford University Press, 1982), vol. 1, 187: "A nursing sow will charge a tiger, and a bitch with pups will not wander far away." Also see *Huainanzi,* "Shuolin," in *A Concordance to the* Huaininanzi, 17/172/30; translated in John S. Major, et al., Huainanzi: *A Guide to the Theory and Practice of Government in Early Han China* (New York: Columbia University Press, 2010), 677: "A nursing bitch will bite a tiger; a brooding hen will peck a fox. When their [maternal] concern has been aroused, they do not take account of [relative] strengths."

66. *Odes, Xiao Ya,* "Xiao Bian," Mao no. 336. Translation based on Legge, *The Chinese Classics,* vol. 4, 338.

67. Liang was another name for the state of Wei and the name of its capital. Wei was one of the successor states of the partitioned state of Jin.

68. Following the text as it appears in the *Taiping yulan,* vol. 4, 513/6A: (至於中心亦已 足矣). See LNZHB, vol. 7, 477.

69. *Odes, Zheng Feng,* "Gao Qiu," Mao no. 80. Translation based on Legge, *The Chinese Classics,* vol. 4, 132; and Waley, *Book of Songs,* 68.

70. Zhuyai was a commandery located in the South China Sea on present-day Hainan Island and considered part of Guangdong province. It became part of the Han empire in 110 BCE but was abandoned in 82 BCE. See *Hanshu* 7, 223; 9, 283.

71. She was twelve years old by current reckoning.

72. Presumably she was returning her husband's remains to his ancestral burial grounds. The rite is mentioned in *Liji,* "Qu Li," part 2, in SSJZS, vol. 1, 3/21B; translated in Legge, *Li Chi,* vol. 1, 89.

73. I follow Wang Zhaoyuan's reading here. See LNZHB, vol. 5, 501.

74. *Analects* XIII:18. Translation based on Legge, *The Chinese Classics,* vol. 1, 270.

75. Heyang was originally associated with the state of Shen (莘). In Warring States times, it was considered part of Wei. It was located in present-day Heyang in Shaanxi province.

76. On the emperor's power to declare amnesties, see Michael Loewe, "The Orders of Aristocratic Rank of Han China," *T'oung Pao* 49, no. 1–3 (1960): 165–171.

77. The Wang Rang of this story cannot be linked to a specific historical person.

78. In general, in Qin and Han times, all males, apart from those who held high aristocratic rank, were required to perform compulsory labor service to the state in their home districts. The labor generally consisted of public works such as road maintenance. See Michael Loewe and Denis Twitchett, eds., *The Ch'in and Han Empires, 221 B.C.–A.D. 220,* vol. 1 of *The Cambridge History of China,* vol. 1, 537; Hulsewe, *Remnants of Ch'in Law: An Annotated Translation of the Ch'in Legal and Administrative Rules of the 3rd Century B.C. Discovered in Yunmeng Prefecture, Hu-pei Province in 1975* (Leiden: Brill, 1985), 11.

79. *Odes, Da Ya,* "Yi," Mao no. 256. Translation based on Legge, *The Chinese Classics,* vol. 4, 515.

80. Reading *ju* (且) as *cu* (徂), "to go to."

81. *Analects* XV:8. Translation based on Legge, *The Chinese Classics,* vol. 1, 297.

6. THE ACCOMPLISHED RHETORICIANS

1. Guan Zhong was minister to Duke Huan of Qi (r. 685–643 BCE). Legend claims that it was the wise counsel of Guan Zhong that allowed Duke Huan to rise to the supreme status of hegemon. Guan Zhong is associated with the *Guanzi.*

2. Ning Qi (also called Ningzi in this story), a man from Wey who served Duke Huan of Qi, is also mentioned in LNZ 2.2. A tale similar to the present biography is told in

Guanzi, "Xiao Wen," in SBCK, vol. 18, 16/51/10B. Here the concubine is not mentioned by name, and the poem is somewhat different. Two texts, the *Lüshi chunqiu*, "Ju Nan," in D. C. Lau, ed., *A Concordance to the* Lüshi chunqiu (Hong Kong: Commercial Press, 1994), 19.8/128/10–15, translated in John Knoblock and Jeffrey Riegel, *Annals of Lu Buwei* (Stanford: Stanford University Press, 2000), 507–508, and the *Huainanzi*, "Dao Ying," in D. C. Lau, ed., *A Concordance to the* Huainanzi (Hong Kong: Commercial Press, 1992), 12/109/1, translated in John S. Major et al., Huainanzi: *A Guide to the Theory and Practice of Government in Early Han China* (New York: Columbia University Press, 2010), 450–451, both relate a similar tale in which the concubine does not appear at all.

3. According to the *Lüshi chunqiu* version of the story, Duke Huan made a habit of coming out of the gates to greet guests. *Shang* was the name of the second tone in the Chinese pentatonic scale. See Kenneth DeWoskin, *A Song for One or Two: Music and the Concept of Art in Early China* (Ann Arbor: University of Michigan Center for Chinese Studies, 1982), 43–44.

4. Zhaoge was known as one of the supplementary capitals of the Shang dynasty. It is also identified as the site at which the Zhou defeated the Shang in the battle of Muye. It is northeast of Qi county in present-day Henan.

5. Taigong Wang, also known as Lü Shang, was a military strategist and army commander under Kings Wen and Wu of the Zhou. Legend has it that King Wen raised Taigong Wang from obscurity to a position of honor. Taigong Wang is traditionally credited with enabling King Wu to overthrow the Shang. For more on this legend, see Sarah Allan, "The Identities of Taigong Wang in Zhou and Han Literature," *Monumenta Serica* 30 (1972–1973): 57–99. Also see *Shiji* 4, 120; 31, 1477–1480; translated in William Nienhauser et al., *The Grand Scribe's Records,* 6 vols. (Bloomington: Indiana University Press, 1994–2006), vol. 1, 59.

6. Yi Yin was minister to Tang, the founder of the Shang dynasty, and regent to Tang's grandson, Taijia. According to legend, Yi Yin accompanied a lady from the clan of Youshen when she was sent out to become one of the consorts of Tang. See notes in LNZ 1.5. For his accomplishments, see *Shiji* 3, 98–99; translated in Nienhauser, *The Grand Scribe's Records,* vol. 1, 45–46.

7. The duties of the "Three Ducal Ministers" (*sangong*), also translated as the "Three Excellencies," are variously described. See *Liji* in SSJZS, vol. 1, 11/94A–97B, 1322–1325, translated in James Legge, *Li Chi: Book of Rites,* 2 vols. (1885; reprint, New York: University Books, 1967), vol. 1, 209–210; *Hanshi waizhuan*, in SBCK, vol. 3, 8/12A, translated in James Hightower, *Han Shih Wai Chuan: Han Ying's Illustrations of the Didactic Application of the Classic of Songs* (Cambridge, Mass.: Harvard University Press, 1952), 274; and *Bohu tong*, in SBCK, vol. 22, 3/A, translated in Tjan Tjoe Som, *Po Hu T'ung: The Comprehensive Discussions in the White Tiger Hall,* 2 vols. (Leiden: Brill, 1952), vol. 2, 410–412. Also see LNZ 1.9 note 101.

8. Yu was a sage ruler of antiquity said to have founded the Xia dynasty. He is mentioned in LNZ 1.4. Gaozi is identified as Yi Bo, the son of Gao Yao, minister to the sage ruler, Shun. See Wang Fu, "Zhi Shi Xing," *Qianfu lun*, in SBCK, vol. 18, 9/5B.

9. The *jueti* was a mule of legendary speed.

10. In early China, people sat on mats rather than chairs, which did not become a feature of Chinese life until the Tang dynasty. To move backward away from one's mat was a sign of respect when addressing a superior.

11. The text varies somewhat from that found in *Guanzi*, "Xiao Wen," in SBCK, vol. 18, 16/51/10B.

12. *Odes, Da Ya*, "Ban," Mao no. 254. Translation based on James Legge, *The Chinese Classics*, 5 vols. (1893; reprint, Hong Kong: University of Hong Kong Press, 1960), vol. 4, 501.

13. This Jiang Yi is not to be confused with another man of a later period with the same name who was noted for his connection with King Xuan of Chu (r. 369–340 BCE).

14. King Gong of Chu reigned from 590 to 560 BCE. According to *Shiji* 40, 1695, Ying became Chu's capital in 690 BCE.

15. Annotations to *Yiwen leiju* 85 state that this passage refers to a law whereby a convicted slanderer was to be charged with and punished for the alleged crime of his slanderous accusation. See Ouyang Xun, *Yiwen leiju* (Shanghai: Shanghai guji chubanshe, 1999), vol. 2, 1462.

16. Sunshu Ao (fl. c. 597 BCE) is also mentioned in LNZ biographies 2.5 and 3.5. He was the prime minister of King Zhuang of Chu (r. 613–591 BCE) and through his wisdom enabled the king to become hegemon.

17. A similar saying is found in the *Shangshu*, "The Announcements of Tang," and "The Great Declaration," in Legge, trans., *The Chinese Classics*, vol. 3, 189, 292–293; the *Mozi*, "Jian Ai," part 2 in SBCK, vol. 21, 4/7B; translated in Ian Johnston, *The Mozi: A Complete Translation* (New York: Columbia University Press, 2010), 145; and the *Lüshi chunqiu*, "Shun Min," in SBCK, vol. 22, 9/3B–4A; translated in Knoblock and Riegel, *Annals of Lü Buwei*, 210.

18. *Odes, Da Ya*, "Ban," Mao no. 254. Translation based on Legge, *The Chinese Classics*, vol. 4, 499.

19. The text identifies the father as a *panren* (繁人) of Jin. On this term, Liang Duan (LNZHB, vol. 7, 490) cites a fragment of the now lost commentary of the *Lienü zhuan* by the Jin dynasty scholar Qimu Sui (綦母邃, whose surname is also sometimes written as Qiwu 綦毋, fl. ca. 345–365 CE) found in the military section of Li Fang, *Taiping yulan*, 7 vols. (Tainan: Pingping chubanshe, 1965), 347/78/8B, where a *panren* is defined as an official in charge of binding armor, and which defines *pan* as an ornamental silk trapping that was bound around the girth of a horse. A story similar to LNZ 6.3 appears in *Hanshi waizhuan*, SBCK, vol. 3, 8/15B, but here it concerns a bow maker from the state of Cai who served Duke Jing of Qi. See translation in Hightower, *Han Shih Wai Chuan*, 281–282.

20. Duke Ping of Jin reigned 557–532 BCE.
21. Gong Liu was an ancient worthy who served as a moral model for the founders of the Zhou dynasty. "Gong" is an honorific used by Zhou historians to refer to their early ancestors. His name thus means "His Honor Liu." See *Shiji* 4, 112–116; translated in Nienhauser, *The Grand Scribe's Records*, vol. 1, 56–57. Some early sources characterize his benevolences as extending to plant life. See, for example, *Qianfu lun* in SBCK, vol. 18, 5/14A. Because of this association, there may have been a tradition that linked Gong Liu to the ode "Xing Wei," which concludes this biography, and which also mentions a concern for all living things. See *Odes, Da Ya*, "Xing Wei," Mao no. 246. Translation based on Legge, *The Chinese Classics*, vol. 4, 474.
22. Duke Mu of Qin reigned from 659 to 621 BCE. This story can be found in *Shiji* 5, 189; translated in Nienhauser, *The Grand Scribe's Records*, vol. 1, 97. Duke Mu lost a prize horse. Though the men who found the horse ate it, Duke Mu offered them wine to drink because of the belief that those who ate horse meat without wine would die. Later, the men repaid him by fighting valiantly for his cause.
23. This story of King Zhuang of Chu (r. 613–591 BCE) is found in *Hanshi waizhuan*, in SBCK, vol. 3, 7/10A–11A; translated in Hightower, *Han Shi Wai Chuan*, 238–239, as follows: "King Chuang of Chu gave a drinking party to his ministers. By evening they were tipsy, while the attendants were all drunk. The lamp in the hall went out and someone tugged at the clothing of the queen, who, [reaching out in the dark], brushed the person's cap tassel and broke it off. She called out to the king, 'Just now when the lights went out someone tugged at my clothing, and I brushed against his [cap] tassel and broke it off. I wish you would quickly make a light to see who has a broken tassel.' The king said, 'Stop!' He immediately issued the order, 'I will not be pleased with those drinking with me who have not broken tassels.' As a result there were no unbroken cap tassels, and it was not known whose cap tassel had been broken by the queen. After that the king went on as before, pleasantly drinking with his ministers. Later Wu raised an army and attacked Chu. There was one man constantly in the van. In five encounters he five times overthrew their ranks and put the enemy to flight. Then he took the leader of the main force [prisoner] and presented him. The king was astonished and asked, 'I have never distinguished you [particularly]; how is it you are so generous to me?' He replied, 'I was the one in the hall with the broken tassel. For a long time I have deserved to have liver and gall smeared on the earth for [what I did] that day. There has never been an occasion for fulfilling [my obligation] until today when I was fortunate enough to be employed as befits a subject and could then defeat Wu and strengthen Chu for Your Majesty.'"
24. See *Han Feizi*, "Wu Du," in SBCK, vol. 18, 49/1B; translated in Burton Watson, *Han Fei Tzu: Basic Writings* (New York: Columbia University Press, 1964), 97–98. Yao was a sage ruler of antiquity.
25. *Odes, Da Ya*, "Xing Wei," Mao no. 246. Translation based on Legge, *The Chinese Classics*, vol. 4, 474. The ode that closes this story is more closely linked to the story than

most in that it refers to ornamental bows and the concern for plant life that is associated with Gong Liu.

26. This story also appears in *Yanzi chunqiu* in SBCK, vol. 14, 2/4A–5B. "Locust tree" is a common translation for the *huai* (槐) tree, though this term probably refers to the *sophora japonica*, also known as the "parasol tree."

27. Duke Jing of Qi reigned from 547 to 490 BCE.

28. On Yanzi (d. 500 BCE), see notes in LNZ 2.12.

29. The six domestic animals were the horse, ox, sheep, pig, dog, and chicken.

30. Duke Jing of Song reigned from 516 to 477 BCE. This attribution is problematic because Duke Jing of Song's reign occurred after that of Duke Jing of Qi (the duke Yanzi served).

31. *Odes, Xiao Ya,* "Chang Di," Mao no. 164. Translation based on Legge, *The Chinese Classics*, vol. 4, 253.

32. Duke Jian of Zheng reigned from 564 to 530 BCE. Jing was another name for the state of Chu.

33. The phrase "to shift blame" comes from *Lunyu* VI:2. Most often, *bu er guo* (不貳過) is translated as "to not repeat the same mistake twice." But that rendering does not make good sense here. I understand the literal meaning of the phrase to be "to not fraudulently lay fault," defining the word *er* as the adverbial equivalent of "double-dealing." Compare with Arthur Waley's translation of the *Analects* passage: "to let others suffer for his faults." See Arthur Waley, *The Analects of Confucius* (New York: Vintage, 1938), 115.

34. There is no precisely corresponding phrase in the *Zhoushu* apart from a passage in the "Hong Fan," which states: "Do not oppress the friendless and childless; do not fear the high and illustrious." Translated by Legge, *The Chinese Classics*, vol. 3, 330. The exact phrase is found in *Shiji* 38, 1614.

35. The exact term she uses here means "mad" or "foolish" (*kuang*). Some annotators suggest that she refers to her husband in this way as a form of self-deprecation. The same term is used by the maiden in LNZ 6.6.

36. *Odes, Xiao Ya,* "Zheng Yue," Mao no. 192. Translation based on Legge, *The Chinese Classics*, vol. 4, 317.

37. This story appears to have been originally devised to illustrate the ode cited at the end of this biography. A similar account, explicitly tied to the ode, is also found in *Hanshi waizhuan*, in SBCK, vol. 3, 1/1B; Hightower translation, *Han Shih Wai Chuan*, 13–15. The story is dismissed as a fabrication in the *Kong Congzi*, 4/4A, in SBBY, vol. 361; a text attributed to Kong Fu (264–208 BCE), an eighth-generation descendant of Confucius, but which is probably a forgery of the third century CE. See translation in Yoav Ariel, *K'ung-Ts'ung-Tzu: The K'ung Family Masters' Anthology* (Princeton: Princeton University Press, 1989), 137.

38. Zigong (fl. ca. 520 BCE) was a disciple of Confucius and an official of the state of Lu. The question of whether or not this woman was worthy of conversation recalls

Analects XV:7, "If he can be talked to and you do not talk to him, you waste the man. If he cannot be talked to and you talk to him, you waste your talk. The knowledgeable will not waste a man but will also not waste his talk." Translated by Bruce Brooks in *The Original Analects: Sayings of Confucius and His Successors* (New York: Columbia University Press, 1998), 132.

39. *Liji*, "Nei Ze," in SSJZS, vol. 2, 27/234C, 1462C; translated in Legge, *Li Chi*, vol. 1, 455–456.

40. The phrase "majestic like a fresh breeze" is taken from the *Odes* as a description of a song made by Yin Jifu, a military commander under King Xuan of Zhou (r. 827/25–782). *Odes, Da Ya*, "Zheng Min," Mao no. 260. Translation based on Legge, *The Chinese Classics*, vol. 4, 545. Wang Zhaoyuan notes that in the parallel passage in the *Hanshi waizhuan*, the text has *sifu* (私復) rather than *hechang* (和暢) "pleasant; a fresh breeze." See LNZHB, vol. 5, 525.

41. I follow Chen Hanzhang in reading *guo* (過) as *yu* (遇). See LNZHB, vol. 8, 660.

42. One *liang* was equivalent to five *xun*, and five *xun* was equivalent to about 10 yards. See *Liji*, "Za Ji," in SSJZS, vol. 2, 43/341C, 1569C; translated in Legge, *Li Chi*, vol. 2, 172.

43. The eight characters at the beginning of this sentence and in the equivalent section of the *Hanshi waizhuan* appear to be corrupt. Also see Hightower, *Han Shih Wai Chuan*, 14.

44. The first phrase (literally, "You have not received early orders," i.e., "you have not yet been ordered by your parents to marry") differs significantly from the text in the *Hanshi waizhuan* version of this tale. One of the rites connected with marriage was making an inquiry about the name of one's future spouse. See Wang Zhaoyuan's comments in LNZHB, vol. 5, 525; and *Ili* in SSJZS, vol. 1, 4/18A, 962; translated in John Steele, *The I-li* (London: Probsthain, 1917), 19.

45. *Odes, Zhou Nan*, "Han Guang," Mao no. 9. Translation based on Legge, *The Chinese Classics*, vol. 4, 15. This ode is also cited in the conclusion to the *Hanshi waizhuan* version of this story.

46. Zhao covered the northern part of modern-day Shanxi province, the southern part of modern-day Hebei province, and part of modern-day Henan. Zhao Jianzi was the chief of the Zhao lineage in Jin who, from 497 BCE onward, headed the state of Jin. He is also mentioned in LNZ 3.11. In 453 BCE, the state of Jin was divided into Zhao, Wei, and Han. In 403 BCE, the heads of those states were officially recognized and allowed to adopt the title of marquis. See *Shiji* 43, 1786–1793.

47. The Nine Rivers refers to rivers in the area of the Yangzi River, and may refer specifically to the rivers that flow into Lake Dongting, such as the Xiang and the Yuan. See speculation on their identification in *Shangshu*, "Yu Gong," translated in Legge, *The Chinese Classics*, vol. 3, 113–114. The Three Huai may refer to three islets in the Huai River. See *Odes, Xiao Ya*, "Gu Zhong," Mao no. 208; translated in Legge, *The Chinese Classics*, vol. 4, 367.

48. I follow Wang Zhaoyuan here. See LNZHB, vol. 5, 528.

49. Murdered innocents were thought to remain on earth and vex the living.

50. Juan seems to have been buying time with this argument. As the ending of this tale suggests, Jianzi's plan to execute the ferryman seems to have been dropped for good.

51. The Ji River disappeared in 1852 when the Yellow River changed its course northward and took over its bed.

52. Tang (r. 1766–1752 BCE) was the founder of the Shang dynasty. He is said to have conquered Jie, the last evil king of the Xia. See LNZ 1.5.

53. King Wu (r. 1049/45–1043 BCE) is traditionally said to have defeated Zhow, the last evil ruler of the Shang (also called the Yin) dynasty. Mount Hua is located in the eastern part of present-day Shaanxi province, and the southern slopes abut the upper part of the Luo River. See *Shiji* 4, 130.

54. After Wang Zhaoyuan, reading *a* (阿) as *ge* (舸). See LNZHB, vol. 5, 529.

55. The presentation of gifts, called either *nacai* or *bicai,* was one of the six rites of marriage. See *Yili* in SSJZS, vol. 1, 4/17A–18A; translated in Steele, *The I-li,* 18. Also see *Zuo zhuan*, Zhuang 24; translated in Legge, *The Chinese* Classics, vol. 5, 107–108. On this passage, Legge says, "The *bi* (幣), used properly of gifts of silks, may also comprehend other offerings,—such as gems."

56. *Odes, Da* Ya, "Quan E," Mao no. 252. Translation based on Legge, *The Chinese Classics,* vol. 4, 491.

57. Zhongmou was located in modern-day Hebei province near Taihe. The term *zai* (宰), "district magistrate," is also often defined as a "steward."

58. This incident of ca. 492 BCE is mentioned in "Dao Ying," *Huainanzi.* See Lau, ed., *A Concordance to the* Huainanzi, 12/111/9–13; translated in Major et al., *The* Huainanzi, 457; as well as in *Hanshi waizhuan* , 6/15A–B; translated in Hightower, *Han Shih Wai Chuan,* 217–218; *Zuo zhuan,* Ai 5; translated in Legge, *The Chinese Classics,* vol. 5, 806; *Lunyu* XVII:7; translated in Legge, *The Chinese Classics,* vol. 1, 321; and *Shiji* 47, 1924, translated by Hsien-yi Yang and Gladys Yang, *Selections from Records of the Historian* (Beijing: Foreign Language Press, 1979), 13.

59. On the term translated here as "taken into custody" *shou* (收), see A. F. P. Hulsewe, *Remnants of Ch'in Law: An Annotated Translation of the Ch'in Legal and Administrative Rules of the 3rd Century B.C. Discovered in Yunmeng Prefecture, Hu-pei Province in 1975* (Leiden: Brill, 1985), 51, note 10.

60. Xiangzi, otherwise known as Zhao Xiangzi (d. 475 BCE), was the son of Zhao Jianzi. Since this incident occurred while Zhao Jianzi was still alive and in charge, Xiangzi is probably a mistake for Jianzi. Jianzi, a high minister of Jin, headed the government and is thus referred to here as "ruler."

61. Here, following the variant noted by Gu Guangqi, I read *chu* (出) as *shi* (使). See LNZHB, vol. 3, 309.

62. *Odes, Da Ya,* "Lu Xiao," Mao no. 173. Translation based on Legge, *The Chinese Classics,* vol. 4, 274.

63. "Lady" (姬 *ji*) was the title of a high-ranking concubine who shared some of the same privileges as wives. See LNZ 5.4 for another example.

64. King Wei of Qi reigned ca. 356–317 BCE.

65. See *Shiji* 46, 1888. The last five words in this sentence were drawn from a *Wenxuan* commentary and restored to the text. See LNZHB, vol. 7, 505.

66. Jimo was a city in Qi located in present-day Pingdu county in Shandong province. E was a city in Qi located southeast of present-day Yanggu county in Shandong province.

67. For the phrase "I waited upon you in your retiring room," see Chen Hanzhang, LNZHB, vol. 8, 663.

68. Liuxia Hui, a virtuous minister from the state of Lu, is said to have offered his own body as a source of warmth for a cold beggar woman without compromising his purity. See discussion in the commentary of the ode "Xiang Bo," in *Odes, Xiao Ya,* "Xiang Bo," Mao no. 200, in SSJZS, vol. 1, 12.3/188B.

69. This proverb warns against innocent actions that may look suspicious to others.

70. The widowed wife most likely refers to the story of Qi Liang's widow. See LNZ 4.8.

71. Some commentators believe that this reference may refer to Duke Wen of Lu's wife, a woman of the Jiang clan known as Ai Jiang, whose son was murdered in a succession struggle. But this identification seems unlikely, since in that story it is Ai Jiang, and not a fugitive officer, who weeps in the marketplace. See *Zuo zhuan,* Wen 18; translated in Legge, *The Chinese Classics,* vol. 5, 282. This event may also refer to an incident in the life of Wu Zixu, for which, see *Zhanguo ce,* in SBCK, vol. 14, 3/44A; translated in James Irving Crump, *Chan-kuo Tse,* 2nd ed., revised (San Francisco: Chinese Materials Center, 1979), 104; and an expanded version quoted in *Taiping yulan,* 827/7A.

72. Here she seems to be interpreting the lack of a Heavenly response as a negative judgment on her worthiness. Wang Zhaoyuan interprets the phrase differently: "No one was able to get redress." See LNZHB, vol. 5, 537.

73. This story, in which Boqi is calumniated by his stepmother and expelled by his father, is quoted in the *Qin Cao* in *Taiping yulan,* 511/9A–B.

74. The story of Shensheng is told in LNZ 7.7.

75. Capital cities during the Warring States period were often divided into two sections—the palace, which was the arena of the court and political authority, and the market, which was the nonofficial sphere where ordinary people, merchants, and craftsmen lived. The market was also the place where officials could make official announcements and stage public events, such as meting out rewards or punishments. To present Yu to the court and the market thus meant that she was rehabilitated in the presence of both the government and the people. On the political significance of the market in Warring States times, see Mark Edward Lewis, *The Construction of Space in Early China* (Albany: State University of New York Press, 2006), 147, 151, 160–164.

76. *Odes, Xiao Ya,* "Chu Ju," Mao no. 168. Translation based on Legge, *The Chinese Classics,* vol. 4, 264.

77. References to Yu "pointing to Heaven above" and Wei overcoming Qin are not specifically discussed in this biography, which suggests the possibility that sections are missing from the received text.

78. Wuyan village is east of present-day Dongping county in Shandong province. King Xuan of Qi reigned from 319 to 301 BCE. See another version of this story in Liu Xiang's *Xinxu* in SBCK, vol. 17, 2/12B–14A.

79. She means that she would like to enter the king's harem, which was located in the rear palace. Furthermore, even a ruler's principal consort would describe her wifely duty as "sweeping and sprinkling."

80. The Sima Gates were the four guarded gates outside of the palace. See Yan Shigu's comment in Ban Gu, *Hanshu* (Beijing: Zhonghua shuju, 1962), 9, 286, note 10; and discussion in Homer Dubs, *The History of the Former Han Dynasty* (Baltimore: Waverly Press, 1944), vol. 2, 316, note 6.9.

81. Several early texts suggest that text is missing from the current version of this tale. See Liang Duan, LNZHB, vol. 7, 509; parallel text in Liu Xiang's *Xinxu* in D. C. Lau, *A Concordance to the* Xinxu (Hong Kong: Commercial Press, 1992), 2.20/12/6; and Li Shan's commentary to Fu Yi's (ca. 35–90 CE) "Rhapsody on Dance," in Xiao Tong, *Wenxuan* (Beijing: Zhonghua shuju, 1981), 17/16A.

82. I follow Liang Duan here, emending *xi* (喜) to *shan* (善). See LNZHB, vol. 5, 6/13B, 510.

83. I follow Liang Duan's rendering of these lines. An alternative reading is that her skill lay in the ability to become invisible. But given the preponderance of early references to riddles in contrast to the absence of those concerning invisibility, Liang's interpretation seems more likely. See discussion in Shimomi Takao, *Ryū kō Retsujoden no Kenkyū* (Tokyo: Tōkaidō daigaku shuppankai, 1989), 729–731. For an example of using riddles as a means of remonstrance, see Lau, ed., *A Concordance to the* Lüshi chunqiu, "Chong Yan," 18.2/110/.3; translated in Knoblock and Riegel, *The Annals of Lü Buwei*, 445–446.

84. Here I follow Xiao Daoguan, LNZHB, vol. 8, 299, though the text remains problematic.

85. An early reference to a riddle book of the same title can be found in *Hanshu* 30, 1753.

86. On the cultural significance of towers and raised platforms, see Lewis, *The Construction of Space in Early China*, 152–159; and Wu Hung, *Monumentality in Chinese Art and Architecture*, 102–104. For a discussion of the term "ruby" (琅玕 *langgan*), see John Knoblock, *Xunzi: A Translation and Study of the Complete Works*, 3 vols. (Stanford: Stanford University Press, 1982), vol. 3, 44, 314, note 112.

87. Lady Wuyan is a name for Zhongli Chun derived from her place of origin.

88. "Loving Matron" (慈母 *cimu*) was an official title for a nurse who assisted in the raising of a child, or a foster mother in the case of an orphan. She was selected from concubines or other suitable women. See "Nei Ze" and "Zeng Wen," *Liji*, in SSJZS, vol. 2, 28/241B, 1469B; 18/165C, 1393C; translated in Legge, *Li Chi*, vol. 1, 473, 326–327.

89. *Odes, Xiao Ya*, "Jing Jing Zhe E," Mao no. 176. Translation based on Legge, *The Chinese Classics*, vol. 4, 280.

90. The term "neck lumps" (瘤 *liu*) most likely refers to scrofula, which is a tuberculosis infection of the skin on the neck. Two medical manuscripts (ca. 168 BCE) found at Mawangdui, the *Zubi shiyi mai jiujing* (Cauterization Canon of the Eleven Vessels of the Foot and Forearm) and the *Shiwen* (Ten Questions), refer to ailments called *lou* (瘻), a word that is interchangeable with *liu* (瘤). See *Mawangdui Han mu boshu*, vol. 4 (Beijing: Wenwu chubanshe, 1985), translation and notes in Donald J. Harper, *Early Chinese Medical Literature: The Mawangdui Medical Manuscripts* (London: Kegan Paul International, 1998), 195–196, 410. In an earlier translation by Albert Richard O'Hara (*The Position of Woman in Early China: According to the* Lieh Nü Chuan *"The Biographies of Chinese Women"* [Taipei: Mei Ya Publications, 1971]), the word *su* (宿) is construed as the woman's surname. *Su* can indeed signify a surname, but if that were the case here, one would expect the term *liu* ("lump") to precede *su* as a modifier. Thus I have construed the meaning of the term *su* as "long-term" or "chronic," as in the term *suji* (宿疾) or "chronic illness," and by extension "large" (i.e., developed over a long period of time). Dongguo refers to the area east of the city wall in Qi's capital.

91. King Min of Qi reigned from 300 to 284 BCE.

92. I am grateful to Eric Henry for pointing out that in eleventh-century Viet Nam, Emperor Ly Thanh Tong (r. 1054–1072) chose the concubine Bac Ninh because she continued to pick mulberry leaves rather than stare at his imperial entourage. See Tran Trong Kim, *Viet Nam Su Luoc* (Saigon: Tan Viet, 1964), 100–101.

93. The term for "a fallen woman" is *bennü* (奔女). It specifically refers to a woman who elopes and marries without her parents' consent.

94. She is quoting Confucius here. See *Analects* XVII:2; translated in Legge, *The Chinese Classics*, vol. 1, 318.

95. For Yao and Shun, see LNZ 1.1; for Jie and Zhow, see LNZ 7.1, 7.2. I transliterate 紂 as Zhow to distinguish this name from that of the dynastic house of Zhou.

96. This event occurred in 288 BCE. See *Shiji* 5, 212; 46, 1898–1900.

97. See *Shiji* 46, 1900–1901, and *Zhanguo ce*, in SBCK, vol. 14, 9/19A; translated in Crump, *Chan-kuo Ts'e*, 526–529.

98. *Odes, Xiao Ya*, "Jing Jing Zhe E," Mao no. 176. Translation based on Legge, *The Chinese Classics*, vol. 4, 279.

99. Jimo was a city in Qi located in present-day Pingdu county in Shandong province.

100. King Xiang reigned from 283 to 265 BCE.

101. This conversation is almost identical to one attributed to Zhao Jianzi (fl. 518 BCE) and a certain Yang Yin as recorded in *Shuoyuan*, SBCK, vol. 17, 8/22B–23A.

102. A "paired-eye fish" is a flatfish. A flatfish, such as the flounder, has both eyes on one side of its head. It was thought that these fish functioned as if they had only one eye and thus needed to swim in pairs to survive.

103. See LNZ 2.5.

104. To attract worthy men to Yan, Guo Wei suggested that the king treat him with great esteem so that those who surpassed Guo in talent would feel assured that they would be well treated in Yan. His strategy was successful, and Yan attracted Yue Yi. See *Shiji* 34, 1558; translated in Nienhauser, *The Grand Scribe's Records*, vol. V.1, 179–180.

105. Because mathematics was held in such low esteem, once the duke honored this humble man, other more worthy scholars were encouraged to offer their services as well. See a similar account in *Hanshi waizhuan* in SBCK, vol. 17, 3/10A–B; translated in Hightower, *Han Shih Wai Chuan*, 95–96.

106. This story is told of Duke Zhuang of Qi in Lau, ed., *A Concordance to the* Huainanzi, 18/199/24–18/200/10; translated in Major et al., *Huaninanzi*, 750–751, and in *Hanshi waizhuan* in SBCK, vol. 3, 8/18A; translated in Hightower, *Han Shih Wai Chuan*, 288. The duke was so impressed with the bravery of a mantis who stood his ground when confronted with the duke's chariot that the duke backed up his vehicle to avoid crushing the mantis and thereby won the allegiance of brave soldiers.

107. See *Xinxu* in SBCK, vol. 3, 5/14A–14B. She was a town located in present-day She county in Henan.

108. *Odes, Qin Feng,* "Ju Lin," Mao no. 126. Translation based on Legge, *The Chinese Classics,* vol. 4, 190.

109. It is not clear what is specifically designated by a "town in the district" (縣邑), but it may refer to the capital of the royal domain of Chu. According to the *Zhugong jiushi* of Yu Zhigu (Tang dynasty), Zhuang Zhi's given name was Xing (娙). See Yu Zhigu, *Zhugong jiushi*, in *Congshu jicheng chubian*, ed. Wang Yunwu, vol. 3175 (Shanghai: Shangwu yinshuguan, 1936), 3/37. King Qingxiang of Chu (r. 298–263 BCE) was the son of King Huai of Chu (r. 328–299 BCE). King Huai had imperiled the state through an unwise alliance with the state of Qin that was crafted by the Qin diplomat Zhang Yi. King Qingxiang continued his father's unsound policies and was known for banishing the loyal statesman and poet Qu Yuan (see further notes below). This biography attributes to King Qingxiang actions that are generally associated with King Huai.

110. Qu Yuan was a loyal minister to King Huai of Chu. He was slandered at court, then banished. See his biography in *Shiji* 84, 2481–2503; translated in Nienhauser, *The Grand Scribe's Records*, vol. 7, 297–309.

111. King Huai rather than King Qingxiang was the target of Zhang Yi's treachery. Zhang Yi tricked Chu into attacking Qi, which had been an ally of Chu. Ultimately, King Huai died abroad due to his ill-placed trust in Qin and the advice of Zilan, King Huai's youngest son, who was later made King Qingxiang's prime minister. See his biography in *Shiji* 70, 2279–2299; translated in Nienhauser, *The Grand Scribe's Records*, vol. 7, 123–138.

112. Tang probably refers to Gaotangguan (高唐觀) in Yunmeng.

113. The three difficulties refer to the conditions alluded to in the riddle concerning the fish, the dragon, and the wall.

114. The Yan River flowed from the northeast of present-day Baokang county in Hubei.
115. Zheng Xiu was the concubine of King Huai and not of King Qingxiang. See *Shiji* 84, 2484; 40, 1725; the first citation is translated in Nienhauser, *The Grand Scribe's Records*, vol. 7, 297. The right side was regarded as the position of honor.
116. She violated ritual rules by disobeying her mother and eloping with the king.
117. *Odes, Bei Feng*, "Bei Feng," Mao no. 41. Translation based on Legge, *The Chinese Classics*, vol. 4, 67; and Arthur Waley, *The Book of Songs* (New York: Grove Press, 1960), 36.
118. According to the *Hanshu*, at the time of the Shang and the Zhou dynasties, "In the winter . . . the women when dwelling in the same lanes did their spinning together at nights. . . .They were required to work in groups, and thereby economize on the expense of light and heat." See *Hanshu* 24A, 1121, translated in Nancy Lee Swann, *Food and Money in Ancient China: The Earliest Economic History of China to A.D. 25* (Princeton: Princeton University Press, 1950), 129.
119. A similar story is told in *Zhanguo ce* in SBCK, vol. 14, 3/27B; translated in Crump, *Chan-kuo Ts'e*, 84; and in *Shiji* 71, 2316, translated in Nienhauser, *The Grand Scribe's Records*, vol. 7, 151–152.
120. Sprinkling was a routine chore used to reduce dust in domestic areas.
121. The text here says "eastern wall." Wang Zhaoyuan, citing the *Zhanguo ce* version of this text (see citation above), points out that here this term means "all four walls" of the woman's house. See LNZHB, vol. 5, 557. Crump translates a variation on this line found in the *Shiji* (citation above), "I cannot buy a candle but, fortunately, you cannot use up all the light from yours."
122. *Odes, Da Ya*, "Ban," Mao no. 254. Translation based on Legge, *The Chinese Classics*, vol. 4, 500.
123. For a full account of Lord Chunyu (ca. 216–150 BCE), see *Shiji* 105, 2794–2817. Also see *Hanshu* 23, 1097–1098, translated in A. F. P. Hulsewe, *Remnants of Han Law* (Leiden: E. J. Brill, 1955), 334–335; *Hanshu* 30, 1780; Michael Loewe, *A Bibliographic Dictionary of the Qin, Former Han and Xin Periods (221 BC–AD 24)* (Leiden: Brill, 2000), 51–53; "The Physician Chunyu Yi and His Historical Background," in *En suivant la Voie Royale: mélanges offerts en homage á Léon Vandermeersch*, ed. Jacques Gernet, Marc Kalinowski, and Jean-Pierre Diény (Paris: Ecole française d'extrême-orient, 1997), 297–313; R. F. Bridgman, "Le Médecine dans le Chine Antique," *Mélanges chinois et bouddhiques* 10, no. 1 (1955): 1–213; and the book-length study by Elisabeth Hsu, *Pulse Diagnosis in Early Chinese Medicine: The Telling Touch* (Cambridge, England: Cambridge University Press, 2010).
124. Emperor Wen reigned from 180 to 157 BCE. Hsu suggests that Chuyu Yi had been sued (or victimized) by a patient he had refused to treat. See Hsu, *Pulse Diagnosis in Early Chinese Medicine*, 49.
125. I follow Hulsewe's rendering of "detain," for the term *ji* (繫). See Hulsewe, *Remnants of Han Law*, 74.
126. This case occurred in 167 BCE. Tiying's memorial, in various versions, is cited in the "Treatise on Punishments and Laws" in *Hanshu* 23, 1098–1100, and translated in

Hulsewe, *Remnants of Han Law*, 334–335. The abrogation of punishments by mutilation is also mentioned in *Shiji* 10, 427; and *Hanshu* 4, 125, translated in Dubs, *History of the Former Han Dynasty*, vol. 2, 255. For speculation on the legal process connected with Tiying's memorial, see Oba Osamu, "The Ordinances on Fords and Passes Excavated from Han Tomb Number 247, Zhangjiashan," *Asia Major*, 3rd series, 14, part 2 (2001): 119–141. In Li Shan's commentary to the examination essay of Wang Rong, he cites a lost passage from the *Lienü zhuan* biography of Tiying, in which Tiying is said to have sung two odes—Mao nos. 96, 132. See *Wenxuan* 36/10A–11B.

127. These reforms differ from those mentioned in *Hanshu* 23.

128. *Odes, Da Ya*, "Ban," Mao no. 254. Translation based on Legge, *The Chinese Classics*, vol. 4, 500.

7. THE DEPRAVED AND FAVORED

1. Given that all of the other prefaces are ten lines long, Gu Guangqi (ca. 1766–1835) conjectures that four lines of the preface are missing. See LNZHB, vol. 3, 279.

2. *Guoyu*, 2 vols. (Shanghai: Guji chubanshe, 1978), "Jinyu," part 1, item 2, relays that when Jie attacked the state of Youshi (有施), the people of Youshi gave Mo Xi to Jie. In his annotations, Wei Zhao (204–273) states that Xi is the clan name of the state of Youshi. According to traditional historiography, Jie was the last evil king of the Xia dynasty, the period that is said to have preceded the Shang (ca. 1554–1045 BCE). See *Shiji* 2, 88, translated in William Nienhauser et al., *The Grand Scribe's Records*, 6 vols. (Bloomington: Indiana University Press, 1994–2006), vol. 1, 38. On the debate concerning the existence of a dynasty that referred to itself as the Xia, see Michael Loewe and Edward L. Shaughnessy, eds., *The Cambridge History of Ancient China: From the Origins of the Civilization to 221 B.C.* (Cambridge, England: Cambridge University Press, 1999), 71–72.

3. In early China, "wine" was perhaps closer to a kind of ale, as it was made of fermented grains rather than grapes. Methods for making much more potent distilled rather than fermented alcohol require more sophisticated equipment and processes that were not developed until a much later period, possibly between the sixth and twelfth centuries. See Joseph Needham, *Science and Civilisation in China*, vol. V, part 4 (Cambridge, England: Cambridge University Press, 1980), 78–79, 121–158; Mu-Chou Poo, "The Use and Abuse of Wine in Ancient China," *Journal of the Economic and Social History of the Orient* 42, no. 2 (May 1999): 123–151; and Roel Sterckx, *Food, Sacrifice, and Sagehood in Early China* (Cambridge, England: Cambridge University Press, 2011), 95–106.

4. Long Feng almost certainly refers to a figure called Guan Longfeng (關龍逢), who is mentioned in the same historical context in the *Bamboo Annals* and the *Hanshi waizhuan*. He is said to have served as an official of the Xia dynasty. See *Zhushu jinian*, "Di Gui"; translated in James Legge, *The Chinese Classics*, 5 vols. (1893; reprint,

Hong Kong: University of Hong Kong Press, 1960), vol. 3, "Prolegomena," 126; and *Hanshi waizhuan* in SBCK, vol. 3, 4/1A; translated in James Hightower, *Han Shih Wai Chuan: Han Ying's Illustrations of the Didactic Application of the Classic of Songs* (Cambridge, Mass.: Harvard University Press, 1952), 125–126.

5. See *Shangshu*, "Tang Shi," translated in Legge, *The Chinese Classics*, vol. 3, 175, and *Shiji* 3, 95, translated in Nienhauser, *The Grand Scribe's Records*, vol. 1, 44.

6. Uttering words that were regarded as inauspicious was roughly equivalent to uttering a curse; that is, making a statement that carried with it a supernaturally injurious effect.

7. Tang was the founder of the Shang dynasty and the leader of the rebellion against Jie. See *Shiji* 2, 88; translated in Nienhauser, *The Grand Scribe's Records*, vol. 1, 38.

8. Mingtiao was located in present-day Henan province, north of the Yellow River and northeast of Kaifeng. Liang Duan notes the possibility that the concubines mentioned here might be associated with the two women mentioned by Shen Yue (502–557 CE) in his annotations to the *Bamboo Annals* passage concerning Jie's downfall. See *Zhushu jinian*, "Di Gui"; translated in Legge, *The Chinese Classics*, vol. 3, "Prolegomena," 125–126.

9. There is a great deal of debate over the identification of the place where Jie ended his days. *Shiji* 2, 88, claims that he died in Mingtiao, where he had been exiled. Nanchao is associated with Chaoxian in present-day Anhui province. Compare this account with the *Shangshu*, "Announcement of Zhong Hui," translated in Legge, *The Chinese Classics*, vol. 3, 177–183. For detailed discussion, see Shimomi Takao, *Ryū kō Retsujoden no Kenkyū* (Tokyo: Tōkaidō daigaku shuppankai, 1989), 778–780.

10. *Odes, Da Ya*, "Zhan Yang," Mao no. 264. Translation based on Legge, *The Chinese Classics*, vol. 4, 561.

11. In this chapter, the "man of discernment's" comments are missing from biographies 7.1–7.7, 7.9–7.10, and 7.12–7.15.

12. According to Sima Qian, Xiahou is the clan name of Jie, based on the name of the state of Xia, which had been given to his ancestor as a feudal territory. See *Shiji* 1, 45; 2, 89; translated in Nienhauser, *The Grand Scribe's Records*, vol. 1, 17, 38.

13. *Guoyu*, "Jinyu," part 1, item 2, states that when the last ruler of the Shang attacked the state of Yousu (有蘇), the Yousu lineage gave Da Ji to him. Wei Zhao relates that Ji (己, not to be confused with 姬) is the clan name of the state of Yousu. I romanize the name of the tyrant 紂 as Zhow to distinguish his name from the dynastic house of Zhou (周). The *Hanshu* mentions that Emperor Cheng (r. 32–7 BCE) owned a screen that depicted the story of Da Ji, the favorite concubine of King Zhow of the Shang dynasty. See *Hanshu* 100A, 4200–4201.

14. Yin is another name for the Shang dynasty (ca. 1554–1045 BCE) and seems to have been used not by the Shang themselves but as a term devised in the Zhou. See Loewe and Shaughnessy, *The Cambridge History of Ancient China*, 232–233. Zhow, the last ruler of the Shang, is also called Di Xin (帝辛) and reigned from 1086 to 1045 BCE.

According to the *Shiji*, the name Zhow, which means "cruel," was an epithet conferred on him by the people. See *Shiji* 3, 105 (which this biography follows closely); translated in Nienhauser, *The Grand Scribe's Records*, vol. 1, 49.

15. The *Shiji* states that he ordered his music master, Shi Juan, to create these musical and dance compositions. See *Shiji* 3, 105; translated in Nienhauser, *The Grand Scribe's Records*, vol. 1, 49. According to Takigawa, the "northern district" refers to the area north of Zhaoge, the former Shang capital, located in present-day Henan, northeast of Qi county. See Takigawa Kametarū, *Shiki kaichū kōshō* (Taibei: Hongye shuju, 1977), 3/26.

16. A bronze inscription ca. 1005–978 BCE notes the role of alcohol in the fall of the Shang. See Sterckx, *Food, Sacrifice, and Sagehood*, 96–97.

17. Bi Gan was Zhow's paternal uncle and may have served as Zhow's Lesser Tutor. See Nienhauser, *The Grand Scribe's Records*, vol. 1, 51, note 129.

18. According to *Shiji* 3, 108, the Viscount of Ji was either an uncle or a half-brother of Zhow. See Nienhauser, *The Grand Scribe's Records*, vol. 1, 51, note 128. He served as Zhow's Grand Tutor. In an effort to escape from Zhow, he feigned madness but was soon imprisoned. The Viscount of Wei was the elder half-brother of Zhow. See *Shiji*, 38, 1607; translated in Nienhauser, *The Grand Scribe's Records*, vol. 5.1, 267. After unsuccessful attempts to reason with Zhow and in an effort to preserve the ancestral sacrifices, the Viscount of Wei fled after the death of Bi Gan.

19. Muye was near Zhow's capital at Zhaoge, about thirty miles south of present-day Anyang in Henan province. For more information on this battle, see Loewe and Shaughnessy, *The Cambridge History of Ancient China*, 309–310. King Wu of Zhou reigned from 1049/45 to 1043 BCE.

20. The troops refused to fight.

21. Most sources mention the Lu (Deer) Tower, not the Lin Tower. For a discussion of jade suits, see Wu Hung, *The Art of the Yellow Springs: Understanding Chinese Tombs* (Honolulu: University of Hawai'i Press, 2010), 131–138.

22. *The Book of Documents*, "Mu Shi"; translation based on Legge, *The Chinese Classics*, vol. 3, 302–303.

23. *Odes, Xiao Ya*, "Qiao Yan," Mao no. 198. Translation based on Legge, *The Chinese Classics*, vol. 4, 341.

24. Bao is a place name, thus her name can also be rendered, "the lady of the Si clan who came from Bao." Bao was located northwest of modern Hanzhong in Shaanxi province. *Guoyu*, "Jinyu," part 1, item 2, states that when the last ruler of the Western Zhou attacked Youbao (有襃), the people gave Bao Si to him. (Some early Chinese place names that simultaneously function as clan names are preceded with the word *you*, possibly meaning "possessing." Youbao and Bao are thus the same place.) Wei Zhao relates that Si is the clan name of the state of Youbao. Si was also the clan name of the ruling house of Xia. King You of Zhou reigned from 781 to 771 BCE. This story is also told in *Guoyu*, "Zhengyu," item 1 in SBCK, vol. 4, 16/6B–8A; *Lüshi chunqiu*, "Yi Si,"

in D. C. Lau, ed., *Concordance to the* Lüshi chunqiu (Hong Kong: Commercial Press, 1994), 22.3/146/3; translated in John Knoblock and Jeffrey Riegel, *The Annals of Lü Buwei* (Stanford: Stanford University Press, 2000), 573–574; and *Shiji* 4, 147–149; translated in Nienhauser, *The Grand Scribe's Records*, vol. 1, 73–74. For a modern historical account of this story, see Li Feng, *Landscape and Power in Early China: The Crisis and Fall of the Western Zhou, 1045–771 BC* (Cambridge, England: Cambridge University Press, 2006), 193–232. For the term that I translate as "female slave" (童妾 tongqie), though the word *tong* means "youth," it also means "slave" or "servant," while the word *qie*, which is often translated as "concubine," also means "female." Further, the *Shuowen jiezi* states that women who had undergone criminal punishment and been made into government slaves were referred to as *qie*. See Xu Shen, *Shuowen jiezi zhu*, 3 vols., ed. Tang Kejing (Hunan: Yuelu shushe, 1997), vol. 1, 370–371.

25. The Xia dynasty was the period that is said to have preceded the Shang (ca. 1554–1045 BCE).

26. The technique he used was oracle-bone divination, which involved applying heat to bones and interpreting the resulting pattern of cracks. See Loewe and Shaughnessy, *The Cambridge History of Ancient China*, 236–245.

27. The *Guoyu* places the word *er* (而) after the word *li* (黎).

28. The suburban sacrifices were made to Heaven and earth.

29. King Li of Zhou reigned from 857/53 to 842/28 BCE.

30. Nudity served as an apotropaic.

31. According to ancient notions of child development, girls lost their baby teeth around the age of seven *sui* (age six by modern reckoning). For references, see note 32 below.

32. "Taking the hairpin" was the ritual acknowledgment of female adulthood and was generally marked at a girl's betrothal. Because the text states that the girl had no husband, the phrase simply indicates that she had come of age. Early Chinese texts note that girls achieved menarche around fourteen *sui*. See *Hanshi waizhuan*, in SBCK vol. 3, 1/9A–B; translated in Hightower, *Han Shih Wai Chuan*, 27–28.

33. King Xuan of Zhou reigned from 827/25 to 782 BCE.

34. According to Bray (see later in this note), there are no early images of winnowing baskets. Much later illustrations suggest that a winnowing basket tended to be a broad object shaped like a round tray or dustpan, with a rounded lip at the top and square and flat at the bottom. It is hard to imagine that anything apart from a long tubular shape would be useful as a quiver, though it is possible that the shape of a quiver could resemble an elongated variation of a winnowing basket. Likewise, it is hard to imagine anything but a broad object serving as a winnowing basket. I therefore follow the *Hanshu* reading of "grass/reed" (萁 *ji*) for "winnowing basket" (箕 *ji*). See *Hanshu* 27, part 3.1, 1465–1466. It is also possible, however, that (箕 *ji*) simply refers to a quiver made from basketry materials. On winnowing baskets, see Francesca Bray, *Science and Civilisation in China*, vol. 6, part II, gen. ed. Joseph Needham (Cambridge, England: Cambridge University Press, 1984), 363; and Dieter Kuhn, *Chinese Baskets and Mats* (Wiesbaden: Franz Steiner Verlag, 1980), 72–73.

35. Liang Duan surmises that the word "daughter" is missing from the text here. See LNZHB, vol. 7, 533.

36. See *Guoyu*, "Jinyu," part 1, item 2, in SBCK, vol. 14, 7/7A.

37. Shen was a state that lay in the vicinity of Nanyang in Henan. Li Feng distinguishes this Shen as located south of the Western Zhou capital of Hao from another Shen, namely Western Shen, that lay west of the capital (in the northern part of the Ping-liang region of modern Gansu province), and speculates that Yijiu is associated with Western Shen. See Li Feng, *Landscape and Power in Early China*, 220–228.

38. The Marquis of Shen was the father of King You's first queen and the maternal grand-father of the expelled former heir apparent of King You, namely, Yijiu. Zeng was the name of a state and also written as 鄫. It was attacked by Zhou troops in 780 BCE. See *Zhushu jinian* in Legge, *The Chinese Classics*, vol. 3, "Prolegomena," 157. It may have been located in near present-day Tengxian and Ningyang in Shandong. See Li Feng, *Landscape and Power in Early China*, 317. The Quan Rong are also known as the Western Rong because their territory lay northwest of the Zhou state.

39. Li Mountain was about 25 miles east of Xi'an in modern Shaanxi province.

40. King Ping of Zhou reigned from 770 to 720 BCE.

41. *Odes, Xiao Ya*, "Zheng Yue," Mao no. 192. Translation based on Legge, *The Chinese Classics*, vol. 4, 318.

42. In point of fact, although the Marquis of Shen deposed King You, he did not put an end to the ancestral sacrifices of the house of Zhou.

43. As a daughter of the ruler of Qi, her clan name is Jiang, while "Xuan" refers to Duke Xuan of Wey, who reigned from 718 to 699 BCE. For events connected with Xuan Jiang, see *Zuo zhuan*, Huan 16 (696 BCE), Min 2 (660 BCE); translated in Legge, *The Chinese Classics*, vol. 5, 66–67, 129. For a study of Xuan Jiang in relation to Mao's commentary on the *Odes,* see Anne Behnke Kinney, "The Book of Odes as a Source for Women's History," in *Overt and Covert Treasures: Essays on the Sources for Chinese Women's History*, ed. Clara Wing-chung Ho (Hong Kong: Chinese University of Hong Kong Press, 2012), 61–111.

44. Officials displayed flags on their vehicles to signify their ranks.

45. Duke Hui of Wey reigned from 699 to 669 BCE.

46. Following Duke Yi (r. 668–661 BCE), Duke Dai of Wey reigned from 660 to 659 BCE. Earlier, during the reign of Shuo, Duke Hui (699–669 BCE), a figure named Qianmou seized the throne and held it for eight years (696–688 BCE). If this is counted as a separate reign, and if the same is done for the reign of Shuo after his reinstatement (688–669), then this would provide some basis for saying "five reigns."

47. *Odes, Bei Feng*, "Ri Yue," Mao no. 29. Translation based on Legge, *The Chinese Classics*, vol. 4, 45.

48. Wen Jiang's first name means "cultured." It is a posthumous name. Jiang is her clan name. Although Wen Jiang's father is not named here, in all likelihood she was the daughter of Duke Xi of Qi (r. 730–698 BCE). Her marriage is noted in *Zuo zhuan*, Huan 3, translated in Legge, *The Chinese Classics*, vol. 5, 42–43. Duke Huan of Lu

reigned from 711 to 694 BCE. The present story is told in *Zuo zhuan*, Huan 18; translated in Legge, *The Chinese Classics*, vol. 5, 70; and in *Shiji* 32, 1483; translated in Nienhauser, *The Grand Scribe's Records*, vol. V.1, 52.

49. Duke Xiang of Qi, who was, in fact, a marquis, reigned from 697 to 686 BCE. At the time of his dalliance with his sister he was known as Prince Zhuer (諸兒).

50. Duke Li of Zheng reigned from 700 to 697 BCE; see *Zuo zhuan*, Huan 15; translated in Legge, *The Chinese Classics*, vol. 5, 64. At this time, having been ousted by the usurper Zhai Zhong, he fled his own state.

51. Propriety did not allow women to go outside of the borders of their husbands' states without good cause. This proviso was meant to safeguard women from sexual liaisons. See, for example, "The Minor Preface" to Mao no. 54, "Zai Chi," translated by Legge, *The Chinese Classics*, vol. 4, 45; and *Guliang zhuan*, Zhuang 5, in SSJZS vol. 2, 5/17C, 2381. When aristocratic men married, they were allotted rooms in their fathers' household where they would live with their wives. The word "room" thus became a metonym for "wife." See *Liji*, "Nei Ze," in SSJZS, vol. 2, 28/243B (including Zheng Xuan's note); translated in James Legge, *Li Chi: Book of Rites*, 2 vols. (1885; reprint, New York: University Books, 1967), vol. 1, 478.

52. Pengsheng was the half-brother of Duke Xiang of Qi.

53. According to *Zuo zhuan*, Zhuang 22; translated in Legge, *The Chinese Classics*, vol. 5, 103, Wen Jiang lived another twenty-two years, until 672 BCE.

54. *Odes, Da Ya*, "Zhan Yang," Mao no. 264. Translation based on Legge, *The Chinese Classics*, vol. 4, 561.

55. Ai Jiang's first name means "sorrowful." Ai is her posthumous name. Jiang is her clan name. Duke Zhuang of Lu reigned from 693 to 662 BCE. This marriage took place in 670 BCE, in the twenty-fourth year of Duke Zhuang's reign. Also see *Zuo zhuan*, Zhuang 23; translated in Legge, *The Chinese Classics*, vol. 5, 106. Ai Jiang's father was Duke Xiang of Qi (see LNZ 7.5). Duke Zhuang of Lu was therefore marrying the daughter of the man who had murdered his father, Duke Huan of Lu. For discussion of this account in the *Zuo zhuan*, see Wai-yee Li, *The Readability of the Past in Early Chinese Historiography* (Cambridge, Mass.: Harvard University Asia Center, 2007), 114–116.

56. On this event, see *Zuo zhuan*, Zhuang 22; translated in Legge, *The Chinese Classics*, vol. 5, 104. This visit was contrary to ritual because a ruler should have sent an officer to present gifts to Ai Jiang rather than going himself. According to Legge, it was also irregular that he should have married so soon after the death of his mother, which occurred earlier that year. The haste may have been due to his mother's insistence on her deathbed that he marry Ai Jiang, his mother's niece.

57. Shu Jiang's name means "third-born daughter of the Jiang clan."

58. *Zuo zhuan*, Zhuang 24; translated in Legge, *The Chinese Classics*, vol. 5, 107–108. Here the speaker is not Xiafu Buji but Yusun. The *Guoyu*, "Luyu," part 4, item 4, records the speech and the name (Xiafu Zhan rather than Buji) somewhat differently.

59. Duke Huan of Lu reigned from 711 to 694 BCE. On the renovations Duke Zhuang made to his father's temple, Legge says the following: "According to rule, the pillars were required to be of a very dark color, nearly black. The painting them red, it is understood, was to dazzle the young wife who would soon be appearing in the temple, and to propitiate the spirit of Huan, when the daughter of his murderer should be presented as the wife of his son!" See *Zuo zhuan*, Zhuang 23–24; translated in Legge, *The Chinese Classics*, vol. 5, 105–107.

60. Prince Qingfu and Prince Ya were full brothers but both half-brothers to Duke Zhuang. They both died at the behest of Duke Zhuang's full brother Ji You (also called Chengji You). See *Zuo zhuan*, Zhuang 32; Min 2, translated in Legge, *The Chinese Classics*, vol. 5, 121, 129.

61. Ziban, son of Duke Zhuang, was named Duke Zhuang's heir but was murdered by Qingfu in 662 BCE before succeeding to the throne. His mother was a woman named Meng Ren. See *Zuo zhuan*, Zhuang 32; translated in Legge, *The Chinese Classics*, vol. 5, 120–121.

62. Duke Min of Lu began his reign at age eight. He reigned from 661 to 660 BCE. He was the son of Duke Zhuang and Ai Jiang's younger half-sister, Shu Jiang. See *Zuo zhuan*, Min 2; translated in Legge, *The Chinese Classics*, vol. 5, 129. He was also murdered by Qingfu.

63. The *Zuo zhuan* does not mention Ai Jiang's role in this murder.

64. Bu Yi (or "Diviner Yi") was a disgruntled grandee who had had land taken from him by the duke's tutor. Wuwei was the name of a side gate of the palace. See *Zuo zhuan*, Min 2; translated in Legge, *The Chinese Classics*, vol. 5, 128.

65. Ju was a small state located in the vicinity of present-day Ju county in Shandong province. The state of Zhu, also referred to as Zou (鄒), was located in present-day Zou county in Shandong province.

66. Duke Huan of Qi reigned from 685 to 643 BCE. As hegemon, he helped to maintain order among the feudal lords. Duke Xi of Lu reigned from 659 to 627 BCE. He was the son of Duke Zhuang and a woman named Cheng Feng. See *Zuo zhuan*, Min 2; translated in Legge, *The Chinese Classics*, vol. 5, 131.

67. Details about Ai Jiang's death are less specific in the *Zuo zhuan* account of Min 2.

68. *Odes*, *Wang Feng*, "Zhong Gu You Tui," Mao no. 69. Translation based on Legge, *The Chinese Classics*, vol. 4, 116.

69. According to the *Zuo zhuan*, Li Ji was the daughter of the head of the Li Rong (驪戎), who held the rank of "baron" (男 *nan*) and the clan name Ji (姬). Her name thus refers to her affiliation with the Li, which in itself may be a place name, while Ji is her clan name. The Li Rong were a branch of the Western Rong, a non-Chinese people who lived west of the Chinese cultural sphere from early times onward. For early relations with the Western Rong, see *Shiji* 5, 174–178; translated in Nienhauser, *The Grand Scribe's Records*, vol. 1, 88–89; and Loewe and Shaughnessy, *The Cambridge History of Ancient China*, 921–924. The latter states that "Rong communities were

dispersed over a broad territory across the northern frontier of the Eastern Zhou and
. . . a large number of them had settled within or to the south of the state of Jin . . . .
By the mid-seventh century, the Rong, repeatedly defeated by Jin and hard pressed in
the north by the rapidly growing power of the Di, were for the most part incorporated
by Jin and Qi." Duke Xian of Jin reigned from 676 to 651 BCE. See the *Zuo zhuan*
account of this story in Zhuang 28, Xi 4, 9; translated in Legge, *The Chinese Classics*,
vol. 5, 114, 141–142, 154–155; and *Shiji* 39, 1640–1652; translated in Nienhauser, *The
Grand Scribe's Records*, vol. V.1, 303–317.

70. For the wife of Duke Mu of Qin, see LNZ 2.4.

71. For Chonger, later known as Duke Wen of Jin (r. 636–628 BCE), see LNZ 2.3, 2.4, 3.4.
For Yiwu, known as Duke Hui of Jin (r. 650–637 BCE), see LNZ 2.4, 5.3.

72. The *Zuo zhuan* states that Li Ji's younger sister bore Zhuozi. See Zhuang 28; translated
in Legge, *The Chinese Classics*, vol. 5, 114.

73. Quwo was a walled city located northeast of present-day Wenxi county in Shanxi. It
was the ancient site of an ancestral temple of Jin, which had been established in 746
BCE using territory taken from the Rong and Di people. It served as a secondary capital ruled by a collateral branch of the Jin line to shield against further incursions by
the Rong. In 678, Duke Wu of the junior Quwo branch replaced the mainline house
of Jin and received royal recognition as the duke of Jin. Duke Xian continued the
work of Duke Wu; that is, he annihilated all the branches of his clan that might have
been able to contest his authority. Thus, at the cost of massive bloodshed, he made Jin
into a great and powerful, unified state. See Mark Edward Lewis, *The Construction of
Space in Early China* (Albany: State University of New York Press, 2006), 140–141. Pu
was located northwest of present-day Xi county in Shanxi, while Erqu was northeast
of Ji county in Shanxi province. *Zuo zhuan*, Zhuang 28, assigns this proposal to two
officials.

74. This dialogue follows with some variation *Guoyu*, "Jinyu," part 1, item 6.

75. This dialogue follows with some variation *Guoyu*, "Jinyu," part 1, item 8.

76. Here I follow the wording of the *Guoyu*, which has *jiao li* (交利) rather than *fu li*
(父利).

77. For Zhow and King Wu, see LNZ 7.2.

78. Duke Wu (r. 678–677 BCE) was the first lord of Quwo to replace the mainline house
of Jin and receive official recognition to rule the entire state. See *Shiji* 39, 1635–1639;
translated in Nienhauser, *The Grand Scribe's Records*, vol. V.1, 302–303. He was Duke
Xian's father. Yi, a city in Jin south of Yicheng in Shanxi province, was once the capital
of Jin. It is where Earl Zhuang of Quwo slew Marquis Xiao of Jin (r. 739–724 BCE).
King Mu of Chu (r. 625–614 BCE) is said to have murdered his father, King Cheng
(r. 663–660 BCE), who had tried to remove him from the line of succession. See
Shiji 40, 1698. See LNZ 5.2 and discussion in Anne Behnke Kinney, *Representations
of Childhood and Youth in Early China* (Stanford: Stanford University Press, 2004),
190. However, as commentators point out, Duke Mu of Chu lived well after the time

of Duke Xian of Jin. Therefore, it is not possible that Li Ji could have alluded to this event in her speech to Duke Xian.

79. Jiang of Qi was Shensheng's mother and the duke's deceased first consort. See parallel account in *Guoyu*, "Jinyu," part 2, items 1, 8.

80. Jiang was about 100 miles northwest of modern-day Loyang in Henan province. *Shiji* 39, 1641, states that the older city of Ju (聚) was made Jin's capital and renamed Jiang in 669 BCE. According to *Shiji* 14, 577, Jiang was made Jin's capital as of 668 BCE.

81. Compare with the wording of the *Guoyu*, "Jinyu," part 2, item 1, here: "If you would kill your own father to benefit others, just how could others possibly benefit from such a thing?"

82. The temple at Xincheng refers to the ancestral temple in Quwo. Quwo was called Xincheng (New City) because Shensheng had recently moved there.

83. For more on the eunuch, see *Zuo zhuan*, Xi 24, translated in Legge, *The Chinese Classics*, vol. 5, 191.

84. See LNZ 2.8.

85. Jia Hua was a grandee of Jin. Liang was a state located south of Hancheng in Shanxi province.

86. See *Zuo zhuan*, Xi 10, translated in Legge, *The Chinese Classics*, vol. 5, 154–155.

87. See *Guoyu*, "Jinyu," part 2, item 8, which provides a less dramatic account of Li Ji's death.

88. Duke Hui of Jin reigned from 650 to 637 BCE.

89. On Duke Huai, see LNZ 5.3.

90. Gaoliang was a city in Jin located in present-day Shanxi province, northeast of Linfen. Duke Wen reigned from 636 to 628 BCE. According to the *Zuo zhuan*, Chonger had Duke Huai put to death. See *Zuo zhuan*, Xi 24, translated in Legge, *The Chinese Classics*, vol. 5, 190–192.

91. The five reigns include those of Duke Xian, Xiqi, Zhuozi, and Dukes Hui and Huai.

92. *Odes*, *Da Ya*, "Zhan Yang," Mao no. 264. Translation based on Legge, *The Chinese Classics*, vol. 4, 56.

93. It is not clear who Mu Jiang's father was. If, as is most likely, she was married between the ages of 15 and 20, then she was born sometime in the reign of either Duke Zhao (r. 632–613 BCE) or Duke Yi (r. 612–609 BCE) of Qi. Duke Xuan of Lu reigned from 608 to 591 BCE. We have the account of Xuan's marriage to Mu Jiang in *Zuo zhuan*, Xuan 1. This story is recounted in *Zuo zhuan*, Cheng 16 and Xiang 9; translated in Legge, *The Chinese Classics*, vol. 5, 398–399, 439–440. Mu Jiang was also the mother of Bo Ji of Song, on which see LNZ 4.2. Mu Jiang's son, Duke Cheng of Lu, reigned for 18 years, from 590 to 573 BCE. A detailed study of Mu Jiang can be found in Anne Behnke Kinney, "A Spring and Autumn Family," *Chinese Historical Review* 20, no. 2 (2013).

94. In contrast to the *Lienü zhuan*, the *Zuo zhuan* records the word *mu* of Mu Jiang's posthumous name as "majestic" (穆). He Xiu's commentary to the *Gongyang zhuan*

identifies a Miu Jiang not as Duke Xuan's wife but as the wife of Duke Cheng of Lu, and thus, Mu Jiang's daughter-in-law. See SSJZS, 19/170A, vol. 2, 2301A. The *Yi Zhou shu* (逸周書), chapter 54, "Shi Fa Jie" (諡法解), states, "*Mu* signifies a mismatch between name and reality (名與實爽曰繆)." See *Sibu beiyao* (Taipei: Taiwan Zhonghua shuju, 1965), vol. 101, 6/24B. Nevertheless, 穆 and 繆 were often used interchangeably in early texts.

95. Shusun Xuanbo was also called Shusun Xuanzi; his given name was Qiaoru. He was a great official of the ducal house of Lu and head of the Shusun lineage. As scions of the sons of Duke Huan of Lu (r. 711–694 BCE), the Shusun, Mengsun, and Jisun lineages were known as the "Three Huan" lineages of Lu. They monopolized political power in Lu until their de facto usurpation of power in 562 BCE. As Mu Jiang married Duke Xuan in the first year of his reign, and his reign lasted from 609 to 591 BCE, Duke Cheng was probably about seventeen years old at the time of his accession.

96. Ji and Meng refer to the Jisun and Mengsun lineages.

97. The "duke" is Duke Cheng. Yanling was a city in the state of Zheng, located north of present-day Yanling in Henan.

98. The subject of this sentence is omitted; in attributing this action to Qiaoru, I follow *Zuo zhuan*, Cheng 16. Jisun Hangfu's name is also sometimes romanized as Jisun Xingfu. Here, Qiaoru is spreading disinformation in order to achieve his own agenda, namely, to remove two officers of Lu who obstruct his path to power. He thus tells the state of Jin that Jisun and Zhongsun (also called Mengsun) will destroy Jin's alliance with Lu. But if Jin does as he, Qiaoru, demands, Lu will fall in with Jin's plans. Ultimately Jin smelled a rat and released Jisun. Jisun Hangfu was also known as Ji Wenzi. He was a member of the Jisun lineage, the grandson of Chengji You, and a minister to the state of Lu. Zhongsun Mie was also known as Meng Xianzi. He was a member of the Mengsun lineage, the great grandson of Zhong Qingfu. For Zhong Qingfu, also see LNZ 7.6.

99. The Eastern Palace was the residence of the heir apparent. Her removal from the main palace to the new residence seems to have been a form of house arrest.

100. The divination system of the *Book of Changes* (i.e., the *Yijing* but also called the *Zhou Yi*) comprises sixty-four hexagrams, i.e., diagrams composed of six lines each. Through various forms of random selection, each of the six lines of a given hexagram is determined as solid (unbroken) or divided (broken), and further distinguished by the designations "old" and "new." An "old" line was thought to be on the verge of changing into its opposite and thereby generated a second hexagram indicating future trends. I here conform to the text of the *Zuo zhuan*, which has "eight" rather than the "six" of the *Lienü zhuan*. The significance of the term "eight" in the passage of the *Zuo zhuan* is no longer well understood but is thought to refer to the second unchanging broken line of the hexagram. See Yang Bojun, *Chunqiu Zuo zhuan zhu*, 4 vols. (Beijing: Zhonghua shuju, 1981), 964–965. Here, the second line of hexagram no. 57, "Stopping" (counting from the bottom up), is identical to that of "Following," no. 17, and

both in received versions of the *Yijing* carry inauspicious connotations. See the revised translation of Legge's original in Z. D. Sung, *The Text of Yi King* (Taipei: Wenhua tushu gongsi, 1975), 79–86, 219–222.

101. See Legge's translation of these lines from *Zuo zhuan*, Xiang 9, in *The Chinese Classics*, vol. 5, 440.

102. The *Zuo zhuan* has the word "body" (體 *ti*) rather than "goodness" (善 *shan*) in the first clause of this sentence. It also includes a passage of Mu Jiang's speech that does not appear in the LNZ account of this story.

103. The *Zuo zhuan* has the word "debauched" (姣 *xiao*) rather than the LNZ's "self-indulgent; abandoned" (放 *fang*).

104. See discussion of this passage as it appears in the *Zuo zhuan* in Li, *The Readability of the Past in Early Chinese Historiography*, 222–224. A version of Mu Jiang's speech is included in the ca. fourth century BCE bamboo manuscript of the *Zuo zhuan* that was purportedly stolen from a tomb of the ancient state of Chu, then recovered and recently published by Zhejiang University. See Cao Jinyan, *Zhejiang da xue cang Zhan guo Chu jian* (Hangzhou: Zhejiang daxue chubanshe, 2011), 138–142.

105. *Odes, Wey Feng,* "Mang," Mao no. 58. Translation based on Legge, *The Chinese Classics*, vol. 4, 99.

106. Strictly speaking, Xia Ji was a woman of the state of Zheng and married to a man of Chen. The *Guoyu*, "Chuyu," part 1, item 4, states that Gongzi Xia, the son of Duke Xuan of Chen (r. 692–648 BCE), arranged the marriage between his son, Yushu, and Xia Ji, who was the daughter of Duke Mu of Zheng (r. 627–606 BCE). As a daughter of the ruler of Zheng, her clan name was Ji. Wei Zhao's (204–273 CE) note says that Xia Ji was the daughter of Duke Mu's lesser concubine, a woman named Yao Zi. See *Guoyu* in SBCK vol. 14, 17/6A. Zheng was located in the vicinity of present-day Zhengzhou in Henan.

107. This detail about Xia Ji is not found in any extant earlier sources. On techniques of inner cultivation, see Donald Harper, *Early Chinese Medical Literature: The Mawangdui Medical Manuscripts* (London: Kegan Paul International, 1998), 112–113, 119–121, and Harold Roth, *Original Tao* (New York: Columbia University Press, 1999), 11–12.

108. This statement is not backed up by earlier texts or even by the information included in the present biography. While Xia Ji served three husbands—Xia Yushu, Xiang Lao, and Qu Wuchen—she never possessed the status of queen.

109. His father, Xia Ji's husband, was dead, and Zhengshu was now the head of the family.

110. Gongsun Ning (also called Kong Ning) and Yi Hangfu (also romanized as Yi Xingfu) were high-ranking ministers of Chen. Duke Ling of Chen, whose name was Pingguo, reigned 613–599 BCE.

111. Xie Ye was a grandee of Chen.

112. Compare with the account in *Zuo zhuan*, Xuan 9; translated by Legge, *The Chinese Classics*, vol. 5, 305; *Shiji* 36, 1579; translated in Nienhauser, *The Grand Scribe's Records*, vol. V.1, 226–228; and *Guoyu*, "Zhouyu," part 2, item 7, in SBCK, vol. 14, 2/10B–14A.

113. Gongsun Ning, Yi Hangfu, and the heir apparent fled because Zhengshu's act constituted a *coup d'état*. Other sources suggest that Zhengshu, who was in fact a second
paternal cousin of Duke Ling, had made himself ruler of Chen. See *Zuo zhuan,* Xuan
10; translated by Legge, *The Chinese Classics,* vol. 5, 308; and *Shiji* 36, 1579–1580. I am
grateful to Eric Henry for background information concerning this event.

114. See *Zuo zhuan,* Xuan 11; translated by Legge, *The Chinese Classics,* vol. 5, 310–311. The
LNZ account fails to mention that King Zhuang of Chu (r. 613–591 BCE) annexed
Chen before restoring it to Duke Ling of Chen's son, Duke Cheng.

115. See *Zuo zhuan,* Cheng 2; translated by Legge, *The Chinese Classics,* vol. 5, 347–348.

116. The "duke" was associated with the former state of Shen, which had been absorbed by
Chu early in the seventh century BCE. It was located at the source of the Han River,
where the royal domain and the state of Zheng converged. In Chu, the commanders of
strategic cities—and Shen was eminently strategic—were all called "dukes." Shen was
home to a large garrison stationed there to guard against invasion from the north. The
relationship between Chu kings and these military "dukes" was always tense. See more
on Wuchen at LNZ 3.10.

117. He did this, presumably, to conceal the fact that he had taken her.

118. Zifan (d. 575 BCE) of Chu was also known as Prince Ce.

119. No early extant records describe the nature of Xia Ji's role in the death of her husband,
Yushu. Xia Nan is another name for Xia Ji's son Zhengshu. Kong refers to Kong Ning,
another name for Gongsun Ning, while Yi refers to Yi Hangfu.

120. Xiang Lao's name can also be translated as "Xiang the Elder." His title has also been
translated as Superintendent of Vehicles (*lianyin*).

121. Bi was located in the ancient state of Zheng, northwest of present-day Zhengzhou
and northeast of Rongyang in Henan province. The battle at Bi (597 BCE), one of the
five great battles of the Spring and Autumn period, was waged between Chu and Jin.
An officer of Jin, Zhi Zhuangzi, killed Xiang Lao and took the corpse back to Jin for
use in negotiating the return of his son, who had been taken prisoner by Chu. See *Zuo
zhuan,* Xuan 12; translated by Legge, *The Chinese Classics,* vol. 5, 320.

122. According to *Zuo zhuan,* Cheng 2, Wuchen sent a message to Xia Ji but did not actually meet with her. See translation in Legge, *The Chinese Classics,* vol. 5, 347. Wuchen
then began complicated international negotiations for the return of Xiang Lao's body
and the exchange of hostages between Jin and Chu, all with the private agenda of
moving Xia Ji from Chu back to her native state of Zheng, where he could make her
his bride. The reference to the petition of betrothal indicates that, unlike her other
suitors, Wuchen was offering her the position of wife, brokered with all of the proper
rituals that were required of such a union.

123. King Gong of Chu reigned from 590 to 560 BCE. Wuchen was not able to go to Zheng
until 589 BCE, some nine years after his initial encounter with Xia Ji in Chu.

124. As is made apparent in the more complete account found in the *Zuo zhuan,* this message supplies Xia Ji with an acceptable reason to leave Chu and return home. Naturally,

the King of Chu was unaware of Wuchen's plans for Xia Ji at this time. The sequence of events in LNZ differs from that found in *Zuo zhuan,* Cheng 2.

125. Zifan was, of course, the Chu general who had been dissuaded by Wuchen from pursuing Xia Ji. Zifan and Zichong (also called Prince Yingqi) were both princes of Chu. See *Zuo zhuan,* Cheng 7; translated in Legge, *The Chinese Classics,* vol. 5, 364.

126. *Odes, Yong Feng,* "Di Dong," Mao no. 51. Translation based on Bernhard Karlgren, trans., *The Book of Odes* (Goteborg: Elanders Boktryckeri Aktiebolag, 1950), 33; also see Legge, *The Chinese Classics,* vol. 4, 84; and Arthur Waley, *The Book of Songs* (New York: Grove Press, 1960), 43.

127. Duke Ling of Qi reigned from 581 to 554 BCE. According to the *Zuo zhuan,* the mother of his heir apparent was called Zong Sheng Ji (鬷聲姬). She was the niece of Duke Ling's primary wife, Yan Yi Ji (顏懿姬) of Lu. Zong Sheng would have therefore been regarded as a secondary wife. See *Zuo zhuan,* Xiang 19; translated by Legge, *The Chinese Classics,* vol. 5, 483. Also see LNZ 3.8 for further details about Sheng Ji. Despite the title of this biography, the primary subject is a woman called Sheng Meng Zi, not Sheng Ji, if we rely on the *Zuo zhuan* for identifications of these figures. Wei Zhao's commentary on *Guoyu,* "Zhouyu," part 3, item 1, also identifies Sheng Meng Zi as Duke Ling's mother, not his wife. See discussion in Shimomi, *Ryū kō Retsujoden,* 850, n. 2.

128. The identification of Sheng Ji with the woman called Meng Zi poses difficulties. *Zuo zhuan,* Cheng 16, identifies a Sheng Meng Zi as the mother and not the wife of the duke of Qi. Her clan name was Zi, and the name Meng indicates that she was the eldest daughter of a concubine or secondary consort.

129. The affair was said to have occurred in 574 BCE. See *Zuo zhuan,* Cheng 17; translated by Legge, *The Chinese Classics,* vol. 5, 403. According to the *Zuo zhuan,* Sheng Meng Zi had previously had an affair with another man, Shusun Xuanbo, also called Qiaoru. He was a great official of the ducal house of Lu and had also carried on an affair with Mu Jiang, the wife of Duke Xuan of Lu (LNZ 7.8). After the abortive coup staged by Qiaoru and Mu Jiang in 575 BCE, Qiaoru fled to Qi, where he began an adulterous liaison with Sheng Meng Zi. When history appeared to be repeating itself, Qiaoru fled to Wey, whereupon Qing Ke seems to have filled that particular void in Sheng Meng Zi's life. See *Zuo zhuan,* Cheng 16, 17; translated by Legge, *The Chinese Classics,* vol. 5, 399, 403.

130. He wore concealing clothing to disguise himself as a woman and thus gain access to the women's quarters.

131. Bao Qian was a grandee of Qi; Guo Zuo was a minister.

132. Keling, also called Jialing, was south of present-day Xuchang in Henan. Gaozi, also called Gao Wujiu, was a minister of Qi. Baozi is another name for Bao Qian.

133. Prince Jiao was the son of Duke Qing of Qi (r. 598–582 BCE) and a brother of Duke Ling of Qi.

134. Ju was a small state located in the vicinity of present-day Ju county in Shandong province. The remaining portion of this biography does not correspond to the account in the *Zuo zhuan*.

135. Cui Zhu was an important figure in Qi politics. See LNZ 7.11 and Kinney, *Representations of Childhood*, 191.

136. According to *Zuo zhuan*, Cheng 17, Qing Ke was in fact killed.

137. This detail is not found in the *Zuozhuan* account.

138. *Odes, Da Ya*, "Zhan Yang," Mao no. 264. Translation based on Legge, *The Chinese Classics*, vol. 4, 561.

139. Reading *hao* (好) as *jian* (奸) and *wang* (亡) as *wang* (妄). See emendations of Wang Zhaoyuan and Liang Duan in LNZHB, vol. 5, 593; vol. 7, 549–550.

140. Tang, located in the vicinity of present-day Pingdu county in Shandong province, was a small fief within Qi that belonged to the "duke" of Tang. For discussion of the development of settlements of this sort in the Western Zhou, see Li Feng, *Bureaucracy and the State in Early China* (Cambridge, England: Cambridge University Press, 2008), 173–180, 296. Cui Zhu (also called Cuizi) was head of the aristocratic Cui lineage of Qi that dated back to the tenth century BCE. Cui held power in Qi from 553 to 546 BCE. This story is also told in *Lüshi chunqiu*, "Shenxing," in SBCK, vol. 22, 22/2B–3B; translated in Knoblock and Riegel, *The Annals of Lü Buwei*, 568–569; *Shiji* 32, 1500–1502, translated in Nienhauser, *The Grand Scribe's Records*, vol. V.1, 98–103; and *Zuo zhuan*, Xiang 25, 27, translated in Legge, *The Chinese Classics*, vol. 5, 514–515, 532.

141. Duke Zhuang of Qi reigned from 553 to 548 BCE. He came to the throne through Cui Zhu's efforts but proved to be an incompetent ruler and, after betraying Cui Zhu, was murdered by him in 548 BCE.

142. This act was an outrageous demonstration on the part of the duke that he had been in the private quarters of Cui's home.

143. Men wore their hair bound in topknots.

144. He did this either because he feared he could not escape and expressed his distress in song or because he wished to make his plight known to any who might assist him. In early Chinese literature, people are often shown expressing themselves in song when they know they are about to die.

145. The LNZ text appears to be corrupt here in suggesting that Jiang gave birth to two sons, one named Ming and another named Cheng (成) as distinct from the first wife's son called Cheng (城). *Zuo zhuan*, Xiang 27; translated in Legge, *The Chinese Classics*, vol. 5, 535; and *Shiji* 32, 1502, translated in Nienhauser, *The Grand Scribe's Records*, vol. 5.1, 102, state that Cui and Jiang together produced just one son, who was called Ming, and that Cui Zhu's eldest son was called Cheng (成) not (城). To maintain narrative coherence, I follow the *Zuo zhuan* version, so that all further references to Cheng are to the eldest son of Cui Zhu.

146. Qing Feng was a powerful and wealthy figure in Qi politics. He held the rank of minister in Qi from 573 BCE and joined forces with Cui Zhu to assassinate Duke Zhuang

in 548. Later, he annihilated the Cui lineage and held de facto power in Qi but was expelled in 545 and fled to Wu. He was killed in 538 by Chu forces that had invaded Wu.

147. I follow Liang Duan and Xiao Daoguan's reading of *wei* (唯) as *sui* (雖). See LNZHB, vol. 7, 552; vol. 8, 355.

148. LNZ has "Jiang" rather than "Qiang," but clearly "Qiang" is intended. Lupu Pie was a grandee of Qi and part of Qing Feng's coterie. See Jia Kui's note in *Shiji* 32, 1503, note 5.

149. The three families were the Cui, Tang, and Dongguo.

150. *Odes, Da Ya,* "Dang," Mao no. 255. Translation based on Legge, *The Chinese Classics,* vol. 4, 510. The last character differs from the Mao version of this ode.

151. According to *Zuo zhuan,* Xiang 27, translated in Legge, *The Chinese Classics,* vol. 5, 535; Ming escaped Qing Feng's final attack on the Cui lineage. *Shiji* 32, 1502, translated in Nienhauser, *The Grand Scribe's Records,* vol. 5.1, 103, however, reports that the entire lineage was wiped out in this attack.

152. Nan Zi is famous for her connection with Confucius. See Siegfried Englert and Roderisch Ptak, "Nan-Tzu, or Why Heaven Did Not Crush Confucius," *Journal of the American Oriental Society* 106, no. 4 (Oct.–Dec. 1986): 679–686. Lin Yutang wrote a humorous piece that transformed Nan Zi into "Nancy." See Lin Yutang, *Confucius Saw Nancy: and Essays About Nothing* (Shanghai: Commercial Press, 1936), 1–46. Wey was a state that corresponds roughly to the areas along the Qi (淇) River in present-day northern Henan. Most of it lay north of the Yellow River, and it bordered on Zheng in the south, Song in the east, Lu in the northeast, Qi in the north, Jin in the northwest, and Zhou in the southwest. See Li Feng, *Landscape and Power in Early China,* 66–67.

153. As she was a woman of the state of Song, Zi designates her clan name. Duke Ling of Wey reigned from 534 to 493 BCE.

154. Zichao of Song was a prince of Song. The exact nature of his relationship with Nan Zi is unclear. Legge suggests that he was her brother. See *Zuo zhuan,* Ding 14; translated in Legge, *The Chinese Classics,* vol. 5, 788–789. He is mentioned in *Analects* VI:14 as a handsome man.

155. According to *Zuo zhuan,* Ding 14, Kuaikui clearly intended to kill Nan Zi. The *Zuo* identifies Nan Zi as Kuaikui's mother. It is possible that as the duke's wife, she was officially but not biologically Kuaikui's mother.

156. Duke Chu of Wey reigned from 492 to 481 BCE. His name, Chu (出), means "expelled" and refers to the fact that he was driven from his position as a territorial ruler. He was reinstated in 476 BCE.

157. Bo Ji's name means "eldest daughter of the Ji clan." Kong Wenzi was a grandee of Wey. For earlier accounts of this tale, see *Zuo zhuan,* Ai 15, 16, 17, 18, 25; translated in Legge, *The Chinese Classics,* vol. 5, 843, 846–848, 849–851, 856–857.

158. *Zuo zhuan,* Ai 15 describes Hun Liangfu as a tall and handsome man.

159. To "wear concealing clothing" means that they disguised themselves as women who, according to the *Liji*, were expected to veil their faces when venturing out of doors. See *Liji*, SSJZS, vol. 2, 27/234C, 1462C; translated in Legge, *Li Chi*, vol. 1, 455. The meaning of this phrase is also clarified in the original passage in the *Zuo zhuan*, which states that they had gained admittance to Kong's chambers by claiming that they were serving women. See *Zuo zhuan*, Ai 15, translated in Legge, *The Chinese Classics*, vol. 5, 843.

160. Here, Kuaikui and Bo Ji forced Bo Ji's son, Kong Kui, to shift allegiance from Duke Chu, who at the time reigned as Duke of Wey, to Kuaikui, who had been passed over in the succession.

161. Zilu, a disciple of Confucius, served as Kong Kui's town steward. See *Shiji* 7, 2193; translated in Nienhauser, *The Grand Scribe's Records*, vol. 7, 68–69.

162. Duke Zhuang of Wey reigned from 480 to 478 BCE.

163. According to the *Zuo zhuan*, the murder of his ally, Hun Liangfu, was at the behest of Duke Zhuang's son, Ji. See *Zuo zhuan*, Ai 17; translated in Legge, *The Chinese Classics*, vol. 5, 848. The murder of Nan Zi is not mentioned in the *Zuo zhuan* or other early sources.

164. Rongzhou was a settlement near the Wey border populated by the Rong peoples. According to the *Zuo zhuan*, Duke Zhuang, in a rash move, invaded Rongzhou and died there. See *Zuo zhuan*, Ai 17; translated in Legge, *The Chinese Classics*, vol. 5, 850–851.

165. *Zuo zhuan*, Ai 16 states that Kong Kui took his mother with him when he was expelled from Wey and fled to Song.

166. Duke Chu of Wey reigned from 467 to 449 BCE.

167. *Odes, Yong Feng*, "Xiang Shu," Mao no. 52. Translation based on Legge, *The Chinese Classics*, vol. 4, 84.

168. Her name means eldest daughter (Meng) of the Yao clan. According to a note in *Shiji* 43, 1805, Meng Yao's father, Wu Guang, was a descendant of the sage Shun and is thus associated with the clan name Yao, as Yao is said to have been born in a place called Yaoxu. See Shen Yue's notes to the *Zhushu jinian*; translated in Legge, *The Chinese Classics*, "Prolegomena," 114. Shun also held the clan name Yu (虞), which because of a phonetic similarity is also recorded as Wu (吳). Also see Xu, *Shuowen jiezi*, vol. 3, 1743.

169. Zhao was one of the three successor states of Jin and covered half of modern-day Shanxi, the southern sector of Hebei, and part of Henan. King Wuling of Zhao reigned from 325 to 299 BCE. An earlier and somewhat different version of this story can be found in *Shiji* 43, 1803, 1811–1816.

170. I romanize Han (韓) as Hann to distinguish it from Han (漢). Hann, along with Wei and Zhao, was one of the three successor states of Jin.

171. King Huiwen of Zhao reigned from 298 to 266 BCE.

172. By doing this, King Wuling was voluntarily stepping down from the throne and making himself a sort of "king emeritus," a rare phenomena in pre-Qin China. Dai was in

the vicinity of modern Wei county in Hebei province. Anyang was located near the modern city of the same name.

173. Shaqiu is northwest of modern Guangzong in Hebei province.

174. Li Dui, also known as Lord Fengyang, was Zhao's commander-in-chief and monopolized power in Zhao. See, for example, *Zhanguo ce* in SBCK, vol. 14, 6/15B; translated in James Irving Crump, *Chan-kuo Ts'e*, 2nd ed., revised (San Francisco: Chinese Materials Center, 1979), 295.

175. *Odes, Da Ya,* "Dang," Mao no. 255. Translation based on Legge, *The Chinese Classics,* vol. 4, 507.

176. Although the line of succession had been disturbed by these events, in point of fact, King Huiwen (He) led the state into a period of unprecedented power and prosperity. See Loewe and Shaughnessy, *Cambridge History of Ancient China,* 638–641.

177. King Kaolie of Chu reigned from 262 to 238 BCE. For earlier accounts of this story, see *Zhanguo ce* in SBCK, vol. 14, 5/45A;–47B; translated in Crump, *Chan-kuo Ts'e,* 274–277; *Shiji* 40, 1736; 78, 2396–2399; translated in Nienhauser, *The Grand Scribe's Records,* vol. 7, 229–231.

178. The Lord of Chunshen, whose name was Huang Xie, was an erudite man of Chu who served as prime minister to King Qinxiang of Chu (r. 227–23 BCE). His biography is found in *Shiji* 78, 2396–2399; translated in Nienhauser, *The Grand Scribe's Records,* vol. 7, 229–231. The Lord of Chunshen was one of the "four great patrons" of the Warring States era, the others being Lord Mengchang of Qi, Lord Pingyuan of Zhao, and Lord Xinling of Wei. Each of these figures maintained thousands of retainers in their establishments.

179. "After he completes his hundred years" means "after his death."

180. Jiangdong was the Lord of Chunshen's fief. It was the area along the Yangzi River to the south of modern Wuhu city in Anhui province.

181. King You (幽) (r. 237–228 BCE) was the son of Queen Li.

182. To distinguish two separate names with identical romanization, I transliterate 猶 as "Youu." Youu was enthroned as King Ai (r. 228–227 BCE). King Ai (Youu) and King You were brothers by the same mother, according to *Shiji* 40, 1736.

183. King Fuchu reigned from 227 to 223 BCE. He was the half-brother of King Ai by a concubine. See *Shiji* 40, 1736.

184. After the death of her husband, Queen Li was referred to as the Queen Dowager.

185. *Odes, Xiao Ya,* "Qiao Yan," Mao no. 198. Translation based on Legge, *The Chinese Classics,* vol. 4, 341.

186. King Zhaoxiang of Zhao reigned from 244 to 236 BCE. Handan was the capital of Zhao. It was located in the vicinity of the modern city of the same name in Hebei province.

187. See his biography in *Shiji* 81, 2449–2452; translated in Nienhauser, *The Grand Scribe's Records,* vol. 7, 271–273.

188. *Shiji* 43, 1831, lists his name as King Youmu. He reigned from 235 to 228 BCE.

189. There is uncertainty as to the identification of the Lord of Chunping. See *Shiji* 43, 1830–1831, and Shimomi, *Ryū kō Retsujoden no kenkyū*, 880–881.

190. Jia reigned from 227 to 222 BCE. In *Shiji*, the songstress has no part in the downfall of Li Mu or in receiving bribes from Qin.

191. *Odes, Yong Feng*, "Xiang Shu," Mao no. 52. Translation based on Legge, *The Chinese Classics*, vol. 4, 84.

8. SUPPLEMENTARY BIOGRAPHIES

1. She is mentioned in *Zuo zhuan*, Zhao 29; translated in James Legge, *The Chinese Classics*, 5 vols. (1893; reprint, Hong Kong: University of Hong Kong Press, 1960), vol. 5, 717–718. The suburbs of Zhou refers to the area just outside the Eastern Zhou capital at Chengzhou (成周), located in modern Luoyang in Henan province.

2. King Jing of Zhou reigned from 519 to 476 BCE. On these events, see *Shiji* 4, 156–157; translated in William Nienhauser et al., *The Grand Scribe's Records*, 6 vols. (Bloomington: Indiana University Press, 1994–2006), vol. 1, 77–78.

3. On the earl of Yuan, see *Zuo zhuan*, Zhao 18; translated in Legge, *The Chinese Classics*, vol. 5, 671. On the place called Yuan, see Li Feng, *Landscape and Power in Early China: The Crisis and Fall of the Western Zhou, 1045–771 BC* (Cambridge, England: Cambridge University Press, 2006), 72–73; and Yang Bojun, *Chunqiu Zuozhuan zhu*, 4 vols. (Beijing: Zhonghua shuju, 1981), 77.

4. This date is incorrect; according to the *Zuo zhuan*, it should be "in the 26th year." See *Zuo zhuan*, Zhao 26; translated in Legge, *The Chinese Classics*, vol. 5, 717–718.

5. See *Zuo zhuan*, Zhao 29; translated in Legge, *The Chinese Classics*, vol. 5, 730.

6. *Odes, Da Ya*, "Yi," Mao no. 256. Translation based on Legge, *The Chinese Classics*, vol. 4, 518.

7. Vestiges of this tale are found in Wang Yi's commentary to the poem "Tian Wen." See D. C. Lau, ed., *Concordance to the* Chuci (Hong Kong: Commercial Press, 2000), 3/9/4, and annotations in Hattori Unokichi, *Kanbun taikei* (Taipei: Xinwenfeng chuban gongsi, 1978), vol. 22, 3/25–26.

8. The song is recorded in *Odes, Chen Feng*, "Mu Men," Mao no. 141. Translation based on Legge, *The Chinese Classics*, vol. 4, 210.

9. *Odes, Xiao Ya*, "Jing Jing Zhe E," Mao no. 176; translation based on Arthur Waley, *The Book of Songs* (New York: Grove Press, 1960), 104.

10. This story is also found in *Zhanguo ce*, in SBCK, vol. 14, 8/1B–5B; translated in James Irving Crump, *Chan-kuo Ts'e*, 2nd ed., revised (San Francisco: Chinese Materials Center, 1979), 455–458; and in *Shiji* 86, 2522–2526; translated in Nienhauser, *The Grand Scribe's Records*, vol. 7, 323–325.

11. According to *Shiji* 15, 711, this event occurred in 397 BCE. The location of Puyang corresponds to the area southwest of the modern city of the same name in northeastern

Hebei province. Yan Zhongzi is also known as Yan Sui. According to the *Zhanguo ce*, Xia Lei (who is there called Han Kui) humiliated Yan Sui at court. In response, Yan Sui tried to kill Xia, then fled to Qi. To avenge himself on Xia Lei, he sought the services of Nie Zheng.

12. Rather than "slashed his flesh," both the *Zhanguo ce* and *Shiji* state that he disemboweled himself.

13. Zhi was north of modern Jiyuan in Henan province.

14. *Odes, Xiao Ya*, "Chang Di," Mao no. 164. Translation based on Legge, *The Chinese Classics*, vol. 4, 251.

15. This story is also recounted in *Zhanguo ce*, in SBCK, vol. 14, 4/51B; translated in Crump, *Chan-kuo Ts'e*, 205.

16. King Min of Qi reigned from 300 to 284 BCE.

17. King Min's misdeeds and his assassination are recounted in *Zhanguo ce*, in SBCK 4/50B; translated in Crump, *Chan-kuo Ts'e*, 203–205.

18. Earlier, when the Yan general Yue Yi attacked Qi, Chu sent Nao Chi to assist King Min of Qi. In 284 BCE, King Min made Nao Chi his minister, but Nao later murdered the king and divided Qi with Yan. See *Shiji* 46, 1900. In the *Zhanguo ce* version of this tale, the king flees and Jia becomes separated from him, and only later does Jia learn about the king's murder.

19. Those who chose to join Wangsun Jia were asked to strip their robes off their right shoulders to indicate their willingness to fight.

20. *Odes, Xiao Ya*, "Xiao Yuan," Mao no. 196. Translation based on Legge, *The Chinese Classics*, vol. 4, 334.

21. This story is found in *Shiji* 7, 298; translated in Nienhauser, *The Grand Scribe's Records*, vol. 1, 181–182. Also see Ban Gu, *Hanshu* (Beijing: Zhonghua shuju, 1962), 31, 1797–1798. Ban Biao (3–54 CE) praises Chen Ying's mother in his essay, "Wang Ming Lun"; see *Hanshu* 100A, 4210; translated in William Theodore de Bary, *Sources of Chinese Tradition*, 2 vols. (New York: Columbia University Press, 1960), vol. 1, 176–180. In Han times, Tangyi was first a marquisate and later a county in the area of the modern Liuhe district in Jiangsu province.

22. Dongyang was a commandery in the restored kingdom of Chu.

23. The Second Emperor of Qin reigned from 209 to 207 BCE.

24. Xiang Liang was a powerful military leader in the 209 BCE uprising against the Qin. See *Shiji* 7, 295–303; translated in Nienhauser, *The Grand Scribe's Records*, vol. 1, 179–185.

25. *Odes, Da Ya*, "Wen Wang You Sheng," Mao no. 244. Translation based on Legge, *The Chinese Classics*, vol. 4, 463.

26. Wang Ling (d. 180 BCE) was appointed Chancellor of the Right in 189 BCE. His biography, which this account follows closely, is found in *Shiji* 56, 2059–2060; translated in Burton Watson, *Records of the Grand Historian of China: Translated from the Shi chi of Ssu-ma Ch'ien*, 2 vols. (New York: Columbia University Press, 1961), vol. 1,

163–164. Also see *Hanshu* 40, 2046–2050. Ban Biao praises Wang Ling's mother in his essay, "Wang Ming Lun"; see *Hanshu* 100A, 4210; translated in de Bary, *Sources of Chinese Tradition*, vol. 1, 176–180. Anguo was in the vicinity of present-day Anguo in Hebei province.

27. Gaozu was the founding emperor of the Han dynasty (206 BCE to 220 CE).

28. The King of Han was Gaozu's title before becoming Emperor Gaozu.

29. Xiang Yu was Gaozu's chief opponent in the civil war that erupted after the fall of the Qin dynasty. Gaozu defeated him in 202 BCE.

30. Facing east was the position of honor.

31. *Odes, Bei Feng*, "Gu Feng," Mao no. 35. Translation based on Legge, *The Chinese Classics*, vol. 4, 56.

32. Here, the term *ren* (仁) should be understood in its sense as found in the title of the third chapter of LNZ, "Sympathetic Wisdom" (仁 智 *renzhi*); that is, a form of empathy or sympathy. In this case, Wang Ling's mother was able to grasp intuitively that the King of Han and not Xiang Yu would be able to lead the nation and her own family to peace and stability.

33. Zhang Tang's biography can be found in *Shiji* 122, 3137–3144; translated in Watson, *Records of the Grand Historian of China*, vol. 2, 425–437. Zhang gained Emperor Wu's approval by basing his legal judgments on the classics, which the emperor had recently brought to prominence as the ideological foundation of the early years of his reign. See *Shiji* 122, 3139.

34. Emperor Wu reigned from 141 to 87 BCE. Imperial Counselor was an office second in importance only to the office of Chancellor. According to Michael Loewe, "The post of imperial counselor acted as a further check to ambitious chancellors. Like the chancellor, the imperial counselor was concerned in the promulgation and distribution of orders to the lower-ranking officials; and the imperial counselor bore specific responsibility for the performance of the civil service. At times he was even responsible for examining the chancellor's conduct of affairs, and as keeper of the records of government he was able to check that proposed measures did not conflict with the established provisions of state." See Michael Loewe and Denis Twitchett, eds., *The Ch'in and Han Empires, 221 B.C.–A.D. 220, The Cambridge History of China* (Cambridge, England: Cambridge University Press, 1986), vol. 1, 468.

35. Yan Qingdi (his surname is also written as Zhuang 莊) was appointed as chancellor in 118 BCE. The three chief clerks were Zhu Maichen, Wang Chao, and Bian Tong. All three of these men had previously supervised Zhang Tang but were now his subordinates. Frustrated by Zhang's tyrannical and duplicitous conduct, they conspired to bring about his downfall, which occurred in 115 BCE, when Zhang Tang was charged with a crime and forced to commit suicide. Later, Emperor Wu regretted his treatment of Zhang Tang and executed the three men. Their biographies are included in *Shiji* 122 (cited earlier).

36. In contrast to the term "to detain in prison" (*xi* 繫), the *Shiji* here states that "the case was referred to" (*shixia* 事下) the Superintendent of Trials. See *Shiji* 122, 3142.

The kingdom of Zhao was deeply invested in metallurgical industries. The King of Zhao was frustrated with the central government's handling of these enterprises and brought suit against it. When Zhang Tang repeatedly dismissed these suits, the King of Zhao tried to find other means to prosecute Zhang Tang and thus loosen his control on Zhao's smelting concerns. See *Shiji* 122, 3142.

37. *Odes, Zheng Feng*, "You Nü Tong Ju," Mao no. 83. Translation based on Legge, *The Chinese Classics*, vol. 4, 137.

38. Juan Buyi's biography, which shares elements with the LNZ account, is found in *Hanshu* 71, 3035–3038; translated in Burton Watson, *Courtier and Commoner in Ancient China: Selections from the* History of the Former Han *by Pan Ku* (New York: Columbia University Press, 1974), 158–162. Juan served late in the reign of Emperor Wu, through the time of Emperor Zhao, and died around 81 BCE.

39. On "reviewing the records of prisoners" (*luqiu* 錄囚), see Yan Shigu's note in *Hanshu* 71, 3037.

40. *Odes, Xiao Ya*, "Xiao Min," Mao no. 195. Translation based on Legge, *The Chinese Classics*, vol. 4, 330.

41. Yang Chang's biography is found in *Hanshu* 66, 2888–2889. Yang was made chancellor in 75 BCE. The office of chancellor was the most senior of the *sangong* (三公), the three senior statesmen of the central government. The chancellor served as an assistant to the emperor and the channel through which information flowed from lower officialdom to the throne. Anping was located in the present-day city of the same name in Hebei province.

42. Emperor Zhao was about nine years old when he ascended the throne in 87 BCE and died in 74 BCE. He was succeeded by Liu He, the King of Changyi, who reigned for a total of twenty-seven days but was quickly removed from the throne after engaging in a spree of ritual violations. See Anne Behnke Kinney, *Representations of Childhood and Youth in Early China* (Stanford: Stanford University Press, 2004), 57–58.

43. When Emperor Zhao came to the throne, Huo Guang (d. 68 BCE) was appointed as regent. As both regent and general-in-chief, he was the virtual head of state. Zhang Anshi (d. 62 BCE) was the son of Zhang Tang (see LNZ 8.7) and a highly respected statesman. See *Hanshu* 59, 2617–2653.

44. Tian Yannian committed suicide in 72 BCE amid charges of embezzlement. See *Hanshu* 90, 3665–3666.

45. "Adjusting one's robes" was a euphemism comparable to our "using the lavatory."

46. In the Han central government, three senior statesmen advised the emperor, and the Nine Ministers were ranked directly beneath them. On their duties, see Loewe and Twitchett, *The Ch'in and Han Empires*, 468–370.

47. Emperor Xuan reigned from 74 to 49 BCE.

48. *Odes, Xiao Ya*, "Ju Xia," Mao no. 218. Translation based on Legge, *The Chinese Classics*, vol. 4, 392; Bernhard Karlgren, trans., *The Book of Odes* (Goteborg: Elanders Boktryckeri Aktiebolag, 1950), 172.

49. Information on Huo Xian can be found in *Hanshu* 68, 2950–2951; 97A, 3966; translated in Watson, *Courtier and Commoner in Ancient China*, 121–151; 259–261, and in C. Martin Wilbur, *Slavery in China During the Former Han Dynasty 206 B.C.–A.D. 25* (New York: Russell & Russell, 1967), 366–368. A third-century commentary cites a comment by Xun Shuang (128–190 CE) stating that Huo Xian was the second wife of Huo Guang and born a slave. Bolu was located south of present-day Li county in Hebei province.

50. Huo Guang served as regent to the young Emperor Zhao, who had ascended the throne as a child and reigned from 87 to 74 BCE.

51. I follow the emendation of *nüjian* (女監) to *nüyi* (女醫) based on the text as found in *Hanshu* 97A, 3966.

52. According to the *Hanshu*, a number of people who were suspicious about the manner of Empress Xu's death reported the case to the authorities, and Chunyu Yan was imprisoned as a result.

53. Emperor Xuan was the grandson of Emperor Wu's deposed heir apparent, Liu Ju. Vicious court politics had placed Liu Ju in a military confrontation with his father. As a result, the heir apparent's family was exterminated, except for one infant who was secretly raised as a commoner by eunuchs. He came to the throne as Emperor Xuan after the untimely demise of Emperor Zhao. See Kinney, *Representations of Childhood*, 77–81.

54. A "spirit path" was an entry road leading to a tomb. The concubines mentioned here, called *liangren* (良人), along with the female slaves, were stationed there to tend Huo Guang's tomb. See *Hanshu* 68, 2950.

55. His name was Feng Yin (殷); Zidu appears to be his style name. See *Hanshu* 8, 251; 68, 2950, 2955; Wilbur, *Slavery in China During the Former Han*, 145, 184, 357, 366–368.

56. From the time of Emperor Zhao, Huo Guang's kin held numerous positions in the government; this move was therefore an attempt to eradicate completely their power and presence at court.

57. *Odes, Xiao Ya*, "Si Yue," Mao no. 204. Translation based on Legge, *The Chinese Classics*, vol. 4, 358; and Karlgren, *The Book of Odes*, 156.

58. Yan Yannian's surname is sometimes written as 莊 Zhuang. Yan is included in the "Harsh Officials" chapter in *Hanshu* 90, 3667–3672, where a similar story concerning his mother is also recorded. Yan Yannian died in 58 BCE. Henan was a commandery administered in the vicinity of present-day Loyang in Henan province. Donghai was also a commandery; it was located in the southern portion of present-day Shandong and the northern part of present-day Jiangsu.

59. One picul is equivalent to approximately 30 kilograms, or 64 pounds 8 ounces. Han official salaries were paid in both cash and grain. The amount of grain received therefore reflected a person's rank. According to one account, there were fifteen grades of salary ranging from one hundred to ten thousand piculs. Officials receiving two thousand piculs were ranked just below those receiving ten thousand. See Yan Shigu's note

prefacing *Hanshu* 19A, 721; and Nancy Lee Swann, *Food and Money in Ancient China: The Earliest Economic History of China to A.D. 25*. (Princeton: Princeton University Press, 1950), 46–47.

60. The La festival was the Han festival of the New Year, during which people purified themselves, sacrificed to spirits and the ancestors, and gathered with families and friends to drink and feast. See Derk Bodde, *Festivals in Classical China: New Year and Other Annual Observances During the Han Dynasty 206 B.C.–A.D. 220* (Princeton: Princeton University Press, 1975), 49–74. Also see Roel Sterckx, *Food, Sacrifice, and Sagehood in Early China* (Cambridge: Cambridge University Press, 2001), 23, 102, 113, 162.

61. The implication is that those who make excessive use of execution make themselves vulnerable to retribution. See Yan Shigu's note in *Hanshu* 90, 3672, note 7.

62. The LNZ has *lao dang* (老嘗), in contrast to the *Hanshu* 90, 3672, which has *dang lao*.

63. The La festival was celebrated over a series of days, including the beginning of the lunar New Year. The meaning here is that she completed the important La ceremonies and then left before the New Year. See discussion in Bodde, *Festivals in Classical China*, 58–60.

64. See *Hanshu* 90, 3670–3671. Hulsewe argues that the term *qishi* (棄市) "to cast away in the marketplace" meant "to subject to public beheading." See A. F. P. Hulsewe, *Remnants of Han Law* (Leiden: E. J. Brill, 1955), 109–110.

65. *Odes, Da Ya*, "Zhan Yang," Mao no. 264. Translation based on Legge, *The Chinese Classics*, vol. 4, 563.

66. The biography of Brilliant Companion Feng, whose given name was Yuan, is found in *Hanshu* 97B, 4005–4007; translated in Watson, *Courtier and Commoner*, 277–278. Brilliant Companion was a newly created title designating the highest rank of imperial concubine. In spite of her favor at the court of Emperor Yuan (r. 48–33 BCE), Feng Yuan came to a tragic end in the reign of Emperor Ai (r. 7 BCE to 1 CE) after she was falsely accused of cursing both Emperor Ai and the Empress Dowager Fu. The latter had also served as Brilliant Companion along with Feng during Emperor Yuan's reign. Feng maintained her innocence to the end and died by her own hand in 6 BCE.

67. I follow Burton Watson's translations of these titles. See Watson, *Courtier and Commoner*, 277–278.

68. King Xiao of Zhongshan was the title of Liu Xin, who died in 8 BCE and who fathered Emperor Ping (r. 1 BCE to 6 CE). See Yan Shigu's notes on the title "Favorite Beauty" in *Hanshu* 97A, 3935–3936.

69. *Jianzhao* was one of four periods in Emperor Yuan's reign and lasted from 38 to 34 BCE. For background on animal combat, see Mark Edward Lewis, *Sanctioned Violence in Early China* (Albany: State University of New York Press, 1990), 150–157. This story was included in the "Admonitions Scroll" of Gu Kaizhi (c. 345–406 CE), but only the caption remains, and the illustration has been lost. For this painting and other illustrations of this story, see Shane McCausland, ed., *Gu Kaizhi and the Admonitions Scroll* (London: The British Museum Press, 2003), 65–67, 126–127, 146, 157, 169.

70. Her son was first made the king of Xindu (37 BCE). After Emperor Yuan died (33 BCE), she first became Queen Dowager of Xindu and then later Queen Dowager of Zhongshan. She died by her own hand in 6 BCE after being accused of uttering imprecations against the emperor. See *Hanshu* 97B, 4005–4007.

71. *Odes, Qin Feng*, "Si Tie," Mao no. 127. Translation based on Legge, *The Chinese Classics*, vol. 4, 191.

72. *Analects*, II:24.2. Translation based on Legge, *The Chinese Classics*, vol. 1, 154.

73. Wang Zhang's style name was Zhongqing. He was noted for his loyalty but nevertheless died in prison in 24 BCE after being slandered by the Marshal of State, Wang Feng, whom Wang Zhang had fearlessly criticized. See *Hanshu* 76, 3238–3239.

74. Wang Feng was the eldest brother of Yuandi's empress, Wang Zhengjun, and was thus the maternal uncle of Emperor Cheng (r. 33–7 BCE). Wang Feng was also the uncle of the "usurper" Wang Mang (r. 9–23 CE), a connection that contributed to the negative portrayal of Wang Feng in early sources.

75. See *Hanshu* 97B, 3982. In Han times, celestial events were often interpreted as signs of Heavenly judgment.

76. "Greatly refractory" (大逆 *dani*) was a term used in Han times for an especially abominable crime (such as rebellion) that was often directed against the ruler. See Hulsewe, *Remnants of Han Law*, 156–176.

77. Here I follow the text as it appears in the *Hanshu* 76, 3239.

78. Wang Zhang died in 24 BCE.

79. Hepu was a commandery located northeast of the vicinity of modern-day Hepu in Guangxi province. The transfer was a form of exile.

80. Wang Shang was the half-brother of Wang Feng and Empress Dowager Wang Zhengjun. He died in 12 BCE.

81. According to the *Hanshu*, Wang Zhang's wife and daughter had amassed a large collection of pearls. By selling the pearls, they were able to move back into their former home. See *Hanshu* 76, 3239.

82. The principle of "contracting and expanding" refers to the ability to be flexible and to proceed or withdraw when appropriate.

83. *Odes, Xiao Ya*, "Qiao Yan," Mao no. 198. Translation based on Legge, *The Chinese Classics*, vol. 4, 340.

84. Wang Zhaoyuan's edition includes the word *nü* (女) after the name Ban in the title. See LNZHB, vol. 5, 630. I follow Liang Duan and omit it.

85. Favorite Beauty was the second highest rank of imperial concubine, second only to that of Brilliant Companion. Emperor Cheng reigned from 33 to 7 BCE. This biography follows with minor differences Ban's biography in *Hanshu* 97B, 3983–3988; translated in Watson, *Courtier and Commoner*, 261–265.

86. The Three Epochs are the three dynasties of antiquity, the Xia, Shang, and Western Zhou. The last rulers of the three eras are Jie of the Xia, Zhow of the Shang, and King You of the Zhou. Accounts of their female favorites are found in LNZ 7.1, 7.2, and

7.3, respectively. These rulers were regarded as particularly reprehensible since they are held responsible for destroying their dynasties.

87. See Fan Ji's biography in LNZ 2.5. The empress dowager was Wang Zhengjun (71 BCE to 13 CE), consort of Emperor Yuan and mother of Emperor Cheng.

88. *The Modest and Retiring, Emblems of Virtue,* and *The Instructress* are the titles of lost texts. The first title is a phrase drawn for the first song of the *Odes.*

89. The dates of the *hongjia* period are 20–17 BCE.

90. Empress Wei, a former slave, was the consort of Emperor Wu (r. 141–87 BCE).

91. Zhao Feiyan was a slave who rose to the position of empress. See her biography in LNZ 8.15; and *Hanshu* 97B, 3988–3999; translated in Watson, *Courtier and Commoner,* 265–277. "Uttering imprecations" (i.e., laying spells on or cursing others) was a serious crime in Han times, particularly when the object of the curse was the emperor and his family. See Hulsewe, *Remnants of Han Law,* 167–169. These events occurred around 18 BCE.

92. Her words recall those of Ding Jiang to Duke Xian's brother Zhuan in LNZ 1.7.

93. One *jin* in Western Han times was equivalent to approximately 245 grams.

94. The Eastern Palace was another name for the Palace of Eternal Trust, the residence of the empress dowager.

95. The inner or rear courtyard was the residence of palace women located behind the main palace.

96. Zengcheng was the name of a residence in the palace grounds nearby the imperial harem.

97. According to Yan Shigu's note, when a girl became a bride, her father tied her nuptial sash and gave her words of instruction. See *Hanshu* 97B, 3986, note 5.

98. The "wife who announces the dawn" refers to the subversion of the patriarchal family whereby the wife dictates to the husband, a state of affairs considered to be as unnatural as a hen rather than a cock crowing at dawn. This allusion to Bao Si, the wife of King You of Zhou, comes from "The Speech at Mu," part 3, of the *Shangshu*; translated in Legge, *The Chinese Classics,* vol. 3, 302–303. For Bao Si and King You, see LNZ 7.3.

99. This line is thought to refer to *Odes, Xiao Ya,* "Shi Yue Zhi Jiao," Mao no. 193. Translated in Legge, *The Chinese Classics,* vol. 4, 322. Also see *Hanshu* 85, 3444–3445.

100. On Huang and Ying, see LNZ 1.1.

101. On Ren and Si, see LNZ 1.6.

102. According to Yan Shigu, Yanglu and Zhe Hall were residences in Shanglin Park where Ban gave birth. See *Hanshu* 97B, 3986, note 11.

103. According to Yan Shigu, the term "to provide end-of-life care" (末流 *moliu*) may also mean "the lowest ranks of women attendants." See *Hanshu* 97B, 3986–3987, note 3. Ban Jieyu's mother-in-law, Empress Dowager Wang Zhengjun, lived to be 84, dying in 13 CE, some twenty years after her son, Emperor Cheng. Ban cared for her mother-in-law for about twelve years, from the time when the empress dowager was about age 56 to age 68. Ban then moved to Emperor Cheng's funerary park sometime after his

death in 7 BCE. Given Empress Dowager Wang's active political involvement to the end of her life, she must have enjoyed relatively good health.

104. According the *Xijing zaji* of Ge Hong (284–364 CE), Emperor Cheng's residences at Ganquan included a palace known as the Palace of the Three Clouds, which was decorated with cloud motifs. See *Xijing zaji*, in Tao Zongyi (1279–1368), ed., *Shuofu*, 100 vols. (Shanghai: Shangwu yinshuguan, 1927), vol. 11, 20/16A.

105. *Odes, Bei Feng,* "Lü Yi," Mao no. 27; *Xiao Ya,* "Bai Hua," Mao no. 229; Legge, *The Chinese Classics,* vol. 4, 41–42, 416–418. Both odes are traditionally interpreted as concerned with wives whose positions are usurped by concubines.

106. Emperor Cheng's tomb was called Yanling. See *Hanshu* 10, 330.

107. For Queen Xuan, see LNZ 2.1; Fan Ji, see LNZ 2.5; and Ding Jiang, see LNZ 1.7. The text has Widow Li (李); but I follow Wang Shaolan's suggestion that *li* is an error for "filial" (孝 *xiao*) and that the reference is to the Filial Widow of Chen, whose biography appears in LNZ 4.15. See LNZHB, vol. 8, 393.

108. *Odes, Wey Feng,* "Qi Yu," Mao no. 55. Translation based on Legge, *The Chinese Classics,* vol. 4, 91.

109. Despite the title, this biography deals mainly with Zhao Feiyan's sister, the Brilliant Companion Zhao. This account shares many features with the biography of Zhao Feiyan and her sister found in *Hanshu* 97B, 3988–3999; and translated in Watson, *Courtier and Commoner,* 265–277. Emperor Cheng reigned from 33 to 7 BCE. Chengyang was a district northeast of present-day Xinyang in Henan province.

110. In early China, parents signified their acceptance of a newborn by ritually lifting it up from the ground; children they decided not to raise were left to die or abandoned in the hope that others might raise them. Her survival after three days indicates that she was born with exceptional endowments. See Kinney, *Representations of Childhood,* 97–118.

111. On his incognito wanderings, see *Hanshu* 27B.1, 1395; 59, 3988. LNZ has Heyang while the *Hanshu* has Yang'a. Yan Shigu claims that Yang'a is often erroneously written as Heyang. See *Hanshu* 97B, 3988, note 2. Yang'a was a district northwest of modern Yangcheng in Shanxi province.

112. "Fair Lady" was fifth in the fourteen ranks of imperial concubines. See *Hanshu* 97A, 3935. According to the *Hanshu,* this event occurred in 11 BCE, when Emperor Cheng was 40 years old. See *Hanshu* 97B, 3993.

113. The central palace was where the empress lived.

114. The text here is a contracted version of parallel text in *Hanshu* 97B, 3993.

115. *Hanshu* 97B, 3993, states that the infant was placed in a basket rather than a leather case.

116. According to the *Hanshu,* this event occurred in 12 BCE, when Emperor Cheng was 39 years old. See *Hanshu* 97B, 3990. In contrast to the *Hanshu* account, LNZ reverses the chronological order of the incidents concerning Cao Gong and Fair Lady Xu.

117. The Lateral Courts were residences within the imperial palace that housed the women of the harem. The courts also included a prison, staffed by eunuchs, for women of the

harem. The Yellow Gates led to the women's quarters of the palace. See Hans Bielenstein, *Bureaucracy of Han Times* (Cambridge, England: Cambridge University Press, 1980), 52–53, 171, note 208. According to *Hanshu* 97B, 3991, the Palace Attendant at the Yellow Gates was the eunuch official Tian Ke.

118. According to the *Hanshu*, the letter and medicine were sent by Emperor Cheng. See *Hanshu* 97B, 3991.

119. The peak, which is in fact an inherited genetic trait, showed that Emperor Yuan was the child's grandfather.

120. Emperor Cheng's half-nephew, Liu Xin, who was known as Emperor Ai (r. 7–1 BCE), was enthroned. He was the grandson of Emperor Yuan by a concubine and the son of King Gong of Dingtao by a concubine surnamed Ding. At age three *sui*, he succeeded his father as king.

121. See LNZ 7.3.

122. *Odes, Da Ya,* "Shao Min," Mao no. 265. Translation based on Waley, *The Book of Songs,* 286.

123. Emperor Cheng's maternal uncles, for example, Wang Feng and Wang Shang, dominated the government. See Homer Dubs, *The History of the Former Han Dynasty* (Baltimore: Waverly Press, 1944), vol. 2, 358–361.

124. The implication here is that Emperor Cheng had depleted his own line of descent.

125. Her LNZ biography is similar to that found in *Hanshu* 97B, 4009–4011. Emperor Ping, who came to the throne at age eight, reigned from 1 BCE to 6 CE. Wang Mang, a despised figure in Chinese history, served as Emperor Ping's regent. After the emperor died, he held the title of "acting" (*jia* 假) emperor and dispensed with the title "regent" (*she* 攝) until he finally usurped the throne in 9 CE, when he established his own dynasty. However, modern historians generally believe that the portrait of Wang Mang painted in the *Hanshu* is unjust and that he was an able ruler. Hans Bielenstein attributes his fall to the catastrophic events that arose when the Yellow River changed course. See Loewe and Twitchett, *The Ch'in and Han Empires,* 232–240. The title, An Han Duke, can also be translated as "Duke Giving Tranquility to the Han."

126. Huo Guang, regent to Emperor Zhao (r. 87–74 BCE), saw his six-year-old granddaughter married to the emperor in 83 BCE. She was known as Empress Shangguan. See *Hanshu* 97A, 3957.

127. This event occurred in 3 CE. Wang Mang at first proclaimed with false modesty that his daughter was not worthy of consideration, only to engender protests against her exclusion. On Wang Mang's hypocritical display during his daughter's betrothal, see *Hanshu* 99A, 4051–4053; Dubs, *History of the Former Han Dynasty,* vol. 3, 154–162. On the rites concerning the presentation of betrothal gifts, see *Yili,* "Shi Hun Li," in SSJZS, vol. 1, 4/17B, 962B; translated in John Steele, *The I-li* (London: Probsthain, 1917), 18.

128. On amnesties, see Michael Loewe, "The Orders of Aristocratic Rank of Han China," *T'oung Pao* 49, no.1–3 (1960): 165–171.

129. Following *Hanshu* 97B, 4011, reading *yu* (豫) as (櫞) See LNZHB, vol. 7, 589. Sun Jian (d. 15 CE) was an important general and statesman affiliated with Wang Mang.

130. For historical background, see Loewe and Twitchett, *The Ch'in and Han Empires*, 248.

131. *Odes, Yong Feng*, "Bo Zhou," Mao no. 45. Translation based on Legge, *The Chinese Classics*, vol. 4, 73.

132. After the fall of Wang Mang's Xin dynasty (r. 9–23 CE), Liu Shenggong, the Gengshi Emperor (r. 23–25 CE), was the first emperor of the Later Han. He was nevertheless not regarded as the founder of the Later Han. His name was Liu Xuan; Shenggong was his courtesy name. He was a sixth-generation descendant of Emperor Jing. Liu Xuan's third cousin, Liu Xiu, known as Emperor Guangwu (r. 25–57 CE), went on to become the founder of the Later Han. Lady Hann is mentioned in Fan Ye, et al., *Hou Hanshu* (Beijing: Zhonghua shuju, 1965), 11, 471.

133. Troops composed mostly of commoners from Pinglin (northeast of present-day Dangyang county in Hubei), Xinshi (in the vicinity of modern-day Nanyang in Henan), and the area of the Lower Yangzi River joined together and proclaimed Liu Xuan emperor in 23 CE. See *Hanshu* 99C, 4180; translated in Dubs, *History of the Former Han Dynasty*, vol. 3, 437.

134. Shentu Jian, a general who served the Gengshi Emperor, sent Wang Mang's head to the emperor at Yuan (in the vicinity of modern-day Nanyang in Henan), the site of the provisional capital. See *Hou Hanshu* 11, 469.

135. See LNZ 8.10. Huo Guang, regent to Emperor Zhao, unlike Wang Mang, resisted the temptation to usurp the throne from his underaged ruler.

136. On the demise of the Gengshi Emperor's rule, see Loewe and Twitchett, *The Ch'in and Han Empires*, 248–251, and *Hanshu* 99C, 4190–4193; translated in Dubs, *History of the Former Han Dynasty*, vol. 3, 466–470.

137. Sometime between 3 and 5 CE, the Yellow River broke its dikes and divided, maintaining its original path but opening a new branch. In 11 CE, it shifted again. The ensuing floods created a wave of refugees and famine. Starving peasants organized themselves into a desperate lawless group called the Red Eyebrows, for the red paint they applied to their foreheads to distinguish themselves from government troops that sought to quell their marauding forces. See Loewe and Twitchett, *The Ch'in and Han Empires*, 240–245. The pass refers to the Hangu Pass, which led to the capital, and is located in present-day Lingbao county in Henan province.

138. *Odes, Xiao Ya*, "Xiao Yuan," Mao no. 196. Translation based on Legge, *The Chinese Classics*, vol. 4, 334.

139. Liang Hong's biography, which includes a similar account of his marriage, is found in *Hou Hanshu* 83, 2765–2786; trans. in Burton Watson, "*Hou Han shu*: Biographies of Recluses," *Renditions* 33–34 (1990): 47–48. Also see discussion in Alan J. Berkowitz, *Patterns of Disengagement: The Practice and Portrayal of Reclusion in Early Medieval China* (Stanford: Stanford University Press, 2000), 106–113. Youfufeng was an administrative unit west of present-day Xi'an in Shaanxi province.

140. They took new names to protect their identities. Baling was a district northeast of present-day Xi'an in Shaanxi province.

141. Wang Mang (see LNZ 8.16–17) reigned from 9 to 23 CE.

142. Kauiji was a commandery in the area of present-day Suzhou in Jiangsu province.

143. In the account in the *Hou Hanshu*, it is the wife's reverent treatment of her husband that prompts others to respect him.

144. *Analects,* VII:15. Translation based on Legge, *The Chinese Classics*, vol. 1, 200.

145. Empress Mingde (40–79 CE) was also known as Empress Ma. Her biography is found in *Hou Hanshu* 10A, 407–414. Her father's biography is found in *Hou Hanshu* 24, 827–852. Emperor Ming reigned from 57 to 75 CE. Xinxi was a district in present-day Xi county in Henan province.

146. The heir apparent was the future Emperor Ming.

147. Emperor Ming had probably just come to the throne at this time, but the narrative does not specifically mention his accession. Empress Ma entered the palace around 53 CE, while Emperor Ming came to the throne in 57 CE, and in 60 CE Ma was named empress.

148. The third year of the *yongping* era corresponds to 60 CE. The term "eight concubines," according to Yan Shigu, refers to the traditional view that the ruler marries nine women, that is, one legal wife and eight concubines. See *Hanshu* 27A, 1322, note 2. According to the notes complied by Li Xian (651–684), the Palace of Prolonged Autumn was so named because autumn was the season in which things mature and come into fruition. See *Hou Hanshu* 10A, 408–409.

149. The first emperor of the Later Han abolished the Former Han system of titles used for imperial concubines and employed only three designations, of which "Honorable Lady" was the highest. See *Hou Hanshu* 10A, 400; and Bielenstein, *The Bureaucracy of Han Times*, 74.

150. The Qiang people are thought to be the predecessors of the Tibetans. The Hu are associated with the Xiongnu peoples who lived in the north and northwest. The Wo have been identified with the inhabitants of northern Kyūshū, and the Yue are associated with the area of present-day Viet Nam. See Ying-shih Yü, *Trade and Expansion in Han China* (Berkeley: University of California Press, 1967), 51–53, 185. Empress Ma's father earned renown for his subjugation of both the Qiang and Yue peoples. See Loewe and Twitchett, *The Ch'in and Han Empires*, 271. It is significant that these four groups represent the peoples dwelling at the four corners of the Later Han empire.

151. Here I follow Chen Hanzhang's emendations based on a parallel passage from the *Xu Hou Hanshu*. See LNZHB, vol. 8, 684. The *Hou Hanshu* gives a slightly different account and also states that she was particularly fond of the *Zhou Guan* (Institutes of Zhou) and the works of Dong Zhongshu. See *Hou Hanshu* 10A, 409.

152. Emperor Guangwu (r. 25–57 CE) was her father-in-law.

153. Here I follow the text of *Hou Hanshu* 10A, 410 (囚相證引).

154. The case concerned Liu Ying, the King of Chu (a son of Emperor Guangwu by a concubine), who in 70 CE was deposed and exiled for heterodox religious practices (associated with Huang-Lao and Buddhism) and for making illegal official appointments. Thousands of people were implicated and arrested in connection with this case. See *Hou Hanshu* 2, 117; 42, 1428–1429.

155. Here I follow the parallel reading found in *Dongguan Hanji*. See D. C. Lau, ed., *A Concordance to the* Dongguan Hanji (Hong Kong: The Commercial Press, 1994), 34 (6.2/34/24).

156. The general was the empress's elder half-brother, Ma Liao (d. 92 CE). See *Hou Hanshu* 24, 853–855.

157. The empress's younger half-brothers were Ma Fang (d. 91 CE) and Ma Guang (d.101 CE). See *Hou Hanshu* 24, 855–858.

158. The *yongping* era corresponds to 58–75 CE.

159. Emperor Ming died in 75 CE and was succeeded by Emperor Zhang. Emperor Zhang was the son of the Empress Ma's cousin but had been officially assigned as Empress Ma's son. At the death of her husband, Empress Ma took the title Empress Dowager.

160. The suggestion was to revive the practice of granting to the maternal relatives of the emperor "Grace and Favor" marquisates. Empress Ma was determined not to repeat the mistakes that led to the downfall of the Former Han; that is, the granting of ranks and privileges to the Wang family, the maternal kin of the emperor. See *Hou Hanshu* 10A, 411. For the Wang family, see LNZ 8.16.

161. The King of Chu (Liu Ying, d. 71 CE) and the King of Huaiyang (Liu Yan, d. 89 CE) were sons of Emperor Guangwu.

162. The Yin family was the family of Emperor Guangwu's Empress Yin Lihua (d. 64 CE). She was the mother of Emperor Ming.

163. Clothing was scented with incense.

164. Glittering Dragon Park was located near the north palace.

165. For this reading I follow Wang Zhaoyuan; see LNZHB, vol. 5, 656 (8/35). De Crespigny translates the title "Minister of Agriculture" as "Minister of Finance," as the control of government granaries was only one among many fiscal responsibilities assigned to this official. See Rafe de Crespigny, *A Biographical Dictionary of Later Han to the Three Kingdoms (23–220 AD)* (Leiden: Brill, 2007), 1224.

166. The Palace of Eternal Joy was the residence of the Empress Dowager.

167. Empress Ma's younger half-brother, Ma Fang, served as Colonel of the City Gates, guarding the twelve gates of the capital. Her half-brother Ma Guang served as Colonel of the Elite Cavalry and commanded one of five regiments stationed at camps near Luoyang.

168. The King of Guangping, Liu Xian (d. 96 CE), the King of Julu, Liu Gong (d. 117 CE), and the King of Lecheng, Liu Dang (d. 96 CE), were all Emperor Ming's sons by unknown concubines. One Han dynasty foot was equivalent to approximately 23 cm.

169. Emperor Zhang reigned from 75 to 88 CE. Later Han sumptuary rules prohibited women in this rank from wearing purple. See *Hou Hanshu* 30, 3677. The identity of

the Xinping princess is not clear. Xinping was in Zuopingyi commandery. From 41 to 54 CE it had been the kingdom of Liu Yan (d. 90 CE), the youngest son of Emperor Guangwu by his first empress. Because he was favored by the young Emperor Zhang and resided in the capital at this time, it is possible that this princess was connected with his household. On Liu Yan, see *Hou Hanshu* 42, 1449–1450; 109, 3405–3406. For further speculation, see Chen Hangzhong, LNZHB, vol. 8, 684 (2/15–16). Confucius was famously against wearing purple. See *Lunyu* X:6 and Legge's note at *The Chinese Classics*, vol. 1, 230–231.

170. *Odes, Da Ya,* "Sang Rou," Mao no. 257. Translation based on Legge, *The Chinese Classics*, vol. 4, 524.

171. After the early death of her mother, Lady Liang Yi (62–? CE) and her two sisters were brought up by her aunt, Princess Liu Yiwang. Princess Liu Yiwang, a daughter of Emperor Guangwu, was married to Liang Song (松), the brother of Lady Liang Yi's father, Liang Song (竦). Emperor He reigned from 88 to 106 CE. Liang Yi's sister, Empress Gonghuai, was the concubine of Emperor Zhang (r. 75–88 CE). She did not receive the title of empress until after her death. See *Hou Hanshu* 10A, 417. Fan Diao was a member of the prominent Fan clan and a descendant of the elder brother of Fan Hong, an important ally of Emperor Guangwu.

172. Emperor He, Liu Zhao, was born in 79 CE.

173. Empress Dou (d. 97 CE), was named empress in 78 CE when she was about fifteen years old. In 82 CE, this child, Liu Zhao, the future Emperor He and son of Lady Liang and Emperor Zhang, was named heir to the throne.

174. Liang Song died in 83 CE. Anding is located northwest of present-day Pingliang county in Gansu province. See *Hou Hanshu* 34, 1172. Jiuzhen was located in the southern part of what is now called the "North" of present-day Viet Nam.

175. For details, see Loewe and Twitchett, *The Ch'in and Han Empires*, 274–283.

176. This memorial, with subtle differences, is found in *Hou Hanshu*, 34, 1172–1173.

177. Dou Xian (d. 92 CE) was the brother of Empress Dou. He served as regent to the young Emperor He, and his family members dominated the court. For details, see Loewe and Twitchett, *The Ch'in and Han Empires*, 280–283. The *Hou Hanshu* tells us that Lady Liang and her sister "died of grief," a term that is often employed as a euphemism for a person being persecuted and forced to commit suicide. *Hou Hanshu*, 10A, 416.

178. See *Hou Hanshu*, 34, 1172.

179. As a member of the family of her husband, Fan Diao, she escaped punishment.

180. Liang Tang and his brothers Yong and Di were all sent to Jiuzhen in 83 after their father's execution.

181. Bo Yi was the concubine of Former Han Emperor Gaozu and the mother of Emperor Wen. After the death of Emperor Hui (Emperor Gaozu's son by Empress Lü) and after Empress Lü's effort to install on the throne a number of false sons of Emperor Hui, the son of Bo Yi came to the throne as Emperor Wen. See Dubs, *History of the Former Han Dynasty*, vol. 1, 215–216. Shi Liangdi was the consort of Emperor Wu's first heir

apparent, Liu Ju. Her son, Liu Jin, was the father of Emperor Xuan. Liu Ju and all of his offspring were executed after he had been charged with treason between 92 and 91 BCE. Only one infant, the future Emperor Xuan, survived, having been secretly reared by eunuchs. When Emperor Zhao died with no heirs in 74 BCE, Emperor Xuan was brought to the throne and various privileges were conferred on the Shi family. See Dubs, *History of the Former Han Dynasty,* vol. 2, 183–184.

182. The Dou family had apparently suppressed the identity of the emperor's true mother.
183. A slightly different post is mentioned in his biography. See *Hou Hanshu*, 34, 1173.
184. The three "kingdoms" were the three fiefs conferred upon her brothers.
185. *Odes, Da Ya,* "Wen Wang," Mao no. 235. Translation based on Legge, *The Chinese Classics,* vol. 4, 429.

WORKS CITED

ABBREVIATIONS

LNZHB   *Lienü zhuan huibian* of Zheng Xiaoxia and Lin Jianyu
SBCK   *Sibu congkan zhengbian* of Wang Yunwu
SBBY   *Sibu beiyao* of the Zhonghua shuju
SSJZS   *Shisanjing zhushu* of Ruan Yuan

Allan, Sarah. "The Identities of Taigong Wang in Zhou and Han Literature." *Monumenta Serica* 30 (1972–1973): 57–99.
——. *The Heir and Sage: Dynastic Legend in Early China*. San Francisco: Chinese Materials Center, 1981.
——. "Not the *Lun yu*: The Chu Script Bamboo Manuscript, *Zigao*, and the Nature of Early Confucianism." *Bulletin of the School of African and Oriental Studies* 72, no. 1 (2009): 115–151.
Allen, Joseph Roe. "The End and the Beginning of Narrative Poetry in China." *Asia Major* 2, no. 1 (1989): 1–24.
Ariel, Yoav. *K'ung-Ts'ung-Tzu: The K'ung Family Masters' Anthology*. Princeton: Princeton University Press, 1989.
Ban Gu. *Hanshu*. Beijing: Zhonghua shuju, 1962.
Berkowitz, Alan J. *Patterns of Disengagement: The Practice and Portrayal of Reclusion in Early Medieval China*. Stanford: Stanford University Press, 2000.
Bielenstein, Hans. *The Bureaucracy of Han Times*. Cambridge, England: Cambridge University Press, 1980.
Blakeley, Barry B. "King, Clan and Courtier in Ancient Ch'u." *Asia Major*, 3rd series, 5, no. 2 (1992): 1–39.
——. "Chu Society and State: Image versus Reality." In *Defining Chu: Image and Reality*, ed. Constance Cook and John S. Major, 51–66. Honolulu: University of Hawai'i Press, 1999.

——. "The Geography of Chu." In *Defining Chu: Image and Reality,* ed. Constance Cook and John S. Major, 9–20. Honolulu: University of Hawai'i Press, 1999.

Bodde, Derk. *Festivals in Classical China: New Year and Other Annual Observances During the Han Dynasty 206 B.C.–A.D. 220.* Princeton: Princeton University Press, 1975.

Boltz, William. "Philological Footnotes to the Han New Year Rites." *Journal of the American Oriental Society* 99, no. 3 (July–Sept. 1979): 423–439.

Bray, Francesca. *Science and Civilisation in China.* Vol. 6, part II. General ed. Joseph Needham. Cambridge, England: Cambridge University Press, 1984.

Bridgman, R. F. "Le Médecine dans le Chine Antique." *Mélanges chinois et bouddhiques* 10, no. 1 (1955): 1–213.

Brooks, E. Bruce and Takeo Brooks, trans. *The Original Analects: Sayings of Confucius and His Successors.* New York: Columbia University Press, 1998.

Cao Jinyan. *Zhejiang Daxue cang Zhanguo Chu jian.* Hangzhou: Zhejiang daxue chubanshe, 2011.

Cao Zhaolan. *Jinwen yu Yin Zhou nüxing wenhua.* Beijing: Beijing daxue chubanshe, 2004.

Chang, Kwang chih. *Shang Civilization.* New Haven: Yale University Press, 1980.

Ch'en Ch'i-yun. *Hsün Yüeh: The Life and Reflections of an Early Medieval Confucian.* Cambridge, England: Cambridge University Press, 1975.

——. *Hsün Yüeh and the Mind of Late Han China.* Princeton: Princeton University Press, 1980.

Chen Liping. *Liu Xiang* Lienü zhuan *yanjiu.* Beijing: Zhongguo shehui kexue yuan, 2010.

Chen Zhi. "A New Reading of 'Yen-Yen.'" *T'oung Pao,* 2nd series, 85, no. 1–3 (1999):1–28.

Crump, James Irving. *Chan-kuo Ts'e.* 2nd ed., revised. San Francisco: Chinese Materials Center, 1979.

de Bary, William Theodore. *Sources of Chinese Tradition.* 2 vols. New York: Columbia University Press, 1960.

de Crespigny, Rafe. *A Biographical Dictionary of Later Han to the Three Kingdoms (23–220 AD).* Leiden: Brill, 2007.

DeWoskin, Kenneth. *A Song for One or Two: Music and the Concept of Art in Early China.* Ann Arbor: University of Michigan Center for Chinese Studies, 1982.

Di Cosmo, Nicola. *Ancient China and Its Enemies: The Rise of Nomadic Power in East Asian History.* Cambridge, England: Cambridge University Press, 2002.

Dobson, W.A.C.H. "Linguistic Evidence and the Dating of the *Book of Songs.*" *T'oung Pao* 51, no. 4–5 (1964): 322–334.

Dongguan Hanji zhuzi suoyin. Hong Kong: Commercial Press, 1994.

Dubs, Homer. *History of the Former Han Dynasty.* Baltimore: Waverly Press, 1944.

Dull, Jack L. "Marriage and Divorce in Traditional China: A Glimpse at 'Pre-Confucian' Society." In *Chinese Family Law and Social Change in Historical and Comparative Perspective,* ed. David C. Buxbaum, 23–74. Seattle: University of Washington Press, 1978.

Durrant, Stephen, Wai-yee Li, and David Schaberg, trans. *Zuo Traditions*/Zuozhuan *(Commentary on Spring and Autumn Annals).* Classics of Chinese Thought. Seattle and London: University of Washington Press, 2014.

Englert, Siegfried and Roderisch Ptak. "Nan-Tzu, or Why Heaven Did Not Crush Confucius." *Journal of the American Oriental Society* 106, no. 4 (Oct.–Dec. 1986): 679–686.

Fan Ye, et al. *Hou Hanshu.* Beijing: Zhonghua shuju, 1965.

Fu Sinian. *Fu Sinian quanji.* 7 vols. Taipei: Lianjing chuban gongsi, 1980.

Gai Shanlin. *Helinger Han mu bihua.* Huhehot: Neimenggu renmin chubanshe, 1978.

Guo Moruo. *Zhongguo shigao ditu ji.* Shanghai: Ditu chubanshe, 1979.

Guo Qinghua. *The Minqqi Pottery Buildings of Han Dynasty China 206 BC–AD 220: Architectural Representations and Represented Architecture.* Eastbourne, Sussex, UK: Sussex Academic Press, 2010.

Guoli zhongyang tushuguan. *Guoli zhongyang tushuguan shanben xu, ba, jilu.* 8 vols. Beijing: Guoli zhongyang tushuguan, 1992–1994.

Guoyu. 2 vols. Shanghai: Guji chubanshe, 1978.

Hardy, Grant. *Worlds of Bronze and Bamboo: Sima Qian's Conquest of History.* New York: Columbia University Press, 1999.

Harper, Donald J. "Chinese Demonography of the Third Century B.C." *Harvard Journal of Asiatic Studies* 45, no. 2 (1985): 459–498.

——. *Early Chinese Medical Literature: The Mawangdui Medical Manuscripts.* London: Kegan Paul International, 1998.

Hattori Unokichi. *Kanbun Taikei.* Taipei: Xinwenfeng chubanshe, 1978.

Hawkes, David, trans. *The Songs of the South: An Ancient Chinese Anthology of Poems by Qu Yuan and Other Poets Translated, Annotated and Introduced by David Hawkes.* Harmondsworth: Penguin, 1985.

Henry, Eric. "'Junzi yue' versus 'Zhongni yue' in *Zuo zhuan.*" *Harvard Journal of Asiatic Studies* 59, no. 1 (1999): 125–161.

——. "Anachronisms in *Lüshi Chunqiu* and *Shuo Yuan.*" *Early Medieval China* 9 (2003): 127–138.

——, trans. *Garden of Eloquence.* Seattle: University of Washington Press, forthcoming.

Hightower, James. *Han Shih Wai Chuan: Han Ying's Illustrations of the Didactic Application of the Classic of Songs.* Cambridge, Mass.: Harvard University Press, 1952.

——. "Ch'ü Yuan Studies." *Silver Jubilee Volume of Zinbun-Kagaku-Kenkyusyo, Kyoto* 1 (1954): 192–223.

Hinsch, Bret. "Reading the *Lienüzhuan* (Biographies of Women) through the Life of Liu Xiang." *Journal of Asian History* 39, no. 2 (2005): 129–157.

——. "The Composition of *Lienüzhuan*: Was Liu Xiang the Author or Editor?" *Asia Major,* 3rd series, 20, no. 1 (2007): 1–23.

Ho Che Wah, Chu Kwok Fan, and Fan Siu Piu. *The Gu Lienü Zhuan with Parallel Passages from Other Pre-Han and Han Texts, The Da Dai Liji with Parallel Passages from Other Pre-Han and Han Texts.* Hong Kong: The Chinese University of Hong Kong, 2004.

Hsu, Elisabeth. *Pulse Diagnosis in Early Chinese Medicine: The Telling Touch.* Cambridge, England: Cambridge University Press, 2010.

Huang, Huaixin, annotator. *Xiao Erya huijiao ji shi.* Xi'an: San Qin chubanshe, 2003.

Huang Qingquan, annotator, and Chen Manming, ed. *Xinyi Lienü zhuan*. Taipei: Sanmin shuju, 1996.

Huber, Louisa. "The Bo Capital and Questions Concerning Xia and Early Shang." *Early China* 13 (1988): 46–77.

Hucker, Charles O. *A Dictionary of Official Titles in Imperial China*. Stanford: Stanford University Press, 1985.

Hulsewe, A.F.P. *Remnants of Han Law*. Leiden: E. J. Brill, 1955.

——. *Remnants of Ch'in Law: An Annotated Translation of the Ch'in Legal and Administrative Rules of the 3rd Century B.C. Discovered in Yunmeng Prefecture, Hu-pei Province in 1975*. Leiden: Brill, 1985.

Hung, Chan Man, ed. *Gu Lienü zhuan zhuzi suoyin*. Hong Kong: Commercial Press, 1993.

Johnston, Ian, trans. *The Mozi: A Complete Translation*. New York: Columbia University Press, 2010.

Judge, Joan and Hu Ying, eds. *Beyond Exemplar Tales: Womens' Biography in Chinese History*. Berkeley: University of California Press, 2011.

Karlgren, Bernhard. "Some Fecundity Symbols in Ancient China." *Bulletin of the Museum of Far Eastern Antiquities* 2 (1930): 1–54.

——, trans. *The Book of Odes*. Goteborg: Elanders Boktryckeri Aktiebolag, 1950.

——. *Glosses on the Book of Odes*. Goteborg: Elanders Boktrykeri Aktiebolag, 1964.

Keightley, David N. *The Origins of Chinese Civilization*. Berkeley: University of California Press, 1983.

Kern, Martin. *The Stele Inscriptions of Ch'in-shih-huang: Text and Ritual in Early Chinese Imperial Representation*. New Haven: American Oriental Society, 2000.

Kierman, Frank, trans. *China in Antiquity,* by Henri Maspero. No city: University of Massachusetts Press, 1978.

Kinney, Anne Behnke. "Death by Fire." Available at www2.iath.virginia.edu/xwomen/boji_essay.html.

——. *Representations of Childhood and Youth in Early China*. Stanford: Stanford University Press, 2004.

——. "The Book of Odes as a Source for Women's History." In *Overt and Covert Treasures: Essays on the Sources for Chinese Women's History*, ed. Clara Wing-chung Ho, 61–111. Hong Kong: Chinese University of Hong Kong Press, 2012.

——. "A Spring and Autumn Family," *Chinese Historical Review* 20, no. 2 (2013): 113–137.

——. "The Significance of the Commoner Woman of Qi in the 'Lanming' Chapter of the *Huainanzi*." In *Text in Context: New Perspectives on the Huainanzi,* ed. Sarah Queen and Michael Puett. Leiden: Brill, forthcoming.

Knapp, Keith Nathaniel. "The *Ru* Interpretation of *Xiao*." *Early China* 20 (1995): 195–222.

——. *Selfless Offspring: Filial Children and Social Order in Medieval China*. Honolulu: University of Hawai'i Press, 2005.

Knechtges, David. *Wen xuan*. 3 vols. Princeton: Princeton University Press, 1987–1996.

Knoblock, John. *Xunzi: A Translation and Study of the Complete Works*. 3 vols. Stanford: Stanford University Press, 1982.

Knoblock, John and Jeffrey Riegel. *The Annals of Lü Buwei*. Stanford: Stanford University Press, 2000.

Kuhn, Dieter. "Silk Weaving in Ancient China: From Geometric Figures to Patterns of Pictorial Likeness." *Chinese Science* 12 (1995): 77–114.

——. *Chinese Baskets and Mats*. Wiesbaden: Franz Steiner Verlag, 1980.

——. *Zur Entwicklung der Webstuhltechnologie im alten China*. Heidelberg: Edition Forum, 1990.

——. "Silk Weaving in Ancient China: From Geometric Figures to Patterns of Pictorial Likeness." *Chinese Science* 12 (1995): 77–114.

Kuroda Akira. "Retsujoden zu no kenkyū." *Kyoto gobun* 15 (2008): 1–30.

——. "Retsujoden zu no keifu." *Guoji Hanxue yanjiu tongxun* 4 (2011): 69–133.

Lau, D. C., ed. *A Concordance to the* Huainanzi. Hong Kong: Commercial Press, 1992.

——. *A Concordance to the* Shuoyuan. Hong Kong: Commercial Press, 1992.

—— *A Concordance to the* Xinxu. Hong Kong: Commercial Press, 1992.

——. *A Concordance to the* Gu Lienü zhuan. Hong Kong: Commercial Press, 1993.

——. *A Concordance to the* Dongguan Hanji. Hong Kong: Commercial Press, 1994.

——. *A Concordance to the* Lüshi chunqiu. Hong Kong: Commercial Press, 1994.

——. *A Concordance to the* Xunzi. Hong Kong: Commercial Press, 1996.

——. *A Concordance to the* Chuci. Hong Kong: Commercial Press, 2000.

——. *A Concordance to the* Guanzi. Hong Kong: Commercial Press, 2001.

Lee, Jen-der. "Wet Nurses in Early Imperial China." *Nan Nü* 2, no. 1 (2000): 1–39.

Legge, James, trans. *Li Chi: Book of Rites*. 2 vols. 1885; reprint, New York: University Books, 1967.

——. *The Chinese Classics*. 5 vols. 1893; reprint, Hong Kong: University of Hong Kong Press, 1960.

——. *The Sacred Books of China: The Texts of Confucianism*. Vol. 3 of *The Sacred Books of the East*. Ed. F. Max Müller. Oxford: Clarendon Press, 1899.

Lewis, Mark Edward. *Sanctioned Violence in Early China*. Albany: State University of New York Press, 1990.

——. *Writing and Authority in Early China*. Albany: State University of New York Press, 1999.

——. *The Construction of Space in Early China*. Albany: State University of New York Press, 2006.

Li Fang. *Taiping yulan*. 7 vols. Tainan: Pingping chubanshe, 1965.

Li Feng. *Landscape and Power in Early China: The Crisis and Fall of the Western Zhou, 1045–771 BC*. Cambridge, England: Cambridge University Press, 2006.

——. *Bureaucracy and the State in Early China*. Cambridge, England: Cambridge University Press, 2008.

Li, Wai-yee. *The Readability of the Past in Early Chinese Historiography*. Cambridge, Mass.: Harvard University Asia Center, 2007.

Li Xueqin. *Eastern Zhou and Qin Civilizations*. New Haven: Yale University Press, 1985.

Liang Duan. *Lienü zhuan jiaozhu*. In *Sibu beiyao*. Vol. 104. Taipei: Taiwan zhonghua shuju, 1965.

Liao, W. K. *The Complete Works of Han Fei-tzu*. 2 vols. London: Probsthain, 1939.

Lin Meicun and Li Junming, eds. *Shule heliuhuo chutu Han jian*. Beijing: Wenwu chuban-she, 1984.

Lindell, Kristinia. "Stories of Suicide in Ancient China: An Essay on Chinese Morals." *Acta Orientalia* 35 (1973): 167–239.

Liu, James J.Y. *Chinese Theories of Literature*. Chicago: University of Chicago Press, 1975.

Liu Xie. *Wenxin diaolong zhu*. Taipei: Minglun chubanshe, 1970.

Liu Yiqing. *Shishuo xinyu jiaojian*. Taipei: Letian chubanshe, 1973.

Loewe, Michael. "The Orders of Aristocratic Rank of Han China." *T'oung Pao* 49, no. 1–3 (1960): 165–171.

——. "The Measurement of Grain During the Han Period." *T'oung Pao*, 2nd series, 4, no. 1–2 (1961): 64–95.

——. *Crisis and Conflict in Han China*. London: George Allen and Unwin, 1974.

——. "The Physician Chunyu Yi and His Historical Background." In *En suivant la Voie Royale: mélanges offerts en homage á Léon Vandermeersch*, ed. Jacques Gernet, Marc Kalinowski, and Jean-Pierre Diény, 297–313. Paris: Ecole française d'extrême-orient, 1997.

——. *A Bibliographic Dictionary of the Qin, Former Han and Xin Periods (221 BC–AD 24)*. Leiden: Brill, 2000.

Loewe, Michael and Denis Twitchett, eds. *The Ch'in and Han Empires, 221 B.C.–A.D. 220*. Volume 1 of *The Cambridge History of China*. Cambridge, England: Cambridge University Press, 1986.

Loewe, Michael and Edward L. Shaughnessy, eds. *The Cambridge History of Ancient China: From the Origins of the Civilization to 221 B.C.* Cambridge, England: Cambridge University Press, 1999.

Ma Chiying. *Shiji jinzhu*. 6 vols. Taipei: Taiwan Shangye shuju, 1979.

Ma Zhiquan. "Dunhuang xuanquanzhi *Lienüzhuan* jian kaolun." *Ludong daxue xuebao* 28, no. 6 (2011): 26–29, 65.

Major, John S., Sarah A. Queen, Andrew Seth Meyer, and Harold D. Roth, trans. *The Huainanzi: A Guide to the Theory and Practice of Government in Early Han China*. New York: Columbia University Press, 2010.

Mawangdui Han mu boshu. Vol. 4. Beijing: Wenwu chubanshe, 1985.

McCausland, Shane, ed. *Gu Kaizhi and the Admonitions Scroll*. London: The British Museum Press, 2003.

Murray, Julia K. *Mirror of Morality: Chinese Narrative Illustration and Confucian Ideology*. Honolulu: University of Hawai'i Press, 2007.

Needham, Joseph, et al. *Science and Civilisation in China*. Vol. 5, part IV. Cambridge, England: Cambridge University Press, 1980.

Nienhauser, William. "A Reexamination of 'The Biographies of the Reasonable Officials' in the *Records of the Grand Historian*." *Early China* 16 (1991): 209–233.

Nienhauser, William, et al., trans. *The Grand Scribe's Records*. 6 vols. Bloomington: Indiana University Press, 1994–2006.

O'Hara, Albert Richard. *The Position of Woman in Early China: According to the* Lieh Nü Chuan *"The Biographies of Chinese Women."* Taipei: Mei Ya Publications, 1971.

Osamu, Oba. "The Ordinances on Fords and Passes Excavated from Han Tomb Number 247, Zhangjiashan." *Asia Major*, 3rd series, 14, no. 2 (2001): 119–141.

Ouyang Xun. *Yiwen leiju.* 2 vols. Shanghai: Shanghai guji chubanshe, 1999.

Poo, Mu-Chou. "The Use and Abuse of Wine in Ancient China." *Journal of the Economic and Social History of the Orient* 42, no. 2 (May 1999): 123–151.

Qian Mu. *Han Liu Xiang Xin fuzi nianpu.* Taipei: Taiwan shangwu shuju, 1987.

Qian Tong, et al. *Guoxue jiben congshu.* Shangwu shuju, n.d.

Raphals, Lisa. *Sharing the Light: Representations of Women and Virtue in Early China.* Albany: State University of New York Press, 1998.

Rickett, W. Allyn, trans. *Guanzi: Political, Economic, and Philosophical Essays from Early China.* Princeton: Princeton University Press, 1985.

Riegel, Jeffrey. "Eros, Introversion, and the Beginnings of Shijing Commentary." *Harvard Journal of Asiatic Studies* 57, no. 1 (June 1997): 143–177.

Rosemont, Henry and Roger Ames. *The Chinese Classic of Family Reverence.* Honolulu: University of Hawai'i Press, 2009.

Roth, Harold. *Original Tao.* New York: Columbia University Press, 1999.

Ruan Yuan. *Shisanjing zhushu.* 2 vols. Beijing: Zhonghua shuju, 1979.

Schaberg, David. *A Patterned Past: Form and Thought in Early Chinese Historiography.* Cambridge, Mass.: Harvard University Asia Center, 2001.

Scheidel, Walter. "The Monetary Systems of the Han and Roman Empires." In *Rome and China: Comparative Perspectives on Ancient World Empires,* ed. Walter Scheidel, 137–207. Oxford: Oxford University Press, 2009.

Schneider, Laurence. *A Madman of Ch'u: The Chinese Myth of Loyalty and Dissent.* Berkeley: University of California Press, 1980.

Seidel, Anna. "Buying One's Way to Heaven: The Celestial Treasury in Chinese Religion." *History of Religions* 17, no. 3–4 (1978): 419–431.

Shaughnessy, Edward L. "From Liturgy to Literature: The Ritual Contexts of the Earliest Poems in the *Book of Poetry.*" *Hanxue yanjiu* 13, no. 1 (1995): 133–165.

——. *Before Confucius: Studies in the Creation of the Chinese Classics.* Albany: State University of New York Press, 1997.

——. *New Sources of Early Chinese History: An Introduction to the Reading of Inscriptions and Manuscripts.* Berkeley: The Society for the Study of Early China and the Institute of East Asian Studies, University of California, 1997.

——. *Rewriting Early Chinese Texts.* Albany: State University of New York Press, 2006.

Sheng, Angela. "The Disappearance of Silk Weaves with Weft Effects in Early China." *Chinese Science* 12 (1995): 41–76.

Shih, Vincent Yu-chung. *The Literary Mind and the Carving of Dragons.* New York: Columbia University Press, 1957.

Shimomi Takao. *Ryū kō Retsujoden no Kenkyū.* Tokyo: Tōkaidō daigaku shuppankai, 1989.

Sibu beiyao. 610 vols. Taipei: Taiwan zhonghua shuju, 1965.

Sima Qian. *Shiji*. Beijing: Zhonghua shuju, 1959.

Som, Tjan Tjoe, trans. *Po Hu T'ung: The Comprehensive Discussions in the White Tiger Hall*. 2 vols. Leiden: Brill, 1952.

Steele, John, trans. *The I-li*. London: Probsthain, 1917.

Sterckx, Roel. *Food, Sacrifice, and Sagehood in Early China*. Cambridge, England: Cambridge University Press, 2011.

Sung, Z. D. *The Text of Yi King*. Taipei: Wenhua tushu gongsi, 1975.

Swann, Nancy Lee. *Food and Money in Ancient China: The Earliest Economic History of China to A.D. 25*. Princeton: Princeton University Press, 1950.

Tai Yen-hui. "Divorce in Traditional Chinese Law." In *Chinese Family Law and Social Change in Historical and Comparative Perspective*, ed. David C. Buxbaum, 75–106. Seattle: University of Washington Press, 1978.

Takigawa Kametarū. *Shiki kaichū kōshō*. Taipei: Hongye shuju, 1977.

Tan Qixiang. *Zhongguo lishi ditu ji*. 5 vols. Shanghai: Ditu chubanshe, 1982.

Tang Kejing. *Shuowen jiezi jinshi*. 3 vols. Changsha: Yulu shushe, 1997.

Tao Zongyi, ed. *Shuofu*. 100 vols. Shanghai: Shangwu yinshuguan, 1927.

Teng Zhaozong. "Yinwan Hanmu jiandu gaishu." *Wenwu* 7 (1996): 32–36.

Thatcher, Melvin. "Marriages of the Ruling Elite in the Spring and Autumn Period." In *Marriage and Inequality in Chinese Society*, ed. Rubie S. Watson and Patricia Buckley Ebrey, 25–57. Berkeley: University of California Press, 1991.

Thorp, Robert. *China in the Early Bronze Age: Shang Civilization*. Philadelphia: University of Pennsylvania Press, 2006.

Tsien, Tsuen-hsuin. *Written on Bamboo and Silk: The Beginnings of Chinese Books and Inscriptions*, 2nd ed. Chicago: University of Chicago Press, 2004.

Tran Trong Kim. *Viet Nam Su Luoc*. Saigon: Tan Viet, 1964.

Van Zoeren, Steven. *Poetry and Personality: Reading, Exegesis, and Hermeneutics in Traditional China*. Stanford: Stanford University Press, 1991.

Waley, Arthur. *The Analects of Confucius*. New York: Vintage, 1938.

——. *The Book of Songs*. New York: Grove Press, 1960.

Wang, C. H. *From Ritual to Allegory: Seven Essays in Early Chinese Poetry*. Hong Kong: Chinese University Press of Hong Kong, 1988.

Wang Xianqian. *Shi sanjia yi ji shu*. 2 vols. Beijing: Zhonghua shuju, 2009.

Wang Yunwu, ed. *Sibu congkan zhengbian*. 100 vols. Taipei: Taiwan Shangwu yinshuguan, 1979.

Watson, Burton. *Ssu-ma Ch'ien, Grand Historian of China*. New York: Columbia University Press, 1958.

——. *Records of the Grand Historian of China: Translated from the* Shi chi *of Ssu-ma Ch'ien*. 2 vols. New York: Columbia University Press, 1961.

——. *Han Fei Tzu: Basic Writings*. New York: Columbia University Press, 1964.

——. *The Complete Works of Chuang Tzu*. New York: Columbia University Press, 1968.

——. *Courtier and Commoner in Ancient China: Selections from the* History of the Former Han *by Pan Ku*. New York: Columbia University Press, 1974.

——. *The Columbia Book of Chinese Poetry: From Early Times to the Thirteenth Century.* New York: Columbia University Press, 1984.

——. "*Hou Han shu*: Biographies of Recluses." *Renditions*, nos. 33 & 34 (1990): 47–48.

——. *Records of the Grand Historian: Han Dynasty I.* Hong Kong: Columbia University Press, 1993.

Weld, Susan. "The Covenant Texts from Houma and Wenxian." In *New Sources of Early Chinese History: An Introduction to the Reading of Inscriptions and Manuscripts*, ed. Edward Shaughnessy, 125–160. Berkeley: The Society for the Study of Early China and the Institute of East Asian Studies, University of California, 1997.

Wilbur, C. Martin. *Slavery in China During the Former Han Dynasty 206 B.C.–A.D. 25.* New York: Russell & Russell, 1967.

Wong Siu-kit and Lee Kar-shui. "Poems of Depravity: A Twelfth-Century Dispute on the Moral Character of the *Book of Songs*." *T'oung Pao* 75, no. 4–5 (1989): 209–225.

Wu Hong. "Myths and Legends in Han Funerary Art." In *Stories from China's Past: Han Dynasty Pictorial Tomb Reliefs and Archaeological Objects from Sichuan Province, People's Republic of China*, ed. Lucy Lim, 72–82. San Francisco: The Chinese Culture Foundation of San Francisco, 1987.

——. *The Wu Liang Shrine: The Ideology of Early Chinese Pictorial Art.* Stanford: Stanford University Press, 1989.

——. *Monumentality in Early Chinese Art and Architecture.* Stanford: Stanford University Press, 1995.

——. *The Double Screen: Medium and Representation in Chinese Painting.* Chicago: University of Chicago Press, 1996.

——. *The Art of the Yellow Springs: Understanding Chinese Tombs.* Honolulu: University of Hawai'i Press, 2010.

Xiao Tong. *Wenxuan.* Beijing: Zhonghua shuju, 1981.

Xu Jian. *Chuxue ji.* Taipei: Dingwen shuju, 1972.

Xu Shaohua. *Zhoudai nanwang lishi dili yu wenhua.* Wuhan: Wuhan University Press, 1994.

Xu Shen. *Shuowen jiezi zhu.* 3 vols. Ed. Tang Kejing. Hunan: Yuelu shushe, 1997.

Yang Bojun. *Chunqiu Zuo zhuan zhu.* 4 vols. Beijing: Zhonghua shuju, 1981.

——. *Chunqiu Zuo zhuan cidian.* Beijing: Zhonghua shuju, 1985.

Yang, Hsien yi and Gladys Yang, trans. *Selections from Records of the Historian.* Beijing: Foreign Language Press, 1979.

Yang Kuan. *Zhanguo shi.* Shanghai: Shanghai Renmin chubanshe, 1981.

Yates, Robin. "Purity and Pollution in Early China." *Integrated Studies of Chinese Archaeology and Historiography* 4 (July 1997): 479–536.

Yong Rong (1744–1790). *Siku quanshu zongmu.* 2 vols. Beijing: Zhonghua shuju, 1965.

Yong, Ying. "Gender, Status, Ritual Regulations and Mortuary Practice." In *Gender and Chinese Archaeology*, ed. Katheryn Linduff and Yan Sun, 161–202. Walnut Creek, Calif.: Altamira Press, 2004.

Yü, Ying-shih. *Trade and Expansion in Han China.* Berkeley: University of California Press, 1967.

Yu Zhigu. *Zhugong jiushi*. In *Congshu jicheng chubian*, Vol. 3175, ed. Wang Yunwu. Shanghai: Shangwu yinshuguan, 1936.

Yuan Ke. *Shenhua lunwen ji*. Shanghai: Shanghai guji chubanshe, 1982.

Zeng Yifen and Cui Wenyin. *Zhongguo lishi wenxianxue shi shuyao*. Beijing: Shangwu yinshuguan, 2000.

Zhang Tao. "Liu Xiang *Lienü zhuan* de banben wenti." *Wenxian* (1989): 250–253.

———. *Lienü zhuan yizhu*. Ji'nan: Shandong daxue chubanshe, 1990.

Zhang Xuecheng. *Wenshi tongyi* in *Sibu beiyao*. Vol. 108. 610 vols. Taipei: Taiwan zhonghua shuju, 1965.

Zhang Xunliao. "Sichuan Dong Han mu Qiu Hu xi qi huaxiang zhuan, huaxiang shi yu changqu huayang *Lienü zhuan*." *Xihua daxue xuebao* 5 (2006): 1–10.

Zhang Yanyuan. *Lidai minghua ji*. In *Huashi congshu*, 4 vols. Ed. Yu Anlan. Shanghai: Shanghai renmin chubanshe, 1963.

Zhangsun Wuji, et al. *Suishu jingji zhi*. Shanghai: Shangwu yinshuguan, 1955.

Zheng Liangshu. *Zhujian boshu lunwenji*. Beijing: Zhonghua shuju, 1982.

Zheng Qiao. *Tongzhi*. Taipei: Xinxing shuju, 1959.

Zheng Xiaoxia and Lin Jianyu, eds. *Lienü zhuan huibian*. 10 vols. Beijing: Beijing tushuguan, 2007.

Zhongguo gujin diming dacidian. Shanghai: Shanghai cishu chubanshe, 2005.

Zhou Xibao. *Zhongguo gudai fushi shi*. Beijing: Zhongguo xiju chubanshe, 1996.

INDEX

Guan Zhong, xl, 27, 109–11, 247n1

Guang (son of Duke Ling of Qi). *See* Zhuang, Duke of Qi

Guangping, King of (Liu Xian), 179, 288n168

Guangwu, Emperor (Liu Xiu), 178, 286n132, 287n152, 288n154, 288n161, 289n169, 289n171

Guliang Commentary (*Spring and Autumn Annals*), xvi, xliii, 231n11

Guo Wei, 129, 257n104

Guo Zuo, 148–49, 271n131

Guoyu, xxxi, xlvi; in "Depraved and Favored," 259n2, 260n13, 261n24, 262n27, 264n58, 266n76, 267nn79–81, 267n87, 269n106, 271n127; in "Maternal Models," 204n103, 204n105, 204n107, 205nn112–13, 205nn119–20, 206n124; in "Principled and Righteous," 241n2, 243n27; in "Sympathetic and Wise," 218n1, 219n4, 221n30, 222n38, 222n41, 225n80; in "Worthy and Enlightened," 215n70, 216n79

Guozi of Qi (Guo Zhuangzi; Guo Guifu), 54, 224n62

Gusou (father of Shun), 1–3

Han, King of. *See* Gaozu, Emperor

Han, state of, 252n46, 274n170

Han dynasty, xv–xxi; consort power in, xviii–xxiv; education of women in, xv, xviii, xix, xxi, xxiv–xxvi, xlv. See also *particular emperors*

Han Xuanzi, 57, 226n82

Hann, Lady, 174–75

Hann, state of, l, 152, 159, 229n118, 229n121, 274n170

Hanshi waizhuan, xxxi, 187n63

Hanshu (Ban Gu), xvi–xvii, xxii, xxxv, xxxvi, xlix, 183n4; on *Lienü zhuan,* xxxii–xxxiii; on Liu Xiang, xxxvii

He, Emperor (Han Hedi; Liu Zhao), 180, 289nn171–73

He (Liu He), King of Changyi, 162–63, 279n42

He Lü, King of Wu, 76–77, 237n73

He Xiu, 183n7, 267n94

hegemon (*ba*): in "Accomplished Rhetoricians," 247n1, 249n16; in "Depraved and Favored," 265n66; in "Maternal Models," 12, 203n92; in "Principled and Righteous," 92, 247n1; in "Sympathetic and Wise," 49; in "Worthy and Enlightened," 27, 29, 31–32, 209n11, 210n15, 211n23, 212n38

Helinger murals (Inner Mongolia), xxxvi, 189n101

Hengyang, Princess, 171

Henry, Eric, xxxi, 218, 241, 256n92, 270n113

Heyang, younger sister of, 106–7

Hong Gong, 183n8

hostages, 242n22

Hou Hanshu (Fan Ye), xxxv

Hou Ji (Qi; Prince Millet), 3–4, 195nn15–17

Hu people, 287n150

Hu Yan. *See* Fan

Hua Meng Ji, 72–74

Huai, Duke of Jin (Yu, Ziyu), 29, 90–91, 144, 211n22, 242n21, 267nn90–91

Huai, King of Chu, 257nn109–11, 258n115

"Huai Ying, Consort of Yu of Jin," 90–91

Huainanzi, xli, 189n96, 191n126

Huaiyang, state of, 85, 178, 240n109, 288n161

Huan, Duke of Lu, 140–41, 203n87, 224n63, 263n48, 264n55, 265n59, 268n95

Huan, Duke of Qi: in "Accomplished Rhetoricians," 109–11, 129, 247nn1–2, 248n3; in "Depraved and Favored," 142, 265n66; in "Maternal Models," 12, 203n92; in "Principled and Righteous," 243n27; in "Sympathetic and Wise," 48; in "Worthy and Enlightened," 27–28, 209n9, 210n15

223n52, 227n89, 238n86; in "Worthy and Enlightened," 39, 211n25

naming conventions, l–li, 202n87, 228n106

Nan Zi of Wey, 151–52, 222n45, 273nn152–55, 274n163

Nangong Jingshu, 15, 205n112

Nao Chi (Zhi?), 159, 277n18

Nie Zheng, 158–59, 277n11

Ning Qi (Ningzi), 27, 109–11, 247n2

Nüying (wife of Shun), 1–3

"Old Woman of Quwo of Wei," 62–64

omenology, xxi, xxii, xli, 10. *See also* divination

"Outcast Orphan Maid of Qi," xxix, 128–30

Pei Yin, 194n3

Pengsheng, Prince, 141, 264n52

Ping, Duke of Jin, 57, 112–14, 225n77, 250n20

Ping, Emperor (Han Pingdi), xliii, 173–74, 281n68, 285n125

Ping, King of Chu, 76–78, 236n70, 238n86

Ping, King of Zhou (Yijiu), 138–39, 263nn37–40

Ping Kuo, 35

Pingyuan, Lord of Zhao, 275n178

polygyny: sororal, xviii, xxiii, 1–3; and succession issues, xlvi

prefaces, xxxiv, xxxvii, 259n1. See also *in particular chapters*

"Principled and Righteous," xliv, 87–108

"Principled Aunt of Liang," 103–4

"Principled Wet Nurse of Wei," 102–3

"Principled Woman of the Capital," 107–8

punishments, 240n106, 249n15, 258n126, 262n24

Pusao, battle of, 46, 220n12

Qi (son of Yu), 5–6, 196n30

Qi, Marquis of, 25, 70, 78, 140, 141, 145, 223n51

Qi, state of, xlv; in "Accomplished Rhetoricians," 109, 110–11, 114–15, 122–26, 128–30, 132–33, 247n1, 254n66, 256n99, 257n111; in "Chaste and Compliant," 70, 72, 75, 78, 234n48; in "Depraved and Favored," 138–44, 145, 148, 149–51, 263n43, 264n49, 265n66, 266n69, 271nn129–33, 272n135, 272nn140–46, 273n152; in "Maternal Models," 10–11, 19, 23, 201n63, 203n92; in "Principled and Righteous," 95–97, 243n27, 244n36; in "Supplementary Biographies," 158–59, 277n11, 277n18; in "Sympathetic and Wise," 47–48, 53–55, 61, 62, 63, 218n104, 223nn51–56, 224n62, 227n100, 229n118; in "Worthy and Enlightened," 25, 27–29, 40, 208n3, 210n15, 210n18, 211n25, 217n90

Qi, woman of (Jing), 114–16

Qi, woman of (Zhuang Jiang), 10–11

Qi Liang Zhi of Qi, 75–76, 235n62, 236n65, 254n70

"Qi Lüe" (Seven Summaries; Liu Xin), xvi

Qi Ying, 225n78

Qian Lou of Lu, 38–39, 216n84, 216n88

Qian Tong, 188n78

Qiang people, 287n150

Qianmou, 263n46

Qiaoru. See Shusun Xuanbo

Qimu Sui, 249n19

Qin, Second Emperor of, 160, 238n92, 277n23

Qin, state of: in "Accomplished Rhetoricians," 113, 123–25, 127, 130–31, 255n77, 257nn109–11; in "Chaste and Compliant," 76–77, 80, 90–91, 236n70; in "Depraved and Favored," 142, 144, 154–56, 276n190; in "Maternal Models," 16–17; in "Principled and Righteous," 102–3, 241n9, 242n21, 246n61; in "Sympathetic and Wise," 62–63, 64–65,

tailao, 94, 103, 245n39, 246n63; in
"Worthy and Enlightened," 30, 212n35

Schaberg, David, l

self-cultivation, xxvi, 11, 63

self-mutilation, xv, xlii, 83–84

Shang (Yin) dynasty, xxiv, xxxviii, xlvi, 5, 6,
63, 248n4, 282n86

Shangchen, Price of Chu, 89–90, 242n18

Shangguan, Empress, 285n126

Shangshu. See *Book of Documents*

Shao, Duke of, 230n1

She, Duke of, 129

Shen, Marquis of, 139, 263n42

Shen, state of, 197n35; in "Accomplished
Rhetoricians," 237n75; in "Chaste
and Compliant," 67–68, 230n1; in
"Depraved and Favored," 138, 139,
263nn37–38, 263n42, 270n116; in
"Sympathetic and Wise," 224n69,
225n70, 226n81

Shen Gong, 183n4

Shen Xu, 141

Shen Yue, 260n8

Sheng, Duke Bai of Chu, 79

Sheng Ji, 53, 148–49, 271n128

"Sheng Ji, Wife of Duke Ling of Qi,"
148–49

Sheng Meng Zi, 271nn127–29

Shensheng, Crown Prince of Jin (Prince
Gong), 28–29, 57, 123, 142–45, 210n16,
211nn25–26, 225n75, 254n74, 267n79

Shentu Jia, 240n112

Shentu Jian, 174, 286n134

Shi family, xix, 183n8

Shi Jingbo, 225n80

Shi Juan, 261n15

Shi Liangdi, 183n8, 289n181

Shi Xian (eunuch), xix–xx, 183n8

Shiji (Sima Qian), xxxi, xxxvii

Shijing. See *Book of Odes*

Shimomi Takao, xxxi–xxxii, l

Shishuo (Tales of the World; Liu Xiang),
xvii

Shiwen (Ten Questions), 256n90

Shou, 140

Shu Ji, 56–58, 224n67, 225n70

"Shu Ji of Yang of Jin," 56–58

Shu Jiang, 141, 264n57, 265n62

Shu Wei, 35, 36

Shun (sage king; Youyu), 190n115, 190n117;
in "Accomplished Rhetoricians,"
127, 249n8, 256n95; in "Depraved
and Favored," 274n168; in "Maternal
Models," 1–3, 4, 193n1, 196n30; in
"Supplementary Biographies," 169;
wives of, xxxiv–xxxv, xxxix, 1–3, 169; in
"Worthy and Enlightened," 32

Shunsun lineage, 224n63

Shuo. See Hui, Duke of Wey

Shuowen jiezi, xxxvi

Shuoyuan (Garden of Eloquence; Liu
Xiang), xvii, xxxi

Shusun lineage, 268n95

Shusun Xuanbo (Qiaoru; Shusun Xuanzi),
145–46, 268n95, 268n98, 271n129

Shuxiang (Yangshe Xi), 224n67, 225n70,
226n81

Shuyu (Yangshe Fu), 225n80

Sibu beiyao, xxxiv

Sima Qian, xvii–xviii, xix, xxxvi, xlvii, xlviii,
217n99, 260n12

Sima Zhen, xxxvi

Song, Marquis (Duke) of, 53, 223n51

Song, state of, xli, xlii–xliii; in "Chaste
and Compliant," 68–69, 71, 231n12,
232n20, 233n30; in "Depraved and
Favored," 151, 273nn152–54, 274n165; in
"Supplementary Biographies," 158; in
"Sympathetic and Wise," 53, 223n51; in
"Worthy and Enlightened," 29, 33–34

Song dynasty, xxxiii, xxxiv

Songs of Chu (*Chuci*), 177, 194n10, 243n24

Major Plays of Chikamatsu, tr. Donald Keene 1961

Four Major Plays of Chikamatsu, tr. Donald Keene. Paperback ed. only. 1961; rev. ed. 1997

Records of the Grand Historian of China, translated from the Shih chi of Ssu-ma Ch'ien, tr. Burton Watson, 2 vols. 1961

Instructions for Practical Living and Other Neo-Confucian Writings by Wang Yang-ming, tr. Wing-tsit Chan 1963

Hsün Tzu: Basic Writings, tr. Burton Watson, paperback ed. only. 1963; rev. ed. 1996

Chuang Tzu: Basic Writings, tr. Burton Watson, paperback ed. only. 1964; rev. ed. 1996

The Mahābhārata, tr. Chakravarthi V. Narasimhan. Also in paperback ed. 1965; rev. ed. 1997

The Manyōshū, Nippon Gakujutsu Shinkōkai edition 1965

Su Tung-p'o: Selections from a Sung Dynasty Poet, tr. Burton Watson. Also in paperback ed. 1965

Bhartrihari: Poems, tr. Barbara Stoler Miller. Also in paperback ed. 1967

Basic Writings of Mo Tzu, Hsün Tzu, and Han Fei Tzu, tr. Burton Watson. Also in separate paperback eds. 1967

The Awakening of Faith, Attributed to Aśvaghosha, tr. Yoshito S. Hakeda. Also in paperback ed. 1967

Reflections on Things at Hand: The Neo-Confucian Anthology, comp. Chu Hsi and Lü Tsu-ch'ien, tr. Wing-tsit Chan 1967

The Platform Sutra of the Sixth Patriarch, tr. Philip B. Yampolsky. Also in paperback ed. 1967

Essays in Idleness: The Tsurezuregusa of Kenkō, tr. Donald Keene. Also in paperback ed. 1967

The Pillow Book of Sei Shōnagon, tr. Ivan Morris, 2 vols. 1967

Two Plays of Ancient India: The Little Clay Cart and the Minister's Seal, tr. J. A. B. van Buitenen 1968

The Complete Works of Chuang Tzu, tr. Burton Watson 1968

The Romance of the Western Chamber (Hsi Hsiang chi), tr. S. I. Hsiung. Also in paperback ed. 1968

The Manyōshū, Nippon Gakujutsu Shinkōkai edition. Paperback ed. only. 1969

Records of the Historian: Chapters from the Shih chi of Ssu-ma Ch'ien, tr. Burton Watson. Paperback ed. only. 1969

Cold Mountain: 100 Poems by the T'ang Poet Han-shan, tr. Burton Watson. Also in paperback ed. 1970

Twenty Plays of the Nō Theatre, ed. Donald Keene. Also in paperback ed. 1970

Chūshingura: The Treasury of Loyal Retainers, tr. Donald Keene. Also in paperback ed. 1971; rev. ed. 1997

The Zen Master Hakuin: Selected Writings, tr. Philip B. Yampolsky 1971

Chinese Rhyme-Prose: Poems in the Fu Form from the Han and Six Dynasties Periods, tr. Burton Watson. Also in paperback ed. 1971

Kūkai: Major Works, tr. Yoshito S. Hakeda. Also in paperback ed. 1972

The Old Man Who Does as He Pleases: Selections from the Poetry and Prose of Lu Yu, tr. Burton Watson 1973

The Lion's Roar of Queen Śrīmālā, tr. Alex and Hideko Wayman 1974

Courtier and Commoner in Ancient China: Selections from the History of the Former Han by Pan Ku, tr. Burton Watson. Also in paperback ed. 1974

Japanese Literature in Chinese, vol. 1: Poetry and Prose in Chinese by Japanese Writers of the Early Period, tr. Burton Watson 1975

Japanese Literature in Chinese, vol. 2: Poetry and Prose in Chinese by Japanese Writers of the Later Period, tr. Burton Watson 1976

Love Song of the Dark Lord: Jayadeva's Gītagovinda, tr. Barbara Stoler Miller. Also in paperback ed. Cloth ed. includes critical text of the Sanskrit. 1977; rev. ed. 1997

Ryōkan: Zen Monk-Poet of Japan, tr. Burton Watson 1977

Calming the Mind and Discerning the Real: From the Lam rim chen mo of Tson-kha-pa, tr. Alex Wayman 1978

The Hermit and the Love-Thief: Sanskrit Poems of Bhartrihari and Bilhana, tr. Barbara Stoler Miller 1978

The Lute: Kao Ming's P'i-p'a chi, tr. Jean Mulligan. Also in paperback ed. 1980

A Chronicle of Gods and Sovereigns: Jinnō Shōtōki of Kitabatake Chikafusa, tr. H. Paul Varley 1980

Among the Flowers: The Hua-chien chi, tr. Lois Fusek 1982

Grass Hill: Poems and Prose by the Japanese Monk Gensei, tr. Burton Watson 1983

Doctors, Diviners, and Magicians of Ancient China: Biographies of Fang-shih, tr. Kenneth J. DeWoskin. Also in paperback ed. 1983

Theater of Memory: The Plays of Kālidāsa, ed. Barbara Stoler Miller. Also in paperback ed. 1984

The Columbia Book of Chinese Poetry: From Early Times to the Thirteenth Century, ed. and tr. Burton Watson. Also in paperback ed. 1984

Poems of Love and War: From the Eight Anthologies and the Ten Long Poems of Classical Tamil, tr. A. K. Ramanujan. Also in paperback ed. 1985

The Bhagavad Gita: Krishna's Counsel in Time of War, tr. Barbara Stoler Miller 1986

The Columbia Book of Later Chinese Poetry, ed. and tr. Jonathan Chaves. Also in paperback ed. 1986

The Tso Chuan: Selections from China's Oldest Narrative History, tr. Burton Watson 1989

Waiting for the Wind: Thirty-six Poets of Japan's Late Medieval Age, tr. Steven Carter 1989

Selected Writings of Nichiren, ed. Philip B. Yampolsky 1990

Saigyō, Poems of a Mountain Home, tr. Burton Watson 1990

The Book of Lieh Tzu: A Classic of the Tao, tr. A. C. Graham. Morningside ed. 1990

The Tale of an Anklet: An Epic of South India— The Cilappatikāram of Iḷaṅkō Aṭikaḷ, tr. R. Parthasarathy 1993

Waiting for the Dawn: A Plan for the Prince, tr. with introduction by Wm. Theodore de Bary 1993

Yoshitsune and the Thousand Cherry Trees: A Masterpiece of the Eighteenth-Century Japanese Puppet Theater, tr., annotated, and with introduction by Stanleigh H. Jones, Jr. 1993

The Lotus Sutra, tr. Burton Watson. Also in paperback ed. 1993

The Classic of Changes: A New Translation of the I Ching as Interpreted by Wang Bi, tr. Richard John Lynn 1994

Beyond Spring: Tz'u Poems of the Sung Dynasty, tr. Julie Landau 1994

The Columbia Anthology of Traditional Chinese Literature, ed. Victor H. Mair 1994

Scenes for Mandarins: The Elite Theater of the Ming, tr. Cyril Birch 1995

Letters of Nichiren, ed. Philip B. Yampolsky; tr. Burton Watson et al. 1996

Unforgotten Dreams: Poems by the Zen Monk Shōtetsu, tr. Steven D. Carter 1997

The Vimalakirti Sutra, tr. Burton Watson 1997

Japanese and Chinese Poems to Sing: The Wakan rōei shū, tr. J. Thomas Rimer and Jonathan Chaves 1997

Breeze Through Bamboo: Kanshi of Ema Saikō, tr. Hiroaki Sato 1998

A Tower for the Summer Heat, by Li Yu, tr. Patrick Hanan 1998

Traditional Japanese Theater: An Anthology of Plays, by Karen Brazell 1998

The Original Analects: Sayings of Confucius and His Successors (0479–0249), by E. Bruce Brooks and A. Taeko Brooks 1998

The Classic of the Way and Virtue: A New Translation of the Tao-te ching of Laozi as Interpreted by Wang Bi, tr. Richard John Lynn 1999

The Four Hundred Songs of War and Wisdom: An Anthology of Poems from Classical Tamil, The Puranānūru, ed. and tr. George L. Hart and Hank Heifetz 1999

Original Tao: Inward Training (Nei-yeh) *and the Foundations of Taoist Mysticism*, by Harold D. Roth 1999

Po Chü-i: Selected Poems, tr. Burton Watson 2000

Lao Tzu's Tao Te Ching: A Translation of the Startling New Documents Found at Guodian, by Robert G. Henricks 2000

The Shorter Columbia Anthology of Traditional Chinese Literature, ed. Victor H. Mair 2000

Mistress and Maid (Jiaohongji), by Meng Chengshun, tr. Cyril Birch 2001

Chikamatsu: Five Late Plays, tr. and ed. C. Andrew Gerstle 2001

The Essential Lotus: Selections from the Lotus Sutra, tr. Burton Watson 2002

Early Modern Japanese Literature: An Anthology, 1600–1900, ed. Haruo Shirane 2002; abridged 2008

The Columbia Anthology of Traditional Korean Poetry, ed. Peter H. Lee 2002

The Sound of the Kiss, or The Story That Must Never Be Told: Pingali Suranna's Kalapurnodayamu, tr. Vecheru Narayana Rao and David Shulman 2003

The Selected Poems of Du Fu, tr. Burton Watson 2003

Far Beyond the Field: Haiku by Japanese Women, tr. Makoto Ueda 2003

Just Living: Poems and Prose by the Japanese Monk Tonna, ed. and tr. Steven D. Carter 2003

Han Feizi: Basic Writings, tr. Burton Watson 2003

Mozi: Basic Writings, tr. Burton Watson 2003

Xunzi: Basic Writings, tr. Burton Watson 2003

Zhuangzi: Basic Writings, tr. Burton Watson 2003

The Awakening of Faith, Attributed to Aśvaghosha, tr. Yoshito S. Hakeda, introduction by Ryuichi Abe 2005

The Tales of the Heike, tr. Burton Watson, ed. Haruo Shirane 2006

Tales of Moonlight and Rain, by Ueda Akinari, tr. with introduction by Anthony H. Chambers 2007

Traditional Japanese Literature: An Anthology, Beginnings to 1600, ed. Haruo Shirane 2007

The Philosophy of Qi, by Kaibara Ekken, tr. Mary Evelyn Tucker 2007

The Analects of Confucius, tr. Burton Watson 2007

The Art of War: Sun Zi's Military Methods, tr. Victor Mair 2007

One Hundred Poets, One Poem Each: A Translation of the Ogura Hyakunin Isshu, tr. Peter McMillan 2008

Zeami: Performance Notes, tr. Tom Hare 2008

Zongmi on Chan, tr. Jeffrey Lyle Broughton 2009

Scripture of the Lotus Blossom of the Fine Dharma, rev. ed., tr. Leon Hurvitz, preface and introduction by Stephen R. Teiser 2009

Mencius, tr. Irene Bloom, ed. with an introduction by Philip J. Ivanhoe 2009

Clouds Thick, Whereabouts Unknown: Poems by Zen Monks of China, Charles Egan 2010

The Mozi: A Complete Translation, tr. Ian Johnston 2010

The Huainanzi: A Guide to the Theory and Practice of Government in Early Han China, by Liu An, tr. John S. Major, Sarah A. Queen, Andrew Seth Meyer, and Harold D. Roth, with Michael Puett and Judson Murray 2010

The Demon at Agi Bridge and Other Japanese Tales, tr. Burton Watson, ed. with introduction by Haruo Shirane 2011

Haiku Before Haiku: From the Renga Masters to Bashō, tr. with introduction by Steven D. Carter 2011

The Columbia Anthology of Chinese Folk and Popular Literature, ed. Victor H. Mair and Mark Bender 2011

Tamil Love Poetry: The Five Hundred Short Poems of the Aiṅkuṟunūṟu, tr. and ed. Martha Ann Selby 2011

The Teachings of Master Wuzhu: Zen and Religion of No-Religion, by Wendi L. Adamek 2011

The Essential Huainanzi, by Liu An, tr. John S. Major, Sarah A. Queen, Andrew Seth Meyer, and Harold D. Roth 2012

The Dao of the Military: Liu An's Art of War, tr. Andrew Seth Meyer 2012

Unearthing the Changes: Recently Discovered Manuscripts of the Yi Jing (I Ching) and Related Texts, Edward L. Shaughnessy 2013

Record of Miraculous Events in Japan: The Nihon ryōiki, tr. Burton Watson 2013

Lust, Commerce, and Corruption: An Account of What I Have Seen and Heard, by an Edo Samurai, tr. and ed. Mark Teeuwen and Kate Wildman Nakai with Miyazaki Fumiko, Anne Walthall, and John Breen 2014

Printed in the USA
CPSIA information can be obtained
at www.ICGtesting.com
JSHW021705230724
66900JS00004B/91